Innovation und Entre

Herausgegeben von
N. Franke, Wien, Austria
D. Harhoff, München, Germany
J. Henkel, München, Germany

Innovative Konzepte und unternehmerische Leistungen sind für Wohlstand und Fortschritt von entscheidender Bedeutung. Diese Schriftenreihe vereint wissenschaftliche Arbeiten zu diesem Themenbereich. Sie beschreiben substanzielle Erkenntnisse auf hohem methodischen Niveau.

Herausgegeben von

Professor Dr. Nikolaus Franke,
Wirtschaftsuniversität Wien,
Austria

Professor Dr. Joachim Henkel,
Technische Universität München,
Germany

Professor Dietmar Harhoff, Ph.D.,
Ludwig-Maximilians-Universität München,
Germany

Richard Weber

Evaluating Entrepreneurship Education

With a foreword by Prof. Dietmar Harhoff, Ph.D.

 RESEARCH

Richard Weber
Munich, Germany

Dissertation Ludwig-Maximilians-Universität München, 2011

D 19

ISBN 978-3-8349-3653-0　　　　ISBN 978-3-8349-3654-7 (eBook)
DOI 10.1007/978-3-8349-3654-7

The Deutsche Nationalbibliothek lists this publication in the Deutsche Nationalbibliografie; detailed bibliographic data are available in the Internet at http://dnb.d-nb.de.

Springer Gabler
© Gabler Verlag | Springer Fachmedien Wiesbaden 2012
This work is subject to copyright. All rights are reserved by the Publisher, whether the whole or part of the material is concerned, specifically the rights of translation, reprinting, reuse of illustrations, recitation, broadcasting, reproduction on microfilms or in any other physical way, and transmission or information storage and retrieval, electronic adaptation, computer software, or by similar or dissimilar methodology now known or hereafter developed. Exempted from this legal reservation are brief excerpts in connection with reviews or scholarly analysis or material supplied specifically for the purpose of being entered and executed on a computer system, for exclusive use by the purchaser of the work. Duplication of this publication or parts thereof is permitted only under the provisions of the Copyright Law of the Publisher's location, in its current version, and permission for use must always be obtained from Springer. Permissions for use may be obtained through RightsLink at the Copyright Clearance Center. Violations are liable to prosecution under the respective Copyright Law.
The use of general descriptive names, registered names, trademarks, service marks, etc. in this publication does not imply, even in the absence of a specific statement, that such names are exempt from the relevant protective laws and regulations and therefore free for general use. While the advice and information in this book are believed to be true and accurate at the date of publication, neither the authors nor the editors nor the publisher can accept any legal responsibility for any errors or omissions that may be made. The publisher makes no warranty, express or implied, with respect to the material contained herein.

Cover design: KünkelLopka GmbH, Heidelberg

Printed on acid-free paper

Springer Gabler is a brand of Springer DE. Springer DE is part of Springer Science+Business Media.
www.springer-gabler.de

Foreword

The stimulation of entrepreneurial activity is a core aspect of innovation policies in Europe and the USA, since entrepreneurship is presumed to be an important driver of economic prosperity. University graduates are assigned a particular role in these policies. The qualification and advancement of potential entrepreneurs at tertiary institutions has therefore gained public attention. On both sides of the Atlantic public authorities demand and advance the integration and extension of entrepreneurship education into academic curricula. The increase in resources allocated to this kind of education comes along with a growing demand for a justification of the investments. Yet, so far only limited empirical research regarding the effects of entrepreneurship education is available.

With the present study, Richard Weber seeks to fill this gap by exploiting a unique dataset describing a large-scale compulsory entrepreneurship course. He employs a quasi-experimental approach to evaluate the effects of entrepreneurship education and highlights the important sorting effects it can have for students. Moreover he explores the impact of social interactions among students in building entrepreneurial skills. His analysis introduces new perspectives in measuring the effects of entrepreneurship education and derives important implications on how to improve its design.

With his thesis Richard Weber delivers new research insights, which deepen our understanding of the effects of entrepreneurship education. This book is the result of more than three years of research, which earned the author a doctoral degree at the Ludwig-Maximilians-Universität Munich. The results presented by Richard Weber are a remarkable contribution to the field of entrepreneurship and economics of education. I am sure that these results will find the attention of practitioners and researchers alike.

Prof. Dietmar Harhoff, Ph.D.

Acknowledgements

This dissertation would not have been completed without the help of faculty members, my friends, and my family. I am deeply indebted to all of them and would like to express my gratitude for their continuous encouragement and support. Several deserve special mention.

First and foremost, I would like to thank Dietmar Harhoff, my doctoral advisor, for his outstanding supervision, guidance, and support throughout the past years. In numerous discussions he shared his fascination for academic research with me. I am deeply grateful for his confidence in both my lecturing capability and my research projects, as well as for the remarkable degree of freedom he granted me throughout my stay at his institute. In particular, I wish to thank him for giving me the opportunity to be part of the LMU Entrepreneurship Center team.

Not less important is the role Georg von Graevenitz played for the successful completion of my dissertation. My discussions with him have been a steady source of inspiration and encouragement. He shared his ideas, his knowledge, and his passion for economic research with me, which enormously impacted this dissertation and enabled me to write it as it is today. His motivating words helped me getting through the hard times of my graduate studies. Moreover, I thank Georg for giving me an equal voice in our work together.

I am also grateful to Dieter Frey, my thesis referee and scientific advisor, for his outstanding support and valuable advice. Also beyond this dissertation, Dieter Frey is an important mentor to me.

For introducing me into the scientific community during my Master of Business Research studies I wish to thank my advisors Tobias Kretschmer and Thomas Hess.

My dissertation critically depended on the access to data on the effects of entrepreneurship education. I wish to express my gratitude to the business administration students at the Ludwig-Maximilians-Universität Munich and the

Technical University of Munich for their willingness to participate in my surveys. I also would like to thank Gunther Friedl and Tobias Kretschmer for their support in the collection of control group data in their lectures. For his generous support during my surveys I wish to cordially thank Simon Bierbaum.

For maintaining an atmosphere of high spirits, mutual support and fun I am deeply indebted to my past and current fellow doctoral students and the assistant professors at Dietmar Harhoff's chair. In particular I would like to thank Philipp Sandner, who acted as my "big brother" during my doctoral studies, and Roland Stürz, a brilliant researcher and good friend, who always had a solution to statistical and other challenges. I am deeply grateful to Hortense Tarrade, Nina Schießl, and Robert Redweik, my colleagues at the LMU Entrepreneurship Center. It has been an honor and great fun to be part of this team. Last but not least I have been very fortunate to share an office with Jeannine Sütterlin. She not only has been a great source of advice during the last years, but we also have successfully survived the administrative machinery of the university together and thereby developed a funny sense of humor. I thank Jeannine for our time together and her friendship.

Special thanks go to Rosemarie Wilcox for reviewing my dissertation and eliminating the severe linguistic deficiencies. Thanks also go to Amanda Herbrand, Daniela Hoche, Konstantin Krauss, and Dennis Seidel for their excellent research assistance.

I thank the directors of the LMU Entrepreneurship Center for their confidence in my capabilities and projects, in particular Andrew "Andy" Goldstein. Andy has impressed me with his entrepreneurial spirit and visionary ideas. Working with him has profoundly fostered my professional development.

For providing more than welcome distraction I owe great thanks to my friends. In particular I wish to thank Andrea and Josef Eckl and Daniel Streithoff for keeping me connected to home. I am grateful to Johannes to Baben, Daniel Schmidl, and Dominik Wittmann – we shared the highs and helped each other out of the lows of our dissertation time. Last, but certainly not least, I am indebted to Stefanie Schneider for being a faithful support and wonderful source of energy during the last years.

Acknowledgements

Above all, I wish to thank my beloved ones, first and foremost my girlfriend Silvia. Words would not be sufficient to honor her role during the whole process. Thank you for your love and patience, your encouragement especially in difficult times, as well as your interest in my work. Most especially I am deeply grateful to my parents Maria and Herbert, and to my brothers Stefan and Robert and their families. Your continuous encouragement, loving affection, and endless support made it possible to pursue my goals. Thank you for your belief in me. This book is dedicated to you.

Richard Weber

Index

Foreword V

Acknowledgements VII

Index IX

List of Figures XV

List of Tables XVII

List of Abbreviations XXI

1. Introduction 1
　1.1 Motivation and Structure of this Book 1
　1.2 Definitions and Overview of the Literature 9
　　1.2.1 A Definition of Entrepreneurship 10
　　1.2.2 Classification of Entrepreneurship Education 12
　　1.2.3 Studies on Effects of Entrepreneurship Education 16
　　1.2.4 Critique of Previously Conducted Studies 29

2. Theoretical Foundations 33
　2.1 Introduction 33
　2.2 Psychological and Sociological Views at the Entrepreneur 36
　　2.2.1 Trait Approach 37
　　2.2.2 Demographic-Sociological Approach 39
　　2.2.3 Behavioral Approach 40
　2.3 The Theory of Planned Behavior 44
　　2.3.1 Predictors of Intentions and Behavior 44
　　2.3.2 Origins of Beliefs: the Role of Exogenous Influences 49
　　2.3.3 Challenges to the Theory of Planned Behavior 54
　2.4 The Theory of Planned Behavior in the Entrepreneurship Domain ... 57
　2.5 A Baseline-Model for Evaluating Entrepreneurship Education 60

- 2.5.1 Impact of Entrepreneurship Education on Entrepreneurial Attitudes and Intentions 61
- 2.5.2 Using the Theory of Planned Behavior to Evaluate Entrepreneurship Education 63
- 2.5.3 Additional Relevant Theoretical Constructs for the Baseline Model 65
- 2.5.4 Extensions of the Baseline Model 74
- 2.5.5 Ethical Concerns – Information versus Persuasion 76
- 2.6 Conclusion 77

3. Institutional Setting and Presentation of the Dataset 79
  - 3.1 Introduction 79
  - 3.2 Context 82
    - 3.2.1 Treatment Group 82
    - 3.2.2 Control Group 86
  - 3.3 Data Collection Procedures 87
    - 3.3.1 Treatment Group 88
    - 3.3.2 Control Group 92
  - 3.4 Measures 97
    - 3.4.1 Selection of Measures for the Questionnaire 97
    - 3.4.2 Psychometric Properties of the used Measures 109
  - 3.5 First Data Description 114
    - 3.5.1 Possible Data Biases 114
    - 3.5.2 Sample Composition 133
  - 3.6 Course-Related Variables and Course Evaluation 141
    - 3.6.1 Standard Course Evaluation Questions 142
    - 3.6.2 Entrepreneurial Learning 142
    - 3.6.3 Assessment of Teamwork and the Cooperation with the Entrepreneurs 144
  - 3.7 Appropriateness of the Dataset for this Research Project 146

4. Determinants of Entrepreneurial Intentions 149
  - 4.1 Introduction 149

Index

    4.2 Hypotheses 151
        4.2.1 Hypotheses Derived from the Theory of Planned Behavior 151
        4.2.2 Hypotheses regarding Individual Background Factors 152
    4.3 Test of the Hypotheses and Additional Results 155
        4.3.1 Hypotheses Related to the Theory of Planned Behavior 157
        4.3.2 Hypotheses regarding Demographic Variables 160
        4.3.3 Hypotheses regarding Prior Experiences 161
        4.3.4 Hypotheses regarding Personality Dimensions 162
        4.3.5 Mediating Effects of the Theory of Planned Behavior Variables .. 163
    4.4 Conclusion 164

5. Assessing the Impact of Entrepreneurship Education –
a Quasi-Experimental Approach 167
    5.1 Introduction 167
    5.2 Empirical Strategy 169
        5.2.1 One Group Before and After Design 169
        5.2.2 The Before and After with an Untreated Control Group - Design 171
        5.2.3 Analyzing the Treatment Effect on Different Subsamples
              using a Difference-in-Difference-in-Differences Approach 176
    5.3 Results 179
        5.3.1 Differences 179
        5.3.2 Difference-in-Differences 180
        5.3.3 Difference-in-Difference-in-Differences 190
    5.4 Conclusion 198

6. A Bayesian Updating Approach to Evaluate Entrepreneurship Education .. 201
    6.1 Introduction 201
    6.2 Integrating the Theory of Planned Behavior with a Model of
        Learning 204
        6.2.1 Updating Opinions of Entrepreneurial Aptitude through
              Entrepreneurship Education 205
        6.2.2 Assumptions 207
        6.2.3 Definitions 209

6.3 Empirical Analysis 216
    6.3.1 Description of Variables 217
    6.3.2 Descriptive Results 224
    6.3.3 Test of Hypotheses 234
  6.4 Discussion and Conclusion.. 260

7. Peer Effects in Entrepreneurship Education.. 265
  7.1 Introduction 265
  7.2 Social Interactions in Education and Entrepreneurship.................... 269
    7.2.1 Social Interaction Effects in Schooling 270
    7.2.2 Social Interaction Effects and Entrepreneurial Intentions and Activity 275
    7.2.3 Peer Effects and the Formation of Entrepreneurial Skills during Entrepreneurship Education.. 277
  7.3 Econometric Framework 281
    7.3.1 Mean Peer-Effects 281
    7.3.2 Non-Linear Peer-Effects 286
    7.3.3 Further Methodological Issues 287
  7.4 Dataset and Additional Measures.. 287
    7.4.1 Entrepreneurial Self-Efficacy 287
    7.4.2 Additional Explanatory and Control Variables 290
    7.4.3 Descriptive Statistics 290
  7.5 Results 300
    7.5.1 Test for Random Team Assignment 300
    7.5.2 Descriptive Results regarding Peer Effects 300
    7.5.3 Mean Peer-Effects 304
    7.5.4 Effects of Peers of Different Self-Efficacy Levels 310
    7.5.5 Non-Linearities in Peer-Effects 313
  7.6 Conclusion 318

8. Conclusion and Avenues for further Research....................................... 321

Bibliography... 329

List of Figures

Figure 2.1: Intentions-based process-model
(according to Krueger and Carsrud (1993)) 42
Figure 2.2: The Theory of Planned Behavior (According to Ajzen (1991)) 48
Figure 2.3: Theoretical Model for the Evaluation of Entrepreneurship
Education (own illustration) 66
Figure 3.1: Number of responses for the 2008-09 cohort treatment-group
ex-ante survey by date 90
Figure 3.2: Number of responses for the 2009-10 cohort treatment-group
ex-ante survey by date 91
Figure 3.3: Number of responses for the 2009-10 cohort treatment-group
ex-post survey by date 92
Figure 3.4: Number of responses for the 2009-10 cohort control-group
ex-ante survey by date 94
Figure 3.5: Number of responses for the 2009-10 cohort control-group
ex-post survey by date 94
Figure 3.6: Distribution of ex-ante entrepreneurial intentions
by group sample (N = 509) 136
Figure 3.7: Nationality of the students in the treatment group sample
(N = 403) 138
Figure 3.8: Nationality of the students in the control group sample
(N = 106) 138
Figure 3.9: Breadth of prior exposure to entrepreneurship
(by group sample, N=509) 140
Figure 3.10: Number of ECTS gained by treatment group students
prior to the course (N = 403) 140
Figure 3.11: Evaluation of the course by treatment group students
(N = 403) 142

Figure 3.12: Student assessment of entrepreneurial learning due to the course (N = 403) 144
Figure 3.13: Students' assessment of cooperation with entrepreneur 146
Figure 5.1: Difference-in-differences estimator calculated for Theory of Planned Behavior variables 183
Figure 6.1: Ex-ante and ex-post entrepreneurial intentions of treatment group students 226
Figure 6.2: Ex-ante and ex-post entrepreneurial intentions of control group students 227
Figure 7.1: Shift in individual entrepreneurial self-efficacy during the course 292
Figure 7.2: Shift in entrepreneurial self-efficacy by background characteristics 302
Figure 7.3: Shift in own entrepreneurial self-efficacy during the course by own and peers' level of ex-ante entrepreneurial self-efficacy 304

List of Tables

Table 1.1:	Overview of evaluations of entrepreneurship education	21
Table 3.1:	Schedule for "Business Planning" during winter term 2008-09	85
Table 3.2:	Schedule for "Business Planning" during winter term 2009-10	86
Table 3.3:	Response rates of conducted surveys by cohort and group	96
Table 3.4:	Labels of the seven-point Likert-scale response categories used in surveys	98
Table 3.5:	Item for measuring Entrepreneurial intentions	99
Table 3.6:	Items for measuring Perceived Desirability	99
Table 3.7:	Items for measuring Perceived Social Norm	100
Table 3.8:	Items for measuring Perceived Behavioral Control	101
Table 3.9:	Coding of demographic variables	102
Table 3.10:	Items for measuring Prior Exposure to Entrepreneurship	103
Table 3.11:	Ten-Item Personality Inventory for measuring Big5 personality dimensions	104
Table 3.12:	Construction of the Big5 measures	105
Table 3.13:	Subsamples defined by background factors	106
Table 3.14:	Items for measuring entrepreneurial learning	107
Table 3.15:	Standard course-evaluation items	108
Table 3.16:	Items for measuring the quality of the cooperation with the entrepreneur	109
Table 3.17:	Theory of Planned Behavior-items factor loadings (ex-ante data)	111
Table 3.18:	Theory of Planned Behavior-items factor loadings (ex-post data)	111
Table 3.19:	Item-construct correlations (ex-ante data)	112
Table 3.20:	Item-construct correlations (ex-post data)	113
Table 3.21:	Scale reliability test using Cronbach's alpha for the ex-ante and ex-post questionnaire	113

Table 3.22:	Test for data bias due to non-response	118
Table 3.23:	Interpretations for possible outcome combinations of difference and equivalence test	120
Table 3.24:	Test for equivalence of treatment-group cohorts	122
Table 3.25:	Test for equivalence of control-group cohorts	124
Table 3.26:	Test for equivalence of the pooled treatment and pooled control group	126
Table 3.27:	Test for attrition bias in the treatment group data	130
Table 3.28:	Test for attrition bias in the control group data	132
Table 3.29:	Descriptive statistics (treatment group sample)	134
Table 3.30:	Descriptive statistics (control group sample)	135
Table 3.31:	Descriptive statistics of course-related and situational variables	141
Table 4.1:	OLS regression models of background factors and entrepreneurial attitudes upon entrepreneurial intentions	156
Table 4.2:	Descriptive statistics and Pearson/ point-biserial correlations (treatment group sample)	158
Table 4.3:	Mean ex-ante entrepreneurial intentions by subsample (treatment group sample)	161
Table 5.1:	Differences-approach – t-tests for ex-post/ex-ante differences	180
Table 5.2:	Difference-in-differences approach – t-tests for ex-post/ex-ante differences	181
Table 5.3:	Difference-in-Differences estimations using OLS	185
Table 5.4:	t-tests for differences in entrepreneurial intentions by subsample	192
Table 5.5:	Difference-in-difference-in-differences estimates using OLS and CEM	196
Table 6.1:	Descriptive statistics (treatment group)	220
Table 6.2:	Descriptive statistics (control group)	222
Table 6.3:	Equivalence test on strength of period 1 signals variables (treatment vs. control group)	228
Table 6.4:	Comparison of the strengths of period 2 signals across groups	229

List of Tables

Table 6.5:	Ex-post responses to the entrepreneurial intentions item, by ex-ante responses (treatment group)	231
Table 6.6:	Changes in the response to the entrepreneurial intentions item, by ex-ante responses (treatment group)	232
Table 6.7:	Pattern of changes in responses to the entrepreneurial intentions item (treatment group)	233
Table 6.8:	Pattern of changes in responses to the entrepreneurial intentions item (control group)	234
Table 6.9:	Comparison of ex-ante standard deviation of entrepreneurial intentions by group	235
Table 6.10:	Test of Hypothesis 6.1 (variance in entrepreneurial intentions, ex-ante and ex-post by group)	237
Table 6.11:	Variance in entrepreneurial intentions by subsample	240
Table 6.12:	Test of Hypothesis 6.2 (OLS regressions, treatment group data only)	244
Table 6.13:	Test of Hypothesis 6.2 (OLS regressions, treatment and control group data)	248
Table 6.14:	Test of Hypothesis 6.3 (OLS regressions, treatment group data only)	254
Table 6.15:	Test of Hypothesis 6.3 (OLS regressions, treatment and control group data)	256
Table 7.1:	Items for measuring Entrepreneurial Self-Efficacy	289
Table 7.2:	Descriptive statistics	293
Table 7.3:	Descriptive statistics (data aggregated on team- and tutorial level)	296
Table 7.4:	Test for random team assignment	298
Table 7.5:	Sample size by level of ex-ante entrepreneurial self-efficacy and background variables	301
Table 7.6:	Sample size by own and peers' level of ex-ante entrepreneurial self-efficacy	303
Table 7.7:	Estimation of mean peer effects (OLS regressions)	306

Table 7.8:	Estimation of peer effects (OLS regressions, allowing for non-linearities in peer quality)	308
Table 7.9:	Estimation of peer effects by gender	311
Table 7.10:	Estimation of peer effects by prior exposure to entrepreneurship	312
Table 7.11:	Estimation of peer effects by own and peers' ex-ante entrepreneurial self-efficacy	314
Table 7.12:	Peer effects by different team combinations	315
Table 7.13:	Social gain in entrepreneurial self-efficacy by reshuffling teams	317

List of Abbreviations

a.m.	ante meridiem
BWL	Betriebswirtschaftslehre (Business Administration)
CAD	Canadian Dollar
CEM	Coarsened Exact Matching
DD	difference-in-differences
DDD	difference-in-difference-in-differences
DV	dependent variable
ECTS	European Credit Transfer System
e.g.	exempli gratia
ESE	entrepreneurial self-efficacy
et al.	et alii
etc.	et cetera
EU	European Union
EUR	Euro
GBP	Great Britain Pound
GPA	Grade Point Average
IDA	Integrated Database for Labor Market Research in Denmark
IP	intellectual property
i.e.	id est
LMU	Ludwig-Maximilians-Universität
M	million
MBA	Master of Business Administration
No.	numero
OLS	ordinary least squares
P25	25th percentile
P75	75th percentile
PISA	Programme for International Student Assessment

pp.	pages
PR	public relations
p.	page
p.m.	post meridiem
SAT	Scholastic Aptitude Test
STAR	Student Teacher Achievement Ratio
S.D.	standard deviation
S.E.	standard error
TEA	Total Early-Stage Entrepreneurial Activity
TIMSS	Third International Mathematics and Science Study
TU	Technische Universität (Technical University)
TV	television
US	United States
USA	United States of America
USD	Unites States Dollar
Vol.	Volume

1. Introduction

1.1 Motivation and Structure of this Book

Governmental departments in many countries are convinced that it is possible to motivate students at tertiary institutions of education to become entrepreneurs and to start their own businesses. The importance of entrepreneurship education and training was emphasized at the World Economic Forum recently (World Economic Forum 2009, p. 7-8): "(…) while education is one of the most important foundations for economic development, entrepreneurship is a major driver of innovation and economic growth. Entrepreneurship education plays an essential role in shaping attitudes, skills and culture–from the primary level up. (…) We believe entrepreneurial skills, attitudes and behaviors can be learned, and that exposure to entrepreneurship education throughout an individual's lifelong learning path, starting from youth and continuing through adulthood into higher education–as well as reaching out to those economically or socially excluded–is imperative."

Up to now it is unclear, whether this kind of education meets the expectations of the politicians. Only rarely, if at all, are entrepreneurship courses evaluated. On a more conceptual level, it is also unclear whether the pure "production" of entrepreneurs through entrepreneurship education can be the goal these policies should be aimed at.

In this book, I first discuss this latter issue. Based on widely recognized classifications of entrepreneurship education, I argue that this kind of education does not fulfill a role of social persuasion resulting in the "production" of just more entrepreneurs. Its goal is rather to provide students with information about entrepreneurship and to convey entrepreneurial skills to them. Based on this new information they should then be able to learn about their entrepreneurial aptitude. Entrepreneurship education should enable them, through a better self-assessment, to consciously decide whether they opt for an enterprising career or whether they prefer to employ their newly learned skills as employees in existing organizations. Accordingly, career intentions among students should become more pronounced during an entrepreneurship course, no matter whether with respect to the first or the latter option. The bottom line is that entrepreneurship education has two purposes: to increase students' entrepreneurial skills and to provide impetus to those who are suited to entrepreneurship while discouraging those who are not. This view differs significantly from the implicit notion that entrepreneurship education somehow enhances students' willingness to become entrepreneurs.

In the empirical analyses in this book I present three approaches to evaluate entrepreneurship education with respect to the effects it has on the attending students. These approaches make use of theories from social psychology, economics, and sociology. The combination of theories from different domains allows dealing with three major research questions, which shed light on this topic from different angles. First – from an economic perspective –, has entrepreneurship education any impact on students' career plans at all, and how large is it? Second – exploiting social psychology theories to establish appropriate measures – how can this impact be characterized on an individual level in terms of skill-building and pronouncing career intentions? And third – from a more sociological point of view – how can the population of course attendees as input factor in an educational production function be used to leverage this impact, especially with respect to conveying skills? To answer these questions I study the effects of a large-scale compulsory entrepreneurship course at a major German university, using an ex-ante-test–ex-post-test control group design.

The answers to these questions are important for several stakeholders regarding entrepreneurship education, for politicians and for institutions who provide and who receive funds to establish entrepreneurship education, for course instructors, for students who attend these courses, and of course for other researchers on this topic.

Beginning at the top level, politicians are interested in these questions. Their decision to financially support the establishment of entrepreneurship education at tertiary institutions is motivated by a very rational calculation. The creation of new businesses is an important driver of economic prosperity. That becomes visible in the creation of new jobs, and also in the generation of innovations (e.g. van Praag and Versloot 2007; Fritsch and Müller 2008).

Especially university graduates are assigned a substantial role in this regard. According to empirical evidence this group creates more jobs than entrepreneurs without university degree (Dietrich 1999), and they invest more in their own start-up (Reynolds et al. 1994). In addition, start-ups by entrepreneurs with a degree are more successful than other start-ups (Shane 2004). In general, researchers observe spillover effects of universities on the economy of the surrounding region. Spin-offs are driving the local economy by actively transferring knowledge into the regional value creation (Harhoff 1999; Shane 2004). Being aware of these results, the qualification and advancement of potential entrepreneurs at tertiary institutions gains politicians' attention. It is their goal to establish a culture of entrepreneurship at universities and so foster the international competitiveness. The establishment and extension of entrepreneurship education is considered an effective strategy to achieve this (Liñán 2004; European Commission 2006). On both sides of the Atlantic public authorities demand and advance the integration and extension of entrepreneurship education in curricula at tertiary institutions (Liñán 2004; Kuratko 2005). This postulation has become visible, for example, in the amount of entrepreneurship chairs. In Germany the number of professorships explicitly dedicated to entrepreneurship at tertiary institutions has almost tripled from 21 to 58 between 1998 and 2008 (Klandt and Heil 2001; Klandt et al. 2008). To reach a similar level as in the USA, however, almost 120 professorships would be necessary in Germany (Vesper and McMullan 1997; Hills and Morris 1998; Fiet 2001; Klandt et al. 2008). Aware of the promises of entrepreneurship education and the shortfall in tertiary entrepreneurship education, the German Government initiated the EXIST program. Between 1997 and 2005, public funds in the amount of EUR 46 million have been invested in the establishment of entrepreneurship education in supporting chairs and entrepreneurship centers at tertiary institutions (Kulicke 2006). Between 2006 and 2010, additional EUR 39 million have been invested. This program centers the motivation and qualification of students, who belong to the primary entrepreneurship-potential of tertiary institutions (Isfan et al. 2004). Research on the effects of entrepreneurship education may thus help politicians to understand the size and nature of the consequences regarding their aim to foster economic prosperity. And second, they find out if the public investment is justified.

At this point it becomes clear why my research questions are of interest for the two other stakeholder groups – providers and receivers of funds to establish and extend entrepreneurship education. Not only public authorities provide the financial means for qualifying students and motivate them to pursue an enterprising career. Private institutions as well (companies, foundations, etc.) get involved in these activities. The increasing number of entrepreneurship education programs and the level of resources allocated to it come along with the demand for a justification of these investments. Both public and private fund providers have generated a growing interest in the issue of effectiveness and efficiency of these programs and the identification of best practices (Fiet 2001). New investments in entrepreneurship education at tertiary institutions are only justified when the results meet the goals of fund providers. Klandt et al. (2008) refer to arbitrage effects on part of the universities. Endowed chairs for entrepreneurship or sponsored entrepreneurship centers, for example, are thus often confronted with the task to demonstrate the effects of their activities. But at training institutions, these chairs or centers are first and foremost interested in maximizing the number of participants and take this number as output measure. In most cases they lack the expertise and resources to conduct well-grounded evaluations aimed at measuring the impact of the training. A well-documented research project that presents theories, measures, and processes ensuring reproducibility may reduce the costs of conducting such evaluations. Both the results of this project and the evaluations the institutions conduct themselves provide them with additional arguments when applying for further funds. For fund providers, on the other hand, these findings justify their investments and offer them a kind of controlling tool, or reveal room for improvement and an adjustment of the terms of the investment made.

This identified room for improvement in the entrepreneurship education activities is of course most important for course planners. It is their responsibility to develop course concepts that best inform the participating students about entrepreneurship and qualify them for entrepreneurial tasks. The results obtained in evaluations measuring economically the training impact show whether these goals have been achieved. By grounding these evaluations on theories from social psychology, the course planners can also determine the nature of these effects. The theoretical discussions as well as the derived implications from the conducted studies in this book – and also from other studies pursuing a similar goal – may aide course planners to adjust the course concepts to maximize the intended effects on students.

They, of course, are the fifth stakeholder group having an interest in the answers to the raised research questions. Students expressed an increasing interest about entrepreneurial careers (Kolvereid 1996a). But often students lack the information and experience for a qualified decision about their future career path at the beginning of their studies (Cox et al. 2002). Entrepreneurship courses may thus provide a welcome source of information to that effect. There they often have the possibility to acquire necessary information and skills, and to engage in entrepreneurial activity in the secure environment of an academic exercise. Having gone through a course, students may now be more able to decide for the "right" career path. Even when the student decides to enter a managerial career after the course it may also be considered a success, when he is held off performing a possibly very costly real-world experiment of starting a firm and failing the task.

Finally, considering the last group of stakeholders, other researchers in the entrepreneurship domain may find both the theoretical model as well as the documentation of its practical implication useful. Following my argumentation about the goals of entrepreneurship education and building on my findings related to my research questions they might extend the presented approaches and replicate them to bring forward this young research stream.

Since so many stakeholders have developed substantial interest in the effects of entrepreneurship education, several empirical studies have been conducted to measure its impact, especially during the last decade. These studies found positive effects with respect to both directly observable measures (number of created businesses and jobs) as well as indirect measures such as the perceptions of attractiveness and feasibility of starting a business and entrepreneurial intentions (Cox et al. 2002; Peterman and Kennedy 2003; Henry et al. 2004; Fayolle et al. 2006a; Souitaris et al. 2007; Oosterbeek et al. 2010; von Graevenitz et al. 2010). This work has been recognized both by the scientific and the practice-oriented community. However, to many of them apply methodological caveats, others find contradictory and counterintuitive results. In general, the comparability of the results is questionable due to the use of different theoretical frameworks and different measures for the same theoretical construct. Scholars conclude that the research on entrepreneurship education has not provided resilient empirical determination of the size and nature of its effects (Cox et al. 2002; Souitaris et al. 2007).

Regarding empirical analysis of the effects of entrepreneurship education scholars identified a large research gap (Béchard and Gregoire 2005). All of the identified stakeholder groups keep demanding more empirical research projects to assess the impact of entrepreneurship education on students' entrepreneurial motivation and skills (Kantor 1988; Donckels 1991; Gorman et al. 1997; McMullan et al. 2001; Souitaris et al. 2007).

This research project aims at overcoming the methodological deficiencies of the previous studies and at resolving the contradictions in their findings. Furthermore it introduces new approaches to evaluate the size and nature of the effects of entrepreneurship education, and how to improve its design to achieve the set goals. It should thus bring forward the understanding of the effects of entrepreneurship education on students.

This book contains eight chapters. Each chapter contributes both to the progress of this research project as well as to a gain in insight into the effects of entrepreneurship education.

In the following section of this first chapter, I take one step back and discuss the goals of entrepreneurship education based on widely recognized definitions. I argue that entrepreneurship education should neither fulfill a function of having students create new businesses and jobs directly after a course, nor should it be aimed at uniform-course induced changes in perceptions of attractiveness, feasibility, and intentions towards starting a business. Accordingly, it should enable students to acquire skills necessary for entrepreneurial tasks on the one hand, and also enable students to better self-select into the "right" career path – be it entrepreneurial or managerial – on the other hand. Based on this angle I review the literature and assess both conceptual and methodological approaches of previously conducted studies.

In the conceptual part of this book, I first lay out the theoretical model based upon which I evaluate the effects of entrepreneurship education in chapter 2. This model grounds on the Theory of Planned Behavior (Fishbein and Ajzen 1980; Ajzen 1985). This theory has already been exploited to measure the effects of entrepreneurship education in previous studies (e.g. Fayolle et al. 2006a; Souitaris et al. 2007). I build on this established and validated theory and extend the previously used models by accounting for individual background characteristics. Characteristics such as demographic variables, prior experiences, or personality traits might not only be responsible for existing predispositions in favor or against entrepreneurship, but also play an important role for processing new information received in an entrepreneurship course.

Subsequently, in chapter 3, I discuss in detail the entrepreneurship course under review and the instrument used to measure its effects. During the development I repeatedly consulted the social psychology literature and previous empirical studies on the effects of entrepreneurship education. The detailed description of both the course and the development of instrument as well as the process of data generation should ensure the validity of the used items and a classification of the generated data by other researchers. Furthermore it should facilitate the comparability to the results of other studies and reproduction in subsequent studies.

In the empirical part of this book I take three approaches to evaluate the effects of entrepreneurship education.

Before doing that, however, I use the generated data to test the Theory of Planned Behavior in chapter 4 to see if the hypothesized relationships hold among the considered sample of students.

In chapter 5 I build a bridge to previously conducted studies on the effects of entrepreneurship education. As done there, I employ a difference-in-differences approach exploiting data from the treatment group (the students who attend the entrepreneurship course) and a control group (students who do not attend an entrepreneurship course). Thereby I elicit the effects on mean entrepreneurial attitudes and intentions as proposed by the Theory of Planned Behavior framework. Methodological extensions, compared to other studies following a difference-in-differences approach, promise more reliable results. First I employ a matching method that reduces biases in the results due to systematic differences between the treated and control group students. Second, I investigate whether the sizes of course-induced effects are different for different students according to background variables such as demographics, prior experiences, and personality traits. The results of a difference-in-difference-in-difference approach suggest implications for selectivity guidelines in admission of students to a course when seminar places are limited.

Building on the study by von Graevenitz et al. (2010), chapter 6 follows the new approach of evaluating entrepreneurship education introduced there. The main postulation there is that student behavior is largely driven by Bayesian Updating. During an entrepreneurship course, students update their opinion about their entrepreneurial aptitude. More specifically, initially undecided students should be most likely to change this opinion. Thus, after the course students are more able to determine whether or not they are suited to entrepreneurship. This chapter extends this framework both conceptually and methodically. On the one hand I integrate it with the Theory of Planned Behavior to gain insight into how an entrepreneurship course should be designed to foster these sorting effects. On the other hand I test the model, using data from the control group as well, which was not done in von Graevenitz et al. (2010).

In the last empirical chapter I leave the framework of the Theory of Planned Behavior and focus on the formation of entrepreneurial skills. Thereby

I concentrate on a resource that has been completely ignored by previous studies on effects of entrepreneurship education. I investigate whether externalities by social interactions among students deliver a lever to increase entrepreneurial skills among the population of students. Since teamwork on business planning is a prevalent component of entrepreneurship education anyway, course planners might manage beneficial social interactions by grouping students according to their abilities to efficiently maximize the formation of skills.

In chapter 8 I summarize the findings of the empirical studies and discuss how the several stakeholder groups might use them to achieve their goals. Furthermore I identify avenues for further research.

1.2 Definitions and Overview of the Literature

A central issue of entrepreneurship research has been and still is to find an answer to the question of what triggers and reinforces entrepreneurial intentions[1] and entrepreneurial activity of individuals (Shane and Venkataraman 2000). Pursuing this question, studies in the field of psychology, sociology and economics analyze

a) from an ex-ante perspective the emergence of entrepreneurial intentions and activity (e.g. Kolvereid (1996a); Tkachev and Kolvereid (1999); Kolvereid and Isaksen (2005); Souitaris et al. (2007)),

b) from an ex-post perspective the reasons for an entrepreneur's decision to start up (e.g. Hansemark (2003); Shane et al. (2003); van der Sluis et al. (2005), Zhao et al. (2010)), and

c) individual differences between entrepreneurs and non-entrepreneurs/ managers (e.g. Chen et al. (1998); Stewart (2001); Markman et al. (2002); Stewart and Roth (2007)).

The analyses in this book belong to the first category, looking at the topic from an ex-ante perspective through a psychological and economic, and later on also

---

[1] I.e., the expressed behavioral intention to become an entrepreneur (Bird 1988) or the commitment to start one's own company.

through a more sociological lens. Offering entrepreneurship education is a central strategy at tertiary education institutes to foster entrepreneurial intentions among students (Liñán 2004). The essential precondition behind this strategy is that entrepreneurship is both teachable and learnable. Peter Drucker (1985, p. 450) expressed a very strong opinion about this issue, "It is not magic, it is not mysterious, and it has nothing to do with the genes. It is a discipline. And, like any discipline, it can be learned".

This introductory chapter to this book deals with this measure of forming entrepreneurial intentions among students. It delivers a definition of fundamental terms as well as a classification of different types of entrepreneurship education. I then discuss the goals tertiary education institutes pursue, or should pursue, by offering entrepreneurship education programs. Furthermore, I present results from previously conducted studies trying to measure in how far the offered entrepreneurship education program reached its postulated goals. I conclude with the problems and challenges inherent in such an evaluation.

1.2.1 A Definition of Entrepreneurship

Before giving a definition and a classification for entrepreneurship education, this subsection addresses the definition of "entrepreneurship". In 2005 the entrepreneurship division of the Academy of Management conducted a survey among its members, supplying them with a choice of possible definitions for entrepreneurship, to vote for a statement about the specific domain entrepreneurship division. The majority voted for the following one: "Specific Domain: the creation and management of new businesses, small businesses and family businesses, and the characteristics and special problems of entrepreneurs. Major topics include: new venture ideas and strategies, ecological influences on venture creation and demise, the acquisition and management of venture capital and venture teams, self-employment, the owner-manager, management succession, corporate venturing and the relationship between entrepreneurship and economic development."[2] Due to this variety of topics – including elements of several domains such as economics, sociology, and psychology just to name a few – there is still no generally accepted definition of "entrepreneurship" or the "entrepreneur". In fact, the lack of a commonly recognized definition of these terms is seen as one major obstacle for researchers in contributing to the understanding of this phenomenon (Shane and Venkataraman 2000). A large number of definitions have been given in many research contributions dealing often solely with the issue of defining entrepreneurship. These definitions often focus on certain aspects. Shapero (1975) thinks of entrepreneurship as "(…) a kind of behavior that includes: (1) initiative taking, (2) the organizing or recognizing of social economic mechanisms to turn resources and situations to a practical account, and (3) the acceptance of risk of failure" (p. 187). Gartner (1988) takes a behavioral approach and considers entrepreneurship as "a role that individuals undertake to create organizations" (p. 64). He adds that entrepreneurship ends when the creation stage of the organization ends. The pursuit of opportunities is central to the definition of Stevenson et al. (1989): "Entrepreneurship is a process by which individuals – either on their own or inside organizations – pursue opportunities without regard to the resources they currently control" (p. 23). This definition does not necessarily postulate that the creation of an organization is involved in being an entrepreneur. Entrepreneurship can also occur within organizations, building a bridge to the concept of "intrapreneurship". Finally, Shane and Venkataraman (2000) give a definition of entrepreneurship as a scientific discipline. They define it "(…) as the scholarly examination of how, by whom, and with what effects opportunities to create future goods and services are discovered, evaluated and exploited. Consequently, the field involves the study of sources of opportunities; the process of discovery, evaluation, and exploitation of opportunities; and the set of individuals who discover, evaluate, and exploit them" (p. 218).

---

[2] http://division.aomonline.org/ent/EntprDiv.htm, accessed March 27, 2011

Following this latter definition, I define entrepreneurship in the context of this research project as the discovery, evaluation and exploitation of opportunities to create future goods and services by a natural individual through the creation of a new organization.[3] In this book I call these new organizations start-ups or new businesses and use the term "to start an own business" for any entrepreneurial activity as defined above.

Based on this definition of entrepreneurship, I proceed to a classification of entrepreneurship education in the next subsection.

1.2.2 Classification of Entrepreneurship Education

In a study about entrepreneurs van der Sluis et al. (2005) found that the individual education (measured in years of schooling and studying) positively affects entrepreneurial success. However, studies dealing with causes triggering the decision to start an own business during the time of education, e.g. during the years of study, shed a more differentiated light on the relationship between schooling and entrepreneurial activity. Formal education in general, researchers believe, does not encourage entrepreneurship. Rather, it prepares students for the corporate domain (Timmons 1994), promotes a "take-a-job" mentality (Kourilsky 1995) and suppresses creativity and entrepreneurship (Chamard 1989; Plaschka and Welsch 1990). Hostager and Decker (1999), for example, find that general business management education – unlike entrepreneurial programs – has

---

[3] As is the case with all of the given definitions, the chosen one is by far not unassailable. It completely fades out, for example, a consideration of the variation in the quality of opportunities that different people identify (Shane and Venkataraman 2000). So do Carland et al. (1984) differentiate between entrepreneurs, who establish and manage a business for the principal purpose of profit and growth and who are characterized by innovative behavior (opportunity-driven), and small business owners, who establish a business as the primary source of income that will consume the majority of their time and resources. Although these two concepts are – especially in Germany ("Existenzgründung" and "Unternehmensgründung") – often used synonymously by mistake, they have certain aspects in common, such as the intention to be self-employed in contrast to being organizationally employed. The chosen definition does also not contain any notion of entrepreneurship in established organizations. For this research project, only the creation of new organizations by natural individuals is considered, as this is the outcome policy makers desire from entrepreneurship education.

no significant influence on entrepreneurial propensity. Gupta (1992) in his survey among Indian entrepreneurs obtains a similar result that management education is not an important driver of entrepreneurial attitudes, and Whitlock and Masters (1996) even show that the interest in pursuing an entrepreneurial career dissipates after visiting general business courses. Therefore specialized "entrepreneurship education" is promoted and implemented into curricula of both secondary and tertiary institutions of education in Germany (Klandt 2008), many of the European Community member countries (European Commission 2006) and in the United States (Kuratko 2005). This special education should trigger and foster entrepreneurial activity among students (Gasse 1985; Donckels 1991; Franke and Lüthje 2004). With the emergence of these offers researchers tried to define or classify entrepreneurship education, a task inferring similar difficulties as with the definition of the term "entrepreneurship" itself. Jamieson (1984) proposes a differentiation into three categories and labeled them "Education about Enterprise", "Education for Enterprise", and "Education in Enterprise". Where the first two categories focus on raising awareness for the field of entrepreneurship and to encourage and prepare the start of an own business (e.g. in the form of business planning), the latter is addressed to people who are already entrepreneurs to support them in expanding their business. Garavan and O'Cinneide (1994a) argue for a similar classification and differentiate between "Entrepreneurship Education" and "Education and Training for Small Business Owners". The latter category corresponds to Jamieson's third category, where the goal of "Entrepreneurship Education" is conveying necessary knowledge about starting and leading a business to increase the number of students who are willing to opt for an enterprising career. McMullan and Gillin (1998), based on the theoretical outline previously developed by McMullan and Long (1987), specify six differentiating elements of entrepreneurship education: objectives that are pursued; faculty or teaching team who will be imparting it; participant students; content of the course; teaching methods; and specific support activities for the participants to start their ventures. Brockhaus (1994) points out that objectives are the fundamental question, under which all other elements should be placed. Following this, Curran and Stanworth (1989) define categories of objectives to be pursued by entrepreneurship education. Garavan and O'Cinneide (1994a) adopt these definitions that have been refined by Liñán (2004). His global definition of entrepreneurship education, which is also employed in this book, says: "(...) the whole set of education and training activities – within the educational system or not – that try to develop (...) some of the elements that affect that intention, such as entrepreneurial knowledge, desirability of the entrepreneurial activity, or its feasibility" (Liñán 2004, p. 163), where "intention" means the intention to start an own business. This definition contains the transfer of knowledge and skills to be able to start an own business, but also associated attitudes and personality characteristics. It thus also serves as a borderline to general management education that does not deal with personality, and career attitudes and intentions of the students, but first of all aims at the transfer of practical knowledge. Furthermore, Liñán (2004) lists four categories of entrepreneurship education:

- **Entrepreneurial awareness education**
  The objective here is to convey knowledge about small enterprises, self-employment and entrepreneurship. The goal is not the immediate creation of more entrepreneurs. After taking a course, attendees should be able to make a more educated decision about their future career. Instructors do not actually try to transform attendees into entrepreneurs, but only allow them to make their future professional career choice with a greater perspective.

- **Education for start-up**
  Courses in this category aim at the preparation of individuals to be the owner of a small conventional business (as are the majority of all firms). They address people with already existing entrepreneurial intentions and try to further develop it. They focus on the practical aspects related to the start-up phase, e.g. how to obtain financing, legal regulations, taxation, etc. (Curran and Stanworth 1989).

- **Education for entrepreneurial dynamism**
  This type of entrepreneurship education applies to entrepreneurs who already passed the start-up phase of their business. It promotes dynam-

ic entrepreneurial behaviors after the initial phase. The objective here is that participants acquire knowledge about strategies for expanding their businesses and open up new markets to secure sustainable growth. Garavan and O'Cinneide (1994b) describe examples of this kind of educational programs.

- **Continuing education for entrepreneurs**

  This category is a specialized version of adult education in general, designed to allow improvement of the entrepreneur's existing abilities (Weinrauch 1984). However, the addressees consider these initiatives as too general for the particular needs of their firms.

The courses mostly found in curricula of tertiary education institutions belong to the first category (Garavan and O'Cinneide 1994a), the so-called "Entrepreneurial Awareness Education". Many of the – often short-termed – entrepreneurship courses would be really working as awareness programs (Curran and Stanworth 1989). These courses allow students to assess their own entrepreneurial skills and aptitude and thus to more conscientiously make decisions about their own future career. More precisely, these courses are implemented in undergraduate studies at the beginning of the curriculum, when students' career intentions are still not very pronounced (Cox et al. 2002). Hence also the role of the instructors is clearly defined: they enable students to carry out this self-assessment. The execution of the thereby potentially developed entrepreneurial intentions depends on certain factors (personal situation, business opportunity, resources, etc.) that are not within the instructors' reach (Liñán 2004). Since I look at entrepreneurship education at tertiary institutions of education, I henceforth use the term "entrepreneurship education" for "entrepreneurial awareness education".

The perhaps initially assumed objective of entrepreneurship education at tertiary education institutions, namely the creation of more start-ups and more jobs (as desired by policy makers) may not be the most appropriate one. Preventing a student, who is not suited to an entrepreneurial career, from failing at a costly experiment such as starting an own business can be also considered a success of this kind of education.

Not in all cases should course participants start their own business shortly after attending the course. They even cannot do this, when considering courses in the first semesters of one's studies. The criteria for evaluating the effects of these courses have therefore to be adapted to the respective objective, the target audience and of course the time horizon of entrepreneurship education at tertiary institutions. In the next subsection I present previously conducted studies trying to measure the "success" of entrepreneurship education.

1.2.3 Studies on Effects of Entrepreneurship Education

Research about the effects of entrepreneurship education is still in its infancy (Gorman et al. 1997). Many studies to date simply describe entrepreneurship courses (Vesper and Gartner 1997), discuss the content of good entrepreneurship education (Fiet 2001) or evaluate the economic impact of courses by comparing course attendees versus non-attendees (Chrisman 1997). Some researchers have proposed a positive link between entrepreneurship education and entrepreneurial attitudes, intention or action, but the evidence is not strong.

Career socialization theory proposes that the decision to initiate a career is influenced by many social factors including exposure to educational experiences. For example, Gibb Dyer (1994) claims that specialized entrepreneurship education might give some people the confidence they need to start their own business. It is also pointed out that attitudes toward entrepreneurship are an ideal connecting factor for entrepreneurship education. Robinson et al. (1991) bring the argument closer to the theoretical lens of planned behavior (Ajzen 1985). They claim that the attitude model of entrepreneurship has ramifications for entrepreneurship education programs, as attitudes are open to change and can be influenced by educators and practitioners. Krueger and Brazeal (1994) assert that entrepreneurship education makes seem starting an own business more "feasible". Already several researchers identified the necessity to assess entrepreneurship education to test the aforementioned assertions (Gibb 1987; Curran and Stanworth 1989; Block and Stumpf 1992; Cox 1996; Storey 2000). Until now some studies try to conduct such evaluations, be it by using direct measures (such as the number of started businesses or the number of created jobs) or indirect measures (e.g. increased entrepreneurial intentions among the participants). The first studies, which could be identified during this research project, were conducted in the 1980s and 1990s, and so took place during the time when the USA experienced a massive extension of the offers of entrepreneurship education at tertiary institutions (Kuratko 2005).

Clark et al. (1984) survey US-American students participating in an introductory entrepreneurship course. By the end of the course, 80% intend to start an own business, and indeed these plans have often been executed. Furthermore, 76% declare that attending the course had a strong influence on their decision to enter an entrepreneurial career.

The analysis of an entrepreneurship course in Great Britain shows that the participants act on their existing entrepreneurial intentions earlier than previously planned (Brown 1990).

In a cross-course evaluation of five entrepreneurship courses Garavan and O'Cinneide (1994a) measure the success of these courses by means of the number of started businesses and created jobs. According to their results the 755 participants create 2,665 jobs. They also employed a cost-benefit-calculation and found that each created job cost USD 1,283 when taking the costs for the courses as a basis.

Chrisman (1997) takes a similar approach, however employing different methods. In his examination of the "Venture Development Program" at the University of Calgary he survey 713 companies, where participating students executed entrepreneurial projects during the course. He calculates that this program created 1.23 jobs per company and additional tax revenue between CAD 1.0 M and CAD 4.7 M (compared to program costs of CAD 1.25 M).

Also Henry et al. (2004) take the number of newly created businesses and jobs as evaluation criteria in their analysis of the Irish "Owner-Management Business Planning Programme", which addresses university alumni with a concrete business idea. The 35 participants start eight businesses and 40 new jobs, whereas the 40 members of a control group only create three and 19, respectively.

Lately the approach to evaluate entrepreneurship education on a macroeconomic level using figures such as the number of started businesses or created jobs was heavily criticized (Peterman and Kennedy 2003; Fayolle et al. 2006b; Souitaris et al. 2007). The effects of such a program on an individual is a complex issue, and actually measurable results in the sense of started businesses or created jobs can often only be observed years after the course (Béchard and Toulouse 1998; Fayolle et al. 2006b). Evaluators cannot possibly observe the formation of new businesses during or directly after the course. But the later they conduct an evaluation, the more complicated is it to filter the relevant factors that lead an individual to her decision to start an own business (Block and Stumpf 1992; Fayolle et al. 2006a)[4].

That is why researchers concentrated on the individual attending the course rather than on the aforementioned outcomes, e.g. on the effects that a course had on him. Cognitive and behavioral approaches delivered the central variables of interest to measure the effects of entrepreneurship education on individuals.

Kolvereid and Moen (1997) compare the behavior of business graduates with a major in entrepreneurship and graduates with other majors from a Norwegian business school. The results indicate that graduates with an entrepreneurship major are more likely to start new businesses and have stronger entrepreneurial intentions than other graduates.

Zhao et al. (2005) ask MBA students how much they have learned during their MBA education regarding typical areas of entrepreneurship. Based on data from 265 students, they find that these perceptions of formal learning are positively related to entrepreneurial self-efficacy.

With a strong focus on different effects of entrepreneurship education with respect to gender, Wilson et al. (2007) conduct a survey among MBA students in the USA. They find that attending an entrepreneurship course significantly increases entrepreneurial self-efficacy of females in comparison to males.

In their survey of 111 business administration students at the Technical University of Dortmund, Hack et al. (2008) find that attending an entrepreneur-

---

[4] See also the discussion in subsection 1.2.2.

ship course raises the overall entrepreneurial intentions among students. Also the perceived attractiveness, the perceived pressure, and the perceived entrepreneurial self-efficacy with respect to entrepreneurship are positively affected.

Walter and Walter (2008) generate a cross-university and cross-disciplinary dataset of 2621 computer science, electrical and information engineering, and business administration students at 30 German universities. They differentiate between not-application-based and application-based entrepreneurship education and aim at examining the relationship between the fact that entrepreneurship courses of either type are offered and the entrepreneurial intentions among students. Their results indicate that by offering not-application-based courses a university cannot significantly affect entrepreneurial intentions among students at all, and only male students seem to be attracted by application-based courses.

Other studies are more similar to this research project since they evaluated the effects of a specific entrepreneurship course.
Hansemark (1998) for example examine how attending an entrepreneurship course affected personality traits that are associated with entrepreneurs. He finds that entrepreneurship education participants exhibit a higher need for achievement and locus of control compared to members of a control group.

Another example for this approach is the study by Cox et al. (2002), who achieve unexpected results. They assess the effect of an introductory entrepreneurship course on the level of entrepreneurial self-efficacy among undergraduate business students. Overall, entrepreneurial self-efficacy is lower among students who have completed the course than among students who have not yet begun the course.

Fayolle et al. (2006a) find in their evaluation of a three-day entrepreneurship course at a French university that the effects differ among several subsamples of the surveyed students. They find a positive impact of the course on students' entrepreneurial intentions, who have not previously attended an entrepreneurship course and who have not been exposed to entrepreneurship through their family. Moreover, they find that the impact of the entrepreneurship course on entrepreneurial intentions is dependent on the level of intention when they enter the course. For students with very low ex-ante entrepreneurial intentions the impact of the course is significantly positive, whereas for students with high intentions it is significantly negative.

The studies by Peterman and Kennedy (2003), Souitaris et al. (2007) and Oosterbeek et al. (2010) are, from a methodological point of view, quite similar to the approach of this project. All of them employed a pretest-posttest control-group design to measure the true causal effects of entrepreneurship education. The first one survey Australian high-school students and used data from 109 matched ex-ante and ex-post questionnaires in the treatment group and 111 in a control group. The examined course has a positive impact on the perceived desirability and feasibility of starting an own business. Souitaris et al. (2007) demonstrate that attending an entrepreneurship course raises entrepreneurial intentions. They survey students of natural and engineering sciences at two major European universities and based their empirical analysis on 124 matched questionnaires of the treatment group and 126 of a control group. Oosterbeek's et al. (2010) dataset is interesting as they have access to data from students of a compulsory entrepreneurship course. Their findings are based on data from 104 matched questionnaires of the treatment group and 146 of a control group. Employing a difference-in-differences framework, they show that the program does not have the intended effects, as the effects on students' self-assessed entrepreneurial skills (and traits) are not significantly different from zero. The effect on entrepreneurial intentions is even negative. Finally, von Graevenitz et al. (2010) survey 189 students of a mandatory business-planning course employing a pretest-posttest design.[5] Their findings corroborate the results of Oosterbeek et al. (2010), since here, too, entrepreneurial intentions decline during the course. However, they also found that students' entrepreneurial intentions become more extreme. They assume that students self-select into the "right" career path due to information they receive during the course.

Table 1.1 gives an overview of studies that evaluate entrepreneurship education.

---

[5] Their dataset is part of the dataset used in this book (see chapter 3 for more detailed information).

Table 1.1: Overview of evaluations of entrepreneurship education

Authors (year)	Title and journal (volume)	Characteristics of examined entrepreneurship course	Method (response rates in parentheses)	Relevant variables	Selected results
Studies examining the effects of one specific entrepreneurship course					
Clark/ Davis/ Harnish (1984)	"Do Courses in Entrepreneurship aid in new venture creation?"; Journal of Small Business Management (22)	- "Your Future in Business" (run at a US university) - Lectures, guest lectures by entrepreneurs, case studies	- Survey among the 1855 participants of the years 1978 through 1982 via mail - 1265 responses (68.2%) - 536 phone interviews, 452 responses (84.3%)	- Number of started companies - Number of created jobs	- 129 newly started companies - 813 newly created jobs - Annual sales generated by the started businesses (accumulated) USD 13,5 M.
Brown (1990)	"Encouraging Enterprise: Britain's Graduate Enterprise"; Journal of Small Business Management (28)	- "Graduate Enterprise Program" (country-wide offered program in Great Britain) - Duration: 16 weeks - Business planning, presentation to investors and starting an own business	- Survey among the 214 applicants to the program in 1987 - No information about data collection procedures	- Number of created jobs	- Newly started companies generated 3.3 jobs on average after one and a half years - Annual sales generated by the started companies in the "Graduate Enterprise Program" (accumulated) GBP 8 M.

Garavan/ O'Cinn-eide (1994b)	"Entrepreneurship Education and Training Programmes: A Review and Evaluation - Part 2"; Journal of European Industrial Training (18)	- Different programs at five European universities - Duration (dependent on program): 25 days - twelve months	- Heterogeneous composition of participants - 755 participants - No information about data collection procedures	- Number of started companies - Number of created jobs	- 316 started companies, thereof 253 still existing at the time the study was conducted - 2665 newly created jobs - Cost-return calculation: costs of USD 1,283 per created job (data for three of the five programs)
Chrisman (1997)	"Program Evaluation and the Venture Development Program at the University of Calgary: A Research Note"; Entrepreneurship Theory and Practice (22)	- Course run by the Venture Development Group of the University of Calgary - Mostly project-based work: student teams work on projects submitted by start-ups (market research, feasibility-study, product design, financial planning, etc.)	- Paper-based survey among 713 start-ups that submitted projects between 1990 and 1994 - 181 valid responses (25.4%)	- Number of created jobs - Tax revenue impact - Perceived value added to the start-ups	- 1.23 new jobs generated per start-up - Additional tax revenue estimated to be between CAD 1,019,712 and CAD 4,657,747 (costs for running the course: CAD 1.25 M.) - Overall perceived value added: CAD 700,000
Hansemark (1998)	"The effects of an entrepreneurship programme on Need for Achievement and Locus of Control of reinforcement"; International Journal of Entrepreneurial Behavior & Research (4)	- No information given	- No details about participants - Ex-ante ex-post control group design - Valid responses: treatment group: 19 control group: 51	- Need for achievement (Likert scales) - Locus of control (Likert scales)	- Treatment group members have a higher need for achievement after the course - Treatment group members have a higher locus of control after the course

Cox/ Mueller/ Moss (2002)	"The Impact of Entrepreneurship Education on Entrepreneurial Self-Efficacy"; International Journal of Entrepreneurship Education (1)	- Entrepreneurship course at a university in southwestern USA - Lectures, business planning - Duration: five months	- Simultaneous paper-based surveys among two cohorts: cohort 1 before entering the course (394 subjects) cohort 2 has just finished the course (254 subjects)	- Entrepreneurial Self-Efficacy	- Course affects entrepreneurial self-efficacy negatively
Peterman/ Kennedy (2003)	"Enterprise Education: Influencing Students' Perceptions of Entrepreneurship"; Entrepreneurship Theory & Practice (28)	- "Young Achievement Australia enterprise program" (offered at high-schools) - foundation, establishment, consolidation and improvements and liquidation of a small company - Duration: nine months	- Participants: students from 17 Queensland high-schools - Ex-ante ex-post treatment-control-group design - Matched and valid questionnaires: treatment group: 109 control group: 111	- Entrepreneurial intentions (dummy-variable) - Perceived feasibility (five items, Likert scales) - Perceived desirability (three items, Likert scales) - Prior exposure to entrepreneurship and rating of the experience (eight items, dummy-variables)	- Treatment group exhibits higher breadth and positiveness of prior exposure to entrepreneurship - The course positively affects perceptions of desirability and feasibility (compared to the control group) - The course shows a greater influence on participants with few or negative prior exposure to entrepreneurship

Henry/ Hill/ Leitch (2004)	"The Effectiveness of Training for New Business Creation: A Longitudinal Study"; International Small Business Journal (22)	- "Owner-Management Business Planning Programme" - Duration: six months	- 35 participants with university degree and business idea - Longitudinal study over three years - 33 valid responses - Comparison group (participants of another entrepreneurship course, 38 participants) - Control group (48 participants)	- Number of started companies - Number of created jobs	- eight started businesses (comparison group: nine; control group: three) - 40 created jobs (comparison group: nine control group: 19)
Fayolle/ Gailly/ Lassas-Clerc (2006a)	"Effect and Counter-effect of Entrepreneurship Education and Social Context on Student's Intentions"; Estudios de Economica Aplicada (24)	- Entrepreneurship course at a French university - Evaluation of business ideas - Duration: three days	- 275 participants ("Master of Management" students) - Paper-based ex-ante and ex-post survey - Valid matched responses: 144 (52.0 %)	- Entrepreneurial intentions (three items, Likert scales) - Attitude towards entrepreneurship (32 items, Likert scales) - Perceived social norm (six items, Likert scales) - Perceived behavioral control (six items, Likert scales)	- Course positively affects perceived behavioral control and entrepreneurial intentions for subgroups of the participants: -- participants who never attended an entrepreneurship course before -- participants who do not have an entrepreneur in the family - Course positively influences students with a low initial entrepreneurial intentions, and negatively influences students with a high initial entrepreneurial intentions

Souitaris/ Zerbinati/ Al-Laham (2007)	"Do entrepreneurship programmes raise entrepreneurial intention of science and engineering students? The effect of learning, inspiration and resources"; Journal of Business Venturing (22)	- Similar courses at universities in London and Grenoble for natural and engineering science students - Lectures, business planning	- Ex-ante ex-post treatment-control group design - Participants: Treatment group: 232 (154 in London, 78 in Grenoble) Control group: 220 (148 in London, 72 in Grenoble) - Valid matched responses: Treatment group: 124 (79 + 45; 51.3 % and 57.7 %) Control group: 126 (84 + 42; 56.8 % and 58.3 %)	- Attitude towards entrepreneurship (33 items, Likert scales) - Perceived social norm (six items, Likert scales) - Perceived behavioral control (six items, Likert scales) - Entrepreneurial intentions (three items, Likert scales) - Emerging entrepreneurial activity during the course (19 items, dummy-variables) - Program benefit: Learning (five items, Likert scales) Inspiration (seven items, dummy-variables) Resource utilization (eleven items, Likert scales)	- No relationship between entrepreneurial intentions and emerging entrepreneurial activity at the end of the course - Course positively affects perceived social norm and entrepreneurial intentions - Inspiration through the course positively affects perceived social norm and entrepreneurial intentions

Oosterbeek/ van Praag/ IJsselstein (2010)	"The Impact of Entrepreneurship Education on Entrepreneurship Competencies and Intentions: An Evaluation of the Junior Achievement Mini-Company Program"; European Economic Review (54)	- "Junior Achievement Young Enterprise Student Mini-Company Program" at the AVANS Hogeschool - Creation, management and liquidation of a small business - Duration: nine months	- Ex-ante ex-post treatment-control group design - Treatment group: 219 participants control group: 343 participants - Valid matched questionnaires: treatment group: 104 (47.0%) control group: 146 (43.0%)	- Personality traits (all Likert scales) -- Need for achievement (ten items) -- Need for autonomy (nine items) -- Need for power (eight items) -- Social orientation (eight items) -- Self efficacy (nine items) -- Endurance (eleven items) -- Risk taking propensity (six items) - Skills (all Likert scales) -- Market awareness (ten items) -- Creativity (eleven items) -- Flexibility (seven items) - Entrepreneurial intentions (one item, Likert scale)	- Course has no significant influences on any of the personality traits or skills - Course significantly negatively affects entrepreneurial intentions

von Graevenitz / Harhoff / Weber (2010)	"The Effects of Entrepreneurship Education"; Journal of Economic Behavior and Organization (54)	- "Business Planning" at the Ludwig-Maximilians-Universität Munich - Lectures, business planning - Duration: four months	- Ex-ante ex-post design - 409 participants - Valid matched questionnaires: 189 (46.2%)	- Entrepreneurial intentions (one item, Likert scale)	- Entrepreneurial intentions decline during the course - Entrepreneurial intentions become more extreme, i.e. the course helps students self-select into the "right" career path

Studies examining the general effects of having attended an entrepreneurship course

Kolvereid/ Moen (1997)	"Entrepreneurship among business graduates: does a major in entrepreneurship make a difference?"; Journal of European Industrial Training (21)	---	- Paper-based survey among all alumni of the course of study "Siviløkonom" at the Bodø Graduate School of Business, Sweden, between 1987 and 1994 - Population: 720 students - 374 valid responses (51.8 %)	- Entrepreneurial intentions (Likert scale) - Entrepreneurial activity (dummy-variable) - Entrepreneurship major chosen (dummy-variable)	- Alumni with entrepreneurship-major have higher entrepreneurial intentions - Alumni with entrepreneurship-major have started an own business more often than other students
Zhao/ Seibert/ Hills (2005)	"The Mediating Role of Self-Efficacy in the Development of Entrepreneurial Intentions"; Journal of Applied Psychology (90)	---	- Surveys at two points of time (t1 and t2) among MBA students at US universities - Population: 778 - Valid matched questionnaires: 265 (34.0 %)	- Perception of formal learning during MBA education (four items, Likert scales)	- Perceptions of formal learning in entrepreneurship-related courses positively related to entrepreneurial self-efficacy

Wilson/ Kickul/ Marlino (2007)	"Gender, Entrepreneurial Self-Efficacy, and Entrepreneurial Career Intentions: Implications for Entrepreneurship Education"; Entrepreneurship Theory & Practice (31)	---	- Survey between 2002 and 2004; -- Population sample: 5'126 MBA students in seven US graduate programs -- 933 valid responses (18.2 %)	- Entrepreneurial self-efficacy (six items, Likert scales) - Entrepreneurship concentration chosen (dummy-variable)	- Entrepreneurship education significantly increased and heightened the self-efficacy of females in comparison to the males
Hack/ Rettberg/ Witt (2008)	"Gründungsausbildung und Gründungsabsicht: Eine empirische Untersuchung an der TU Dortmund"; Zeitschrift für KMU und Entrepreneurship (56)	---	- Paper-based survey among business students at the TU Dortmund, Germany -- Population: 1172 students; -- 111 valid responses (9.5%)	- Entrepreneurial intentions (one item, Likert scale)	- Entrepreneurship education significantly increased intention
Walter / Walter (2008)	"Deutsche Universitäten als Gründungsinkubatoren: Der Beitrag der Gründungsausbildung zur Gründungsintention von Studierenden"; Schmalenbachs Zeitschrift für betriebswirtschaftliche Forschung (60)	---	- Paper-based survey among computer science, electrical and information engineering, and business administration students at 30 German universities - Population: 5962 - 2721 valid responses (45.64%)	- Entrepreneurial intentions (one item, Likert scale) - Application-based and non-application-based entrepreneurship education (dummy-variables)	- Only application-based entrepreneurship education significantly raises intentions, but only for male students

1.2.4 Critique of Previously Conducted Studies

The studies presented above show that entrepreneurship education at tertiary institutions of education can generate impetus towards entrepreneurial activity. However, the findings have often been criticized for methodological deficiencies (Gorman et al. 1997; Peterman and Kennedy 2003; Souitaris et al. 2007).

This criticism starts at the choice of the variables of interest when evaluating entrepreneurship education (Wyckham 1989). The evaluation criteria have to be adapted to the status of education, the objectives of the course and the target audience (Béchard and Toulouse 1998). The goal of university entrepreneurship education is just not necessarily that all participants start their own businesses in the short run as argued in subsection 1.2.2 (Curran and Stanworth 1989). In addition the evaluation of entrepreneurship education based on figures such as the number of started businesses or created jobs is problematic. The often perennial latency between completing an entrepreneurship course and the formation of a new business as well as the many – by the university – not influenceable general conditions affecting entrepreneurial activity hinders the establishment of a causal connection (Cox et al. 2002). Even a longitudinal study could face difficulties to derive an appropriate causality, since it would become more and more challenging to filter the impact of a single entrepreneurship course on the decision to start a company the later the measurement is carried out (Lüthje and Franke 2002; Fayolle et al. 2006b). Accordingly descriptive or retrospective approaches (for example in the studies of McMullan et al. (1985), McMullan and Gillin (1998), Garavan and O'Cinneide (1994a), Chrisman (1997), and Henry et al. (2004)) might deliver no convincing evidence that entrepreneurial activity is affected by entrepreneurship education (Gorman et al. 1997; Alberti 1999).

Therefore the effects of entrepreneurship education should be evaluated directly after finishing a course (Block and Stumpf 1992). Evaluators have to take different evaluation criteria into account, and this is why the participating individual got in the focus of such evaluations, and also the effects the studied course had on the focal individual (this change in approaches in the late 1990s is also demonstrated by Table 1.1). First studies taking this point of view analyzed the effects of entrepreneurship courses on personality traits that are associated with entrepreneurs and that are considered to differentiate entrepreneurs from non-entrepreneurs (see subsection 2.2.1). However, these personality traits are presumed to be relatively stable and difficult to influence (Robinson et al. 1991), explaining for example the results of Oosterbeek et al. (2010). They could not confirm that the course had a significant impact on personality traits. Cognitive constructs such as "perceived feasibility" or "perceived desirability" of starting a business, or entrepreneurial intentions have been identified as appropriate target variables. This will be discussed more profoundly in the next chapter.

But even studies with these measures exhibit methodological deficiencies. First, although evaluating the effects using the same outcome variables, the studies use different items to measure them. This complicates a comparison and validation of the results, questioning the derived implications from these studies regarding the course design. Second, some of them do not employ control groups to validate the findings (as is the case in Cox et al. (2002), Fayolle et al. (2006b), and von Graevenitz et al. (2010)). Also fundamental controls, i.e. ex-ante and ex-post surveys, have not been conducted (see Kolvereid and Moen (1997), Cox et al. (2002), Zhao et al. (2005) Wilson et al. (2007), Hack et al. (2008), or Walter and Walter (2008)). Third, most studies assume that entrepreneurship education has the same effects on all students regardless of their individual background, such as demographic characteristics or prior exposure to entrepreneurial behavior (e.g. Souitaris et al. 2007). Lüthje and Franke (2002), however, state that this is not the case. Oosterbeek et al. (2010) explicitly investigate whether the course they survey yields different effects on female and male students. They do indeed find that female students are more subject to course-induced influences than male students. In almost all studies I presented above, however, the researchers surveyed students who self-selected into the analyzed entrepreneurship course. This potentially biases the results in favor of educational interventions, as one could argue that the students attending the course already had a certain positive disposition towards entrepreneurship (Lüthje and

Franke 2002). When researchers evaluate a compulsory course as did Oosterbeek et al. (2010), the results could look significantly different regarding effects on entrepreneurial intentions and attitudes. And finally from a conceptual point of view, none of the presented studies discussed in depth the issue of the goals of entrepreneurship education. Currently, there is also no agreement on what would constitute a suitable conceptual model for the analysis of the effects of entrepreneurship education. Most studies measure the impact of entrepreneurship education merely by searching for uniform course-induced positive changes in entrepreneurial intentions. I argue that this approach may be misleading because it masks important sorting effects. Entrepreneurship courses may fulfill a function of informing students about future career options and help them to better self-select into the right career path (see subsection 1.2.2. for a discussion on the goals of entrepreneurship education, and also von Graevenitz et al. (2010)). This effect can be socially positive even if entrepreneurial intentions decline as a consequence of entrepreneurship training.

While this literature has generated interesting insights, the effects emanating from entrepreneurship education are still poorly understood and the research in this domain still has huge gaps. Not surprisingly, several researchers have called for more research to answer the question if entrepreneurship education can influence entrepreneurial perceptions and intentions (Kantor 1988; Donckels 1991; Krueger and Brazeal 1994; McMullan et al. 2001). Descriptive and retrospective studies are not sufficient to provide convincing evidence for the presumed effects (Matthews and Moser 1996; Gorman et al. 1997; Alberti 1999). Peterman and Kennedy (2003) call for the development of credible methods of testing preconceived hypotheses, using large sample sizes and control groups, in order to move this young field of research beyond its exploratory stage (Alberti, 1999).

At the beginning of each chapter, I will briefly discuss its contribution in overcoming these criticisms presented in this section.

2. Theoretical Foundations

2.1 Introduction

This research project aims at assessing the effects of entrepreneurship education on students' ability to discover whether an entrepreneurial career suits them. In the previous chapter I argued that this assessment has to be done directly after students have finished the course. But neither instructors nor researchers conducting this assessment may expect that those students who are encouraged to start an own business do so right at this time. Thus one has to first think of a suitable theoretical framework that allows predicting entrepreneurial activity when there is a time lag expected between the end of the course and the start of the business.

In this chapter I propose a theoretical framework to evaluate the size and nature effects of entrepreneurship education on individual career attitudes and intentions. This framework also permits an assessment of what course components provide information based upon which students adjust these attitudes and intentions. And third, a consequent use of this framework enables researchers to compare different courses and derive implications for their design to maximize the desired outcomes. This theoretical model makes heavy use of theories from social psychology, which have already been applied to the entrepreneurship domain.

Early entrepreneurship research tried to do this based on personality or demographic characteristics of individuals (Brockhaus 1980; McClelland 1961). Researchers strove to identify a pattern of personality or personal environment that allows differentiating between entrepreneurs and managers. However, empirically the related variables were found to be poor predictors of entrepreneurial activity. The "typical" entrepreneur remained elusive (Autio et al. 1997).

A more promising way of looking at the prediction of entrepreneurial activity offers the study of the entrepreneurial process by applying a behavioral approach using intention models (Bird 1988; Shapero and Sokol 1982). Research in social psychology suggests that intentions proved to be a robust predictor of planned behavior such as starting a business (Ajzen 1991; Shapero and Sokol 1982; Bird 1988; Katz and Gartner 1988; Krueger and Brazeal 1994). Research into intentions in general is dominated by the work of Ajzen and Fishbein (Ajzen 1991; Fishbein and Ajzen 2010). Their "Theory of Planned Behavior" proposes that the formation of intentions depends on perceived desirability, perceived social norm, and perceived behavioral control towards the behavior in question. The results of several meta-studies suggest a superiority of the behavioral approach using the Theory of Planned Behavior over other approaches to predict future behavior (Kim and Hunter 1993; Armitage and Conner 2001). Also in the entrepreneurship domain, the Theory of Planned Behavior has been widely used to predict entrepreneurial intentions and activity (e.g. Kolvereid 1996a; Tkachev and Kolvereid 1999; Krueger et al. 2000; Kolvereid and Isaksen 2006; Fayolle et al. 2006a).

The Theory of Planned Behavior has also been applied in the context of entrepreneurship education evaluation (Fayolle et al. 2006a; Souitaris et al. 2007). Krueger and Carsrud (1993) explicitly suggested its use: "Researchers might use this model to analyze how (...) entrepreneurial education affects intentions." Its focus on the evolution of intentions and not on the entrepreneurial behavior itself (Fayolle et al. 2006a) is a key argument why the Theory of Planned Behavior is an appropriate framework for that: it does not try to measure these effects directly in terms of actual entrepreneurial activity, which is difficult to determine as discussed in subsection 1.2.4. Moreover, it allows a structured analysis of the impact of entrepreneurship education on the three attitudes that intentions derive from. Relating components of an entrepreneurship course with these attitudes and empirically determining the size and nature of these impacts, the theory allows deriving implications about the optimal design of entrepreneurship education to achieve the desired outcomes.

In this chapter, I lay out the theoretical model based on the Theory of Planned Behavior upon which I will evaluate the effects of entrepreneurship education as proposed by Krueger and Carsrud (1993) and Fayolle et al.

(2006a). The model I propose (and that subsequently delivers the relevant variables in the empirical parts of this book) is thus based on a repeatedly applied and empirically tested and validated theory (and measurement tools). Therefore, using a Theory of Planned Behavior-based model, I circumvent criticism other studies have been exposed to, as mentioned in subsection 1.2.4. Instead of inventing a new model delivering an unproven set of measurement tools, I build on pretested items repeatedly used both to predict entrepreneurial activity and to measure the effects of entrepreneurship education. Moreover, due to the wide acknowledgement of the Theory of Planned Behavior as a framework for evaluating entrepreneurship education, I ensure that the results of the empirical chapters are comparable to those of previously conducted and future studies. I thus address a major critique expressed by Shook et al. (2003): "With regard to theoretical limitations, the entrepreneurial intent literature has not resulted in cumulative knowledge because the various perspectives have been pursued in isolation from other perspectives. (...) Future work on entrepreneurial intentions should attempt to integrate and reduce the number of alternative intention models" (p. 386).

The contribution of this chapter is threefold. First, I review the trait and demographic-sociological approach-based literature on predicting entrepreneurial activity. I conclude that the behavioral approach is the most appropriate for that. Second, I introduce the Theory of Planned Behavior and assess its appropriateness for predicting future behavior in general. Especially relevant here is the discussion of the role of behavioral interventions in the formation of attitudes and intentions. In addition I address theoretical and practical challenges to this theory that may also apply to my research project. Next, I review the Theory of Planned Behavior-based literature on the prediction of entrepreneurial activity. A discussion of its applicability to this specific domain by drawing comparisons to applications regarding other behaviors follows. Finally, I present my Theory of Planned Behavior-based model to evaluate the effects of entrepreneurship education as a behavioral intervention. There I argue that each of the three attitudes identified by the Theory of Planned Behavior may change in response to content taught in an entrepreneurship course. The relations between the attitudes and course content allow deriving implications about course design when tested empirically. Moreover and in contrast to other studies, I explicitly address the role of background variables (demographics, prior experiences, personality) when learning about entrepreneurship. I thus address Franke and Lüthje's (2004) comment that an entrepreneurship course does not have the same effects on all students. Also Henry et al. (2005) state that this is important, as failure to take into account individual background characteristics lead to biases in the measurement of the effects of entrepreneurship education. Due to restricted education budgets an identification of these different effects on different subsamples of the student population may have consequences for the selectivity in student admission to entrepreneurship courses.

This chapter has six sections. In the next section I review the trait, demographic-sociological, and behavioral approach to predict entrepreneurial activity. Next, section 3 introduces the Theory of Planned Behavior, followed by a discussion of its application in section 4. Section 5 provides the theoretical model based upon which I empirically evaluate an entrepreneurship course in later chapters. Section 6 concludes with an assessment of the proposed model with respect to its practical application and the interests of the stakeholder groups of entrepreneurship education discussed in section 1.1.

2.2 Psychological and Sociological Views at the Entrepreneur

As mentioned earlier, the domain of entrepreneurship research is clearly an interdisciplinary one. Psychological and sociological theories contributed to the advancement of the understanding of entrepreneurship and the entrepreneur. Historically researchers proceeded in their efforts by asking questions about who is an entrepreneur (trait approach), what environment forms an entrepreneur (demographic-sociological approach), and why somebody chooses to become an entrepreneur (behavioral approach). Where initially researchers focused on the characteristics of an entrepreneur, currently the behavior itself is the main dimension of interest. The next paragraphs give an overview of the different approaches.

2.2.1 Trait Approach

Psychologists claim that broad dispositional variables can predict some behaviors. This stream of thought was also transferred to the entrepreneurship domain. Early entrepreneurship research aim at defining and characterizing entrepreneurs (and his entrepreneurial decisions) based on personality traits and try to delineate them from non-entrepreneurs (McClelland 1961; Brockhaus 1980; Brockhaus and Horwitz 1982). Others follow, exploring traits such as the propensity to act, internal locus of control, creativity, need for achievement, innovativeness, proactivity, propensity to take risks, problem-solving style, need for autonomy, and tolerance of ambiguity and uncertainty (see e.g. Robinson et al. 1991). The reasoning behind this research is based on the assumption that the performance of the new businesses depends first and foremost on the entrepreneur. The hope is to be able to develop tests with which one could identify the "ideal" entrepreneur and so decrease the risk of a depreciatory investment by a potential venture capitalist.

However, the trait approach delivered a large number of lists of characteristics and traits associated with an entrepreneur, leading to confusions among the entrepreneurship community rather than to a gain in insight (Shane et al. 2003; Rauch and Frese 2007). Not surprising, from a theoretical point of view this approach is heavily criticized (Gartner 1988; Krueger et al. 2000). It exhibits methodological weaknesses (instruments were borrowed from psychology and inappropriately applied to entrepreneurship (Hornaday 1982), only few instruments were specifically designed to explain entrepreneurship (Wortman 1986)) and yields only poor new insights (Gartner 1988; Krueger et al. 2000). Another problem is that different instruments intended to measure the same concept lack convergent validity (Robinson et al. 1991), such that the existing literature might contain misleading information about the traits associated to entrepreneurship. Moreover, this approach is more appropriate to measure general tendencies (Abelson 1982; Epstein 1984). It loses its efficacy when applied to a specific domain such as entrepreneurship (Mischel 1968; Carsrud et al.

1987; Krueger and Carsrud 1993).[6] Finally, another issue of the trait approach in entrepreneurship research emerges from its ex-post focus. The traits associated with entrepreneurs have been determined in surveys among entrepreneurs. Researchers assume that an entrepreneur exhibits these traits already before he starts his business, and that these traits are not a consequence of his behavior when starting and managing the business (Gartner 1988). To prove causality one would have to observe the focal individual also prior to the entrepreneurial activity, what is done in behavioral approaches.

Reviews of literature conclude that there is no consistent relationship between personality and entrepreneurship. Thus personality traits alone are only weak predictors of entrepreneurial activity. In addition, in the entrepreneurship education evaluation literature the trait approach yields poor findings. In their prominent study Oosterbeek et al. (2010) measure the impact of an entrepreneurship course on personality traits and find no significant differences after the course compared to before. This finding is not surprising, given that personality traits are considered extremely stable over time (Epstein and O'Brien 1985) and thus not likely to be manipulable by a short-term intervention such as an entrepreneurship course.

The failure of the trait approach to significantly predict entrepreneurial activity calls for another approach to evaluating entrepreneurship education. But although it is postulated that future research using the trait paradigm should be completely abandoned (e.g. Brockhaus and Horwitz (1982); Gartner (1988), Zhao et al. (2010)), this approach could still be valuable. Despite their low explanatory power in predicting propensity to entrepreneurship when considered on their own, researchers hypothesize an indirect influence between traits and specific actions, greatly attenuated by other, more immediate factors (Ajzen and Fishbein 1980) (see subsection 2.2.3). The same is true for the demographic-sociological approach.

---

[6] And this is not unique to research about entrepreneurs. Traits are found to have limited predictive power and inconsistent correlations with regard to any particular behavior. And even when obtaining significant correlations, these were of rather low magnitude (Mischel 1968; Fishbein and Ajzen 2010).

2.2.2 Demographic-Sociological Approach

Researchers hypothesize that demographic or sociological variables are linked to differences in behavior (Fishbein and Ajzen 2010). The demographic-sociological approach focuses on individual background characteristics and the social environment of the individual, analyzing it regarding its impact on the individual's emergence as entrepreneur. It assumes that people having a similar background also have similar characteristics, and the reasoning behind it is quite similar to the one with regard to the trait approach – identifying socio-demographic characteristics of known entrepreneurs would render it possible to predict entrepreneurial activity in unknown populations, delivering the same advantages as mentioned with the trait approach. Demographic variables that are often examined in the entrepreneurship domain are, e.g., family background and experiences such as birth order, role models, marital status, age, gender, education level of parents and of oneself, socioeconomic status, previous work experience, and work habits (see Robinson et al. (1991)), and sociologists conducting entrepreneurship research focus on neighborhood and social interaction effects (see subsection 7.2.2 for a review of this literature).

Similar to the trait approach, however, the demographic-sociological approach in the entrepreneurship domain is challenged by researchers. Researchers argue that it is not a given set of demographic characteristics that leads to the decision to enter an entrepreneurial career, but specific reactions to circumstances – even if similar demographic backgrounds lead to similar experiences, it is the conclusions one draws and acts upon that determines entrepreneurship (Robinson et al. 1991). And these conclusions do not have to be static over time, as an individual gathers more and perhaps different experiences, leading to a re-evaluation of decisions associated to entrepreneurship (Fishbein and Ajzen 2010).

So again, variables employed in this approach yield inconsistent and conflicting results and have limited predictive power (Robinson et al. 1991). Thus they are poor predictors of entrepreneurial activity (Krueger et al. 2000). But as already mentioned in the preceding subsection, researchers argue that socio-demographic variables could have an indirect impact on specific actions, affecting more immediate antecedents (Fishbein and Ajzen 2010).

Although both the trait and the demographic-sociological approach are strongly challenged, they both contribute to the understanding of the emergence of entrepreneurship, advancing the domain within the limits of the respective paradigm. In order to advance this understanding, an alternative paradigm has to include both approaches and their strengths and simultaneously overcome the deficiencies. The behavioral approach to entrepreneurship, examining entrepreneurial intentions, promises to do both.

2.2.3 Behavioral Approach

The study of intentions to perform a certain behavior is considered very promising when researchers want to better understand the antecedents, context and consequences of the behavior in question (Ajzen and Fishbein 1980; Ajzen 1987; Fishbein and Ajzen 2010). I use Bird's (1988, p. 442) widely recognized definition of intention: "Intentionality is a state of mind directing a person's attention (and therefore experience and action) toward a specific object (goal) or a path in order to achieve something (means)."[7] Intentions encompass motivational aspects influencing the behavior in question and are indicators for how much effort individuals have to exert to execute this behavior. Every planned behavior can be best predicted by studying an individual's intentions regarding this behavior, and not her personality or demographic characteristics (Bagozzi and Yi 1989). Research in social psychology found that the intention is the single best predictor of any planned behavior (Bagozzi and Yi 1989) even when this behavior is rare, hard to observe or involves unpredictable time lags between intention and action (Ajzen 1991). Typical examples are decisions regarding the future career path (Lent 1994). Compared to the actual behavior intentions are measurable without delay and unaffected by distorting influences.

---

[7] Although stemming from the entrepreneurship literature I use this definition for intentions also on a general level.

In addition, intentions are not subject to any ex-post rationalization of the observed individual. In general: the stronger the intention, the higher is the probability that the intention predicts an actual execution of the behavior in question (Ajzen 1991).

Thus intentions predict action, while specific attitudes influence intentions. These attitudes in turn are derived from exogenous influences (Ajzen 1987; Bagozzi and Yi 1989). These encompass for example personality traits and socio-demographic variables (Ajzen 1991). The behavioral approach thus fulfills the requirements postulated at the end of the preceding subsection: it integrates the trait and demographic-sociological approaches presented above and can make use of their strengths and can build on established theory.

From this point of view, the poor findings resulting from these approaches are explained: intentions (not to mention actual behavior) are only indirectly affected by these exogenous influences – either by strengthening or weakening the attitudes toward the behavior or by moderating the link between intention and action (i.e. they hinder or boost the transformation of intention into action). Moreover, in addition to the exogenous influences, the attitudes underlying intentions are based on perceptions, which means that they can be influenced (Ajzen 1991). This implies and explains that intentions are different by individual and by situation. Intention-based theories therefore suggest that exogenous influences affect individual attitudes and – indirectly – intentions, and in the end actual behavior (Ajzen 1987, see also Figure 2.1).

A strong intention towards a specific behavior should therefore result in an actual attempt to execute the behavior. In their meta-analytic review of 48 studies from various fields of behavior, Armitage and Conner (2001) report a mean intention-behavior correlation of .47, explaining 22% of the variance. Others report a range for correlation coefficients of .45 - .62 (Randall and Wolff 1994; Notani 1998).

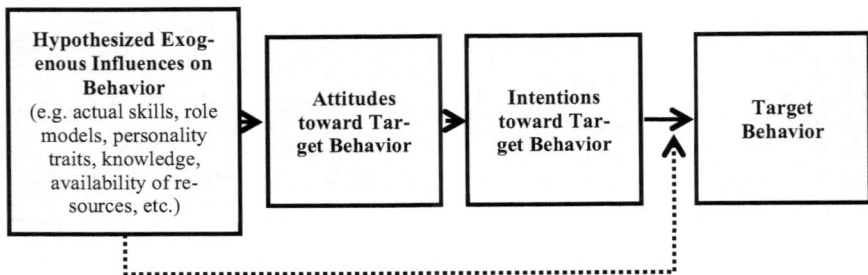

Figure 2.1: Intentions-based process-model (according to Krueger and Carsrud (1993))

"Given the impressive success of a cognitive approach in other fields (e.g., psychology, education), there are grounds for predicting that it may also yield positive results when applied to the field of entrepreneurship" (Baron 2004, p. 237). Thus the behavioral approach is seen as the most promising one for predicting entrepreneurial activity. Many researchers consider entrepreneurship as a typical example of intentionally planned, however with a certain time lag, emerging behavior (e.g. Shapero and Sokol 1982; Bird 1988; Katz and Gartner 1988; Krueger and Brazeal 1994).[8] Derived from the previously mentioned definition by Bird (1988), Krueger (1993) defines entrepreneurial intentions as the commitment to starting a new business. The study of entrepreneurial intentions is considered very promising, because researchers get a better understanding for background factors, accompanying environment factors (e.g. the availability of resources such as the offer of entrepreneurship courses) and the final consequences of the behavior (i.e. the decision for a specific career) without having to observe the transformation of intentions into action. Moreover, this approach leads to insights why many entrepreneurs decided to pursue an entrepreneurial career long before they identified an appropriate business idea (Brockhaus 1987; Krueger et al. 2000). Individuals identify goals (for example the start of an own business) before they implement measures they have to execute to fulfill this goal (such as the identification of a business idea) (Ajzen 1987; Tubbs and Ekeberg 1991). Especially important for this research project

---

[8] The presence of business planning in literally every course concept at tertiary institutions underlines this (Krueger et al. 2000).

is the fact that theories based on the behavioral approach can explain how entrepreneurship education as exogenous influence can affect the perceptions-based attitudes, and so indirectly entrepreneurial intentions. This is particularly true for intentions regarding career choice. These intentions are even more subject to influences by exogenous interventions compared to other examples as studied by Ajzen (1991; 2002) that are only dependent on the volitional control of the individual (such as the decision to quit smoking, or short-term voting preferences).

Despite the proven superiority of the behavioral approach over the trait or demographic-sociological approach, some issues remain when applied to the entrepreneurship domain (but are generally true for other domains as well). Researchers often conducted "ad-hoc" studies, developing questionnaires without theoretical base, calling it attitude approach and thus failed to develop standard scales and follow validation procedures. Moreover, they ignored already used and validated standard scales developed in social psychology research that could have easily been applied to the entrepreneurship domain.

To overcome these issues, since the 1990s, researchers in the entrepreneurship domain made heavily use of well-established behavioral theories in social psychology. There the research is dominated by models going back to the work of Icek Ajzen and Martin Fishbein, who developed a theoretical framework to predict a broad range of behaviors. The latest version of this framework is called "Theory of Planned Behavior". In the following section I present this theory on a general level, before discussing its application to the entrepreneurship domain. Later I discuss its applicability to the evaluation of entrepreneurship education and that this theory is ideally suited for this purpose, as they propose an indirect way to assess their influence on downstream actual behavior (Fayolle et al. 2006a). It helps to avoid the criticisms mentioned in this sector and issues with ad-hoc evaluations based on e.g. the number of created businesses (see subsection 1.2.4).

2.3 The Theory of Planned Behavior

Ajzen and Fishbein (1980) developed a theoretical frame accounting for the cognitive processes underlying intentionally planned behavior. The latest version is the "Theory of Planned Behavior", which still dominates the social psychology research about intentions. This model promises researchers to gain more insight into hypothesized influences on the behavior in question. They not only better understand which exogenous influences are significant antecedents of attitudes and intentions, but also how they affect the execution of the target behavior. In the following, I present this theory and its application to the prediction of entrepreneurial intentions.

2.3.1 Predictors of Intentions and Behavior

The Theory of Planned Behavior emerges from Fishbein's and Ajzen's Theory of Reasoned Action (Fishbein and Ajzen 1975; Ajzen and Fishbein 1980). According to the Theory of Reasoned Action there are two antecedents of the intention regarding a specific behavior, the attitude towards the behavior (or perceived attractiveness/desirability of the behavior) and the perceived social norm (or perceived social pressure) to exhibit the behavior in question.

However, researchers criticized the Theory of Reasoned Action for not being able to conclusively explain the link between intention and action. Intention alone cannot be the exclusive determinant in cases where the individual has no or not complete control over the behavior, or put differently: it may be that an individual has the intention to perform the behavior, but the lack of confidence to be able to execute the behavior impedes it. With the Theory of Planned Behavior Ajzen (1985) himself has revised the Theory of Reasoned Action. To the two aforementioned factors he adds the perceived behavioral control, which indicates if the behavior in question seems controllable or feasible for the individual or not. Personality traits, socio-demographic characteristics etc. represent background factors that indirectly affect intentions (see subsection 2.3.2). Exogenous circumstances do not directly influence behavior, but result in a (conscious or unconscious) analysis of individual beliefs, where the individual ponders the different possible alternatives (Ajzen 1991). In the following I deal with each of the three attitudinal factors (in the following referred to as "attitudes").

- Perceived desirability[9]

    The perceived desirability of the behavior in question is the degree to which an individual positively or negatively values the behavior.[10] The perceived desirability is determined by the set of information-based and accessible[11] behavioral beliefs. A behavioral belief is the subjective probability that the behavior will produce a given (positive or negative) outcome. The strength of each behavioral belief weighted by the subjective evaluation of the possible consequences inherent in the execution of the behavior determines the perceived attractiveness/ desirability.

- Perceived social norm

    People tend to conform due to punishments of violations against rules. Influences of the social environment on intentions and actions are captured in this factor. The perceived social norm is the perceived social pressure to engage or not to engage in the behavior in question. The perceived social norm is determined by the set of information-based and accessible normative beliefs. These beliefs indicate if an individual's referent groups (e.g., the individual's spouse, family, friends or others, depending on the population and behavior studied) prescribe or proscribe the performance of the behavior. The strength of each normative belief weighted by the motivation to comply with the respective referent determines the perceived social norm/pressure.

---

[9] This factor is often referred to as „Attitude towards the behavior". However, to not run the risk of confusion between "attitudes" and "Attitude towards the behavior", I use „perceived desirability" for this first attitudinal factor.

[10] Researchers distinguish between desirability and affect. Affect is related to mood, emotions and arousal, whereas desirability is assessed in terms of overall evaluation (see for example Giner-Sorolla 1999)

[11] A person may hold many behavioral beliefs with respect to any behavior, however only a relatively small number (five to nine, Miller 1956) may be readily acessible at a given moment (so-called "salient" beliefs, see subsection 2.3.1).

- Perceived behavioral control[12]
  Successful performance of any behavior depends not only on a favorable intention, but also on a sufficient level of behavioral control (see also the discussion above about the development from the Theory of Reasoned Action to the Theory of Planned Behavior). Available resources, skills, opportunities and other prerequisites needed to exhibit the behavior of interest are referred to as "actual behavioral control". However, from a psychological point of view (especially when studying future behavior) the perception of controllability and its influence on intention and action is much more interesting. When individuals perceive that the execution of a behavior is within their capacity to act, they exert more effort to actually perform the behavior of interest (Liñán 2004). Perceived behavioral control can serve as a proxy for actual control to predict future behavior. It refers to an individual's perception of her ability to perform a given behavior (i.e. the perception of how difficult or easy it is to exhibit this behavior). The perceived behavioral control is determined by the set of accessible control beliefs, i.e. the perception of the presence of factors that may facilitate or impede the performance of a behavior (e.g. experiences, "second-hand" information about the behavior in question, and role models). The strength of each control belief weighted by the perceived power of the control factor determines the perceived behavioral control.

---

[12] There are major overlaps between perceived behavioral control and "perceived self-efficacy" derived from Bandura's "Social Learning Theory" (Bandura 1977, 1982). Bandura (1991, p. 257) defined perceived self-efficacy as "(...) people's belief about their capabilities to exercise control over their own level of functioning and over events that affect their lives." It thus describes the self-assessment of the ability to execute necessary courses of action and accomplish future tasks as well as how effectively an individual can transform these skills into desired outcomes. It is based upon past experience and anticipation of future obstacles and determines perceptions whether or not certain goals are attainable.
An important aspect is that perceived self-efficacy is considered to be task- and domain-specific. So an individual can exhibit a very strong self-efficacy in one domain and be convinced to be able to successfully perform the behavior, whereas in another domain the opposite is true (Bandura 1977, 1982, 1997).

It should be noticed that attitudes exist at a general and specific level. Applied to specific behaviors, also the measurement of the attitudinal factors has to be adapted to ensure the accuracy of measurement (Ajzen and Madden 1986; Ajzen 1991; Fishbein and Ajzen 2010).

The Theory of Planned Behavior imposes the hypothesis that the more pronounced these three attitudinal factors are, the higher is the probability that an individual will perform the behavior of interest (or refrains from doing so). However, it does not impose a hypothesis about the relative contribution of the three attitudinal factors. It is rather expected that their contribution to the prediction of intentions varies from person to person, from group to group and from one behavior to another (Ajzen and Madden 1986; Ajzen 1991; Fishbein and Ajzen 2010). Relative weights of the three components are mostly estimated empirically without prior hypotheses about the relative importance of the different components. Predictions on an intuitive basis or based on other theories may be however possible (Ajzen and Madden 1986; Ajzen 1991; Fishbein and Ajzen 2010).

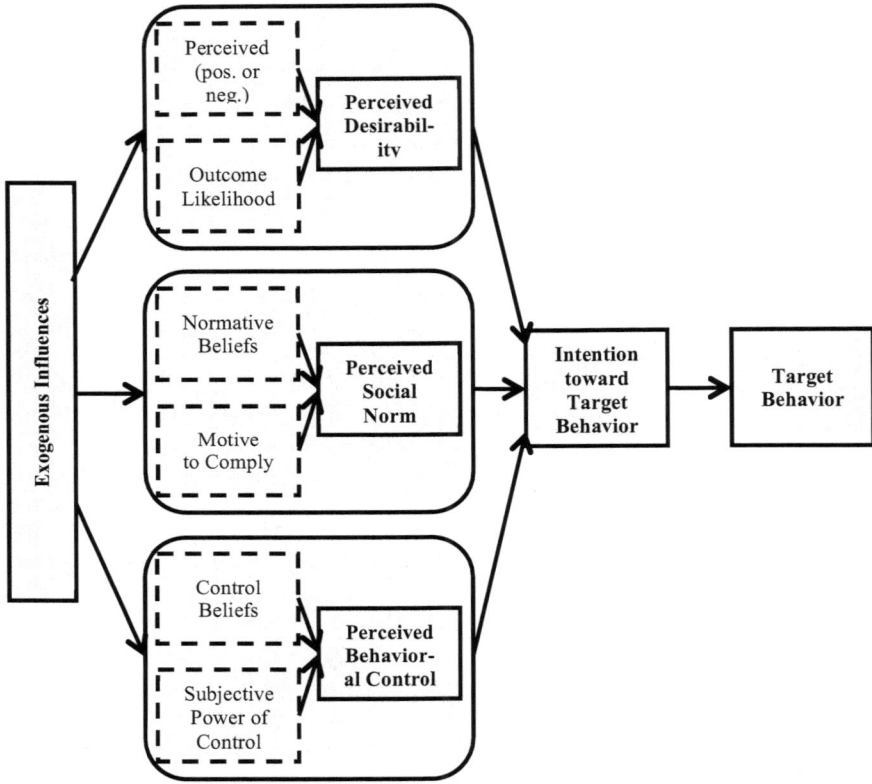

Figure 2.2: The Theory of Planned Behavior (According to Ajzen (1991))

In meta-analyses researchers were able to show that intentions can be predicted with ample accuracy for a wide array of behaviors. Correlations with intentions range from .45 - .60 for perceived desirability, from .34 - .42 for perceived social norm, and from .35 - .46 for perceived behavioral control (e.g. Armitage and Conner (2001) and Fishbein and Ajzen (2010)). Armitage and Conner (2001) further find that the Theory of Planned Behavior accounts for 39% of the variance in intention and 27% of the variance in behavior. This favorably compares to 10% of the variance regarding the behavior in question explained by personality traits alone (Ajzen 1987), demonstrating the superiority of the behavioral approach using the Theory of Planned Behavior over trait approaches. Other studies (see e.g. Armitage et al. (2002)) report similar results with regard to demographic-sociological approaches to predict specific behaviors. The application and assessment of the Theory of Planned Behavior in the entrepreneurship domain will be discussed in detail in section 2.4.

Having discussed the link between attitudinal factors and intention, I consider the belief and thus attitude formation in the next subsection. One paragraph there is devoted to behavioral interventions as one source of information aiding belief and attitude formation. Education can be considered as a special kind of behavioral intervention, which closes the circle to entrepreneurship education as a source of information to form beliefs, attitudes and – in the context of undergraduate studies ultimately (see discussion in subsection 1.2.2) – intentions.

2.3.2 Origins of Beliefs: the Role of Exogenous Influences

According to the Theory of Planned Behavior, individuals form their attitudes toward a specific behavior based on behavioral, normative and control beliefs. They are perceptions-based and this means that learning plays a significant role in belief and attitude formation. This in turn means that attitudes underlying the intention to perform a given behavior can be influenced, in direct as well as indirect ways. At a given point of time, people differ in their beliefs because they are different with respect to certain background variables, such as personality traits or socio-demographic characteristics. On the other side, on an ongoing basis people continue to form and re-evaluate beliefs by direct observation and the acquisition of information. Observed differences in beliefs must therefore be the result of differential learning experiences (Fishbein and Ajzen 2010). In the following I discuss these origins of beliefs.

2.3.2.1 Differences in Beliefs: the Role of Individual Background

Due to different background variables (traits, socio-demographic characteristics) people have made different experiences, could have been exposed to different sources of information, have drawn different conclusions from certain experiences and will therefore most likely differ in the beliefs they hold. Recognizing this potential with regard to the formation of beliefs, Fishbein and Ajzen integrated these factors in the Theory of Planned Behavior as "exogenous influences" (see Figure 2.2).

- **Personal dispositions**

    The TPB hypothesizes an indirect influence of personality traits or prior experiences related to the behavior in question on intentions and actual behavior. These effects are largely mediated by the three attitudinal factors by influencing behavioral, normative and control beliefs. In general however reviews show some inconsistency in the effects of specific traits on intentions and behavior (Fishbein and Ajzen 2010)[13].

    Other personal dispositions that might affect intentions and behavior are mood and emotions, also called "affect" (Giner-Sorolla 1999). Social learning theory argues that the own physiological state, i.e. factors such as physical condition, personality traits or emotions and mood, when confronted with certain tasks might affect perceived self-efficacy. Anxiety about performing a certain task, for example, may contribute to the likelihood of failure and so an individual may refrain from actually executing the behavior in question (Gist and Mitchell 1992).

- **Demographic characteristics**

    Demographic characteristics such as gender, age, birth order, socio-economic status, or others might also lead to different experiences an individual could have been exposed to, or to different cognitive processes of how to evaluate new information. These experiences and conclusions could lead to different formations of behavioral, normative and control beliefs among different subpopulations. The Theory of Planned Behavior therefore argues that demographic variables also

---

[13] See also the discussion on the trait approach to predict entrepreneurial activity (subsection 2.2.1).

tend to influence intentions indirectly through the three attitudinal factors and the underlying beliefs (Ajzen 1991).

2.3.2.2 Re-evaluating Beliefs: the Role of Encounters with the Real World

The Theory of Planned Behavior assumes further, as already mentioned, that beliefs are not stable over time. This means that in daily encounters with the real world an individual "learns" and re-evaluates her beliefs and forms perhaps different attitudes toward a specific behavior. This learning style is most likely again a function of the above mentioned background variables, but also of other, more immediate origins of belief formation.

- **Direct observation**
  According to the social learning theory, direct observation of other people can provide vicarious experience that affects attitudes by a process of social comparison with the potential role models (Wood and Bandura 1989). When an individual perceives similarities between himself and the role model (in terms of personality or skills) and when the observed behavior produces obvious consequences or measurable success (Bandura 1986; Gist and Mitchell 1992), individuals tend to infer that the same outcomes would occur when performing the behavior themselves. This influences one's behavioral beliefs. Also, direct observation might affect normative beliefs through social persuasion by these role models. When the observed role models tell an individual what to do, she tends to conform to this advice (Fishbein and Ajzen 2010). Lastly, noticing – by observation of others – what barriers or facilitating factors an individual might face when performing a specific behavior, control beliefs are affected.

- **Social interactions**
  Where psychologists focus on individuals, sociologists consider the influences of the social environment, also called peer-effects. When belonging to the same group, individuals tend to behave in a similar way.

This is not disjunctive with the consideration of role models, see below, and is surely also a function of traits and demographic characteristics and all other variables that define a group of people. Sociologists however explicitly explore a more aggregate level of data and social interactions within one of these groups and hypothesize mutual effects regarding the execution of a specific behavior (Manski 1993, 2010).[14]

- **Explicit acquisition of information**

  Attitudes may also be formed by receiving information provided by an outside source (TV, radio, internet, newspapers, books, lecturers, friends, relatives, coworkers) that affects the underlying beliefs. For example, information about successful entrepreneurs on TV could influence behavioral beliefs, or feedback from others helps individuals to realistically assess their own skills (Gist and Mitchell 1992), which in turn might affect normative and control beliefs.

- **Behavioral interventions**

  Sometimes individuals are exposed to a special kind of source of information, namely behavioral interventions or "behavior change interventions". Generally speaking, in behavioral interventions individuals are confronted with aspects associated with the behavior in question. Thus they learn about this specific behavior and form behavioral, normative and control beliefs. The goal of behavioral interventions is to alleviate a "social problem". Because many social problems are caused by human behavior, social scientists reasonably set up attempts to change the behavior of a given population. This should ultimately lead to producing or reinforcing the behavior in question. In a meta-analysis of 47 studies examining the effects of behavioral interventions (from a broad range of behaviors) in an experimental framework Webb and Sheeran (2006) found that they produce rather large changes in intentions (mean = .66) that also result in a considerable change in actual

---

[14] While neglected in the first three chapters of the empirical part of this theses (chapters 4 to 6), chapter 7 is fully dedicated to the analysis of social interactions happening during entrepreneurship education.

behavior (mean = .36). The Theory of Planned Behavior provides a useful framework both for designing and evaluating behavioral intervention, since it allows identifying the most important beliefs to be addressed when considering a specific behavior, and to identify those beliefs which are affected by actually being exposed to a behavioral intervention (Fishbein and Ajzen 2010).[15]

The Theory of Planned Behavior assumes that people act reasonably upon their beliefs, thinking that their beliefs, and therefore the information they have about the behavior in question, are valid (Ross and Ward 1996).[16] This also means that forgetting or encountering contradictory information can reduce the strength of beliefs (Fishbein and Ajzen 2010). All the above mentioned variables might influence intentions and actual behavior indirectly by affecting attitudes and the underlying behavioral, normative and control beliefs. However, if there is a connection between these variables and beliefs or attitudes, or even intentions, is an empirical question (Fishbein and Ajzen 2010).

It is also an empirical question, whether a special intervention regarding a specific behavior, e.g. entrepreneurship education to change entrepreneurial intentions and behavior, affects beliefs and attitudes underlying this behavior. The Theory of Planned Behavior provides a useful framework to examine the nature of these connections. It allows evaluating the usefulness of entrepreneurship education towards the goal to provide information about entrepreneurial careers and so to change entrepreneurial intentions. But before I discuss the application of the Theory of Planned Behavior in the entrepreneurship domain and its applicability to the evaluation of entrepreneurship education, I point out some challenges to it.

---

[15] The goal of this research project is to evaluate a special kind of behavioral intervention, namely entrepreneurship education to alleviate a specific social problem that is a lack of knowledge about the properties of an entrepreneurial career among undergraduate students. Since this is a cornerstone of my research project, I do not go into the details regarding behavioral interventions here but devote an extra section to this topic, section 2.5.

[16] This also implies that people can just persuade others by providing them with wrong or misleading information, e.g. in behavioral interventions. For an ethical discussion about that issue, I refer to subsection 2.5.2, where I discuss the applicability of the Theory of Planned Behavior to the evaluation of behavioral interventions.

2.3.3 Challenges to the Theory of Planned Behavior

Although the Theory of Planned Behavior is widely recognized in many scientific domains and was applied in hundreds of empirical studies, it is not free of criticism. In this subsection I acknowledge the criticism since it has implications for the set-up of my research project and for possible caveats of the results, without claiming that the list of issues mentioned here is exhaustive.

2.3.3.1 Challenges from a Theoretical Point of View

The first issue is the question of sufficiency. According to the Theory of Planned Behavior, intentions are formed based on the perceived desirability, perceived social norm, and perceived behavioral control. The theory's sufficiency assumption states that the inclusion of additional variables at this level should not improve the prediction of either intention or action. This assumption has repeatedly been challenged (see e.g. Conner and Armitage (1998)), and earlier treatments of the theory even leave open the addition of more predictors (Ajzen and Fishbein 1980; Ajzen 1991). Challenges of the sufficiency assumption focus on three candidates: past behavior, self-identity, and anticipated affect (Fishbein and Ajzen 2010).

- **Past behavior** has been shown to be a good predictor of future behavior due to habit formation. Its inclusion produces a substantial increase in the amount of explained variance in intentions and later behavior (Ouellette and Wood 1998; Sandberg and Conner 2008). Its relation to future behavior seems not to be fully mediated by the three attitudinal factors of the Theory of Planned Behavior (Ajzen 1991). Therefore researchers repeatedly argued for adding past behavior as predictor in the model. However, past behavior does not meet the causality criterion. Unlike the three antecedents of intention in the Theory of Planned Behavior, frequency of past behavior cannot readily be used to explain performance of later action. To argue that behavior now is a function

of past behavior leads to the question why an individual started to behave in a certain way previously (Fishbein and Ajzen 2010).
- Role theory and social identity theory state that people's **self-identity** can influence their intentions and actions. If they take on a certain role or identify with a social category, they are expected to act consistent with that role (Armitage and Conner 1999). However, existing measures of self-identity do not seem to give new insights that could not be delivered by the three attitudinal factors already contained in the Theory of Planned Behavior (Fishbein and Ajzen 2010).
- The Theory of Planned Behavior is often criticized for being too rational, negating effects of affective or emotional reactions (see also below). Research on **anticipated affect** assumes that anticipated affective reactions have also a direct effect on intentions and action (Sandberg and Conner 2008). But again, also this factor does not seem to add value to the Theory of Planned Behavior, as it seems to play a role in assessing the desirability of behavioral alternatives (Fishbein and Ajzen 2010).

The second big issue from a theoretical side, often raised in discussions of the Theory of Planned Behavior, is the question of rationality. It is said to be too rational, focusing on deliberative mode of operation in the exclusion of an intuitive or spontaneous mode. Fishbein and Ajzen counter this criticism by pointing out that the theory does not suggest that people are rational (Ajzen and Fishbein 1980; Fishbein and Ajzen 2010). They argue that people's attitudes and intentions follow spontaneously from their beliefs, and that these beliefs are derived both by deliberative inference processes as well as intuition, and are both based on logical thoughts as well as wishful thinking, or other motives. Another facet of the question of rationality is the question whether the Theory of Planned Behavior is applicable also to non-western cultures, as is the case with every behavioral model developed in individualistic Western countries that are to be used, for example, in more collectivistic cultures.[17]

---

[17] As this issue is not affecting the setting of this research project I refer interested readers to the book by Fishbein and Ajzen (2010) for a detailed discussion.

2.3.3.2 Challenges from a Practical Point of View

When employing the Theory of Planned Behavior to predict specific intentions or actions, researchers also have to take into account some methodological issues. Usually these research set-ups involve the distribution of questionnaires to a group of people. Questionnaires based on the Theory of Planned Behavior face the same challenges, as do those based on most other theories.

First and foremost researchers are confronted with the question of the validity of questionnaire measures. Within the Theory of Planned Behavior framework, there is a certain possibility that responding to the questionnaire makes individuals reflect the behavior in question. As a consequence, the act of responding could make salient certain behavioral, normative, and control beliefs that would otherwise not have been accessible. This could even lead to a process of creating or changing desirability, norm, control, and intentions rather than just measuring them (Ogden 2003).

Another aspect of the validity of measures is the consistency bias. Self-presentational concerns could encourage participants to create a degree of consistency among their responses to the questionnaire measures, resulting in an overestimation of correlation among the components of the Theory of Planned Behavior in the statistical examination of the data afterwards (Budd 1987).

A further issue is the question of the validity of self-reports. Self-reports are almost always used when applying the Theory of Planned Behavior due to their practical advantages. However, negative aspects of self-reports are raised, too. Respondents may not recall past behavior or choose not to report it accurately due to self-representation or social desirability concerns, which depend heavily on the behavior in question. Researchers can reduce these kinds of biases by encouraging people to tell the truth and respond spontaneously to questionnaire items and to assure them confidentiality. Lastly, using questionnaires, there may also occur "floor- and ceiling effects". Likert-type scales are widely used in questionnaires based on the Theory of Planned Behavior. When two respondents indicate for example an extreme desirability (meaning that they tick the boxes with the highest value in the items that measure desirability), researchers cannot further distinguish between these two individuals with respect to their desire to engage in the behavior in question. And when employing the Theory of Planned Behavior for evaluating behavioral interventions, researchers cannot investigate further if this desire even got stronger after the intervention, when an individual checked the boxes with the highest value both times.

Despite these challenges the Theory of Planned Behavior is widely recognized in various scientific fields, and by now researchers applied it in over 1,000 studies in a broad array of behaviors. This is also true in the entrepreneurship domain to predict entrepreneurial activity. Having now laid the theoretical foundations of the constructs and strengths of the Theory of Planned Behavior, I now discuss its application in the entrepreneurship domain and present studies that tried to predict entrepreneurial intentions and activity in the following section. Finally I conclude this chapter by arguing that the Theory of Planned Behavior is very well applicable to the evaluation of entrepreneurship education and select the relevant theoretical constructs for this research project.

2.4 The Theory of Planned Behavior in the Entrepreneurship Domain

Acknowledging the benefits, the Theory of Planned Behavior promises to predict entrepreneurial attitudes and intentions and has frequently been used to predict entrepreneurial and career choice intentions (see section 2.4 below for a literature review). According to Ajzen's (1991) postulation each of the constructs has to be adapted to this specific kind of behavior:
- "perceived desirability" reflects the difference in the (after consideration of the available information) evaluations of the outcomes of being self-employed versus being organizationally employed,
- "perceived social norm" means the perceived pressure from other people to enter an entrepreneurial career or to pursue an organizational employment,

- and "perceived behavioral control" refers to the subjectively perceived controllability over starting and running an own business and to successfully accomplish the tasks associated with being an entrepreneur.

According to Krueger (1993), I define entrepreneurial intentions as the commitment to starting a new business. In the following I, will call the three attitudinal factors of the Theory of Planned Behavior "entrepreneurial attitudes" within the entrepreneurship domain.

As mentioned earlier, there is no a priori hypothesis about the relative contribution of these three attitudinal factors to explaining entrepreneurial intentions. This remains an empirical question for each specific behavior (Ajzen 1991, 2002), in this case actually starting an own business.

The Theory of Planned Behavior promises valuable insights into the emergence of entrepreneurial activity. There is a vast literature on the intent to start a business, and researchers in this literature stream frequently use the Theory of Planned Behavior to predict entrepreneurial activity. In this subsection, I will only deal with studies that fully applied the Theory of Planned Behavior.

Kolvereid (1996a) does so to predict entrepreneurial activity and generates his findings based on 128 questionnaires from Norwegian students. He confirms the applicability of the TPB in entrepreneurship research: entrepreneurial intentions derive from (by order of the strength of the influence) the perceived behavioral control, the perceived subjective norm, and the perceived desirability.

The study by Tkachev and Kolvereid (1999) to determine the antecedents of entrepreneurial intentions delivers largely identical results. They also use the Theory of Planned Behavior and surveyed 561 Russian students at a medical and two technical universities.

Kolvereid and Isaksen (2006) test the Theory of Planned Behavior in their study using data from questionnaires from 297 Norwegian entrepreneurs. Their findings confirm the hypothesized positive link between perceived desirability and social norm on the one side and entrepreneurial intentions on the other side. However, their data fail to support the hypothesis of the positive influence of perceived behavioral control on entrepreneurial intentions. They explain this with the very good general conditions for entrepreneurs in Norway.

Also the (already in subsection 1.2.3 cited) studies by Fayolle et al. (2006a) and Souitaris et al. (2007) confirm the hypothesized relationships of the Theory of Planned Behavior. They test the model both before and after the course. In contrast to findings in other studies that employed the Theory of Planned Behavior (both in the entrepreneurship and other domains) the perceived social norm has the largest (positive) influence on entrepreneurial intentions.

German students are surveyed by Hack et al. (2008) in their study, which I also already cited in subsection 1.2.3. Their data support every hypothesized relationship in the Theory of Planned Behavior, whereupon the perceived desirability had the strongest (positive) influence on entrepreneurial intentions, followed by perceived behavioral control and perceived social norm.

In addition, some researchers developed their own conceptual models based on the Theory of Planned Behavior, each emphasizing difference constructs (e.g. Davidsson 1995; Autio et al. 1997; Lüthje and Franke 2002).

To sum up, it can be stated that most empirical studies show that entrepreneurial potential is determined by three attitudinal factors that can be found in the presented intentions-based models: is starting an own business desirable (for the individual), is it feasible, and what is the opinion of the individual's referent groups regarding entrepreneurship. Based on the studies above that employ the full Theory of Planned Behavior I am able to calculate mean correlations between attitudes and intentions specifically for the prediction of entrepreneurial intentions. These range from .33 - .56 for perceived desirability (mean r = .44), from .31 - .60 for perceived social norm (mean r = .49), and from .25 - .61 for perceived behavioral control (mean r = .42). Taking the mean over all studies, the Theory of Planned Behavior accounts for 36% of the variance in entrepreneurial intention[18]. All these figures lie in the same range reported by Armitage and Conner (2001) in their meta-analysis covering a broad range of behaviors (I briefly report their results in subsection 2.3.1). Moreover

---

[18] Kolvereid (1996a) does not report the R-squared.

the explained variance in entrepreneurial intentions compares favorably to 20% explained by personality alone, as found for example by Frank et al. (2007) in their study among students of 14 Austrian schools.

Actually, there is a lack of methodologically exact empirical studies dealing with the link between intentions and action. Katz (1992) even challenges this link in the entrepreneurship domain, Reynolds (1997) points out the significant latency between intention and action particularly in entrepreneurship[19]. Nevertheless, is the Theory of Planned Behavior is appropriate for the evaluation of interventions such as an entrepreneurship course. The goal of such an intervention is, as discussed in subsection 1.2.2, to influence the attitudes of the participants regarding entrepreneurial intentions and actions. The actual founding of a new business is normally not within reach of the instructor. In the following section I deal with the applicability of the TPB to evaluate such behavioral interventions in more detail and formulate a theoretical baseline-model for this research-project.

2.5 A Baseline-Model for Evaluating Entrepreneurship Education

Up to this point in this chapter I discussed that information and beliefs, and therefore attitudes toward a specific behavior, originate from a variety of sources. This can be background variables such as personality traits or socio-demographic characteristics or in encounters with "the real world" through TV, radio, internet, interactions with family and friends, or formal education. Human behavior then follows reasonably or spontaneously from these beliefs and information. Therefore, the acquisition of new information about the behavior in question can change beliefs. Behavioral interventions are thus considered an effective way of changing intentions and action (Webb and Sheeran 2006, see also paragraph 2.3.2.2).

---

[19] In fact, Kolvereid and Isaksen (2006) do report correlations between attitudes and entrepreneurial activity, being $r = .24$ for perceived desirability and $r = .21$ for perceived social norm. As they measured perceived behavioral control by means of perceived entrepreneurial self-efficacy the correlation coefficient reported is not comparable to the others. The same holds for the variance in entrepreneurial activity explained, which is reported to be 41%.

This research project deals with the evaluation of a specific behavioral intervention – entrepreneurship education at tertiary institutions – regarding its effects on the change of specific – i.e. entrepreneurial – intentions. The Theory of Planned Behavior delivers an ideal framework for this purpose. In this section I present the theoretical model I use in the empirical analyses to answer the question whether entrepreneurship education has effects on entrepreneurial attitudes and intentions at all, what the size and nature of these effects are, and how these findings can be used to derive implications for the design of entrepreneurship courses.

2.5.1 Impact of Entrepreneurship Education on Entrepreneurial Attitudes and Intentions

Entrepreneurship education conveys knowledge and skills meant to reduce the cost of becoming an entrepreneur. However, there are generic components in the pedagogical approaches (e.g. knowing how to write a business plan is also helpful in established corporations). From this point of view, entrepreneurship education will not influence entrepreneurial intentions by much. However, according to the behavioral approach to predict entrepreneurship, where such an intervention also affects attitudes it may affect intentions, and so downstream action. Moreover, entrepreneurship education allows students to engage in entrepreneurial activity in an experimental setting, e.g. in start-up simulations or in real-life projects. That would help reduce students' uncertainty about the suitability of an entrepreneurial career. The most important effect of entrepreneurship education may so lie in acquiring information, i.e. learning, about entrepreneurship. This information allows students to form beliefs and thus entrepreneurial attitudes and intentions.

For example could informative signals cause changes in behavioral beliefs (perceived desirability) regarding one's entrepreneurial aptitude. "Emitters" of such signals might be lecture sessions with successful and unsuccessful entrepreneurs to inform students if entrepreneurship pays off (Krueger and Brazeal 1994). The interaction with an entrepreneur when developing a business plan together could also generate signals affecting the attitude towards self-employment as students get to know the entrepreneur's daily business. Students could receive positive or negative signals for their own entrepreneurial aptitude. Changes in normative beliefs (perceived social norm) can emerge through feedback by educators and even fellow students or family when discussing the performance in the entrepreneurship course (Krueger and Carsrud 1993). Discussions with for example fellow students about one's own performance in a possible team-project could increase or diminish the perceived pressure to start a company. These signals, too, may be processed and lead to an update of the assessment of one's entrepreneurial aptitude.

Finally students can also receive informative signals due to the change in control beliefs (perceived behavioral control) by accumulating tacit knowledge (Reuber et al. 1990; Krueger and Brazeal 1994). Often entrepreneurship courses contain "learning-by-doing"-elements such as writing a business plan or playing a start-up simulation. Students can so discover if starting a company seems controllable for them and strengthen their self-confidence regarding entrepreneurial tasks. In the end, they would choose the career path (entrepreneur or not) they feel they have more control over (Bandura 1977). Perceptions of behavioral control are thus affected by course components focusing on the skills needed by an entrepreneur.

In line with the assumptions of the behavioral approach to predict entrepreneurship, Minniti and Bygrave (2001) stated, that "(…) entrepreneurship is a process of learning, and a theory of entrepreneurship requires a theory of learning" (p. 7). And further, "entrepreneurs learn by updating a subjective stock of knowledge accumulated on the basis of past experiences" (p. 5).

In order to be able to systematically assess the effects of entrepreneurship education regarding the change in entrepreneurial attitudes and intentions, researchers needed a conceptual framework with a proven set of methods and procedures. The Theory of Planned Behavior promises to deliver this.

2.5.2 Using the Theory of Planned Behavior to Evaluate Entrepreneurship Education

The Theory of Planned Behavior defines a causal sequence that describes the emergence of human behavior. Behavioral, normative, and control beliefs are formed or interpreted based on an individual's available information toward a specific behavior. To the extent that these beliefs are salient, they lead to the formation of perceptions of desirability, social norm, and control. The intention to carry out this behavior or refrain from doing so emerges from these attitudes (Fishbein and Ajzen 2010). Behavioral interventions are an effective way to provide individuals with information about a certain behavior and thus allow them to form, re-evaluate or make beliefs about it salient. The Theory of Planned Behavior can be used as a conceptual and methodological framework for the evaluation of behavioral intervention, for all kinds of behaviors (see paragraph 2.3.2.2), and as pointed out by Krueger et al. (2000) especially for evaluating the effects of entrepreneurship education on entrepreneurial attitudes and intentions as well. The advantage of using the Theory of Planned Behavior for this purpose is that it concentrates on rather few variables, and assumes that these are sufficient to understand and change entrepreneurial intentions and behavior: the change in one, two, or all three attitudinal factors should be accompanied by a change in entrepreneurial intention as well. This simple but efficient mechanism provides two important kinds of information:

- **Information about the effectiveness of entrepreneurship education**
  The intensive use of the Theory of Planned Behavior in a wide range of domains and especially in the entrepreneurship domain provides researchers with a set of proven methods and procedures in order to measure entrepreneurial attitudes and intentions before and after the behavioral intervention. Together with the focus on only a small number of variables these methods allow to identify the factors that have changed due to the intervention and thus deliver a means for evaluating its effectiveness in intention change.

- **Information about how to design entrepreneurship education**

  When the entrepreneurship course has been found to be effective in producing a change in intentions, the Theory of Planned Behavior allows identifying the impact more accurately by examining which one of the entrepreneurial attitudes produced this change. Moreover, it might in turn allow researchers to draw conclusions about which individual background characteristics and what course components led to a formation or re-interpretation of beliefs, or to making behavioral, normative, and control beliefs salient, upon which the entrepreneurial attitudes are formed. On the other hand, when the course failed in producing any change, the evaluator could identify reasons for this failure. This not only opens the way to improving the design of entrepreneurship courses and thus to enhancing future effectiveness (see subsection 2.5.1 for a discussion on how different course characteristics might affect behavioral, normative, and control beliefs). It may also enlighten the issue, which students – based on their background variables – are affected by entrepreneurship education at all. This may provide instructors with information about which students they should accept for a course when being under cost constraints (Lüthje and Franke 2002).

The advantages the Theory of Planned Behavior delivers call for an application in evaluating entrepreneurship education, as already proposed by Krueger et al. (2000). Several researchers already responded to this call; see for example the studies by Fayolle et al. (2006a), Souitaris et al. (2007), or Hack et al. (2008) which were discussed earlier.[20] In the following I introduce additional relevant theoretical constructs for a baseline model to evaluate entrepreneurship education. I conclude this chapter then with a wrap-up of this model.

---

[20] When examining the effects of a behavioral intervention, researchers usually administer questionnaires to the participants, one before the intervention has started, and one after the intervention has ended. In an experimental or quasi-experimental setting, they also retrieve data from a control group that is not exposed to this intervention. When doing so for entrepreneurship education, the difference in entrepreneurial attitudes and intentions (eventually compared to the differences in the constructs in the control group data) opens room for interpretations regarding the causes for the observed changes and to draw implications about the effectiveness of the course and about a better design of the course.

2.5.3 Additional Relevant Theoretical Constructs for the Baseline Model

Entrepreneurship education will not have homogeneous effects on all participating students' entrepreneurial attitudes and intention (Lüthje and Franke 2002). According to the Theory of Planned Behavior, certain background variables such as demographic variables, prior experiences, and personality traits, influence intentions indirectly through perceived desirability, perceived social norm, and perceived behavioral control. Therefore, dependent on the individual differences regarding these background variables, some students already enter entrepreneurship training with a certain predisposition towards entrepreneurship and may already be more able to assess their aptitude for entrepreneurship more realistically (Ajzen 1991; Ajzen 2002).

On the other hand, these individual differences may influence how people remember and interpret existing information and beliefs, and also how they interpret new information they receive during entrepreneurship education. So these background characteristics do not only determine the level of entrepreneurial attitudes and intentions when entering the entrepreneurship course, but also how the existing beliefs about those are re-considered and re-evaluated. This in turn leads to the claimed inhomogeneous effects of an entrepreneurship course on students. First, these effects depend on the degree the students are willing and able to process new information. And second, the intensity of this new information has to be sufficient enough to change the individually existing predispositions toward entrepreneurship. Only then students will – with the words of Minniti and Bygrave (2001) – learn and "update [sic!] a subjective stock of knowledge accumulated on the basis of past experiences" (p. 7, see also above).

In an attempt to improve effectiveness of training and due to restricted education budgets, researchers cope with this issue in education and learning and try to forecast a trainee's potential for academic success (De Raad and Schouwenburg 1996; Goldstein and Ford 2002). This would reduce instructional costs and increase the desired learning outcome.

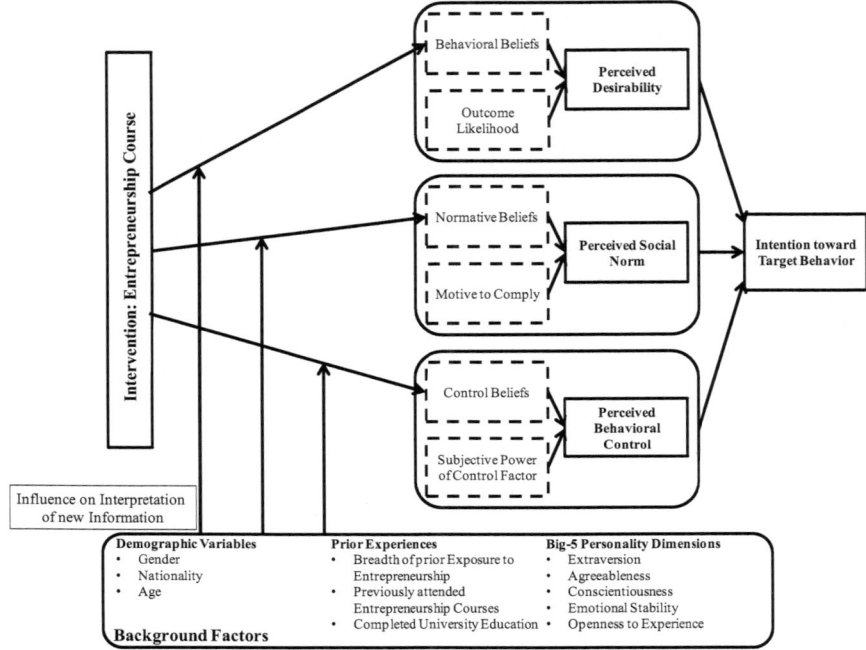

Figure 2.3: Theoretical Model for the Evaluation of Entrepreneurship Education (own illustration)

In the theoretical model, I introduce three groups of background factors accounting for individual differences that have frequently been used in studies about training proficiency and entrepreneurship. These are demographic characteristics, relevant prior experiences, and personality traits.

2.5.3.1 Demographic Variables

If individuals exhibit different learning and interpretation styles due to different experiences that can be traced back to demographic variables, then also these characteristics have to be taken into account when examining the effects of entrepreneurship education. The link between demographic variables and entrepreneurial intentions has frequently been analyzed. However, there is little research about the link between demographics and training outcomes, and even fewer regarding entrepreneurship education. The two demographic variables appearing most often in studies about training are gender, age and a potential migration background (Colquit et al. 2000).

Gender

Previous research with respect to training proficiency has failed to establish a significant link to training outcome (Webster and Martocchio 1995; Colquit et al. 2000). Research about gender-differentiated effects of entrepreneurship education does not deliver a consistent picture. Wilson et al. (2007) find that entrepreneurship education significantly increases the entrepreneurial self-efficacy of females in comparison to males in their MBA-student sample. Oosterbeek et al. (2010), on the other hand, find that being exposed to the entrepreneurship program affects entrepreneurial intentions negatively both for female and male students, but the negative impact is stronger for women. Although these two findings are different in the direction, it seems that the effects of entrepreneurship education are more prominent for female than for male students. The relationship between gender and entrepreneurial intentions has extensively been analyzed. In general, there is evidence that women and female youths both have less interest in entrepreneurial careers as well as lower entrepreneurial intentions than men and boys (Scherer et al. 1989; Matthews and Moser 1996; Kolvereid 1996a; Chen et al. 1998; Kourilsky and Walstad 1998; Delmar and Davidsson 2000; Gatewood et al. 2002; Veciana et al. 2005; Zhao et al. 2005). Bandura (1992) asserts that the reason for this is that women more likely limit their career aspirations due to the perceived lack of necessary skills. This seems to play an even bigger role regarding entrepreneurial tasks (Bandura et al. 2001).

Age

Many studies provide evidence for a negative relationship between age and learning (see Colquit et al. 2000 for an overview). However, as it can be reasonably assumed that students who attend the same entrepreneurship course belong to the same age group, I will not discuss potential different effects of entrepreneurship education associated with this variable.

Nationality

Previous research reveals the existence of different entrepreneurial cultures in different countries and examines the reasons for that (Hayton et al. 2002). Mueller and Thomas (2001) define culture as the underlying system of values peculiar to a specific group or society. Looking at the facts presented by the Global Entrepreneurship Monitor, the Total Early-Stage Entrepreneurial Activity (TEA) index for Germany is 4.2, and thus among the lowest in the EU (Kelley et al. 2010). Students coming to Germany for a semester abroad may have faced a stronger exposure to entrepreneurship than their German fellow students. Moreover, self-employment is often used as a way to establish immigrant groups in the economy when other career options are closed (see e.g. Hagen 1962). Although not all ethnic minority groups have a higher propensity to become self-employed (Shapero and Sokol 1982; Delmar and Davidsson 2000), students who were born in immigrant households in Germany could have experienced a different exposure to entrepreneurship than their native German fellow students. The Theory of Planned Behavior was very rarely applied to different cultures in the entrepreneurship domain. Autio et al. (2001) and Liñán and Chen (2009) are two of the few examples. The latter argue that the values shared within a culture would affect entrepreneurial attitudes. And further, as the perceived social norm reflect the felt social pressure to start an own company, the influence of cultural values would be stronger on this factor of the Theory of Planned Behavior. Thus students who have come to Germany as immigrants with their parents or who just spend a semester abroad coming from another country to study at a German university could exhibit different, i.e. higher, entrepreneurial attitudes and intentions than their native German fellow students. As a consequence, the effects of entrepreneurship education could be different for these two groups.

2.5.3.2 Prior Experiences

Individuals are exposed to different experiences during their life, so they can already have accumulated knowledge about and interest in an entrepreneurial career (Cooper 1985; Cooper 1993). This knowledge refers to individual distinctive information one has about entrepreneurship (Venkataraman 1997). Recent results associate prior knowledge with a greater awareness about the existence of that professional career option (Liñán 2004) as well as with the identification of a greater number of entrepreneurial opportunities and with ones that are more innovative (Shane 2000; Shepherd and DeTienne 2005). Prior experiences might already have formed some career intentions when entering an entrepreneurship course, and so most likely this intervention will have different effects for differently framed students (Fayolle et al. 2006a).

Prior exposure to entrepreneurship – role models and past behavior

This framing is for example a result of observing role models, prior work experience, or previously experienced education. Role models are considered very important in the accumulation of knowledge (Carrier 2005; Matthews and Moser 1996; Rondstadt 1990) and have been found to be a strong determinant of career choices (Katz 1992). Role modeling occurs when social behavior is informally observed and then adopted by a learner who has learned by example rather than by direct experience (Bandura 1977). According to social learning theory, role models are important environmental factors for career intentions (Mitchell et al. 2002). Shapero and Sokol (1982) state that the immediate family, and in particular the parents, play the most powerful role in forming a notion of desirability and credibility of entrepreneurial actions. Empirical evidence for a relationship between the presence of parental entrepreneurial role models and the preference for a self-employment career has been repeatedly reported (Scott and Twomey 1988; Scherer et al. 1989; Matthews and Moser 1996; Peterman and Kennedy 2003). Boyd and Vozikis (1994) show that entrepreneurial intentions are stronger with a growing degree of entrepreneurial self-efficacy due to the presence of entrepreneurial role models among close relatives. In the Theory of Planned Behavior framework, role models are expected to have an influence mostly on perceived behavioral control, and a weaker impact on perceived desirability and perceived social norm (Scherer et al. 1989). Furthermore there is also empirical evidence that personal experience of owning or operating a small firm or working in a young company contributes to higher entrepreneurial attitudes and intentions (Matthews and Moser 1996). I already discussed the role of past behavior in paragraph 2.3.3.1. These experiences could affect entrepreneurial attitudes and intentions and make an entrepreneurial career seem rewarding and manageable or not. Results in management research suggests that that top managers share breadth and quality of business experiences (McCall et al. 1988), a result that is later confirmed by Krueger (1993) in the entrepreneurship domain. Therefore, breadth of experience should predict entrepreneurial attitudes better than any single type of experience. Krueger (1993) suggests four likely sources of exposure: one's family business, a business started by another relative or friend, working in someone else's small business, and starting one's own business.

Previously attended entrepreneurship courses

Students who already have attended an entrepreneurship course prior to the course that is taken as behavioral intervention probably already acquired all the information they can get out of entrepreneurship education. Depending on how they have processed this information, they might already exhibit a stronger predisposition towards or against entrepreneurship.

Previously completed general education

Another source for the emergence of career intentions might be the already completed education. At tertiary level, students get prepared for a career as non-entrepreneurs, and the courses taken convey a "take-a-job" mentality. Whitlock and Masters (1996) for example find that the interest in pursuing an entrepreneurial career decreases after attending general business administration courses. Also the chosen major (and potentially also minors) could play a role in forming entrepreneurial attitudes – business majors for example could already have a higher awareness of becoming an entrepreneur as a viable career option compared to students who chose other majors.

2.5.3.3 Personality Dimensions

Some researchers hypothesize a relation between individual differences in specific personality traits and learning success (Rothstein et al. 1994). As learning is an event of information processing affected by perceptions, non-cognitive personality factors may play a moderating role by interacting with this processing sequence (Lindsay and Norman 1977). However, only scant research has investigated the relation of individual measures of personality to measures of training readiness and training success (De Raad and Schouwenburg 1996), and even fewer in the specific setting of entrepreneurship education. A framework for recent analyses of the relations between personality traits and academic performance is provided by the Big5 model of personality structure (Dean et al. 2006). This model serves as taxonomy to catalogue "all aspects of human personality which are or have been of importance, interest or utility" (Cattell 1943). According to Norman (1963) these five dimensions are labeled extraversion, conscientiousness, and openness to experience, agreeableness, and emotional stability. With the help of this framework, some studies tried to give profile descriptions of "ideal" students (see e.g. Gough (1966); Middleton and Guthrie (1959); Oakland (1969); Schmit and Ryan (1993)).

On the other side, the Big5 model was used in entrepreneurship studies to find differences between entrepreneurs and non-entrepreneurial managers. There is empirical evidence that the conviction to start up a new venture is at least to some extent a question of personality structure (Brockhaus and Horwitz 1982). Zhao et al. (2010) are the first to examine the relationship of personality and entrepreneurial intentions. In the analyses in this book, I employ this framework for a similar purpose in the entrepreneurship education setting. In light of this, I discuss the five personality dimensions below. Traits do not change within a short period of time (Fishbein and Ajzen 2010) and are therefore assumed not to be affected by the training (Oosterbeek et al. 2010).

Extraversion

People who are high on extraversion are considered as active, energetic, vigorous and being sociable, gregarious, assertive and active. This dimension taps traits that are important for learning new things. In their review, De Raad and Schouwenburg (1996) find that successful students score low on extraversion, as extraverted students would rather socialize instead of concentrating on their work (Eysenck 1992). However, Barrick and Mount (1991) find that extraversion predicts training proficiency, especially in training programs that require high levels of energy and interaction. There, learning is more effective when the learner is active rather than passive (Burris 1976). On the other hand, these traits are often associated with entrepreneurs, whose tasks are also highly interactive. Furthermore, extraversion is the strongest predictor of leadership, which is also a useful characteristic for an entrepreneur (Zhao et al. 2010). Extraverts should therefore be more attracted to enterprising (Costa et al. 1984). In their meta-analysis of relevant studies, Zhao et al. (2010) report that extraversion is a significant predictor of entrepreneurial intentions.

Conscientiousness

Traits associated with conscientiousness – or often called "need for achievement" – are being organized, systematic, efficient, practical, steady, dependable, careful, thorough, responsible, hardworking, achievement-oriented and persevering (Goldberg 1992). Regarding training proficiency, conscientiousness is seen as a main psychological resource in learning and education (De Raad and Schouwenburg 1996). There is some evidence for a positive correlation between conscientiousness and training performance (Salgado 1997). Students high on conscientiousness are considered to be more motivated to perform well (Chamorro-Premuzic and Furnham 2005). McClelland (1961) – among others – relates conscientiousness with job performance. Individuals who score high in this dimension should be more attracted to work situations in which they personally have control over outcomes, face moderate risk of failure and get direct feedback on their performance. According to McClelland, entrepreneurship – as opposed to most other forms of employment - offers more of these conditions. The importance of other traits associated with conscientiousness, such as persistence and motivation, are emphasized by Chen et al. (1998). Thus highly conscientious people should be more attracted to an enterprising career. This is also confirmed by Zhao et al. (2010).

Openness to experience

Individuals who are open for experience are imaginative, cultured, curious, original, broad-minded, intelligent, creative and steadily seek out new ideas. Regarding learning ability, Salgado (1997) finds that this factor is a valid predictor of training proficiency as the mentioned characteristics are associated with positive attitudes toward learning experiences and a higher motivation to learn when entering a training program. So a high score on openness to experience may identify individuals who are "training ready" (Barrick and Mount 1991). Zhao et al. (2010) conclude that individuals who are high on openness to experience are more attracted to entrepreneurship, as this factor is linked to a critical task of an entrepreneur, opportunity recognition.

Emotional Stability Traits associated with the inverse to emotional stability – neuroticism – are anxiety, depression, anger, embarrassment, emotionality, worry, and insecurity. Barrick and Mount (1991) consider emotionally stable students to have an edge over highly neurotic students. They state that highly neurotic individuals would be unable to function on their own. This means that these individuals most likely will not pursue an entrepreneurial career. Entrepreneurs are hardy, optimistic individuals who are steady in the face of social pressure, stress or uncertainty. These pressures could include the heavy workload, critical decision making with little guidelines and of the unsure financial consequences. Therefore Zhao et al. (2010) hypothesize a positive correlation between emotional stability and entrepreneurial intentions.

Agreeableness This dimension predicts engagements in interpersonal relationships. Traits associated with this factor are courtesy, flexibility, trust, cooperation, forgiving, modesty, altruism, and tolerance. According to De Raad and Schouwenburg (1996), this factor does not provide direct clues about the nature of the correlation with academic performance. Regarding predispositions towards entrepreneurship, Zhao et al. (2010) state that highly agreeable people could be too trusting for being entrepreneurs and are more attracted to social occupations.

Given the subject of entrepreneurship education, one could argue for two points of view: Regarding the interpersonal energy-demanding nature of the training subject matter, individuals high on extraversion, conscientiousness, openness to experience, and emotional stability have a high training proficiency and should therefore learn more (Dean et al. 2006). Thus they better find out if they are really able to perform in entrepreneurial tasks, and we would expect a high change in entrepreneurial attitudes and intention. On the other hand, individuals ranking high on these dimensions could already be highly attracted to entrepreneurship. So they would not be much affected by a short-term intervention, for example an entrepreneurship education, and the observed change in entrepreneurial attitudes and intention would be minimal.

My empirical analyses in chapters 4 through 6 will deliver insights into this question.

2.5.4 Extensions of the Baseline Model

Up to now the theoretical considerations have dealt with exogenously given characteristics. However, course- and course-environment-related variables could also have an influence on the change of attitudes and intentions.[21]

Social interactions

In economics of education, peer quality and behavior – i.e. the quality and behavior of the other students in the classroom – is seen as one of the most important determinants of student outcomes. The most influential study in this field, the "Coleman Report" of 1966, reports that school performance of disadvantage is more amenable to improvement through manipulation of peer influence than by increased per-student expenditures (Coleman et al. 1966). Correlations between peer characteristics and academic performance measures (GPA, achievements) are frequently reported (see for example Sacerdote (2001);

---

[21] In the empirical analyses in chapters 4 to 6 I focus on the baseline model. Peer effects in entrepreneurship education are investigated separately in chapter 7. All other constructs in this subsection are used descriptively to assess students' perceptions of the quality of the course I employ as behavioral intervention.

Schneeweis and Winter-Ebmer (2007)). Facteau et al. (1995) argue that trainees can better transform learned skills on the job with the help of their peers. Recently, also the entrepreneurship literature strongly considers peer effects. Several studies find that social interactions among entrepreneurship-exposed individuals could function as social multipliers regarding entrepreneurial activities (Gompers et al. 2005; Nanda and Sørensen 2010). In a school setting, Falck et al. (2010) find that the presence of entrepreneurial peers at school has positive effects on an individual's entrepreneurial intentions. So apparently, also the composition of one's peer group during entrepreneurship training could influence the changes in entrepreneurial attitudes and intentions due to this intervention.

Learning

Johannisson (1991) develops a conceptual framework with five levels of learning from entrepreneurship education (see also Souitaris et al. (2007)): Why entrepreneurs act (values, motivation), what needs to be done (knowledge), how to do it (abilities, skills), who should we know (social skills, networks) and finally when to act (experience and intuition). The role of accumulated knowledge has been discussed in paragraph 2.5.3.2 above. Also the knowledge gained in an entrepreneurship course could therefore have an impact on how students evaluate or re-evaluate their beliefs and therefore contribute to a change of entrepreneurial attitudes and intentions.

Additional course-related variables

Dependent on the structure of the entrepreneurship course in question, additional variables could enter the evaluation. An Example could be academic faculty who run the course. They become key persons for the students, as they are providing theory-based knowledge and new research findings, and might also give feedback on the performance during the course. In addition, Lüthje and Franke (2002) argue that these instructors should be joined by business practitioners, who can authentically provide hands-on experience and insights into the roles and tasks of an entrepreneur. This supports the transfer of tacit knowledge between entrepreneurs and students. This allows students to gain additional information whether an entrepreneurial career is desirable or feasible. Other examples could be students' assessment of teamwork if they created a business plan in teams, general assessments of how satisfied students were with the course or any other variable that represents the characteristics of the examined entrepreneurship course.

In this section I argue that an entrepreneurship course will not have the same effect on all students. All these background variables – and potentially many more – might play a role when researchers want to examine the patterns of the effects of entrepreneurship education. However, as stated earlier and according to Fishbein's and Ajzen's work, it is not clear whether or not there is a connection. This is an empirical question which I try to answer in the empirical studies I present in chapters 4 to 6.

One issue that belongs to behavioral interventions is still open. Whatever effects entrepreneurship education has on different individuals, the instructors ex-ante aimed at changing beliefs and downstream behavior. Ultimately, the instructors exert influence over future career paths. If they are aware of that or not, it raises an ethical concern about how they use this "power", and even if they should make use of this power at all.

2.5.5 Ethical Concerns – Information versus Persuasion

Fishbein and Ajzen (2010) point out the importance of the ethical concerns raised in behavioral interventions. In general, people consider it acceptable and even desirable when someone provides them with information upon which they are able to make more competent decisions with a better feeling. On the other hand, it is unethical to provide information aiming to persuade somebody to adopt a certain behavior that is desirable by the provider of that information.

Instructors of entrepreneurship education face exactly this issue. They have to ensure that the information provided in the course is accurate, based on latest scientific knowledge, and not dependent on their own entrepreneurial attitudes, intentions or behavior. However, it seems impossible to provide information about a behavior that does not have the potential to persuade. Having said that, it is important to note that people are free to accept or reject the information provided during the entrepreneurship course. Moreover, there is also an ethical concern about not intervening to change entrepreneurial intentions during the students' university life[22]. In chapter 1 I argued that entrepreneurship education should enable students to decide more consciously about their future career.

2.6 Conclusion

In this chapter I present a theoretical framework for evaluating the effects of entrepreneurship education. This framework is based on the widely acknowledged Theory of Planned Behavior, that has frequently been used to predict entrepreneurial activity and thus provides sufficiently tested and validated concepts and measurement tools (see next chapter).

My Theory of Planned Behavior-based framework provides several advantages in evaluating entrepreneurship education. First, it goes beyond measures of micro-economic impact such as the number of created businesses and jobs, which are inappropriate when evaluating entrepreneurship education (see subsection 1.2.2 for a discussion). It rather focuses on the evolution of students' entrepreneurial attitudes and intentions during an entrepreneurship course. These concepts provide an indirect way to measure the impact of an entrepreneurship course on students' career aspirations appropriately directly at the end of the course. Second, the focus on relatively few but sufficient relevant concepts (perceived desirability, perceived social norm, and perceived behavioral control) allows a purposeful assessment of the effects. The variations of the changes in the beliefs underlying these three attitudes may inform about which components of the course generated relevant information that led to an adjustment of students' career aspirations. This in turn opens avenues into considerations of better designs of entrepreneurship courses to achieve the intended goals of enabling students to more consciously decide about their future career

---

[22] In other domains, there could even be an ethical obligation to try to persuade people to change their behavior. Examples could be the attempt to reduce smoking or to increase the usage of condoms.

path. Third, the framework allows including background variables that play an important role in the formation and re-evaluation of beliefs underlying the three attitudes. Entrepreneurship education will not have the same effects on all students. When exhibiting certain background characteristics (demographics, prior experiences, personality traits) students might not respond to the stimuli generated during an entrepreneurship course. This raises an issue on the supply side of entrepreneurship education due to restricted education budgets in most public universities. When universities only have a limited number of places in lectures or seminars, these should be offered to students who are open to these learning experiences. Finally, and from a more application-oriented point of view, this framework grounds on a proven and validated set of concepts and measurement tools. Using pretested questionnaire-items based on the Theory of Planned Behavior to predict entrepreneurial activity avoids unnecessary issues in measuring the concepts. Moreover, as the application of the Theory of Planned Behavior is widely acknowledged in the entrepreneurship domain, and more specifically in the literature on the evaluation of entrepreneurship education, the obtained results are comparable to the findings of other studies. This in turn allows a classification of the own findings and strengthens the derived implications for course design and student selection.

In the next chapter I persist in the application-oriented view. That chapter contains the presentation of my research design and the entrepreneurship course I evaluate. Moreover I introduce the used questionnaire items and present results of validity tests of those, and descriptive results about the composition of the student sample attending the course.

3. Institutional Setting and Presentation of the Dataset

3.1 Introduction

Overall, this book aims at discussing and determining the effects of entrepreneurship education on entrepreneurial attitudes and intentions, both from a theoretical, but also from an empirical perspective. Having laid out the theoretical foundations in the previous chapter, I now describe my research design and the generation of a dataset based upon which I can empirically measure the size and nature of the effects of entrepreneurship education in the following chapters. I argued that my theoretical framework has some advantages compared to those of previously conducted studies (see subsection 1.2.4). In this chapter I discuss the practical application of this framework. On the other hand, I discuss several caveats emanating from the data that have to be kept in mind when interpreting the findings of the following chapters. I also present the data collection processes in detail to prove the validity of my data and to make a reproduction of this design possible for a further validation of my findings.

The optimal research design when evaluating the effects of entrepreneurship education would be a controlled experiment. For this, it would first be necessary to identify an entrepreneurship course that students have been exogenously randomly assigned to (treatment group), and other students not (control group). To ensure statistical power in the empirical analyses, the sample sizes should be as large as possible. A second component of the optimal research design is the data collection. In a controlled experiment using this framework, researchers should survey the students twice: the first time before the course has begun to measure the initial attitudes and intentions when entering the course (ex-ante test), and the second time when the course has finished (ex-post test). Doing so in both the treatment and control group enables the researcher to exactly determine the changes in attitudes and intentions (following the theoretical model presented in chapter 2) among the treatment group compared to those of the control group. These comparisons deliver the true causal effects of the entrepreneurship course. When collecting the data the researcher also has to ensure that students respond to both surveys, as otherwise the data would be subject to attrition bias. This bias introduces a discount of subjects for whom the researcher has complete data for the ex-ante test, but was not able to successfully match this observation to a complete ex-post questionnaire (Heckman 1979). Third, the questionnaires used for both the ex-ante and the ex-post test should be based on established theory and previously used items. The researcher has to ensure validity of the measures, reproducibility of the research design, and comparability of the obtained results to those of other studies.

In practice, however, a research setting like this is hard to obtain, or even impossible when demanding that the experiment is controlled. Only few studies employ an ex-ante and ex-post test control group design. I already emphasized the studies by Peterman and Kennedy (2003), Souitaris et al. (2007) and Oosterbeek et al. (2010) who do so.

However, other issues remain, for example regarding the choice of treatment and control group. In most cases, also in the three mentioned studies, students self-select into entrepreneurship courses, i.e. they decide themselves to attend a course or not. As a consequence, these students may enter the course with already existing predispositions towards (or against) entrepreneurship. This in turn leads to a bias in the interpretation of the information these students receive during a course, and so to a bias in the adjustment of behavioral, normative and control beliefs, as argued in subsection 2.5.3. Moreover, although treatment and control groups in these studies are not random, no explicit tests for the equivalence with respect to background variables of the two groups are conducted. In the previous chapter I stressed the importance of background characteristics when interpreting information obtained during an entrepreneurship course. Therefore, the disregard of the differences between treated and untreated students with respect to, for example, prior entrepreneurship-related experiences when interpreting the results may lead to biased conclusions. In addition, due to the young age of entrepreneurship as field of study at tertiary institutions (see section 1.1), class sizes are rarely large. In contrast to other disciplines, entrepreneurship courses are still not mandatory for most students, especially in non-business studies. Accordingly, the sample sizes are not very large in previously conducted studies (see subsection 1.2.3). Finally, these studies use different instruments to measure the same constructs. Therefore, a comparison of the results found in these studies is difficult.

In this chapter I present my research design and data in six sections. The research design aims at overcoming methodological deficiencies of previously conducted studies and to be as close to the ideal design as possible. First it contains a description of the treatment and control group I use for an ex-ante and ex-post test design together with a detailed presentation of the entrepreneurship course that I employ as behavioral intervention. Unlike other studies (except the one by Oosterbeek et al. (2010)) the course is mandatory for the students. This minimizes potential biases due to self-selection into the course. In the third section I give an overview of the data collection procedures with detailed time lines of the conducted surveys. In section four, I present the items used to measure the theoretical constructs introduced in my theoretical model in section 2.5. My choice of the instruments is grounded on the theoretical work on the Theory of Planned Behavior by Ajzen (1985; 1991) and Fishbein and Ajzen (2010) as well as on existing empirical literature on the prediction of entrepreneurial intentions (see section 2.4). This ensures the comparability of my findings in later chapters to other studies. Both the detailed presentation of the data collection processes and the questionnaire items should make a reproduction of this research project possible for a validation of my findings in chapters 4 to 7. The fifth section of this chapter assesses several possible sources of bias in my data. This section also includes a test for equivalence between the treatment and control group. This kind of test is not employed in previous studies. Section four also presents descriptive statistics regarding sample composition. Results of general course evaluation questions are shown in section six. This chapter concludes with a discussion of the appropriateness of the dataset and potential caveats regarding the empirical analyses in chapters 4 to 7. I also debate in how far the implications regarding course design derived from the findings in these chapters can be generalized to entrepreneurship education in general, given that the results are based on a single course concept.

3.2 Context

Here I give a detailed presentation of the entrepreneurship course I use as behavioral intervention. Based upon the data collected among the students who have attended this course and using the theoretical model presented in section 2.5 I evaluate the effects of entrepreneurship education on entrepreneurial attitudes and intentions of students. Following the research designs of Peterman and Kennedy (2003), Souitaris et al. (2007) and Oosterbeek et al. (2010) I also collect data from untreated students (i.e. students who have not attended an entrepreneurship course during the same period of time). Comparing the changes in entrepreneurial attitudes and intentions among the treated students to the changes among the untreated students allows determining the true causal effects of the course.

3.2.1 Treatment Group

As the context for the empirical tests I selected 3rd semester business administration students of the Munich School of Management at the Ludwig-Maximilians-Universität Munich. In this semester the students have to take the mandatory course "Business Planning", which is offered by the Institute for Innovation Research, Technology Management and Entrepreneurship, and the LMU Entrepreneurship Center[23]. As the course is mandatory, I do not face any self-selection issues regarding course participation. Moreover I can be sure that this is the first university course with entrepreneurship content the students attend and can so analyze the "true" effects of an entrepreneurship course. Furthermore, 3rd semester students are not likely to have already formed very

---

[23] Although I am a staff member at both institutions, I was not involved in any aspect of "Business Planning" at any time.

strong career intentions, so an entrepreneurship course as a sort of information source about future careers could still possibly impact students' plans. And third, since this research project is also set up to capture not only the overall impact on attitudes and intentions, but also the effects of background variables on these measures, I have chosen a course that is regarded as best practice.

The objectives of this course are i) to teach students basic capabilities needed in the planning and management of a start-up enterprise, in particular to convey the necessary knowledge and skills for crafting a complete business plan; ii) to raise awareness for the option to pursue an entrepreneurial career: students are supposed to acquire knowledge about small enterprises, self-employment and entrepreneurship so that they can make rational career decisions; iii) to allow students to gain practical experience by interaction with real-world entrepreneurs. The objectives of this course do not encompass any notion of convincing students to become entrepreneurs or to describe entrepreneurship as a particularly desirable option. While the economic importance of entrepreneurship is clearly signaled, students are not meant to be indoctrinated.

The course "Business Planning" is organized as follows: Every year, the 3rd semester students take the course in the winter term that lasts from October to February. During this time all students (approximately 400 per year) attend the so-called plenum sessions (90 minutes per session). In these sessions, faculty staff is teaching basic principles about entrepreneurship and how to write a business plan. Additionally, guest speakers such as entrepreneurs, marketing or finance experts give practical advice. Parallel to the lectures in the plenum sessions the students work together in teams of four to six in order to develop a business plan. Each of these teams cooperates with a Munich-based founder who is providing his business idea for the business-planning task. This allows the students to leave the purely academic setting and to take insight into the daily tasks of a real-world entrepreneur. Furthermore, four of these teams at a time attend one of 20 weekly tutorials (or discussion sessions)[24] (90 minutes per session) led by Munich School of Management faculty. In these discussion

---

[24] Students were grouped in teams and scheduled to the discussion sessions by LMU Entrepreneurship Center staff.

sessions the teams present their business-planning progress to the faculty and to the other teams and get feedback. The students had also access to an e-learning platform where they could download the lectures of the plenum sessions as podcasts. At the end of the course, the student teams have to submit a complete business plan of 15 pages and give a 20 minute presentation to faculty staff who acts as hypothetical investors. Grades are based largely on team performance in the written business plan and presentation and secondly on individual achievements (each team-member is "responsible" for one chapter of the business plan). Additionally but not linked to grading, there is also an award for the ten best business plans, and every student gets a certificate for accomplishing the course. All in all, every year approximately 400 3rd semester business students attend "Business Planning", grouped in 80 teams with four to six students each, cooperating with 40 founders (one founder cooperates with two teams).

Table 3.1 and Table 3.2 give an overview over the class schedules of "Business Planning" in the winter terms 2008/09 (cohort 1) and 2009/10[25].

In the following I will call students who have attended "Business Planning" the "treatment group" or "treated students".

---

[25] The parts shaded in grey are no lectures, but refer to the examination process.

Table 3.1: Schedule for "Business Planning" during winter term 2008-09

Calendar week	Plenum Sessions (Tuesdays)	Discussion Sessions (Mondays through Thursdays)
42	Kick-Off	
43	Entrepreneurship: Overview and Essentials	Kick-Off
44	Product- and Service-Mix, Business Modeling	First presentation of the business idea
45	Financial Planning	Presentation of the product-/ service mix and business model
46	Market and Competition	
47		Presentation of the market and competitive analysis
48	Sales / Marketing / PR	
49		Presentation of the sales, marketing and PR strategy
50	Growth and Start-up Financing, IP	
51		Presentation of the growth plan and targeted financing sources
3	Submission of business plans	
4	Presentation of business planning results	
5	Closing Ceremony and awarding of best business plans	

Table 3.2: Schedule for "Business Planning" during winter term 2009-10

Calendar week	Plenum Sessions (Mondays)	Discussion Sessions (Mondays through Thursdays)
43	Kick-Off	Kick-Off
44	Entrepreneurship Overview & Essentials, Product- and Service-Mix	
45	Efficient Teamwork	Presentation of the business idea and the product-/ service mix
46	Market and Competition	
47	Presentation Skills	Free teamwork
48	Marketing and Sales	Presentation of market and competitive analysis
49	Rhetoric	Presentation of marketing and sales strategy
50	Team, Organization, Growth and Start-up Financing	
51	Efficient Teamwork 2	
2	Submission of business plans	
3	Presentation of business planning results	
4	Closing Ceremony and awarding of best business plans	

3.2.2 Control Group

I am interested in the true causal effect "Business Planning" has on entrepreneurial attitudes and intentions. This calls for a quasi-experimental design (see chapter 5). To distinguish between differences attributable to the exposure to the course and differences caused by other influences, I also had to collect data from a comparison group[26] that has not been exposed to an entrepreneurship course during the time period the treatment group has attended "Business Planning". Otherwise the students in the control group should be as similar as possible to the students in the treatment group with respect to, for example, demographic variables.

---

[26] In the literature the terms control group and comparison group are used synonymously. Hereinafter the term control group is used.

The most intuitive way to find a control group in the winter term 2008-09 (cohort 1) was to look at the second big university in Munich, the Technical University of Munich, in its School of Management. I identified an appropriate group in the lecture "Controlling", a mandatory lecture for all business administration students in their third semester. These students were not exposed to entrepreneurship courses by then.

In the winter term 2009-10 (cohort 2) I had to look for another solution and surveyed the first semester students of the Munich School of Management of the Ludwig-Maximilians-Universität Munich. The best way to approach this group was lecture "Einführung in die BWL" ("Introduction to Business Administration"), which is mandatory for every business administration student beginning his studies.

In the next section I describe how I proceeded with regard to the data collection in the treatment and control group in cohorts 1 and 2.

3.3 Data Collection Procedures

To collect data I used either online- or paper-based questionnaires. The online-surveys were created and conducted by using LimeSurvey[27], an open-source survey application that I hosted on a server at the data center of the Ludwig-Maximilians-Universität Munich and that I could feed with the email addresses of the enrolled students. I obtained these addresses from the examination office. Using LimeSurvey allowed me to create personalized invitation-links for every student and thus to keep trace about who already answered the survey and to send out reminders to the right group of students who have not responded by then. It is important to note that I was not able to connect the submitted questionnaire to the personalized link or even to the email address.

I made clear to all students that the survey is for research purposes only, that their participation in the survey is voluntary and that their data will not affect their grades. Both ex-ante and ex-post questionnaires were reviewed by

---

[27] http://www.limesurvey.org/

three academic staff members and five non-participating students to ensure clarity of wording and validity of the constructs. To reduce biases due to self-presentational and social desirability issues (see subsection 2.3.3.2), I assured the students in all invitations to respond to the questionnaire and in the introductory section of the questionnaires, that their data will be analyzed anonymously, and asked them to answer honestly, spontaneously and not to go backwards once having entered their data. Moreover I incentivized students to respond to the questionnaires by assuring them that the data will be used to improve the course and additionally offered some premiums (see below).

To ensure a clear arrangement, I grouped items together and showed one group of items after another in online-questionnaires and also presented the items in the same groups in paper-based questionnaires.

As I am interested in the individual changes of entrepreneurial attitudes and intentions, I had to match the ex-ante and ex-post questionnaires that belonged to the same individual. The matching was achieved through a structured identification code[28]. A transcript of the questionnaire is available from the author on request.

All in all there were four groups of students, two treatment- and two control group cohorts, of which each was asked to answer to two surveys. I also discuss the response rates of the eight surveys, the overall response rate of the pooled sample, and the results of the matching of questionnaires.

3.3.1 Treatment Group

Both cohorts filled out questionnaires before the first session (ex-ante test) of the course and directly after they submitted their final business plan, but before the grades were communicated (ex-post test).

---

[28] The code consisted of the first letter of the first name of the student's mother, the last letter of the student's name, the first digit of the student's month of birth, and the first letter of the student's place of birth.

3.3.1.1 Data Collection

Timeline cohort 1 The ex-ante questionnaire for cohort 1 was online. I gathered email-addresses of all enrolled students via the examination office of the Munich School of Management. I sent out invitations to respond to the questionnaire on October 2, 2008 (0.00 a.m.), asking students to respond by October 14, 2008, the day the course started. I deactivated the link when the kick-off began (2.00 p.m.). As incentive to respond, I raffled off ten Amazon vouchers at 25 Euros each. In addition, students could indicate their willingness to take part in an experiment as one of 50 subjects where they could possibly win up to 300 Euros. On October 9 and October 13 (both 0.00 a.m.) I sent out reminders to those students who did not answer by then. The ex-post questionnaire was paper-based. As students had to fetch certificates of attendance in calendar week 6, 2009, I considered having them respond to the questionnaire when they did so the most efficient and effective way. This also reduced the cost of filling out the questionnaire for students, so I did not give away any additional incentives, except for a new request to indicate their willingness to participate in an experiment, as one of 100 subjects, where they could again win up to 300 Euros.

Timeline cohort 2 Since I experienced some issues with missing values in the paper-based questionnaires in cohort 1, both ex-ante and ex-post questionnaire were online for cohort 2. Again I gathered the email-addresses of all enrolled students via the examination office of the Munich School of Management. I sent out the invitations with personalized links for the ex-ante questionnaire on October 6, 2009 (0.00 a.m.) and asked the students to respond by October 19, 2009. Again I deactivated the link when the kick-off began (2.00 p.m.). This time students were asked to respond to the survey as a prerequisite to register for the e-learning platform where they could also see the discussion session they were assigned to. However, the students were not forced to fill out the questionnaire, since we also offered them to provide them with a link to directly apply to the e-learning platform. The students who did not answer by then received two reminders on October 10 and October 18, 2009 (both 0.00 a.m.). The links with the requests to respond to the ex-post survey were sent out directly after the closing ceremony on January 25, 2010 (4 p.m.), asking the students to respond by February 10, 2010 (11.59 p.m.). I sent out two reminders to those students who did not respond by then on January 31 and February 5, 2010 (both 0.00 a.m.). As an incentive to answer the survey I offered to send the course certificates via mail instead of having the students fetch them at the LMU Entrepreneurship Center, asking them to submit their postal address that was stored in a different database.

3.3.1.2 Response Rates

Cohort 1 In the winter term 2008-09, 409 students were enrolled in "Business Planning". A total of 357 (87.143 %) students responded either to the ex-ante or ex-post survey. 311 (76.0 %) of these questionnaires were complete. 280 (68.5 %) students answered the ex-ante questionnaire, 254 (62.1 %) of the questionnaires were complete.

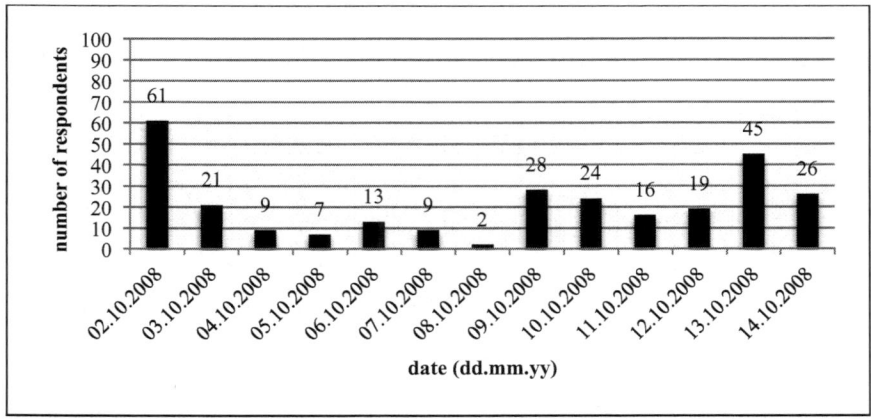

Figure 3.1: Number of responses for the 2008-09 cohort treatment-group ex-ante survey by date

The ex-post test was answered by 276 (67.5 %) students, 255 (62.3 %) of these questionnaires were complete. Of the 254 ex-ante and 255 ex-post questionnaires I was able to match 177 (43.3%) to the right counterpart of the ex-ante questionnaires. Unfortunately I experienced some difficulties in reconstructing the structure of the teams the students worked in together. As I am also interested in peer-effects that may arise within the teams, I decided to respect this structure and therefore had to drop 31 more matched ex-ante ex-post observations. Thus I can use 146 (35.7%) complete and valid ex-ante ex-post questionnaire pairs.

Cohort 2 405 students were enrolled in the 2008-09 "Business Planning" course. I received responses to either the ex-ante or the ex-post survey from 353 (87.2 %) students, 331 (81.7 %) of them were complete. 342 (84.4 %) students complied with my request to answer the ex-ante questionnaire, 340 (84.0 %) were complete and valid.

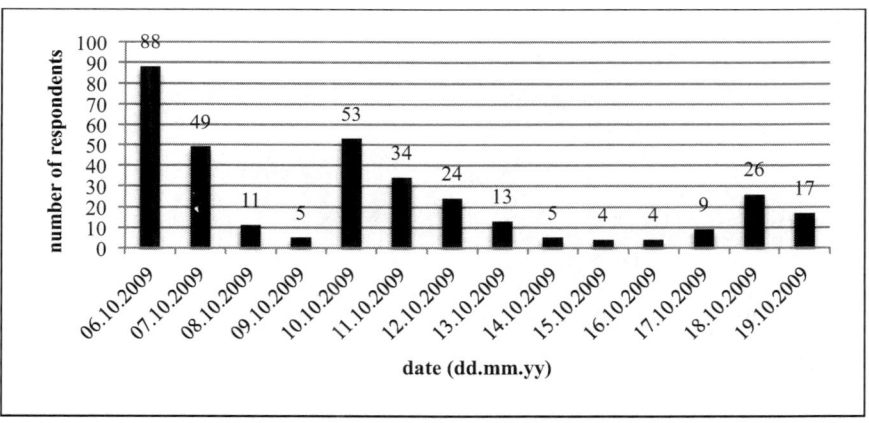

Figure 3.2: Number of responses for the 2009-10 cohort treatment-group ex-ante survey by date

290 (71.6 %) students answered the ex-post test, 270 (66.7 %) were complete and valid.

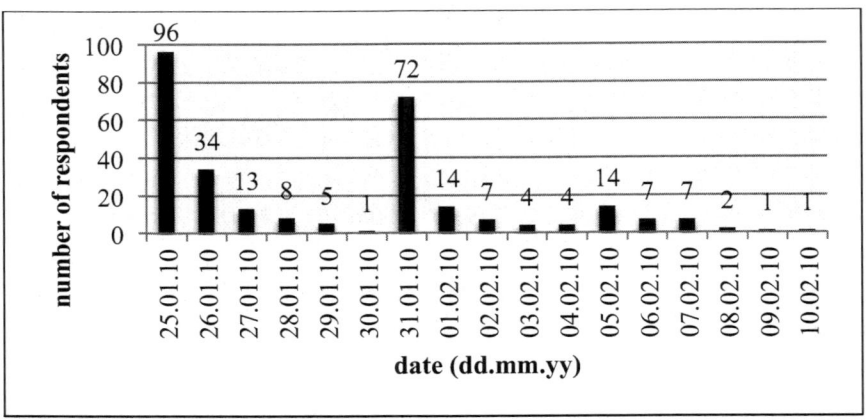

Figure 3.3: Number of responses for the 2009-10 cohort treatment-group ex-post survey by date

Overall I received 257 (63.5 %) complete and valid ex-ante ex-post questionnaire pairs.

3.3.2 Control Group

Both cohorts filled out questionnaires at the same point of time as the treatment group, i.e. the ex-ante test at the time when "Business Planning" started and the ex-post test at its end.

3.3.2.1 Data Collection

Timeline cohort 1 I did not have the opportunity to collect the email addresses of the students enrolled in "Controlling", so both the ex-ante and ex-post test were paper-based. With permission by the professor to do so at the end of the lecture, I asked the students to fill out the questionnaire during the last 10 minutes of the second session on October 23, 2008 (i.e. one week later than the kick-off of "Business Planning"). Again, I announced that I would raffle off ten Amazon-vouchers at 25 Euros each among all students who completed the questionnaire to incentivize them. Under the same circumstances I was allowed to conduct the ex-post test in the last session of the lecture on January 21, 2009.

Timeline cohort 2 For the cohort 2 control group I was able to get the email-addresses of all enrolled students for "Einführung in die BWL" via the examination office of the Munich School of Management, and thus put both the ex-ante and ex-post test online. I sent out the invitations for the ex-ante test on October 8, 2009 (0.00 a.m.) and left the link active till November 1, 2009 (11.59 p.m.). Two reminders were sent out on October 15 and October 27, 2009 (both at 0.00 a.m.). Again I used ten Amazon vouchers at 25 Euros as incentives and pointed out that the LMU Entrepreneurship Center would use the data to improve "Business Planning" that the students would attend in their third semester.[29] The students received the invitations for the ex-post test on January 24, 2010 (0.00 a.m.) with the request to answer by February 11, 2010, and in addition two reminders on January 31 and February 5, 2010 (both at 0.00 a.m.), with the same incentive used in the ex-ante test.

3.3.2.2 Response Rates

Cohort 1 308 students were enrolled in "Controlling" at the Technical University of Munich in the winter term 2008-09. 166 (53.9 %) answered either to the ex-ante or ex-post questionnaire, where 150 (48.7 %) were complete. In the ex-ante survey, I received 131 (42.5 %) questionnaires, and 116 (37.7 %) of them were complete and valid. The ex-post survey generated 79 (25.6 %) answers, and 78 (25.3 %) were complete and valid. The matching of questionnaires led to 40 (13.0 %) complete and valid ex-ante ex-post questionnaire pairs.

Cohort 2 "Einführung in die BWL" counted 540 enrolled students in the winter term 2009-10, and I received 310 (57.4 %) answers to either the ex-ante or ex-post survey, where 247 (45.7 %) were complete. The ex-ante survey was answered by 273 (50.6 %) students, 234 (43.3 %) were complete and valid.

---

[29] In fact, the results of this project should help to improve the course concept.

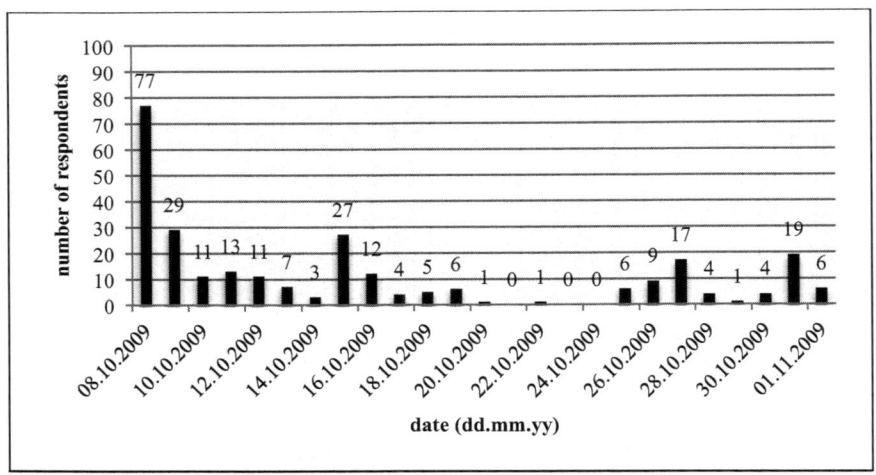

Figure 3.4: Number of responses for the 2009-10 cohort control-group ex-ante survey by date

150 (27.8 %) students filled out the ex-post questionnaire, 123 (22.8 %) were complete.

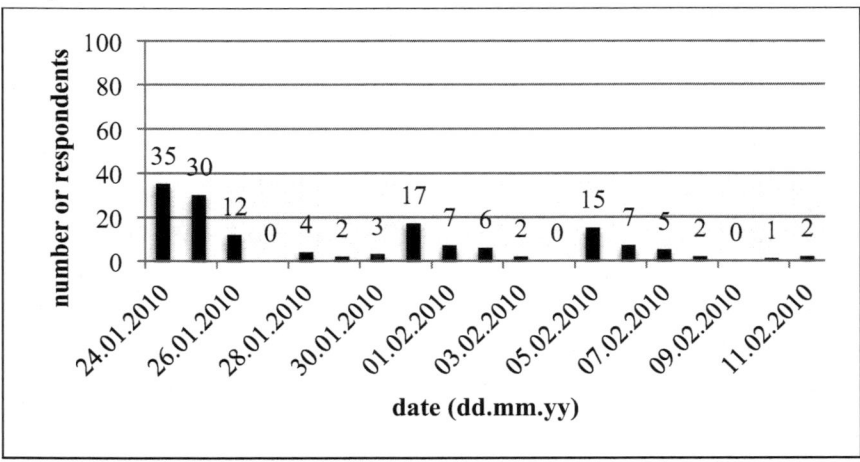

Figure 3.5: Number of responses for the 2009-10 cohort control-group ex-post survey by date

All in all I was able to receive 86 (15.9 %) complete and valid ex-ante ex-post questionnaire pairs.

For the empirical analyses in chapters 4 through 7, I will pool both cohorts. In my opinion this is justified, because the entrepreneurship content the two cohorts of the treatment group were exposed to in "Business Planning" did not differ dramatically. In addition, I test for statistical equivalence of the cohorts and groups in paragraph 3.5.1.3. Hence the final sample consists of 403 (response rate of 49.8 %) matched and valid ex-ante ex-post questionnaire pairs for the treatment group. From the 126 (14.9 %) complete questionnaire pairs of the control group I disregard seven from the 2008 cohort and 13 from the 2009 cohort in the evaluation of the course effects as these subjects indicated that they attended an entrepreneurship course during the ex-ante and ex-post test. This leaves me with a control group of 106 (12.5 %) subjects who were not exposed to an entrepreneurship course during the time in question.

I will test whether there are significant differences between the two cohorts with respect to background variables and initial entrepreneurial attitudes and intentions to see if these groups can be considered equivalent. But before being able to make statements about possible biases in the data, I have to verify that the scales I use in the questionnaire are reliable and valid.

Table 3.3 summarizes the response rates for both cohorts of the treatment and control groups.

Table 3.3: Response rates of conducted surveys by cohort and group

	Cohort 1						Cohort 2						Pooled					
	Treatment group				Control group		Treatment group				Control group		Treatment group				Control group	
	ex-ante		ex-post		ex-ante	ex-post	ex-ante		ex-post		ex-ante	ex-post	ex-ante		ex-post		ex-ante	ex-post
Enrolled students	409		276		308		405		290		540		814		566		848	
Responses to either ex-ante or ex-post survey	357				166		353				310		710				476	
	87.3%				53.9%		87.2%				57.4%		87.2%				56.1%	
Thereof complete	311				150		331				247		642				397	
	76.0%				48.7%		81.7%				45.7%		78.9%				46.8%	
Number of responses	280		276		131	79	342		290		273	150	622		566		404	229
	68.5%		67.5%		42.5%	25.6%	84.4%		71.6%		50.6%	27.8%	76.4%		69.5%		47.6%	27.0%
Thereof complete	254		255		116	78	340		270		234	123	594		525		350	201
	62.1%		62.3%		37.7%	25.3%	84.0%		66.7%		43.3%	22.8%	73.0%		64.5%		41.3%	23.7%
Complete matched and used questionnaires	146				40		257				86		403				106	
	35.7%				13.0%		63.5%				15.9%		49.8%				12.5%	

3.4 Measures

In this section I present the items used to measure the variables in question. The order in which I present the measures mirrors the order I followed in the theoretical considerations in subsection 2.5.3.

The ex-ante questionnaire for the treatment group was structured into two sections. The first section asked for the identification code for the matching of ex-ante and ex-post questionnaires. The second section contained (in this order) questions for demographic background, prior exposure to entrepreneurship through family and acquaintances and own entrepreneurship experiences, the elements of the Theory of Planned Behavior, and personality traits.

The ex-post questionnaire had an additional third section. It gave students the opportunity to evaluate the course "Business Planning". Apart from that the questionnaire contained basically the same questions, however I did not (for some exceptions making the matching of questionnaires easier) include questions from the ex-ante test whose answers would not change over time (demographics, personality traits).

The ex-ante and ex-post questionnaire for the control group was exactly the same as for the treatment group, logically leaving out the course evaluation questions in the ex-post test.

3.4.1 Selection of Measures for the Questionnaire

The items I employed to measure the constructs of the Theory of Planned Behavior and other variables of interest is based on existing theoretical and empirical literature in the psychological and entrepreneurship domain. A full transcript of the questionnaire used in the surveys is available from the author on request. The answering time to complete the questionnaire varied between 10 and 20 minutes.

3.4.1.1 Measures for the Elements of Theory of Planned Behavior

To develop the questionnaire sections dealing with the elements of the Theory of Planned Behavior I reviewed the instruments of the studies in section 2.4 and also the entrepreneurship education evaluation studies presented in subsection 1.2.3. Later I cross-checked with the recommendations by Liñán and Chen (2009). Throughout the process of developing the questionnaire I consulted Ajzen's work on the evolution of the Theory of Planned Behavior (Ajzen 1985; Ajzen and Madden 1986; Ajzen 1991, 2002). As recommended in these studies, all items were queried with 7-point Likert scales. To be consistent and not to confuse the students, every scale had the same seven labels. I asked the students to indicate their agreement to presented statements by choosing one of the following options:

Table 3.4: Labels of the seven-point Likert-scale response categories used in surveys

German original	English translation	Coded as (for the empirical analyses)
"ich stimme überhaupt nicht zu"	"I completely disagree"	1
"ich stimme nicht zu"	"I disagree"	2
"ich stimme eher nicht zu"	"I rather disagree"	3
"weder noch"	"neutral"	4
"ich stimme eher zu"	"I rather agree"	5
"ich stimme zu"	"I agree"	6
"ich stimme voll und ganz zu"	"I completely agree"	7

Entrepreneurial intentions Armitage and Conner (2001) find that a behavioral measure of intention seems superior to the two other kinds of intentions measures – desire and self-prediction. Following that, I measured *entrepreneurial intentions* by one item initially proposed by Shapero and Sokol (1982).

Table 3.5: Item for measuring Entrepreneurial intentions

Item	German item in the questionnaire	English Translation
1	"Ich strebe an, innerhalb der nächsten fünf bis zehn Jahre mein eigenes Unternehmen zu gründen."	"I intend to start my own business in the next five to ten years"

Perceived desirability In the existing literature, perceived desirability is measured both by belief-based scales (e.g. in Kolvereid (1996b)) and by aggregate scales (e.g. Kolvereid and Isaksen (2006)). In this latter study, in addition, entrepreneurial intentions are regressed on both types of measures, where the aggregate type was a significant regressor, and the belief-based type was not. Moreover, Ajzen (1991) show that correlations between belief-based measures and aggregate measures are sometimes disappointing. For this reason I also decided to use an aggregate measure of perceived desirability. I used a four-item measure first developed by Gundry and Welch (2001) and subsequently adopted by Kolvereid and Isaksen (2006), who add a fifth item.

Table 3.6: Items for measuring Perceived Desirability

Item	German item in the questionnaire	English translation
1	"Ich würde lieber mein eigenes Unternehmen besitzen, als in einem Angestelltenverhältnis mehr Geld zu verdienen."	"I would rather own my own business than earn a higher salary employed by someone else."
2	"Ich bin lieber mein eigener Chef, als in einem Angestelltenverhältnis Karriere zu machen."	"I would rather own my own business than pursue a promising career employed by someone else."
3	"Um mein eigener Chef zu sein, bin ich bereit, erhebliche persönliche Opfer zu bringen."	"I am willing to make significant personal sacrifices in order to stay in my own business."
4	"Ich würde nur so lange als Angestellter arbeiten bis ich die Möglichkeit habe, ein eigenes Unternehmen zu gründen."	"I would work somewhere else only as long as I make another attempt to start my own business."
5	"Ich bin bereit, in meinem eigenen Unternehmen bei gleichem Gehalt mehr zu arbeiten denn als Angestellter in einer Organisation."	"I am willing to work more with the same salary in my own business, than as employed in an organization."

The scores on the items are averaged to obtain an overall measure of *perceived desirability* (Gundry and Welch 2001).

Perceived Social Norm In the entrepreneurship domain this factor is sometimes simply omitted (Krueger 1993; Chen et al. 1998). Other studies ask for the opinions of three important reference groups – closest family, friends, and other important people – whether one ought to become an entrepreneur or not and amended questions about the respective "motive to comply" (Kolvereid 1996a; Tkachev and Kolvereid 1999; Kolvereid and Isaksen 2006; Souitaris et al. 2007). I adopted this three-item indicator of these studies. I included an additional item about the opinions of fellow students, as this perception becomes important in a setting such as an entrepreneurship course, where the students receive repeatedly feedback from this group.

Table 3.7: Items for measuring Perceived Social Norm

Item	German item in the questionnaire	English translation
1-1	"Ich glaube, dass meine engste Familie findet, dass ich ein Unternehmen gründen sollte."	"My closest family thinks that I should start my own business."
1-2	"Die Erwartungen meiner engsten Familie sind mir wichtig."	"The expectations of my closest family are important to me."
2-1	"Ich glaube, dass meine engsten Freunde finden, dass ich ein eigenes Unternehmen gründen sollte."	"My closest friends think that I should start my own business."
2-2	"Die Erwartungen meiner engsten Freunde sind mir wichtig."	"The expectations of my closest friends are important to me."
3-1	"Ich glaube, dass meine Kommilitonen finden, dass ich ein eigenes Unternehmen gründen sollte."	"My fellow students think that I should start my own business."
3-2	"Die Erwartungen meiner Kommilitonen sind mir wichtig."	"The expectations of my fellow students are important to me."
4-1	"Ich glaube, dass andere mir nahe stehende Personen finden, dass ich ein eigenes Unternehmen gründen sollte."	"Other people who are close to me think that I should start my own business."
4-2	"Die Erwartungen anderer mir nahe stehenden Personen sind mir wichtig."	"The expectations of other people who are close to me are important to me."

The items 1-1, 2-1, 3-1, and 4-1 were transformed to yield symmetric scales from -3 to 3, which were then multiplied by a weight indicating to which extent the respondent cares about the expectation of the respective group. Following Kolvereid (1996a) and Souitaris et al. (2007), the scores are added to obtain an overall measure of *perceived social norm*.

Perceived Behavioral Control Previous studies measure perceived behavioral control through specific – "entrepreneurial" – self-efficacy (Chen et al. 1998; Zhao et al. 2005; Kolvereid and Isaksen 2006). However, Ajzen (2002) considers perceived behavioral control as a concept somewhat wider than self-efficacy. Therefore I looked for other measures and finally adopted a six-item battery developed by Kolvereid (1996a), which is subsequently used by Tkachev and Kolvereid (1999) and Souitaris et al. (2007).

Table 3.8: Items for measuring Perceived Behavioral Control

Item	German item in the questionnaire	English translation
1	"Selbständig zu sein würde mir sehr leicht fallen."	"For me, being self-employed would be very easy."
2	"Wenn ich wollte, könnte ich ganz leicht einen Karriereweg als Selbständiger einschlagen."	"If I wanted to, I could easily pursue a career as self-employed."
3	"Wenn ich selbständig wäre, hätte ich vollständige Kontrolle über meine Situation."	"As self-employed, I would have complete control over the situation."
4	"Die Anzahl der Ereignisse, die mich davon abhalten könnten, mich selbständig zu machen, ist sehr hoch."	"The events outside my control which could prevent me from being self-employed are numerous."
5	"Wenn ich selbständig werden würde, wären die Erfolgschancen sehr hoch."	"If I become self-employed, the chances of success would be very high."
6	"Wenn ich einen Karriereweg als Selbständiger einschlagen würde, wäre die Aussicht auf Misserfolg sehr hoch."	"If I pursue a career as self-employed, the chances of failure would be very high."

Responses to items 4 and 6 become recoded (1=7, 2=6, etc.) and the scores on the six items are then averaged to obtain an overall measure of *perceived behavioral control* (Kolvereid 1996a; Souitaris et al. 2007).

3.4.1.2 Background Factors

In the following I deal with measures of several background factors that enter my empirical studies according to the theoretical considerations of subsection 2.5.3.

3.4.1.2.1 Demographic Variables

In the questionnaire I asked the students for several demographic characteristics: gender, age, nationality, marital status, and religious denomination. The variable *age* and the dummy-variables *female (0/1)* and *foreign (0/1)* are included in the empirical analyses[30]:

Table 3.9: Coding of demographic variables

Variable	Coded as (for the empirical analyses)
age	years
female (0/1)	= 0 if student is male = 1 if student is female
foreign (0/1)	= 0 if student is German = 1 if student is non-German

3.4.1.2.2 Prior Experiences

Three subcategories are associated with prior experiences: role models, own prior exposure to entrepreneurship and prior completed education before the course.

Prior exposure to entrepreneurship To obtain a measure about prior exposure to entrepreneurship I included two yes-no items, asking if parents or acquaintances have ever started an own business following Krueger (1993). Two dummy-variables accounting for role models enter the empirical analyses, *parents self-employed (0/1)* and *acquaintances self-employed (0/1)*. Once again following Krueger (1993) I included two questions whether the students ever worked for a start-up or if they even already have started their own business once. In addition, I added one item asking for previously attended entrepreneurship courses. I include two dummy-variables in the empirical analyses, *worked for*

---

[30] I left out marital status in the empirical analyses since there were only four treated and none of the untreated students who were not single.
In addition, I left out religious denomination, because for ethical reasons it was a voluntary question in the questionnaire and many students left this field blank. In order not to loose observations, I decided this way.

start-up (0/1) and *entrepreneur (0/1)*. Following Krueger (1993) and the theoretical motivation in subsection 2.5.3, I constructed the variable *breadth of prior exposure* to entrepreneurship. This variable is the sum of the answers to the four yes-no questions.

Previously attended entrepreneurship courses To account for prior exposure to entrepreneurship through completed entrepreneurship education, I asked the students how many courses they already attended. The variable *attended entrepreneurship courses* is the number of previously attended courses.

Table 3.10: Items for measuring Prior Exposure to Entrepreneurship

Variable	German item in questionnaire	English translation	Coded as (for the empirical analyses)
parents self-employed (0/1)	"Sind oder waren Ihre Eltern selbständig bzw. haben sie ein Unternehmen gegründet?"	"Are your parents self-employed or have ever started an own business?"	= 0 if answer is "no" = 1 if answer is "yes"
acquaintances self-employed (0/1)	"Gibt es in Ihrem Bekanntenkreis jemanden, der sich selbständig gemacht bzw. ein Unternehmen gegründet hat?"	"Do you have any acquaintances who are self-employed or have ever started an own business?"	= 0 if answer is "no" = 1 if answer is "yes"
worked for start-up (0/1)	"Haben Sie selbst jemals für ein neugegründetes oder junges Unternehmen gearbeitet?"	"Have you ever worked for small or new company?"	= 0 if answer is "no" = 1 if answer is "yes"
entrepreneur (0/1)	"Haben Sie selbst sich jemals selbständig gemacht bzw. ein eigenes Unternehmen gegründet?"	"Have you ever started an own business?"	= 0 if answer is "no" = 1 if answer is "yes"
attended entrepreneurship courses	"Wie viele unternehmensgründungsbezogene Kurse haben Sie schon besucht?"	"How many entrepreneurship courses have you already attended?"	number of attended courses

Previously completed university education A B.Sc. in Business Administration at the Ludwig-Maximilians-Universität requires 180 ECTS (European Credit Transfer System) credits. I obtain a measure of the extent of courses taken before entering the entrepreneurship course by the number of ECTS credits collected so far. In contrast to the previous variables, this was no questionnaire-item, but I received this information from the examination office of the Munich School of Management. The variable *ECTS* capturing the number of collected ECTS prior to "Business Planning" enters the empirical analyses.

3.4.1.2.3 Big5 Personality Dimensions

To obtain measures for the Big5 personality dimensions extraversion, agreeableness, conscientiousness, emotional stability, and openness to experience I employed the Ten-Item Personality Inventory developed by Gosling et al. (2003). I asked students on seven-point Likert scales in how far they agree with the following statements (with the labels presented in Table 3.4).

Table 3.11: Ten-Item Personality Inventory for measuring Big5 personality dimensions

Item	German item in the questionnaire	English version as in Gosling et al. (2003)
	"Ich betrachte mich selbst als ..."	"I see myself as ..."
1	"extrovertiert, begeisterungsfähig"	"extraverted, enthusiastic"
2	"kritisch, streitbar"	"critical, quarrelsome"
3	"gewissenhaft, selbstdiszipliniert"	"dependable, self-disciplined"
4	"nervös, leicht erregbar"	"anxious, easily upset"
5	"offen für neue Erfahrungen, aufgeschlossen"	"open to new experiences, complex"
6	"reserviert, zurückhaltend"	"reserved, quiet"
7	"sympathisch, umgänglich"	"sympathetic, warm"
8	"unorganisiert, unachtsam"	"disorganized, careless"
9	"entspannt, emotional stabil"	"calm, emotionally stable"
10	"konventionell, unkreativ"	"conventional, uncreative"

The variables that enter the empirical analyses are constructed as follows by taking the average of the two respective items:

Table 3.12: Construction of the Big5 measures

Variable	Items
extraversion	1, 6 (reverse-scored)
agreeableness	2, 7 (reverse-scored)
conscientiousness	3, 8 (reverse-scored)
emotional stability	4, 9 (reverse-scored)
openness to experiences	5, 10 (reverse-scored)

The respective two scores then get averaged to obtain an overall measure of each personality dimension.

3.4.1.3 Subsamples of Students

In the empirical chapters 4, 5, and 6, I sometimes split up the sample of students along demographic, prior experiences, and personality variables in two subsamples, for example to compare extravert versus introvert students. Every pair of subsamples is defined by a dummy-variable built using the variables above. The following table gives an overview of these dummy-variables.

Table 3.13: Subsamples defined by background factors

Subsample	Dummy-variable defining the subsample	Definition
demographic variables		
female students	*female (0/1)*	as before
foreign students	*foreign (0/1)*	as before
prior experiences		
students with self-employed parents	*parents self-employed (0/1)*	as before
students with self-employed acquaintances	*acquaintances self-employed (0/1)*	as before
students who worked for a start-up	*worked for start-up (0/1)*	as before
students who have been self-employed	*entrepreneur (0/1)*	as before
students who already have attended an entrepreneurship course	*attended entrepreneurship course (0/1)*	= 1 if *attended entrepreneurship courses* > 0 = 0 else
students who are advanced in their studies	*high ECTS (0/1)*	= 1 if *ECTS* > 51 (median) = 0 else
personality dimensions		
extravert students	*extravert (0/1)*	= 1 if *extraversion* > 4 = 0 else
agreeable students	*agreeable (0/1)*	= 1 if *agreeableness* > 4 = 0 else
conscientious students	*conscientious (0/1)*	= 1 if *conscientiousness* > 4 = 0 else
emotionally stable students	*emotionally stable (0/1)*	= 1 if *emotional stability* > 4 = 0 else
students open to new experiences	*open to experience (0/1)*	= 1 if *openness to experience* > 4 = 0 else

3.4.1.4 Situational Variables

As motivated in subsection 2.5.4, also course-related variables could contribute in the explanation of in how far students re-evaluate their beliefs and therefore change their entrepreneurial attitudes and intentions.[31] To a large extent these variables depend on the structure of the course in question.[32]

learning - Following Johannisson (1991) and his conceptual framework Souitaris et al. (2007) develop a perceptions-based instrument to measure entrepreneurial learning. I used this instrument in my questionnaire asking students on seven-point Likert scales in how far they agree with the following statements that reflect (in this order) the know-why, know-what, know-how, know-who, and know-when levels according to Johannisson's work (with the labels presented in Table 3.4). The scores on the six items are averaged to obtain an overall measure of learning.

Table 3.14: Items for measuring entrepreneurial learning

Item	German item in questionnaire	English version in Souitaris et al. (2007)
	"Der Kurs hat dazu beigetragen, …"	"The course contributed …"
1	"dass ich die Einstellungen, Werte und die Motivation von Unternehmern besser verstehe."	"to my better understanding of the attitudes, values and motivation of entrepreneurs."
2	"dass ich die Schritte besser verstehe, die man unternehmen muss, um ein Unternehmen zu gründen."	"to my better understanding of the actions someone has to take in order to start a business."
3	"meine praktischen Management-Fähigkeiten, um ein Unternehmen zu gründen, zu verbessern."	"to enhancing my practical management skills in order to start a business."
4	"meine Fähigkeit, Netzwerke zu knüpfen, zu verbessern."	"to enhancing my ability to develop networks."
5	"meine Fähigkeit, Geschäftsmöglichkeiten zu erkennen, zu verbessern."	"to enhancing my ability to identify an opportunity."

---

[31] Although discussed in section 2.5, I will not introduce peer variables at this point. Chapter 7 of this book is dedicated to peer effects during the entrepreneurship course, therefore I introduce these variables there.

[32] To avoid any endogeneity issues in the empirical analyses, I use these variables to descriptively assess the students' perceptions of the quality of the course.

course evaluation - To capture the students' general opinion about "Business Planning", I included four statements and asked the students to indicate in how far they agree (on 5-point Likert scales, ranging from 1 – "does not apply to me at all" to 5 – "completely applies to me"). I chose these items after reviewing several course evaluation forms of the Department for Psychology at the Ludwig-Maximilians-Universität. The scores on the four items are averaged to obtain a measure of how satisfied the student was with the course.

Table 3.15: Standard course-evaluation items

Item	German item in the questionnaire	English translation
1	"Durch die Veranstaltung habe ich viel gelernt."	"I learned a lot during the course."
2	"Die Ziele der Veranstaltung habe ich erreicht."	"I accomplished the goals of the course."
3	"Die beabsichtigten Effekte der Veranstaltung sind meiner Meinung nach erreicht worden."	"In my opinion, the intended effects of the course have been achieved."
4	"Ich würde die Veranstaltung anderen Studierenden weiterempfehlen."	"I would recommend this course to other students."

assessment of teamwork – With a single item I asked students to rate the overall quality of their teamwork by a grade ranging from 1 (very good) to 5 (poor).

student commitment – To capture a student's commitment to the business planning project I asked how many hours they spent in developing the business plan in total per week.

cooperation with entrepreneur – To assess the quality of the interaction with the founder the team cooperated with, I included five statements and asked students in how far they agree (on 5-point Likert scales, ranging from 1 – "I do not agree at all" to 5 – "I completely agree"). The scores on the five items are averaged to obtain a measure of how satisfied the student was with cooperation with the entrepreneur.

Table 3.16: Items for measuring the quality of the cooperation with the entrepreneur

Item	German item in the questionnaire	English translation
1	"Die Geschäftsidee unseres Gründers ist vielversprechend."	"The business idea of our entrepreneur is promising."
2	"Unser Gründer ist motiviert, seine Idee tatsächlich umzusetzen."	"Our entrepreneur is motivated to execute his business idea."
3	"Unser Gründer unterstützte unser Team durch persönlichen Zeiteinsatz."	"Our entrepreneur invested a lot of time in supporting our team."
4	"Insgesamt war die Zusammenarbeit zwischen unserem Team und unserem Gründer erfolgreich."	"The cooperation between our entrepreneur and our team was successful."
5	"Die von unserem Team geleistete Arbeit schafft unternehmerischen Mehrwert für unseren Gründer."	"Our team's achievements provide added value to our entrepreneur."

entrepreneur commitment – To measure the entrepreneur's commitment, I asked students for an estimate how many hours the founder spent in the joint development of the business plan in total over the whole course duration.

prize (1/0) – This measure indicates if the team's business plan was awarded a prize at the end of the course. In contrast to the previous variables, this was no questionnaire-item, but I obtained this information from LMU Entrepreneurship Center staff, who has run the course.

team size – indicates the size of the team a student worked in during the course.

cohort 2009 (0/1) – This dummy-variable takes on a value of 1 if the observed student belongs to the 2009 cohort, and 0 if he belongs to the 2008 cohort.

treatment (0/1) – This dummy-variable marks observations in the treatment (value of 1) and the control group (value of 0).

3.4.2 Psychometric Properties of the used Measures

To analyze the psychometric properties of the ex-ante and the ex-post instrument, I use the whole sample of 529 matched and valid ex-ante ex-post questionnaire pairs from both cohorts and both the treatment and control group. I will focus on the measures associated with the elements of the Theory of Planned Behavior, as these are the most important variables in my analyses. The tests involve two steps: first I conduct a validity analysis, and then I test the reliability of the scale.

Chandler and Lyon (2001) give an overview over several possible procedures to execute validity analysis that have also been considered by Liñán and Chen (2009): structural, content validity and convergent and discriminant validity. Just as the latter did in their study, I carefully considered structural and content validity in the development of the instrument, and ensured that the used items are both relevant and representative of the construct being measured. Next, I use factor analysis to assess convergent validity (Liñán and Chen 2009). Sufficient correlations in the data matrix are a critical assumption when using factor analysis. A first step is the visual inspection of the correlations, which reveals that all correlations are significant at the 1% level. This provides an excellent basis for factor analysis. The Bartlett test of sphericity, which provides the statistical probability that the correlation matrix has significant correlations among at least some of the variables, assesses the overall significance of the correlation matrix. The results were significant, both for the ex-ante data $\chi^2(df=105, N=529) = 4808.043\ (p=0.000)$, and for the ex-post data $\chi^2(df=105, N=529) = 5354.008\ (p=0.000)$, which is a clear indication of suitability of factor analysis. Next I computed the Kaiser-Meyer-Olkin (KMO) measure of sampling adequacy to quantify the degree of intercorrelations among the variables. The results indicate an index of 0.919 for the ex-ante data and 0.922 for the ex-post data, both "marvelous" signs of adequacy for factor analysis as characterized in Kaiser (1970). Both statistics – Bartlett's test and KMO – suggest that data are suitable for factor analysis.

Table 3.17 and Table 3.18 present the rotated factor matrix for the ex-ante and the ex-post data respectively. Following Liñán and Chen (2009) I do not show loadings below 0.4. As may be observed, all items loaded on the expected factor only.

Table 3.17: Theory of Planned Behavior-items factor loadings (ex-ante data)

Item	Factor		
	Perceived Desirability	Perceived Social Norm	Perceived Behavioral Control
Perceived Desirability item 1	0.742		
Perceived Desirability item 2	0.749		
Perceived Desirability item 3	0.673		
Perceived Desirability item 4	0.697		
Perceived Desirability item 5	0.476		
Perceived Social Norm item 1		0.764	
Perceived Social Norm item 2		0.869	
Perceived Social Norm item 3		0.727	
Perceived Social Norm item 4		0.859	
Perceived Behavioral Control item 1			0.636
Perceived Behavioral Control item 2			0.660
Perceived Behavioral Control item 3			0.534
Perceived Behavioral Control item 4			
Perceived Behavioral Control item 5			0.578
Perceived Behavioral Control item 6			0.473

Notes: Rotated factor matrix (ex-ante data); extraction method: principal factors; rotation method: orthogonal varimax (Kaiser off); loadings below 0.4 not shown; N = 529.

Table 3.18: Theory of Planned Behavior-items factor loadings (ex-post data)

Item	Factor		
	Perceived Desirability	Perceived Social Norm	Perceived Behavioral Control
Perceived Desirability item 1	0.750		
Perceived Desirability item 2	0.790		
Perceived Desirability item 3	0.748		
Perceived Desirability item 4	0.717		
Perceived Desirability item 5	0.596		
Perceived Social Norm item 1		0.772	
Perceived Social Norm item 2		0.848	
Perceived Social Norm item 3		0.763	
Perceived Social Norm item 4		0.814	
Perceived Behavioral Control item 1			0.638
Perceived Behavioral Control item 2			0.721
Perceived Behavioral Control item 3			0.595
Perceived Behavioral Control item 4			
Perceived Behavioral Control item 5			0.615
Perceived Behavioral Control item 6			

Notes: Rotated factor matrix (ex-post data); extraction method: principal factors; rotation method: orthogonal varimax (Kaiser off); loadings below 0.4 not shown; N = 529.

As one can learn from the table, the Perceived Behavioral Control item 4 in the ex-ante data and the Perceived Behavioral Control items 4 and 6 in the ex-post data do not load on any of the three factors with a loading above 0.4. Therefore I will leave out these two items when building both the ex-ante and ex-post measure of Perceived Behavioral Control.

I assess discriminant validity by looking at correlations. The respective items should correlate more with their own construct than with the others. This indicates that the students perceive the items as belonging to their theoretical construct (Liñán and Chen 2009). I computed the item-construct correlations and display the results in Table 3.19 for the ex-ante data and Table 3.20 for the ex-post data. As may be observed, correlations of each item to other constructs are always below the correlations with their own construct.

Table 3.19: Item-construct correlations (ex-ante data)

Item	Entrepreneurial Intention	Perceived Desirability	Perceived Social Norm	Perceived Behavioral Control
Entrepreneurial Intentions	1.000	0.663	0.614	0.506
Perceived Desirability item 1	0.567	0.861	0.554	0.463
Perceived Desirability item 2	0.562	0.878	0.564	0.519
Perceived Desirability item 3	0.595	0.845	0.567	0.477
Perceived Desirability item 4	0.676	0.873	0.623	0.532
Perceived Desirability item 5	0.468	0.727	0.416	0.407
Perceived Social Norm item 1	0.582	0.611	0.912	0.524
Perceived Social Norm item 2	0.571	0.609	0.944	0.492
Perceived Social Norm item 3	0.486	0.508	0.829	0.501
Perceived Social Norm item 4	0.577	0.604	0.934	0.512
Perceived Behavioral Control item 1	0.460	0.508	0.486	0.854
Perceived Behavioral Control item 2	0.408	0.438	0.445	0.865
Perceived Behavioral Control item 3	0.390	0.437	0.405	0.803
Perceived Behavioral Control item 5	0.436	0.464	0.489	0.763
Entrepreneurial Intentions	1.000			
Perceived Desirability	0.663	1.000		
Perceived Social Norm	0.614	0.648	1.000	
Perceived Behavioral Control	0.506	0.564	0.557	1.000

Note: N = 529

Table 3.20: Item-construct correlations (ex-post data)

Item	Entrepreneurial Intention	Perceived Desirability	Perceived Social Norm	Perceived Behavioral Control
Entrepreneurial Intentions	1.000	0.746	0.692	0.592
Perceived Desirability item 1	0.686	0.887	0.610	0.531
Perceived Desirability item 2	0.665	0.898	0.591	0.559
Perceived Desirability item 3	0.651	0.889	0.608	0.527
Perceived Desirability item 4	0.748	0.896	0.669	0.555
Perceived Desirability item 5	0.606	0.810	0.549	0.501
Perceived Social Norm item 1	0.646	0.629	0.920	0.549
Perceived Social Norm item 2	0.671	0.663	0.957	0.564
Perceived Social Norm item 3	0.575	0.584	0.872	0.480
Perceived Social Norm item 4	0.649	0.627	0.923	0.520
Perceived Behavioral Control item 1	0.604	0.604	0.592	0.880
Perceived Behavioral Control item 2	0.523	0.494	0.546	0.913
Perceived Behavioral Control item 3	0.392	0.376	0.328	0.803
Perceived Behavioral Control item 5	0.449	0.469	0.481	0.806
Entrepreneurial Intentions	1.000			
Perceived Desirability	0.746	1.000		
Perceived Social Norm	0.692	0.683	1.000	
Perceived Behavioral Control	0.592	0.581	0.578	1.000

Note: N = 529

Reliability is defined as "(...) the degree to which measures are free from error and therefore yield consistent results" (Peter 1979, p. 6). To test scale reliability I use Cronbach's alpha. According to Nunnally (1978), the threshold level is .7. In this case, the values range from 0.815 to 0.916 for the ex-ante questionnaire, and from 0.846 to 0.930 for the ex-post questionnaire (see Table 3.21 below). Thus the theoretically developed scales may be considered reliable.

Table 3.21: Scale reliability test using Cronbach's alpha for the ex-ante and ex-post questionnaire

Scale	Ex-ante	Ex-post
Perceived Desirability (5 items)	0.879	0.915
Perceived Social Norm (4 items)	0.916	0.930
Perceived Behavioral Control (4 items)	0.815	0.846

Note: N=529

These results suggest that my instrument fulfills reliability and validity requirements, allowing me to use the chosen measures in the empirical studies. In the next sections, I will have a closer look at the data generated in my surveys.

3.5 First Data Description

This section focuses on the data generated in my surveys, which I will use in the empirical studies in chapters 4 through 7. In particular, I first assess whether my data is subject to non-response or attrition bias. Moreover I investigate if the chosen treatment and control group may be considered equivalent with respect to background variables. Thereafter I report descriptive statistics on sample composition. I conclude this section by showing students' responses to questions on general course evaluation and the assessment of the teamwork, and the cooperation with the entrepreneur.

3.5.1 Possible Data Biases

Possible systematic biases in my data could emerge from five sources: the choice of treatment and control groups, non-observation, the pooling of two treatment and two control groups, significant pre-treatment differences between treatment and control group, and attrition. I deal with all five in the following.

3.5.1.1 General Sample Selection Issues

In this section I discuss potential selection biases. Selection bias occurs if the selected sample shows systematic differences from the population it intends to represent. As discussed in subsection 2.3.2, the effects of entrepreneurship education may vary among students due to their different background variables. Moreover, the attended course itself will play a role with respect to the changes in entrepreneurial attitudes and intentions. Different content or course format will most likely result in different effects. In sum, there are some sample selection issues I face in this research project.

On an individual level, one can argue, that I survey a very "special" group of third semester students, to be specific students who decided to study business administration at the Ludwig-Maximilians-Universität Munich, one of Germany's "elite universities" at that time. Even the choice for Munich and its prospering economic environment could have turned the balance regarding the decision to come to this city for studies, and that could be the reason why this group of students is so special. Or, of course, the choice of the major – in this case business administration – could infer a certain bias in the results which could only be resolved if this research project was executed across several disciplines. However, I am not able to test whether students in Munich are different from students in other German university locations. Or from a more comprehensive point of view: I completely fade out cultural differences between German or Munich-based students and students of other nationalities, although this could also be important with respect to the effects of entrepreneurship education, see subsection 2.5.3. I can, however, compare my treatment group with a control group, giving me the relative impact of entrepreneurship education on entrepreneurial attitudes and intentions. This should minimize at least this latter bias.

On a course level, another argument why I am confronted with sample selection bias is that I only considered one special kind of entrepreneurship education. I chose "Business Planning" at the Ludwig-Maximilians-Universität Munich mostly for two reasons. First, it is a mandatory course, so I do a priori not face any self-selection issues (a problem other studies had to deal with, see subsection 1.2.4). And second, business planning is regarded a standard format for introductory entrepreneurship education (Hills 1988; Honig 2004). This allows me to derive the most general implications possible about effectiveness of entrepreneurship education and about an optimal design of an entrepreneurship course under the restriction that I only look at one course, which certainly is a cost-related trade-off in this research project. Another noteworthy advantage of picking this course is that every student is obligated to register on an online-communication platform where students have access to all course documents.

This opens the possibility to conduct follow-up surveys beyond this research project and do further evaluations according to the framework by Block and Stumpf (1992). And surely another reason was that I am staff member of the LMU Entrepreneurship Center. Thus I was able to have a close look at the course at any time without being involved in any of the operations that belonged to it. Admittedly, based on this data I am not able to derive any implications regarding entrepreneurship education in general. Currently I am not aware of any study that employed a research design to exploit different formats of entrepreneurship courses to derive implications about how an "optimal" entrepreneurship course should be designed.

Some criticism may also be raised for the choice of the control group. Here I looked for students who can be considered to be as similar as possible to the treatment group. The choice fell on the students' "counterparts" at the Technical University of Munich, as they have the same age, can be considered to have the same level of experience, chose business administration as their studies and Munich as the location to do so. However it could be argued that these two groups differ with respect to their interests. For example, the students of the Technical University might be more interested in technology, as their business administration studies include a minor in natural, computer or engineering sciences. In a more pragmatic manner I chose the first semester business administration students of the Ludwig-Maximilians-Universität. I assume that they have the same interests as the third semester students in "Business Planning" as they chose the same school. On the other hand, they surely are younger and thus have a lower experience level and perhaps also even less idea about their future careers.

3.5.1.2 Non-Observation Bias

The first concrete bias to consider is the response bias, which might occur if the group of respondents systematically differs from the group of non-respondents (Sapsford 2007). In this case, the term "non-respondents" refers to those from whom I do not have complete matched ex-ante ex-post questionnaires; therefore I will call this kind of bias "non-observation bias" in the following.

I have only a limited way in which I can ascertain that my sample of complete matched questionnaires is random for the treatment group, and unfortunately no possibility for a test of the control group data. From 784 of 814 enrolled students in the treatment group, I have data on gender and the number of collected ECTS credits prior to "Business Planning" in my final dataset (I obtained this data from the examination office). To test for non-observation bias I employ a probit technique. In my model the selection equation's dependent variable *observed (0/1)*, indicating matched and usable questionnaires, is equal to one if an individual returned completed ex-ante and ex-post questionnaires (403 students) and zero otherwise. Independent variables include the two aforementioned and the cohort-dummy. The resulting estimation equation has the following functional form:

$$\text{prob}(y = 1) = \text{prob}(\alpha + \sum_{i=1}^{3} x_i \beta_i + \varepsilon) > 0$$

Equation 3.1: Test for data bias due to non-response

where y is the dichotomous dependent variable (*observed (0/1)*), α is a constant, i is an index, β_i is a vector of coefficients, and ε is the error term. The independent variables x_i are:

$x_1 = $ *female (0/1)*
$x_2 = $ *ECTS*
$x_3 = $ *cohort 2009 (0/1)* .

Probit results are presented in Table 3.22. I find that the number of collected ECTS credits increases the likelihood of responding to both survey rounds, while the effect of gender is insignificant. This may reflect students' behavior. Students with less progress in their studies may feel more pressure and are thus less willing to invest time to answer both survey rounds. And since I had difficulties in reconstructing the team memberships and therefore had to drop observations in the 2008 cohort, it is not surprising that the dummy for the 2009 cohort is also highly significant.

Table 3.22: Test for data bias due to non-response

Variable	Mean	Median	S.D.	Min	Max	Observations	Probit coefficients	Probit marginal effects
observed (0/1)	0.495	-	-	0	1	814	DV (yes=1)	DV (yes=1)
female (0/1)	0.535	-	-	0	1	806	-0.036	-0.014
							(0.095)	(0.038)
ECTS	42.706	47	16.447	0	72	792	0.024***	0.009***
							(0.003)	(0.001)
cohort 2009 (0/1)	0.498	0	-	0	1	814	1.043***	0.398***
							(0.102)	(0.036)
constant	-	-	-	-	-	-	-1.465***	
							(0.180)	
Obs							784	
Pseudo R2							0.123	
ll							-476.228	
LR chi2							133.781	
Prob > chi-squared							0.000	

Notes: standard errors in parentheses; * significant at 10%; ** significant at 5%; *** significant at 1%

3.5.1.3 Group and Cohort Equivalency

The use of an ex-ante ex-post test control-group design in a quasi-experimental setting (see chapter 5) allows investigating certain threats to validity. However, because the treatment and control groups are not equivalent by definition, selection bias might be present. The ex-ante test makes it possible to explore the size and direction of that bias.[33]

Another source of bias in this research setting is the pooling of the 2008 and 2009 cohorts. The two ex-ante tests for both the treatment group and the control group can be used to assess this bias. Exploration of this kind of bias is usually done by seeing if two groups differ significantly at ex-ante test. This might preferably be done by using equivalency testing methods (Rogers et al. 1993). These procedures are used to determine if two groups are sufficiently near each other to be considered equivalent. They are appropriate when the investigator is able to specify a small, nonzero difference between the treatment and control group that would serve to define an "equivalence interval" around a difference of zero (*delta*). Differences falling within that equivalence interval are considered practically unimportant. These methods are considered more sensitive to detecting differences than standard differences tests, although failure to find differences does not prove that groups are equal, because they may still differ on unobserved variables. I used two-tailed t-tests as difference test and the Westlake version as equivalence test (Westlake 1976, 1988). In the equivalence test, two one-sided hypothesis tests must be performed. The first test seeks to reject a null hypothesis asserting that the difference between two means is less than or equal to *delta*. The second test seeks to reject a null hypothesis asserting that the difference is greater than or equal to *delta*. Because delta is the minimum difference that would make a difference in the means, the goal is to demonstrate statistically that an observed difference between two means is simultaneously too large and too small to have come from a distribution with mean of *delta*. Both one-sided null-hypotheses must be rejected to establish equivalency.[34]

---

[33] This project does not intend to conduct comparisons of students of one Munich university with those of the other one. I also will not interpret the findings in a way that tries to explain possibly existing differences with potential university-related characteristics.

[34] Rogers et al. (1993) provide an excellent introduction to equivalence tests and more detail about the Westlake version.

Rogers et al. (1993) argue that it can be informative to compare the results of the difference and equivalency test. The interpretations for the four possible combinations are shown in Table 3.23.

Table 3.23: Interpretations for possible outcome combinations of difference and equivalence test

Difference test	Equivalence test	
	reject null	do not reject null
reject null	difference larger than standard null, but not as large as *delta*	different
do not reject null	equivalent	insufficient evidence

Table 3.24 and Table 3.25 show the results of the equivalence tests between the 2008 and 2009 cohorts for each the treatment and control group, Table 3.26 shows the results of the tests comparing the pooled treatment with the pooled control group. As *delta*, I used 20% of the control group or 2008 cohort group mean respectively, as suggested in Rogers et al. (1993).

The equivalence analysis in Table 3.24 shows that the two cohorts of the treatment group can be considered equivalent with respect to three elements of the Theory of Planned Behavior: entrepreneurial intentions, perceived desirability and perceived behavioral control, as well as with respect to age, gender, the aggregate measure of prior exposure to entrepreneurship, already attended entrepreneurship courses, and the Big5 personality dimensions. Further the data suggest that the two cohorts differ significantly with respect to previously gained ECTS credits and to students who have self-employed parents and acquaintances. For all other variables neither the t-test nor the equivalence test yielded significant results, including perceived social norm. Therefore I cannot accurately determine if the two cohorts are different or equivalent for these variables. Nevertheless, the two groups seem to be largely equivalent with respect to the most important variables, and therefore I conclude that it is justified to pool the two cohorts for the further analysis.

I ran the same analysis with the two cohorts of the control group, and received almost the same results as with the treatment groups. Table 3.25 shows that the two control group cohorts may be considered equivalent with respect to entrepreneurial intentions, perceived desirability, and perceived behavioral control, as well as age[35]. Further the significant difference in the gender composition seems to be practically unimportant. The tests for all other variables fail to obtain statistical difference or equivalence, including perceived social norm. As above, I argue that the two groups seem to be largely equivalent with respect to the elements of the Theory of Planned Behavior, and that therefore pooling the two cohorts for further analyses is justified.[36]

---

[35] This was one major concern: the chosen control group for the 2008 wave of the survey was one year ahead with their studies compared to the chosen control group for the 2009 wave.

[36] Unfortunately, I have no data on the personality dimensions of the 2008 control-group students.

Table 3.24: Test for equivalence of treatment-group cohorts

Variable	Treatment group 2008 N=146		Treatment group 2009 N=257		Difference		Difference test two-tailed t-test		Equivalence test Westlake version		
	Mean	S.D.	Mean	S.D.	Mean	S.E.	|t|	p	criterion	|z|	p
Theory of Planned Behavior variables											
entrepreneurial intentions	4.089	1.823	4.230	1.756	-0.141	0.185	0.762	0.447	0.818	3.670	0.000+
perceived desirability	4.363	1.407	4.233	1.425	0.130	0.147	0.881	0.379	0.873	5.054	0.000+
perceived social norm	-4.555	29.970	-5.027	28.685	0.472	3.022	0.156	0.876	0.911	0.145	0.442
perceived behavioral control	4.199	0.947	4.193	1.018	0.006	0.103	0.059	0.953	0.840	8.102	0.000+
demographic variables											
age	21.726	1.974	21.622	2.224	0.103	0.221	0.467	0.641	4.345	19.152	0.000+
female (0/1)	0.527	-	0.537	-	-0.010	0.052	0.185	0.854	0.105	1.851	0.032+
foreign (0/1)	0.137	-	0.171	-	-0.034	0.038	0.902	0.368	0.027	0.180	0.429
prior experiences											
parents self-employed (0/1)	0.397	-	0.526	-	-0.128	0.052	2.486	0.013*	0.079	0.943	0.173
acquaintances self-employed (0/1)	0.788	-	0.607	-	0.181	0.048	3.770	0.000*	0.158	0.483	0.315
worked for start-up (0/1)	0.267	-	0.257	-	0.010	0.046	0.226	0.821	0.053	0.945	0.172
entrepreneur (0/1)	0.055	-	0.062	-	-0.007	0.025	0.304	0.762	0.011	0.142	0.443
breadth of prior exposure	1.507	0.998	1.451	0.988	0.055	0.103	0.540	0.590	0.301	2.393	0.008+
attended entrepreneurship courses	0.021	0.185	0.089	0.410	0.069	0.036	1.925	0.055	0.004	1.811	0.035+
ECTS	52.562	12.412	41.230	12.593	11.332	1.298	8.728	0.000*	10.512	0.631	0.264

Notes: equivalence criterion is +/- 20% of the 2008 cohort's mean; the highest p-value of the two one-sided tests are reported; * significant at 5% for two-tailed t-test; + significant at 5% for equivalence test

Table 3.24 (continued): Test for equivalence of treatment-group cohorts

Variable	Treatment group 2008 N=146		Treatment group 2009 N=257		Difference		Difference test two-tailed t-test		Equivalence test Westlake version		
	Mean	S.D.	Mean	S.D.	Mean	S.E.	|t|	p	criterion	|z|	p
personality dimensions											
extraversion	5.045	1.040	4.881	1.184	0.163	0.118	1.389	0.166	1.009	7.197	0.000+
agreeableness	4.428	0.783	4.523	0.743	-0.095	0.079	1.213	0.226	0.886	10.062	0.000+
conscientiousness	5.318	1.055	5.510	1.139	-0.191	0.115	1.663	0.097	1.064	7.587	0.000+
emotional stability	4.736	1.179	4.759	1.160	-0.022	0.121	0.186	0.853	0.947	7.646	0.000+
openness to experience	5.397	0.906	5.463	1.034	-0.066	0.103	0.641	0.522	1.079	9.882	0.000+

Notes: equivalence criterion is +/- 20% of the 2008 cohort's mean; the highest p-value of the two one-sided tests are reported; * significant at 5% for two-tailed t-test; + significant at 5% for equivalence test

Table 3.25: Test for equivalence of control-group cohorts

Variable	Control group 2008 N=33		Control group 2009 N=73		Difference		Difference test two-tailed t-test		Equivalence test Westlake version		
	Mean	S.D.	Mean	S.D.	Mean	S.E.	|t|	p	criterion	|z|	p
Theory of Planned Behavior variables											
entrepreneurial intentions	3.576	1.521	3.507	1.692	0.069	0.344	0.200	0.842	0.715	1.877	0.030+
perceived desirability	3.939	0.882	3.772	1.420	0.167	0.268	0.622	0.535	0.788	2.315	0.010+
perceived social norm	-19.636	22.174	-12.411	26.863	-7.225	5.352	1.350	0.180	3.927	0.616	0.269
perceived behavioral control	4.061	0.986	3.983	1.069	0.778	0.219	0.355	0.723	0.812	3.352	0.000+
demographic variables											
age	21.182	1.446	20.658	2.029	0.524	0.392	1.337	0.184	4.236	9.468	0.000+
female (0/1)	0.424	-	0.658	-	-0.233	0.102	2.291	0.024*	0.085	3.125	0.001+
foreign (0/1)	0.152	-	0.110	-	0.042	0.069	0.605	0.547	0.030	0.168	0.433
prior experiences											
parents self-employed (0/1)	0.515	-	0.493	-	0.022	0.106	0.208	0.836	0.103	0.765	0.222
acquaintances self-employed (0/1)	0.667	-	0.534	-	0.132	0.104	1.275	0.205	0.133	0.009	0.497
worked for start-up (0/1)	0.406	-	0.301	-	0.105	0.100	1.045	0.299	0.081	0.235	0.407
entrepreneur (0/1)	0.121	-	0.055	-	0.066	0.056	1.195	0.235	0.024	0.759	0.224
breadth of prior exposure	1.697	1.075	1.384	0.952	0.313	0.208	1.507	0.135	0.339	0.125	0.450
attended entrepreneurship courses	0.636	3.141	0.178	0.674	0.458	0.384	1.194	0.235	0.127	0.862	0.194

Notes: equivalence criterion is +/- 20% of the 2008 cohort's mean; the highest p-value of the two one-sided tests are reported; * significant at 5% for two-tailed t-test; + significant at 5% for equivalence test

Table 3.25 (continued): Test for equivalence of control-group cohorts

Variable	Control group 2008 N=33		Control group 2009 N=73		Difference		Difference test two-tailed t-test		Equivalence test Westlake version		
	Mean	S.D.	Mean	S.D.	Mean	S.E.	|t|	p	criterion	|z|	p
personality dimensions											
extraversion	-	-	4.535	1.106	-	-	-	-	-	-	-
agreeableness	-	-	4.415	0.712	-	-	-	-	-	-	-
conscientiousness	-	-	5.627	1.120	-	-	-	-	-	-	-
emotional stability	-	-	4.704	1.221	-	-	-	-	-	-	-
openness to experience	-	-	5.162	1.020	-	-	-	-	-	-	-

Notes: equivalence criterion is +/- 20% of the 2008 cohort's mean; the highest p-value of the two one-sided tests are reported; * significant at 5% for two-tailed t-test; + significant at 5% for equivalence test

Table 3.26: Test for equivalence of the pooled treatment and pooled control group

Variable	Treatment group (pooled) N=403 Mean	S.D.	Control group (pooled) N=106 Mean	S.D.	Difference Mean	S.E.	Difference test two-tailed t-test |t|	p	Equivalence test Westlake criterion	|z|	p
Theory of Planned Behavior variables											
entrepreneurial intentions	4.179	1.780	3.528	1.634	0.650	0.191	3.404	0.001*	0.706	1.931	0.024+
perceived desirability	4.280	1.418	3.825	1.275	0.456	0.152	3.005	0.003*	0.765	2.037	0.020+
perceived social norm	-4.856	29.120	-14.660	25.612	9.804	3.103	3.159	0.002*	2.932	2.214	0.013+
perceived behavioral control	4.195	0.992	4.007	1.040	0.188	0.109	1.717	0.087	0.801	5.612	0.000+
demographic variables											
age	21.660	2.135	20.821	1.876	0.839	0.227	3.689	0.000*	4.164	14.615	0.000+
female (0/1)	0.533	-	0.585	-	-0.051	0.054	0.945	0.345	0.117	1.205	0.114
foreign (0/1)	0.159	-	0.123	-	0.036	0.039	0.924	0.356	0.025	0.297	0.383
prior experiences											
parents self-employed (0/1)	0.479	-	0.500	-	-0.021	0.055	0.386	0.700	0.100	1.444	0.074
acquaintances self-employed (0/1)	0.672	-	0.575	-	0.097	0.052	1.868	0.062	0.115	0.349	0.364
worked for start-up (0/1)	0.261	-	0.333	-	-0.073	0.049	1.487	0.138	0.067	0.125	0.450
entrepreneur (0/1)	0.060	-	0.075	-	-0.016	0.027	0.600	0.549	0.015	0.031	0.488
breadth of prior exposure	1.471	0.991	1.481	0.997	-0.010	0.108	0.089	0.929	0.296	2.646	0.004+
attended entrepreneurship courses	0.065	0.347	0.321	1.834	-0.256	0.097	2.638	0.009*	0.064	1.978	0.024+

Notes: equivalence criterion is +/- 20% of the control group's mean; the highest p-value of the two one-sided tests are reported; * significant at 5% for two-tailed t-test; + significant at 5% for equivalence test; reduced control-group sample for personality dimensions variables (N=73)

Table 3.26 (continued): Test for equivalence of the pooled treatment and pooled control group

Variable	Treatment group (pooled) N=403		Control group (pooled) N=106		Difference		Difference test two-tailed t-test		Equivalence test		Westlake	
	Mean	S.D.	Mean	S.D.	Mean	S.E.	$|t|$	p	criterion		$|z|$	p
personality dimensions												
extraversion	4.940	1.135	4.535	1.106	0.405	0.146	2.784	0.006*	0.907		3.447	0.000+
agreeableness	4.489	0.751	4.415	0.712	0.073	0.097	0.758	0.449	0.883		8.370	0.000+
conscientiousness	5.440	1.112	5.627	1.120	-0.186	0.143	1.300	0.194	1.125		6.554	0.000+
emotional stability	4.751	1.166	4.704	1.221	0.046	0.151	0.307	0.759	0.941		5.920	0.000+
openness to experience	5.439	0.989	5.162	1.020	0.277	0.128	2.167	0.031*	1.032		5.904	0.000+

Notes: equivalence criterion is +/- 20% of the control group's mean; the highest p-value of the two one-sided tests are reported; * significant at 5% for two-tailed t-test; + significant at 5% for equivalence test; reduced control-group sample for personality dimensions variables (N=73)

Table 3.26 shows the results for the test of equivalence of the pooled treatment and pooled control group. They suggest that the two groups are statistically equivalent regarding perceived behavioral control, and that the differences in the three other elements of the Theory of Planned Behavior are practically irrelevant. The latter is also true for the variables *age* and *attended entrepreneurship courses* as well as for the two personality dimensions *extraversion* and *openness to experience*. With respect to all other Big5 personality dimensions as well as to the aggregate measure of *breadth of prior exposure* the two groups are statistically equivalent. All other reported variables are not statistically significant either by the t-test or by the equivalency test. The variability in these variables was too great to allow an accurate appraisal given the sample size. Thus the two groups can be considered equivalent with respect to the most important variables, the elements of the Theory of Planned Behavior. Therefore I conclude that there are no major biases stemming from non-equivalence between treatment and control group in my data. This provides an excellent starting position for the quasi-experimental study in chapter 5 and further analyses of the course effects in chapter 6.

However, even when equivalence tests do not detect any (or only small) differences in selected baseline parameters, selection bias is still a threat in quasi-experimental settings (as employed in chapter 5) evidencing attrition. I investigate whether my data is affected by attrition biases in the next paragraph.

3.5.1.4 Attrition Bias

Attrition bias is a kind of sample selection stemming from the loss of participants during the ex-ante and ex-post test (Heckman 1979), discounting subjects for whom I have complete data for the ex-ante test, but was not able to successfully match this observation to a complete ex-post questionnaire. The loss of subjects in the treatment as well as in the control group might change the characteristics of the groups and the outcomes of the empirical analyses irrespective to the intervention.

A first indication that I do not face major bias due to attrition in the treatment group can be taken from Table 3.27. This table reports descriptive statistics and results from two-tailed t-tests for differences between two groups of students with respect to the variables of the baseline model: those who responded to the ex-ante survey but for whom I was not able to match an ex-post questionnaire and those for whom I have a valid matched ex-ante / ex-post questionnaire pair and who therefore enter the empirical analyses. It is noteworthy that the latter group scores lower in entrepreneurial attitudes and intention (although not significantly) than the group of students I only have ex-ante data for. One might have expected differently, that students who score high in these variables and therefore indicate a certain a priori interest in entrepreneurship are more willing to also complete the second survey. The same holds for the variables related to prior experiences. Three variables are apparently significantly affected by attrition: *ECTS, age* and *foreign (0/1)*. This indicates that students who are performing relatively bad during their studies, older students and students with a nationality other than German more often failed to complete the ex-post test. I could not perform the test for the Big5 personality dimensions, as these items were included in the ex-post questionnaire.

Table 3.27: Test for attrition bias in the treatment group data

Variable	Ex-ante response only N=191		Matched responses N=403		Difference		Test statistic	
	Mean	S.D.	Mean	S.D.	Mean	S.E.	|t|	p
Theory of Planned Behavior variables								
entrepreneurial intentions	4.236	1.856	4.179	1.780	0.057	0.159	0.375	0.708
perceived desirability	4.352	1.379	4.280	1.418	0.072	0.124	0.610	0.542
perceived social norm	-4.613	26.912	-4.856	29.120	0.243	2.497	0.081	0.936
perceived behavioral control	4.199	1.043	4.195	0.992	0.004	0.088	0.138	0.890
demographic variables								
age	22.063	2.665	21.660	2.135	0.403	0.204	2.001	0.046*
female (0/1)	0.592	-	0.533	-	0.059	0.044	1.330	0.184
foreign (0/1)	0.283	-	0.159	-	0.124	0.035	3.567	0.000*
prior experiences								
parents self-employed (0/1)	0.513	-	0.479	-	0.034	0.044	0.777	0.437
acquaintances self-employed (0/1)	0.696	-	0.672	-	0.024	0.041	0.582	0.561
worked for start-up (0/1)	0.272	-	0.261	-	0.011	0.039	0.302	0.763
entrepreneur (0/1)	0.094	-	0.060	-	0.034	0.023	1.541	0.124
breadth of prior exposure	1.576	0.937	1.471	0.991	0.105	0.086	1.221	0.222
attended entrepreneurship courses	0.137	0.684	0.065	0.347	0.072	0.042	1.709	0.088
ECTS	41.206	16.772	45.335	13.649	-4.129	1.438	2.872	0.004*

Note: * significant at 5% for two-tailed t-test

In the control group data, on the other hand, two important variables seem to be affected by attrition. Table 3.28 reports the results of the two-tailed t-tests for differences between the two groups of students as specified above in the treatment case. As in the treatment case, the group for whom I was able to gather matched responses scores – against expectations – generally lower in entrepreneurial intentions and attitudes than the group I only have the ex-ante data for. Three of these variables seem to be significantly affected by attrition: *entrepreneurial intentions, perceived desirability*, and *perceived social norm*. With the exception of *acquaintances self-employed (0/1)* students I have matched responses for score higher on variables related to prior exposure to entrepreneurship than students I only have ex-ante data for, what I would have expected. In addition, one of these variables, *worked for start-up (0/1)*, seems to be significantly affected by attrition.

Thus attrition bias seems to be existent, driven largely by the control group sample. However, considering the important variables, the elements of the Theory of Planned Behavior, the values for students who answered the ex-ante questionnaire only are higher than those from students who responded to both surveys. This is counterintuitive, as one would expect that students with higher values in these variables are more interested in entrepreneurship and therefore more likely to answer both the ex-ante and ex-post questionnaire. Hence, these differences will only introduce a conservative bias into my results, if any. Moreover, attrition bias in the treatment group seems to be negligible, so I conclude that I can interpret my findings nearly uninfluenced by attrition.

Table 3.28: Test for attrition bias in the control group data

Variable	Ex-ante response only N=244		Matched responses N=106		Difference		Test statistic	
	Mean	S.D.	Mean	S.D.	Mean	S.E.	|t|	p
Theory of Planned Behavior variables								
entrepreneurial intentions	4.205	1.658	3.528	1.634	0.677	0.192	3.524	0.001*
perceived desirability	4.243	1.276	3.825	1.275	0.418	0.148	2.817	0.005*
perceived social norm	-6.947	27.746	-14.660	25.612	7.714	3.155	2.445	0.015*
perceived behavioral control	4.188	0.864	4.007	1.040	0.180	0.107	1.685	0.093
demographic variables								
age	21.205	3.258	20.821	1.876	0.384	0.339	1.134	0.257
female (0/1)	0.537	-	0.585	-	-0.048	0.058	0.828	0.408
foreign (0/1)	0.119	-	0.123	-	-0.004	0.038	0.100	0.920
prior experiences								
parents self-employed (0/1)	0.439	-	0.500	-	-0.061	0.058	1.060	0.290
acquaintances self-employed (0/1)	0.664	-	0.575	-	0.088	0.056	1.583	0.114
worked for start-up (0/1)	0.226	-	0.333	-	-0.107	0.051	2.100	0.037*
entrepreneur (0/1)	0.049	-	0.075	-	-0.026	0.027	0.972	0.332
breadth of prior exposure	1.377	0.950	1.481	0.997	-0.104	0.112	0.928	0.354
attended entrepreneurship courses	0.262	0.844	0.321	1.834	-0.058	0.143	0.409	0.683

Note: * significant at 5% for two-tailed t-test

3.5.2 Sample Composition

This subsection sheds light on the composition of the treatment and control group regarding entrepreneurial attitudes and intentions (at the beginning of the course) and background characteristics. Table 3.26 already gives some information about how the treatment and control sample are composed and examines statistical equivalence. However this subsection is dedicated to a more detailed description of the samples. To begin, I report overall descriptive statistics, for the treatment group in Table 3.29, for the control group in Table 3.30. Subsequently I will discuss several background factors separately for each group.[37]

---

[37] As before, I will not make any assumptions about possible differences in values being related to characteristics of the two Munich universities.

Table 3.29: Descriptive statistics (treatment group sample)

Variable	N	Mean	Median	S.D.	Min	Max
ex-ante Theory of Planned Behavior variables						
entrepreneurial intentions	403	4.179	4.0	1.780	1	7
perceived desirability	403	4.280	4.2	1.418	1	7
perceived social norm	403	-4.856	0.0	29.121	-78	84
perceived behavioral control	403	4.195	4.0	0.992	1	7
ex-post Theory of Planned Behavior variables						
entrepreneurial intentions	403	3.859	4.0	1.845	1	7
perceived desirability	403	4.333	4.4	1.519	1	7
perceived social norm	403	-1.782	0.0	30.494	-84	84
perceived behavioral control	403	4.346	4.3	1.069	1	7
demographic variables						
age	403	21.660	21.0	2.135	19	34
female (0/1)	403	0.533	-	-	0	1
foreign (0/1)	403	0.159	-	-	0	1
prior experiences						
parents self-employed (0/1)	403	0.479	-	-	0	1
acquaintances self-employed (0/1)	403	0.672	-	-	0	1
worked in start-up (0/1)	403	0.261	-	-	0	1
entrepreneur (0/1)	403	0.060	-	-	0	1
breadth of prior exposure	403	1.471	1.0	0.991	0	4
attended entrepreneurship courses	403	0.065	0.0	0.347	0	4
ECTS	403	45.335	51.0	13.649	9	71
personality dimensions						
extraversion	403	4.940	5.0	1.135	1	7
agreeableness	403	4.489	4.5	0.758	1	7
conscientiousness	403	5.440	5.5	1.112	1	7
emotional stability	403	4.751	5.0	1.166	1	7
openness to experience	403	5.439	5.5	0.989	1	7
additional control variables						
team size	403	5.072	5.0	0.408	4	6
cohort 2009 (0/1)	403	0.638	-	-	0	1

First Data Description 135

Table 3.30: Descriptive statistics (control group sample)

Variable	N	Mean	Median	S.D.	Min	Max
ex-ante Theory of Planned Behavior variables						
entrepreneurial intentions	106	3.528	3.0	1.634	1	7
perceived desirability	106	3.825	3.6	1.275	1	7
perceived social norm	106	-14.660	-12.0	25.612	-72	45
perceived behavioral control	106	4.007	4.0	1.040	1.25	6.75
ex-post Theory of Planned Behavior variables						
entrepreneurial intentions	106	3.396	3.0	1.637	1	7
perceived desirability	106	3.891	4.0	1.345	1	6.6
perceived social norm	106	-15.028	-16.0	27.173	-72	62
perceived behavioral control	106	3.943	4.0	1.056	1	7
demographic variables						
age	106	20.821	20.0	1.876	18	28
female (0/1)	106	0.585	-	-	0	1
foreign (0/1)	106	0.123	-	-	0	1
prior experiences						
parents self-employed (0/1)	106	0.500	-	-	0	1
acquaintances self-employed (0/1)	106	0.575	-	-	0	1
worked in start-up (0/1)	106	0.333	-	-	0	1
entrepreneur (0/1)	106	0.075	-	-	0	1
breadth of prior exposure	106	1.481	1.0	0.997	0	4
attended entrepreneurship courses	106	0.321	0.0	1.834	0	5
personality dimensions						
extraversion	73	4.535	4.5	1.106	2	7
agreeableness	73	4.415	4.5	0.712	2.5	6
conscientiousness	73	5.627	6.0	1.120	2	7
emotional stability	73	4.704	5.0	1.221	1.5	6.5
openness to experience	73	5.162	5.0	1.020	2.5	7
additional control variables						
cohort 2009 (0/1)	106	0.689	-	-	0	1

3.5.2.1 Theory of Planned Behavior-Variables

Although the equivalence tests in the previous subsection suggest that the two groups are statistically equivalent with respect to the ex-ante values of the Theory of Planned Behavior-variables, the treated students' ex-ante values are higher than those of the control group students. The treatment group means are all near to the middle of the scale, which is 4 for intentions, desirability and behavioral control and 0 for social norm, the control group means are all below this points. The interpretation of this observation is that the students are on average uncertain about their aptitude for entrepreneurship.

Especially with regard to chapters 5 and 6 I take a closer look at the ex-ante entrepreneurial intentions distribution of the treatment and the control group. Figure 3.6 shows the percentage of students by response category for the ex-ante question for entrepreneurial intentions. It tells that the ex-ante distribution of the treatment group is more or less bell-shaped, and that most of the students took an answer that indicates uncertainty about career intentions ("rather disagree", "neutral", or "rather agree"). The – on average – lower value of entrepreneurial intentions for the control group at the beginning of the course is apparently largely driven by the quarter of students who "disagreed" and by the very small share of students who "completely agreed" to the statement of starting an own business within the next five to ten years.

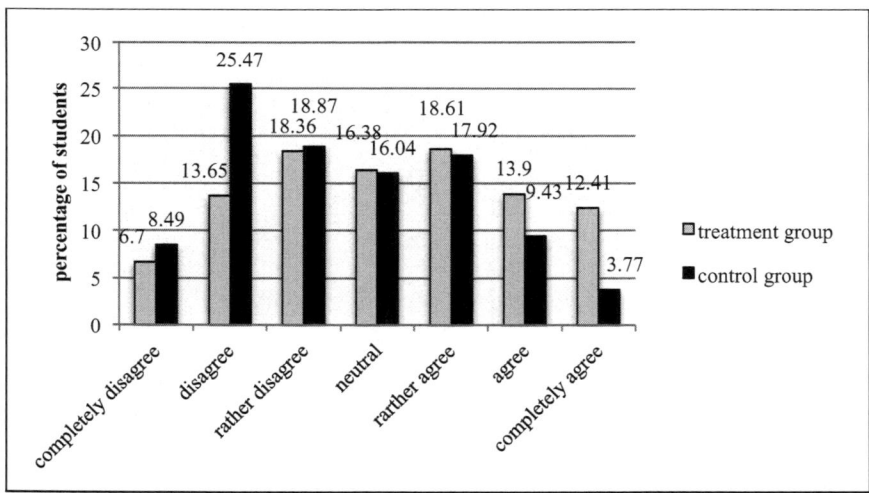

Figure 3.6: Distribution of ex-ante entrepreneurial intentions by group sample (treatment: N = 403; control: N = 106)
Notes: students were asked to indicate in how far they agree to the statement "I intend to start my own business in the next five to ten years".

3.5.2.2 Demographic Variables

For the available demographic variables, the equivalence tests were not conclusive, as reported in Table 3.26. Not surprisingly, the students of the treatment and control group are in the same age range. The minimum age of the control group students is one year lower than the one of the treatment group students, as the 2009 cohort control group is one year behind the treated students with respect to the course of study. About two thirds of the treated students are 21 or younger, as are three quarters of the control group. Few students are older than 25, only 22 in the treatment and six in the control group.

Both in the treatment and the control group I observed more female students than male (53.5% and 58.3% of the respective group are female students). For the treatment group, this value for the observed students does not deviate from the value when calculating the mean of all 814 students who attended "Business Planning", as already suggested by Table 3.22 reporting the tests for non-response bias.

The share of foreign students among the observed students is slightly higher in the treatment than in the control group (15.9% versus 12.3%). Figure 3.7 and Figure 3.8 below give information about the nationality of the foreign students. Surprisingly, the biggest group of foreign students in the observed treatment group does not come from one of Germany's neighboring countries. The biggest group comes from Bulgaria (eleven students), followed by Ukraine (eight) and China, Russia and Turkey (four). Smaller groups come from the Czech Republic, Italy, and Poland (three), and Bosnia, Croatia, Hungary, Luxembourg, Moldova, Romania and Serbia (two). Other countries, represented by one student each, include Albania, Belarus, Denmark, Georgia, Greece, Slovakia, Slovenia, Tunisia, USA, and Vietnam. The 13 foreign students in the control group have Bulgarian (four students), Austrian (3), and Ukrainian (2) nationality, the remaining come from Ecuador, Romania, Switzerland, and Vietnam.

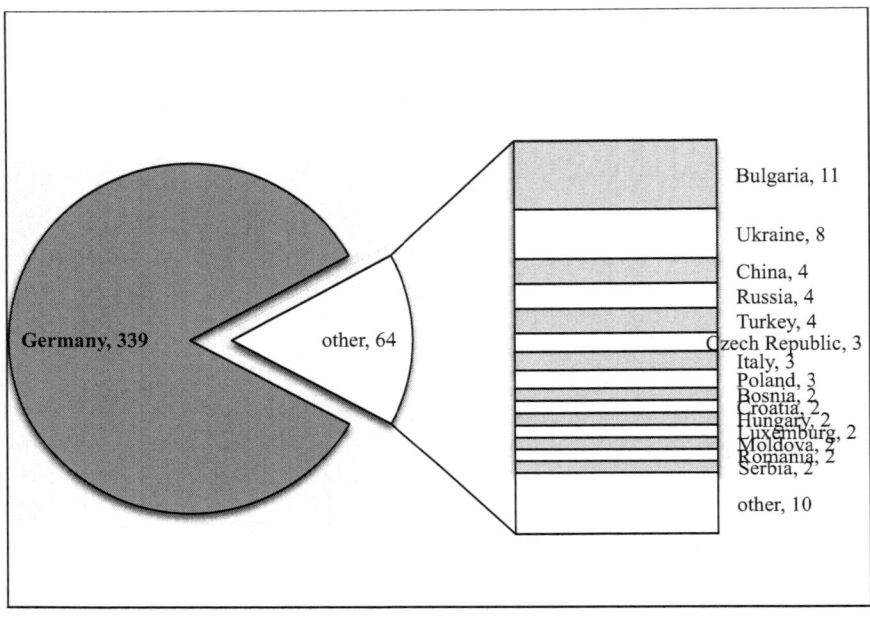

Figure 3.7: Nationality of the students in the treatment group sample (N = 403)

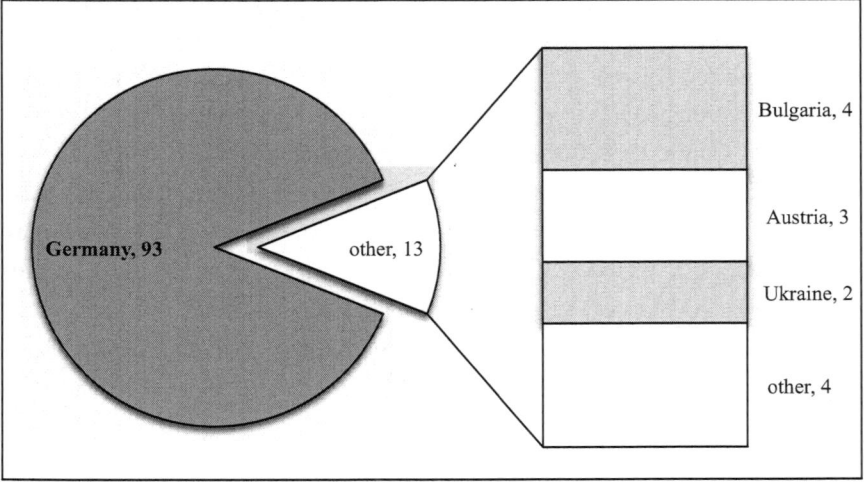

Figure 3.8: Nationality of the students in the control group sample (N = 106)

3.5.2.3 Prior Experiences

Regarding the variables characterizing prior experiences, the test for equivalence of treatment and control group suggested that treated and control group students can be considered statistically equivalent with respect to *breadth of prior exposure* and *attended entrepreneurship courses*.

The equivalence tests were inconclusive for the four dummy-variables determining the breadth of prior exposure. On average, control group students are slightly more likely to have self-employed parents, to have worked for a start-up and to be entrepreneurs themselves. This reflects also the aggregate variable *breadth of prior exposure*. Figure 3.9 shows the distribution of this variable. Accordingly, about 85% of the students of both groups have answered at least one question about prior exposure to entrepreneurship with "yes". Moreover it suggests that the breadth of prior entrepreneurship-related experiences is nearly equally distributed among treated and control group students.

Only very few students from both groups have previously attended entrepreneurship courses at all. Only about 4.5 percent (18 students) of the treated students and 10.4 percent (seven students) of the control group students have done so.

The last characteristic to consider here is the gained number of ECTS credits when entering "Business Planning". I have only data for the treated students on that. Table 3.29 above informs that on average students have gained 45 credits, i.e. about one fourth of the needed number of credits to graduate as bachelor in business administration at the LMU Munich. The distribution displayed in Figure 3.10 tells that about 22 percent of the students have already collected 60 ECTS credits or more. Under the assumption of an equal distribution of the overall 180 ECTS credits across the recommended time for the completion of the bachelor degree (six semesters), this would propose that more than three quarters of the students are not as far in their studies as they should be at the beginning of the third semester.

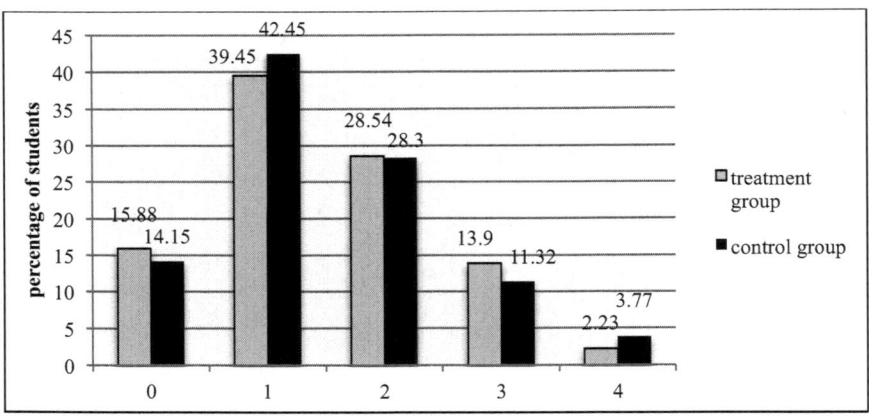

Figure 3.9: Breadth of prior exposure to entrepreneurship (by group sample, N=509)

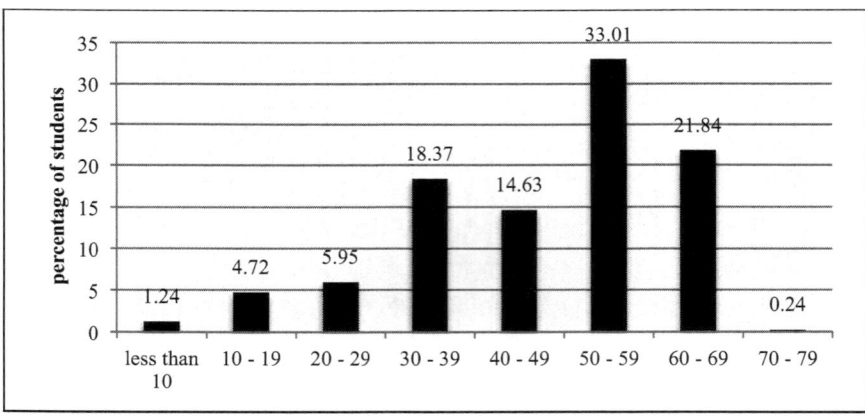

Figure 3.10: Number of ECTS gained by treatment group students prior to the course (N = 403)

3.5.2.4 Personality Dimensions

The tests for equivalence suggest that treatment and control group students can be considered as statistically equivalent with respect to all Big5 personality dimensions. Overall, it seems that the students from both groups are overly conscientious and open to experiences.

3.6 Course-Related Variables and Course Evaluation

Before proceeding with the empirical analyses about the course impact on entrepreneurial intentions and attitudes, this section presents descriptive results of the student evaluation questions about the course and its characteristics. As in all tertiary institutions, the Munich School of Management asks students to fill out an evaluation form that asks for the students' opinion of the course. I also present additional descriptive results related to the structure of the course. Table 3.31 gives an overview of these. In the following subsections, I discuss the variables in more detail. Beginning with the bottom of the table, one can see that 14 percent of the observed students were awarded a prize. Overall, about ten percent of all students have been awarded a prize for their achievement at the end of "Business Planning".

Table 3.31: Descriptive statistics of course-related and situational variables

Variable	N	Mean	Median	S.D.	Min	Max
learning	403	4.873	5	1.138	1	7
course evaluation	403	3.834	4	0.804	1.25	5
assessment of teamwork	403	3.883	4	1.132	1	5
student commitment	403	8.063	6	8.199	0	70
cooperation with entrepreneur	403	3.480	3.6	0.927	1	5
commitment of entrepreneur	403	16.868	10	29.223	1	250
prize (0/1)	403	0.139	-	-	0	1
team size	403	5.072	5	0.408	4	6
cohort 2009 (0/1)	403	0.638	-	-	0	1

3.6.1 Standard Course Evaluation Questions

On average, the course was ranked with 3.8 on the scale from 1 to 5, where 1 would indicate a low and 5 a high grade for the course. Figure 3.11 shows the results of the course evaluation questions asked in the ex-ante questionnaires. I recoded the 5-point scale into "negative" (response categories 1 and 2), "neutral" (3) and positive (4 and 5).

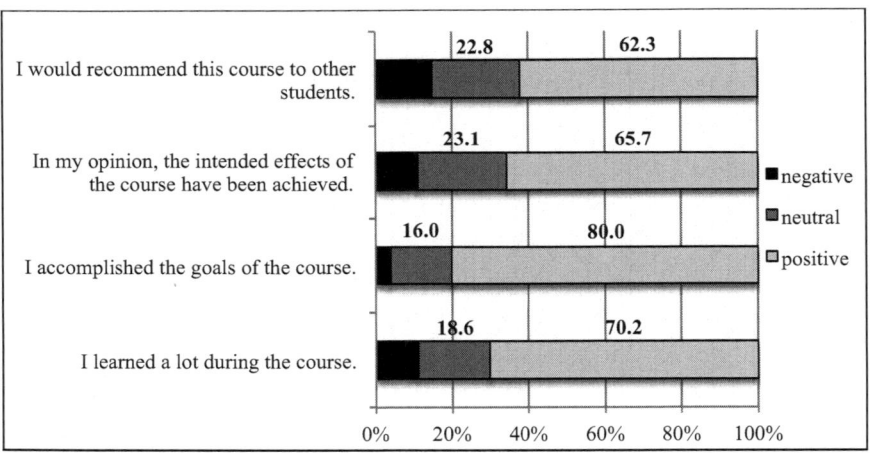

Figure 3.11: Evaluation of the course by treatment group students (N = 403)

This figure draws an overall positive picture of the students' opinion about the course. Two thirds of the students would recommend the course to other students, and over 70 percent stated that they learned a lot during the course. The results in the next subsection further corroborate this latter finding.

3.6.2 Entrepreneurial Learning

The aggregate measure of entrepreneurial learning based on the framework by Johannisson (1991) yields an average value of 4.9, the highest value being 7.0. So the students indeed did learn something about entrepreneurship. Figure 3.12

displays the responses to each item, the response categories recoded to "negative" (response categories 1 to 3), "neutral" (4), and "positive" (5 to 7).

As already suggested by other findings above, the course received an overall positive feedback, indicating that students learned about entrepreneurship in every category of Johannisson's framework. Apparently, the students profited from the course particularly in the first three dimensions captured by the framework. These reflect learning about attitudes and motives of entrepreneurs (69 percent of the students assessed the course positively with respect to this learning-dimension), the knowledge about what someone has to do in order to start a business (over 86 percent positive answers), and necessary entrepreneurship related abilities and skills (70 percent positive answers). The somewhat smaller effect in the first dimension is probably due to the fact that student teams engaged in considerable division of labor, and that only some students within the respective teams directly interacted with the cooperating entrepreneurs. 49 percent and 58 percent of the students respectively confirmed an improvement in the remaining two dimensions reflecting social skills and necessary entrepreneurship-related intuition.

Hence the course was obviously well-received by the students, both with respect to standard evaluation questions as well as to the entrepreneurship-related learning dimensions. Therefore I do not assume that course outcomes are affected by a negative reception of the course organization or course content. However, one special characteristic of "Business Planning" is the teamwork and cooperation with a Munich-based entrepreneur. I present descriptive results of the assessments of this part of the course in the next subsection.

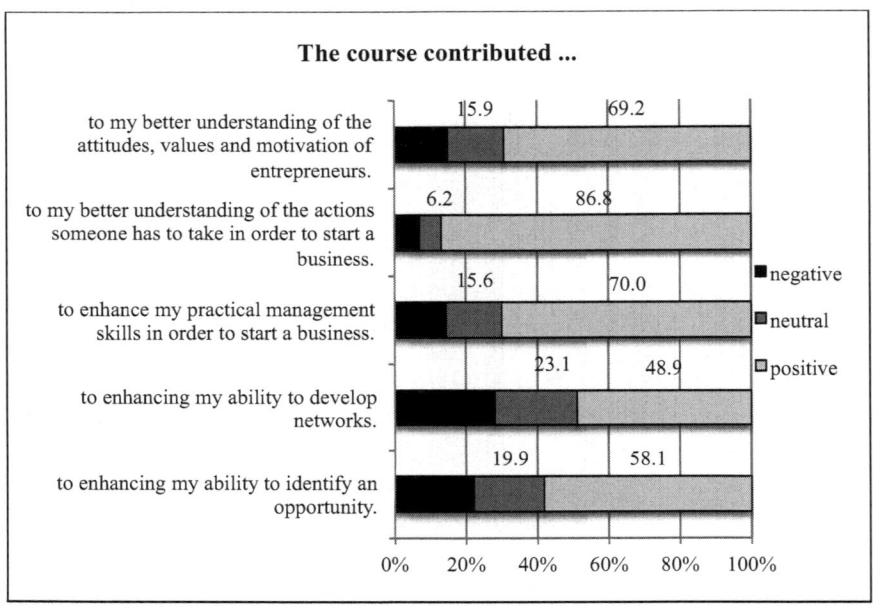

Figure 3.12: Student assessment of entrepreneurial learning due to the course (N = 403)

3.6.3 Assessment of Teamwork and the Cooperation with the Entrepreneurs

Table 3.29 informs that on average students rated the teamwork with 3.9 out of maximum 5.0 points. Moreover it tells that on average the students spent about eight hours per week working on the business plan-project (variable *student commitment*). Ten students indicated that they spent 30 hours or more on the project. This may be more considered as "perceived" effort: according to qualitative feedback, students feel that the project is too time-consuming. It may be that they are more committed – or feel more pressure – to deliver good results and therefore invest more time in the project compared to other seminars, because it is a real-life project in direct cooperation with an entrepreneur. Therefore the perceived effort in "Business Planning" may be higher than in other seminars where students also work on real-life projects. In those, however, it is more common to cooperate anonymously with a Munich-based firm instead of with a single person. Probably the formation of a "team-identity" is stronger in "Business Planning" than in other seminars. Students may thus feel more committed or even pressurized in the project, because their actions directly influence another person's life.

Almost naturally in these combinations, conflicts of interest may occur: the students want to get good grades and accomplish the academic task, the entrepreneur wants to get the most out of the project for his start-up. The results of the students' assessment of the cooperation with the founders also mirror these latent conflicts. This cooperation was on average ranked with 3.5 out of a maximum of 5.0 points. Figure 3.13 sheds more light on this assessment. Again I recoded the 5-point scale into "negative" (response categories 1 and 2), "neutral" (3) and positive (4 and 5).

The students' perceptions of the quality of the entrepreneurs' business ideas are mixed. The largest share of students (41 percent) judge those as not very promising, further 24 percent do not have a strong opinion about the quality of the founders' ideas. Despite that, the students acknowledge the motivation of the entrepreneurs to execute their business ideas. Almost two thirds of the students expressed a positive opinion on that. The results regarding the two items capturing the direct interaction with the entrepreneur provide support for my assertions above. By the majority, the students were not satisfied with the time investment and support of their founders. Only 47 percent felt being supported enough. Table 3.29 informs that on average a founder spent 17 hours together with the student team on the project. However, over 60 percent of the students stated that the entrepreneur spent only ten hours or less on supporting the students in their project. The result on the question, whether the students thought if the cooperation with their entrepreneur had been a success, reveals a similar picture. Only just over half of the students answer this question positively. The teams' own contribution to the entrepreneurs' start-up project was considered substantial. Almost 76 percent of the students claimed that they provided added value to the entrepreneur and her or his project.

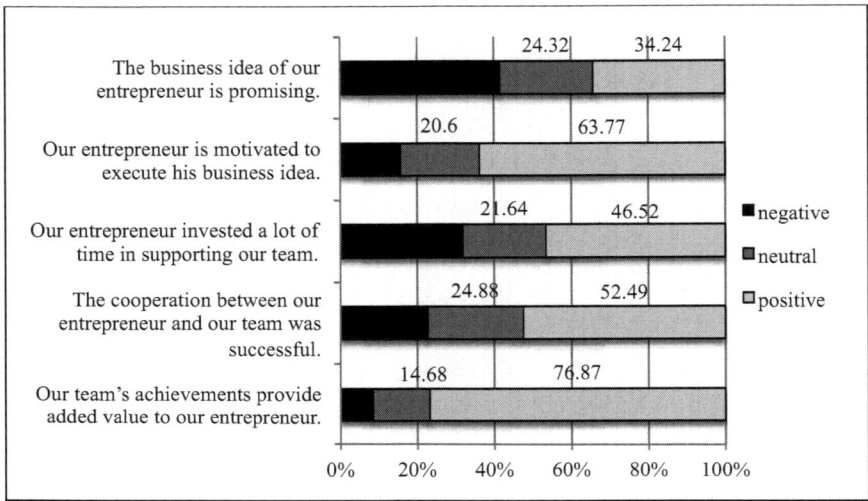

Figure 3.13: Students' assessment of cooperation with entrepreneur

3.7 Appropriateness of the Dataset for this Research Project

This chapter has set out the description of the entrepreneurship course I take as behavioral intervention, the process of data collection, tests for the validity of the data with respect to the research design, and first descriptive results about the impact of the course. The research design I employ has several advantages compared to previously conducted studies from a practical point of view (advantages stemming from my theoretical framework have been discussed at the end of the previous chapter).

First, I surveyed both treated and untreated students, administering questionnaires both before and after the course. This allows me to run a quasi-experiment (see chapter 5 and 6) to determine the true causal effects of the entrepreneurship course on entrepreneurial attitudes and intentions. Second, the treatment group students have not self-selected themselves into this course as it is mandatory for all students of the considered population. Researchers argue that surveying students that have chosen themselves to attend the course biases the results in favor of the intervention (Gorman et al. 1997). The choice of a mandatory course to conduct the evaluation thus minimizes the inaccuracy of the assessments presented in the following chapters. Other advantages stem from the practical application of my theoretical model. The choice of the questionnaire items is grounded on previously conducted studies employing the Theory of Planned Behavior. Thus these items have been pre-tested and validated, and I do not face any pitfalls due to measurement errors when applying ad-hoc measures developed on my own. As the items have become somewhat "standard" in this literature, I am also able to classify my findings and compare them to those of other studies. This strengthens the reliability of my findings. Lastly, I employ various tests to prove validity and reliability of my items and the appropriateness of the treatment and control group data. Only rarely are issues such as non-response and attrition bias, and never the issue of equivalence of treatment and control group, considered in other studies, thus introducing some tentativeness on the findings.

However, several caveats apply. First to mention is the issue of whether these particular course-participants are representative of the target population as a whole. Both Munich universities have been awarded the title of "University of Excellence" by the German Science Council and German Research Foundation. The results of the empirical analyzes could be biased in the way that students with specific characteristics, motivations, and aspirations apply for studies at these universities. Therefore, the sample composition may be systematically different to those found at other universities. Second, the generalizability of the results on course effects provided in chapters 5 to 7 are questionable, as they are based on only one course. This issue may be partly resolved by considering the course "Business Planning" as a blueprint of entrepreneurship courses. Krueger et al. (2000) point out that business planning as an entrepreneurship course component is strongly emphasized at tertiary institutions. Accordingly entrepreneurship course concepts such as "Business Planning" are found at most of these institutions. Thus the findings may be generalizable to the extent that one might understand them as emanating from a business planning course concept involving teamwork on an entrepreneurial project. For this reason I provided in-depth information on the set-up of "Business Planning". Third, the sample size of the control group is not very large. Therefore the tests in chapters 5 and 6 may lack statistical power. Moreover the various tests on the data suggest that the control group data is subject to attrition bias. An additional downside regarding the control group is of course the lacking data on the personality dimensions for the 2008 cohort. In the following chapters I therefore employ two sets of control variables – one with the personality dimensions (resulting in a loss of observations), and one without. Another group of methodological issues has already been discussed in paragraph 2.3.3.2, including the issue of students giving socially desired answers and floor- and ceiling effects when employing 7-point Likert scales.

4. Determinants of Entrepreneurial Intentions

4.1 Introduction

Researchers in the field of entrepreneurship aim at developing a better understanding of individual deliberations regarding the attraction of an entrepreneurial career. The Theory of Planned Behavior has become a widely used theoretical framework to predict entrepreneurial activity and explore the reasons for entering such a career. However, Kolvereid (1996a) and subsequently Souitaris et al. (2007) call for more research to confirm whether their results about the attitudes-intentions link can be generalizable to other contexts. Therefore, to replicate and confirm early results about the linking of entrepreneurial attitudes with intentions I test the Theory of Planned Behavior based on my data in this chapter.

I draw upon the Theory of Planned Behavior and additional theoretical concepts discussed in chapter 2 to develop two groups of hypotheses. The first group is concerned with the attitudes-intentions link postulated by the Theory of Planned Behavior, the second group with the relationship between background variables (demographic, prior experiences, and personality dimensions) and intentions. To test the hypotheses I use the ex-ante data of the pooled control group.

All three hypotheses derived from the Theory of Planned Behavior receive strong support. With respect to demographic variables the results suggest that female students have lower and foreign students have higher entrepreneurial intentions, thus confirming earlier findings reported in paragraph 2.5.3.1. A broad prior exposure to entrepreneurship (role models and own entrepreneurial activity) is positively related to entrepreneurial intentions. On the other hand, with advancing completion of general university education, entrepreneurial intentions decline. Both results confirm the expected relationships and confirm the results of previously conducted studies (see paragraph 2.5.3.2). However, having already attended entrepreneurship courses has no statistical significant influence on entrepreneurial intentions, but the size of the subsample of students who had attended a course already is very small. Zhao et al. (2010) examined the relationships between the Big5 personality dimensions and entrepreneurial intentions. They find that (ordered by strength of influence) openness to experience, conscientiousness, emotional stability, extraversion and agreeableness are all significantly related to entrepreneurial intentions, whereupon the first four have a positive, and agreeableness has a negative sign. I can confirm this order for the first three dimensions, and agreeableness also exerts the weakest influence. Extraversion is not significantly related to intentions. A somewhat surprising finding is the negative sign with the relation between conscientiousness and intentions. Perhaps, at this stage of their life, students leverage this characteristic in their studies rather than in preparing the step into an entrepreneurial career. Finally, the results suggest that the background variables are mediated by the entrepreneurial attitudes as predicted by the Theory of Planned Behavior. Thus they have an indirect effect on entrepreneurial intentions through perceptions of desirability, social norm, and behavioral control.

This chapter contributes both to the literature on entrepreneurial intentions and to the progress of my analyses. First, it adds to the emerging literature on predicting entrepreneurial activity using the Theory of Planned Behavior. It illustrates that the Theory of Planned Behavior is appropriate for research into entrepreneurial activity. Second, this chapter sheds light on the importance of background variables such as demographics, prior experience, and personality dimensions for the formation of entrepreneurial intentions. Third, on a more general level, the study also contributes to the literature on the Theory of Planned Behavior itself by confirming the attitude-intentions link and by testing the effects of exogenous influences on entrepreneurial intentions.

With respect to the following empirical analyses this chapter also contributes to this research project as a whole by getting more insights in the initial entrepreneurial attitudes and intentions of the treatment group. It sheds light on existing predispositions of several subsamples defined by background characteristics and thus adds to a more reliable interpretation of the results in the following chapters. Variances in entrepreneurial intentions across several subsamples defined by background characteristics may also imply more general consequences for planning an entrepreneurship course. For some students an entrepreneurship course may provide more valuable information than for others.

The remainder of this chapter contains three sections. First, I derive hypotheses about the attitudes-intention link as well as about the influence of background variables on entrepreneurial intentions in the next section, thereby relying heavily on the theoretical discussions in chapter 2. Section 3 provides the empirical tests of these hypotheses. Section 4 concludes and discusses implications for the following chapters.

4.2 Hypotheses

The first three hypotheses are directly derived from the Theory of Planned Behavior. The following set of nine hypotheses deal with direct effects of background factors (demographics, prior experiences, personality dimensions) on entrepreneurial intentions.

4.2.1 Hypotheses Derived from the Theory of Planned Behavior

According to the Theory of Planned Behavior positive or negative subjective evaluations of possible outcomes when starting a business (compared to becoming employed) determine the perceived desirability of becoming an entrepreneur. The positive effect of perceived desirability on entrepreneurial intentions has been broadly confirmed in the entrepreneurship literature (see section 2.4). The following relationship is expected:

H 4.1: The higher the perceived desirability with respect to starting an own business, the stronger the entrepreneurial intentions.

Also expectations and opinions of important reference people play a role in the formation of entrepreneurial intentions. The strength of this factor depends on an individual's motive to comply with these expectations. Some empirical studies fail to show a significant relationship between perceived social norm and entrepreneurial intentions. Other results suggest that it exhibits an important influence (see section 2.4), hence:

H 4.2: The higher the perceived social norm with respect to starting an own business, the stronger the entrepreneurial intentions.

In general individuals have a higher propensity to act regarding behaviors they feel to be capable of performing, i.e. if this behavior seems to be feasible or controllable for them (Bandura 1986; Ajzen 1991; Dutton 1993). According to the Theory of Planned Behavior the perceived behavioral control, i.e. the perceived capability to start and run an own business, exhibits a positive influence on entrepreneurial intentions. Many studies confirmed this relationship empirically (see section 2.4). The following hypothesis is proposed:

H 4.3: The higher the perceived behavioral control with respect to starting an own business, the stronger the entrepreneurial intentions.

4.2.2 Hypotheses regarding Individual Background Factors

Building strongly on the theoretical discussion in subsection 2.5.3, I derive some hypotheses about the role of individual background factors as determinants of entrepreneurial intentions.

4.2.2.1 Demographic Variables

The following two hypotheses are directly derived from the discussion in paragraph 2.5.3.1[38]:

H 4.4: Female students have lower entrepreneurial intentions than male students.

H 4.5: Foreign students have higher entrepreneurial intentions than male students.

4.2.2.2 Prior Experiences

There is considerable evidence that many entrepreneurs had role models of some kind (see paragraph 2.5.3.2). For example, many entrepreneurs have entrepreneurial parents. However, entrepreneurs' children do not disproportionately become entrepreneurs themselves (Brockhaus and Horwitz 1982). Scott and Twomey (1988) argue that multiple role models play a role in forming career preferences. As presented in paragraph 2.5.3.2, several studies confirm a positive relationship between role models and the preference for an entrepreneurial career. Also, past behavior in terms of entrepreneurial activity plays a substantial role in the formation of career intentions. Following the discussion there I suggest the following hypothesis:

H 4.6: The breadth of prior exposure to entrepreneurship will be positively related to entrepreneurial intentions.

In paragraph 2.5.3.2 I presented arguments of some researchers claiming that general education prepares students for the corporate domain (Timmons 1994) and promotes a "take-a-job" mentality (Kourilsky 1995). Especially general business courses seem to have a negative impact on entrepreneurial intentions

---

[38] Due to practically no variation in the variable age, I do not state a hypothesis about the relationship between age and entrepreneurial intention here.

(Whitlock and Masters 1996). With my sample being business administration students, I suggest:

H 4.7: The amount of completed university education is negatively related to entrepreneurial intentions.

At this point, I will not state a hypothesis about the relationship between the number of previously attended entrepreneurship courses and entrepreneurial intentions due to the contradictory findings in the literature of entrepreneurship education evaluation. The further exploration of this issue is one goal of this research project.[39]

4.2.2.3 Personality Dimensions

The following hypotheses about the relationship between the Big5 personality dimensions and entrepreneurial intentions are directly derived from paragraph 2.5.3.3 and were already stated in Zhao et al. (2010).

H 4.8: Extraversion will be positively related to entrepreneurial intentions.
H 4.9: Agreeableness will be negatively related to entrepreneurial intentions.
H 4.10: Conscientiousness will be positively related to entrepreneurial intentions.
H 4.11: Emotional Stability will be positively related to entrepreneurial intentions.
H 4.12: Openness to experience will be positively related to entrepreneurial intentions.

---

[39] However, I will include the variable attended entrepreneurship courses in the empirical analyses to provide information in how far students are "anchored" in their attitudes and intentions when entering the entrepreneurship course. This anchor will play a role when interpreting the results in the following chapters.

4.3 Test of the Hypotheses and Additional Results

The operationalization of all used variables is already described in section 3.4[40]. To test the hypotheses, I report the correlation matrix and run OLS regressions of the variable *entrepreneurial intentions* on the variables of the Theory of Planned Behavior and on the background variables. For the background variables, I also report t-tests comparing entrepreneurial intentions in subsamples of the treated students. Along each of these factors, I divided the whole sample in two groups according to the dummy-variables in Table 3.13. This is a rougher analysis with respect to the background variables; however I will split the sample in these subsamples in later analyses, too. The reported results will provide a point of reference there. As mentioned before, I only consider the ex-ante data.

Table 4.2 sets out the correlations of all considered variables and for additional variables with respect to prior experiences. The correlations of the latter variables serve as robustness checks for the results regarding the more aggregated breadth of prior exposure variable. In Table 4.1 I present the regressions with standardized coefficients. Note that the dependent variable *entrepreneurial intentions* can be treated as a continuous variable, so that I use OLS estimation. I report 6 regressions: model 1 contains the entrepreneurial attitude constructs of the Theory of Planned Behavior, model 2 to 4 the demographic, prior experiences, and personality dimension variables, respectively. Model 5 contains all of the considered variables. Model 6 is a copy of model 1, however with the respective ex-post values of entrepreneurial intentions and attitudes.

---

[40] Remember that completed university education is operationalized by the number of gained ECTS credits (variable *ECTS*).

Table 4.1: OLS regression models of background factors and entrepreneurial attitudes upon entrepreneurial intentions

dependent variable entrepreneurial intentions	Model 1 TPB	Model 2 demographic variables	Model 3 experiences variables	Model 4 personality dimensions	Model 5 background and TPB	Model 6 TPB (ex-post)
Theory of Planned Behavior variables						
perceived desirability	0.414***				0.391***	0.459***
perceived social norm	0.295***				0.280***	0.291***
perceived behavioral control	0.103**				0.086*	0.136***
demographic variables						
age		-0.029			-0.041	
female (0/1)		-0.221***			-0.027	
foreign (0/1)		0.212***			0.091**	
prior experiences						
breadth of prior exposure			0.262***		0.045	
attended entrepreneurship courses			-0.032		-0.026	
ECTS			-0.106**		-0.055	
personality dimensions						
extraversion				0.040	0.019	
agreeableness				-0.102**	-0.041	
conscientiousness				-0.120**	0.035	
emotional stability				0.107**	0.010	
openness to experience				0.214***	0.038	
test statistics						
observations	403	403	403	403	403	403
adj. R-squared	0.506	0.073	0.080	0.072	0.515	0.614
F-test (df)	138.11(3)	11.52(3)	12.64(3)	7.278(3)	31.53(14)	213.68(3)
F-test sig	0.000	0.000	0.000	0.000	0.000	0.000

Note: standardized coefficients reported; * significant at 10%; ** significant at 5%; *** significant at 1%

4.3.1 Hypotheses Related to the Theory of Planned Behavior

Table 4.2 shows that *perceived desirability, perceived social norm*, and *perceived behavioral control* are all positively and significantly related to *entrepreneurial intentions: r = .66* for *perceived desirability, r = .62* for *perceived social norm*, and *r = .51* for *perceived behavioral control*. Regression model 1 shows an adjusted R-squared of 0.51 and significant standardized coefficients with the hypothesized sign for all three entrepreneurial attitudes. Therefore, hypotheses 4.1 – 4.3 are accepted.

The values found here compare favorably to the correlation coefficients and variance explained reported in the studies presented in section 2.4. The mean correlation coefficients in the studies presented there are r = .44 for perceived desirability, r = .49 for perceived social norm, and r = .42 for perceived behavioral control. The mean variance explained in entrepreneurial intentions employing the Theory of Planned Behavior is 36%. Moreover, from the standardized coefficients reported in model 1, Table 4.1, one learns that perceived desirability is the strongest determinant of entrepreneurial intentions within the Theory of Planned Behavior framework, followed by perceived social norm and far behind perceived behavioral control. At first sight, this seems a bit surprising, given the pronounced importance of perceived behavioral control in general and that some studies even fail to show a significant relationship between perceived social norm and entrepreneurial intentions. Perhaps the students in this sample are at this time more driven by the possible outcomes of entrepreneurial activity and by advice from others than by perceptions of their own skills to perform an entrepreneur's tasks. One reason could be that at this point in their young life they lack the necessary experience and information to tell if they have the necessary skills. Although the picture remains the same after the entrepreneurship course, the difference between the standardized coefficients of *perceived social norm* and *perceived behavioral control* on the other side got smaller (model 6 in Table 4.1). This could be an indication that after having received information in the entrepreneurship course students are more able to

Table 4.2: Descriptive statistics and Pearson/ point-biserial correlations (treatment group sample)

		Mean	S.D.	1	2	3	4	5	6	7
Theory of Planned Behavior variables										
1	entrepreneurial intention	4.17	1.78	1.00						
2	perceived desirability	4.28	1.42	0.66*	1.00					
3	perceived social norm	-4.85	29.12	0.62*	0.65*	1.00				
4	perceived behavioral control	4.19	0.99	0.51*	0.57*	0.57*	1.00			
demographic variables										
5	age	21.66	2.14	-0.01	-0.02	0.02	0.04	1.00		
6	female (0/1)	0.53	-	-0.19*	-0.27*	-0.20*	-0.27*	-0.03	1.00	
7	foreign (0/1)	0.16	-	0.18*	0.09	0.10	0.07	0.04	0.28*	1.00
prior experiences										
8	parents self-employed (0/1)	0.49	-	0.21*	0.17*	0.21*	0.14*	0.05	0.05	-0.04
9	acquaintances self-employed (0/1)	0.67	-	0.17*	0.14*	0.25*	0.15*	0.07	0.01	0.34*
10	worked for start-up (0/1)	0.26	-	0.13*	0.13*	0.12*	0.19*	0.13*	-0.06	0.22*
11	entrepreneur (0/1)	0.06	-	0.12*	0.14*	0.10*	0.13*	0.09	-0.15	-0.18
12	breadth of prior exposure	1.47	0.99	0.27*	0.24*	0.30*	0.25*	0.14*	-0.01	0.10*
13	attended entrepreneurship courses	0.07	0.35	-0.02	-0.04	0.04	0.06	-0.03	-0.06	-0.06
14	ECTS	45.34	13.65	-0.14*	-0.10	-0.07	-0.07	-0.19*	-0.06	-0.22*
personality dimensions										
15	extraversion	4.94	1.14	0.14*	0.08	0.17*	0.19*	0.07	0.02	-0.00
16	agreeableness	4.49	0.76	-0.07	-0.06	-0.01	0.02	-0.06	0.13*	-0.07
17	conscientiousness	5.44	1.11	-0.06	-0.13*	-0.14*	-0.04	0.03	0.19*	0.00
18	emotional stability	4.75	1.17	0.15*	0.16*	0.17*	0.22*	-0.04	-0.20*	-0.06
19	openness to experience	5.44	0.99	0.22*	0.17*	0.23*	0.23*	0.04	0.12*	0.07

Note: * significant at 5%

	8	9	10	11	12	13	14	15	16	17	18	19
1												
2												
3												
4												
5												
6												
7												
8	1.00											
9	0.16	1.00										
10	0.20*	0.32*	1.00									
11	0.19	0.33*	0.51*	1.00								
12	0.62*	0.63*	0.64*	0.43*	1.00							
13	0.05	-0.02	0.02	0.07	0.04	1.00						
14	-0.15*	0.02	-0.07	-0.08	-0.12*	-0.06	1.00					
15	0.16*	0.17*	0.14*	0.05	0.23*	0.06	-0.05	1.00				
16	0.01	-0.10	-0.13*	-0.02	-0.10*	-0.04	0.01	0.04	1.00			
17	0.07	-0.05	-0.02	-0.06	-0.01	0.06	0.11*	0.08	0.05	1.00		
18	0.08	0.04	-0.01	0.00	0.05	0.12*	-0.02	0.25*	0.13*	0.10*	1.00	
19	0.24*	0.08	0.10*	0.12*	0.23*	0.06	-0.19*	0.41*	0.11*	0.23*	0.29*	1.00

tell whether they have the necessary skills. And if yes, this could mean that the influence of others' advice is getting smaller due to this ability to judge one's own skills. Moreover, model 6 shows that hypotheses 4.1 – 4.3 also hold with the values of the variables after the course, with even better test statistics.

4.3.2 Hypotheses regarding Demographic Variables

Table 4.3 tells that male students enter the course with significantly higher average entrepreneurial intentions than female students (4.537 vs. 3.865, p = 0.000). The same is true for foreign students compared to their German fellow students (4.906 vs. 4.041, p = 0.000). Accordingly, the variables *female (0/1)* and *foreign (0/1)* are both significantly related to entrepreneurial intentions in the expected way ($r = -.19$ and $r = -.18$ respectively). Regression model 2 in Table 4.1 shows an adjusted R-squared of 0.07 and significant standardized coefficients with the hypothesized sign for both variables. Most likely due to the before mentioned reasons, the coefficient for the variable *age* is insignificant. Therefore, hypotheses 4.4 and 4.5 are accepted.

Table 4.3: Mean ex-ante entrepreneurial intentions by subsample (treatment group sample)

students exhibiting background characteristic			1 no	2 yes	3 difference (2) - (1)	test statistic two-tailed t-test	
						|t|	p-value
demographic variables	female (0/1)	sample size	188	245	403		
		mean	4.537	3.865	-0.672	3.847	0.000***
	foreign (0/1)	sample size	339	64	403		
		mean	4.041	4.906	0.865	3.620	0.000***
prior experiences	parents self-employed (0/1)	sample size	210	193	403		
		mean	3.824	4.565	0.741	4.264	0.000***
	acquaintances self-employed (0/1)	sample size	132	271	403		
		mean	3.742	4.391	0.649	3.482	0.001***
	worked for start-up (0/1)	sample size	298	105	403		
		mean	4.037	4.581	0.544	2.715	0.007***
	entrepreneur (0/1)	sample size	379	24	403		
		mean	4.127	5.000	0.873	2.345	0.020**
	already attended course (0/1)	sample size	385	18	403		
		mean	4.187	4.000	-0.187	0.435	0.664
	high ECTS (0/1)	sample size	181	222	403		
		mean	4.348	4.041	-0.307	1.730	0.084*
personality dimensions	extravert (0/1)	sample size	165	238	403		
		mean	3.915	4.361	0.446	2.491	0.013**
	agreeable (0/1)	sample size	269	134	403		
		mean	4.193	4.149	-0.044	0.234	0.815
	conscientious (0/1)	sample size	107	296	403		
		mean	4.355	4.115	-0.240	1.198	0.232
	emotionally stable (0/1)	sample size	190	213	403		
		mean	3.984	4.352	0.368	2.080	0.038**
	open to experience (0/1)	sample size	102	301	403		
		mean	3.755	4.322	0.567	2.806	0.005***

Notes: * significant at 10%; ** significant at 5%; *** significant at 1% (for two-tailed t-test); subsamples as defined by Table 3.13

4.3.3 Hypotheses regarding Prior Experiences

As expected, students who have already been exposed to entrepreneurship before entering the course have higher average entrepreneurial intentions than students who were not (Table 4.3). This difference is largest for the subsample of self-employed students compared to students who have not started an own business yet (5.000 vs. 4.127, p = 0.020), and second largest for students who have self-employed parents compared to students without a self-employed parent (4.565 vs. 3.824, p = 0.000). Accordingly, the *breadth of prior exposure* to entrepreneurship is significantly related to *entrepreneurial intentions* and has the expected sign (r = .27, see Table 4.2). This result also holds when considering the four dummy variables that together form the breadth-variable. The variables *parents self-employed (0/1), acquaintances self-employed (0/1), worked for start-up (0/1), and entrepreneur (0/1)* are all significantly and positively related to *entrepreneurial intentions (r = .21, r = .17, r = .13, and r = .12* respectively). Moreover and as predicted, the variable ECTS is significantly and negatively correlated to *entrepreneurial intentions (r = -.14)*. Students who already have completed many university courses enter the course with lower average entrepreneurial intentions than other students (4.041 vs. 4.348, p = 0.084). Regression model 3 in Table 4.1 shows an adjusted R-squared of 0.08 with significant standardized coefficients and the predicted signs. Thus hypotheses 4.6 and 4.7 are also accepted. The variable *attended entrepreneurship courses* is not significantly related to entrepreneurial intentions. Therefore previously attended entrepreneurship courses do not seem to provide a career anchor for the students at the pre-university stage of their lives.[41]

4.3.4 Hypotheses regarding Personality Dimensions

Extravert, emotionally stable, and students open to experience enter the course with significantly higher average entrepreneurial intentions than compared to students who are low in the respective dimension (see Table 4.3). Accordingly (Table 4.2), the variables *extraversion, emotional stability,* and *openness to experience* are significantly and positively related to entrepreneurial intentions as hypothesized *(r = .14, r = .15, and r = .22* respectively). There were no significant correlations between *agreeableness* and *conscientiousness* and *entrepreneurial intentions*.

---

[41] However, only 18 students have attended a course before.

Model 4 in Table 4.1 shows a somewhat different pattern. Controlling for the other personality dimensions, the coefficient for extraversion is insignificant, but all other dimensions significantly influence entrepreneurial intentions. However, unexpectedly conscientiousness exerts a negative influence on entrepreneurial intentions. Perhaps students at this stage of their life leverage their personal disposition in this dimension - being organized, systematic, efficient, practical, steady, dependable, careful, thorough, responsible, hardworking, achievement-oriented and persevering (see paragraph 2.5.3.3) – to perform better at university than to pursue entrepreneurial intentions. The coefficients for the dimensions agreeableness, emotional stability and openness to experience have the expected sign. I conclude that hypotheses 4.8, 4.9, 4.11, and 4.12 are accepted, but hypothesis 4.10 is rejected. Thus I cannot confirm the results of the widely acknowledged meta-analysis of Zhao et al. (2010).

As a by-product, model 4 in Table 4.1 delivers additional insights in the relative influence strengths of the personality dimensions. According to the standardized regression coefficients reported there, it seems that the strongest personality effect is for openness to experience, followed by conscientiousness, emotional stability, and agreeableness. This partly confirms the order found in Zhao et al. (2010). They find the same order for the first three dimensions, then followed by extraversion, and agreeableness exerts the weakest influence (however conscientiousness with a positive sign in their study).

4.3.5 Mediating Effects of the Theory of Planned Behavior Variables

Model 5 in Table 4.1 supports the assertion in the Theory of Planned Behavior, that individuals form their attitudes toward a specific behavior largely based on behavioral, normative and control beliefs. At a given point of time, they have formed these beliefs based on their background characteristics (see subsection 2.3.2 for a discussion). Researchers should be able to predict intentions by means of the three attitudinal factors. Therefore, there should be no direct link between those background characteristics and – in this case – entrepreneurial intentions when controlling for attitudes. In model 5 one learns that indeed most of the coefficients of the background variables turn insignificant when controlling for the attitudinal factors, except for *foreign (0/1)*. All of the coefficients belonging to the variables of the Theory of Planned Behavior are significant and strongly influence entrepreneurial intentions, as predicted by the theory.

4.4 Conclusion

Failure as an entrepreneur can be costly both for the individual and for society. A major goal of entrepreneurship research is thus to gain insight into the reasons why individuals aim at entering an entrepreneurial career. Researchers try to develop a deeper understanding of the deliberative processes with respect to such career plans. A widely used theoretical framework promising to deliver these insights is the Theory of Planned Behavior and other concepts stemming from the social psychology literature. This chapter provides a test of the Theory of Planned Behavior based on the ex-ante data of the pooled treatment group as introduced in chapter 3. Moreover I analyzed the importance of several background characteristics (demographic, prior experiences, personality dimensions) as determinants of entrepreneurial intentions.

The findings presented here strongly support the application of the Theory of Planned Behavior in the research on the prediction of entrepreneurial activity. As hypothesized by the theory, perceived desirability, perceived social norm, and perceived behavioral control are significant predictors of entrepreneurial intentions. The effect sizes and the variance in entrepreneurial intentions explained compare favorably to those previously found in other studies in this field. Second, the results suggest that females exhibit lower entrepreneurial intentions than male students, and German students intend less to enter an entrepreneurial career than foreign students. The results on the relationships between prior experiences and entrepreneurial intentions broadly confirm the findings in the existing literature. Broad entrepreneurial experiences in terms of role models and own entrepreneurial activity are significantly and positively related to entrepreneurial intentions. On the other hand, the more university courses a student has completed, the lower his intention to start an enterprising career. The chapter also provides evidence that the Big5 personality dimensions are related to entrepreneurial intentions. Openness to experience and emotional stability appear to be the personality dimensions that are positively related to entrepreneurial intentions, while agreeable and conscientious students exhibit a lower intent to start an own business. Extraversion is not significantly related to intentions. The estimated effect sizes for the Big5 personality dimensions are moderate in magnitude, explaining 7% of the variance in entrepreneurial intention. These findings are not consistent with the results found in the meta-analysis by Zhao et al. (2010), who find another order for the importance of personality dimensions and a positive sign for the relationship between conscientiousness and entrepreneurial intentions. On a more general level this chapter adds to the literature on the Theory of Planned Behavior itself. It provides further evidence that its application in the specific field of career intentions is appropriate. The results also suggest that the impact of exogenous influences on intentions is mediated by the antecedents of intentions as proposed by the Theory of Planned Behavior.

The results found in this chapter have some implications for the following empirical analyses in this book. The ratio behind using the ex-ante data of the treatment group in this chapter is to gain additional insights in the "starting points" of the students. Given the variances in entrepreneurial intentions among different subsamples, it is not likely that an entrepreneurship course has the same effects on all students. Some students already enter the course with a certain predisposition towards entrepreneurship based on their previous experiences or their personality structure, either in favor or against entering an entrepreneurial career. A short-term behavioral intervention like an entrepreneurship course probably cannot change this predisposition by much. Akerlof and Kranton (2000) for example state that individuals will have developed a certain identity during adolescence that will not be subject to course-induced stimuli. Hence it seems worthwhile to differentiate between subsamples of students defined by background characteristics when examining the effects of an entrepreneurship course. The findings also suggest some general implications with respect to entrepreneurship education. Students with an already existing strong predisposition towards or against entrepreneurship might not respond to stimuli provided in an entrepreneurship course. This has implications for the selection of students for admission to an entrepreneurship course, or for course and curricula planners with respect to how and when they offer entrepreneurship education. The low entrepreneurial intention of female students might tell that female students will not process the information given in a course, as they already are determined regarding future career plans. This implies two possible consequences. In a case where only limited seminar places are available, a course planner might decide not to admit female students to the course when his goal is to increase entrepreneurial intentions among students. Or, on the other hand, he might offer a special course addressed to the specific characteristics of female students. Another example is the negative relationship between already completed university education and entrepreneurial intentions. It confirms the point of view that entrepreneurship education should be offered in the early phase of the university curriculum. In a later phase the students might already have a strong predisposition against entrepreneurship, and might not respond to stimuli provided in an entrepreneurship course. Other results in connection with background characteristics may suggest similar consequences. Therefore I will not only analyze the effect of an entrepreneurship course on the whole population, but will also analyze whether some students are more "training ready" than others, as suggested already in subsection 2.5.3.

5. Assessing the Impact of Entrepreneurship Education – a Quasi-Experimental Approach

5.1 Introduction

The studies by Peterman and Kennedy (2003), Souitaris et al. (2007), and Oosterbeek et al. (2010) make important contributions to the literature on the effects of entrepreneurship education. These exploit data from a treatment and control group to determine the true causal effects of entrepreneurship education on overall entrepreneurial attitudes and intentions. However, given the methodological deficiencies of these studies discussed in subsection 1.2.4, I replicate and advance these research designs in this chapter. Two research questions are addressed: What is the size and nature of the course-induced effects on mean entrepreneurial attitudes and intentions? And do these effects appeal to some subsamples of students, defined by demographic variables, prior experiences, or personality dimensions, more than to others?

Here, I too, use a difference-in-differences approach to elicit the true causal effects of "Business Planning" on students' mean entrepreneurial attitudes and intentions. Following Souitaris et al. (2007), I analyze the effects the course had on entrepreneurial intentions as well as on perceptions of desirability, social norm, and behavioral control towards entrepreneurship separately. However, I extend this basic research design in two ways, making it possible to draw more reliable and differentiated interpretations. First, I apply Coarsened Exact Matching (CEM, Iacus et al. 2011) to my data. In paragraph 3.5.1.3, where I conducted the tests on equivalence of treatment and control group, I argued that large differences in background characteristics may bias the estimations of the effects of the course. For a quasi-experimental design, the treated and untreated students have to be as similar as possible (Rogers et al. 1993). The above mentioned studies do not run tests for this precondition or take it into account when estimating the effects of the course. CEM is a method to control for these differences. Second, according to the argumentation in chapters 2 and 4, I respect the possibility that the course may have different effects dependent on the students' background characteristics. From the above mentioned studies, the one by Oosterbeek et al. (2010) does so by reporting the difference-in-differences estimations separately for female and male students. I extend this approach by reporting difference-in-difference-in-differences estimations to elicit the effects an entrepreneurship course has on different subsamples defined by background characteristics. This method allows a simultaneous comparison of the effects on the considered subsample of treated students to both the treated students not being in this subsample, and the untreated students who exhibit the background characteristic that defines the subsample. This provides a more robust way to analyze the effects on a specific subsample than the approach by Oosterbeek et al. (2010).

The results suggest that mean entrepreneurial intentions among the treated students significantly decrease during the course, whereas mean perceptions of social norm and behavioral control experience a positive shift. However, exploiting the data on the control group in addition, the significant effect on entrepreneurial intentions vanishes. The difference-in-differences estimations confirm the significant positive effect on mean perceived social norm and perceived behavioral control, but only when applying CEM to the data. The difference-in-difference-in-differences estimations surprisingly reveal that mean entrepreneurial intentions of students who have already started a business decrease during the time of the course. Regarding entrepreneurial attitudes, this group also experiences a negative shift in their perceptions of perceived behavioral control. Moreover, perceptions of desirability and social norm increase during the course among students with self-employed parents. And students who already attended an entrepreneurship course before experience a positive shift in their perceived desirability.

This chapter adds to the emerging literature on the evaluation of entrepreneurship education. It builds on previously conducted studies by Peterman and Kennedy (2003), Souitaris et al. (2007), and Oosterbeek et al. (2010) and advances the used methodologies. Through these improvements it provides more robust estimations of the effects of entrepreneurship education on entrepreneurial attitudes and intentions. Moreover it delivers insight into how an entrepreneurship course appeals to students with different background characteristics.

The remainder of this chapter contains three sections. In section 2 I present the empirical strategy. I introduce the difference-in-differences and difference-in-difference-in-differences methods and explain the Coarsened Exact Matching method. Section 3 presents the results of the estimations. Section 4 concludes and discusses the implications of the findings.

5.2 Empirical Strategy

This section explains the empirical strategy I use to analyze the course-induced effects on mean entrepreneurial intentions and attitudes.

5.2.1 One Group Before and After Design

For a first assessment of the effects of entrepreneurship education on entrepreneurial attitudes and intentions I use the "one group pretest posttest design" (as it is called in psychology, or "differences" in economics) approach (Shadish et al. 2002). This approach is motivated by the estimation of the equation

$$y_{it} = \alpha + \beta d_t + \varepsilon_{it},$$

Equation 5.1: Differences estimation equation

with pooled data from the two time periods (ex-ante and ex-post). y_{it} is the outcome variable of interest for observation i in period t, $t = 0$ for the time before the treatment (or "ex-ante") and $t=1$ for the time after the treatment ("ex-post"), and $i = 1, ..., N_t$ where N_0 denotes the number of observations ex-ante and N_1 the number of observations ex-post.[42] The dummy-variable d_t denotes the time period, i.e. $d_t = 1$ if t = 1 and $d_t = 0$ otherwise, and β is the causal effect of the treatment on the outcome of interest (Meyer 1995).

The main assumption is that in absence of the treatment the causal effect β would be 0, i.e. there would be no difference in the mean of those in group *t = 0* and group *t = 1*. This condition can be expressed by $E(\varepsilon_{it} \mid d_t) = 0$, i.e. the conditional mean of the error term does not depend on the value of the time-dummy. If this condition holds, the unbiased difference estimator $\hat{\beta}_d$ can be obtained as

$$\hat{\beta}_D = \Delta \bar{y}$$
$$= \overline{y_1} - \overline{y_0}$$
$$= \bar{y}_{ex-post} - \bar{y}_{ex-ante},$$

Equation 5.2: Obtaining the differences estimator

where the bar indicates an average over the individual observations and the subscript on y denotes the time period (Meyer 1995).

To test whether $\hat{\beta}_D$ is statistically different from 0 one can either conduct a t-test testing the null hypothesis that $\hat{\beta}_D = 0$, or directly estimate the parameters of *Equation 5.1* using regression analysis and pooled data from the two time periods. However, the differences-estimator may be confounded for several reasons. First, there could be other and unobserved events other than the experimental treatment (i.e. the entrepreneurship course) that could affect changes between t = 0 and t = 1 with respect to the outcome variable of interest (e.g. changes in law affecting, for example, the perceived desirability to become self-employed). Meyer (1995) calls this "omitted variables bias". Another bias

---

[42] Accordingly it is not necessary to exclude observations who exited the sample between the ex-ante and the ex-post test (attrition), as this equation compares the means of all ex-ante with all ex-post observations. I chose the more conservative approach by only taking complete matched ex-ante and ex-post data as presented in section 3.3 and tested the data for potential attrition bias in subsection 3.5.1. Thus I enforce comparability of the ex-ante and ex-post group, what would otherwise raise some additional concerns with respect to the validity of the results (Meyer 1995).

could be trends in outcomes, meaning that there are processes within the units of observations producing changes as a function of the passage of time per se, e.g. aging (see Meyer (1995) for a more detailed discussion). To circumvent these problems it is necessary to assess the outcomes for similar groups that did not receive the treatment, but would most likely also be affected by these influences.

5.2.2 The Before and After with an Untreated Control Group - Design

When such a control[43] group is present, i.e. a group that did not receive the experimental treatment but experienced the same other influences that affected the treated group and that exhibits similar background characteristics, one can employ a quasi-experimental design (Shadish et al. 2002). Using this design allows measuring the true causal effect of the course on entrepreneurial attitudes and intentions. It is then possible to compare the outcome of the treatment and control group and to differentiate between changes in the outcome variables caused by the course and changes caused by other influences. The term quasi-experimental emphasizes that one important characteristic of a "true" experiment is missing: a randomized assignment of the units of observation to the treatment and the control group. Instead, the units are sorted into the two groups by self-selection[44].

One of the most often used quasi-experimental designs is called "the untreated control group design with pretest and posttest" (Meyer 1995, p. 154) in psychology, or "difference-in-differences" in economics. In the special case of this study, the design is also called the untreated control group design with dependent pretest and posttest samples, as I gathered ex-ante and ex-post data from the same units.

---

[43] In the literature the terms "control group" and "comparison group" are used synonymously. Henceforth I use the term "control group".
[44] This self-selection as a source of bias in the data has been discussed in chapter 3.

For this design, the underlying model is of the form

$$y_{it}^j = \alpha + \alpha_1 d_t + \alpha^1 d^j + \beta d_t^j + \varepsilon_{it}^j,$$

Equation 5.3: Difference-in-differences estimation equation

where the outcome y is now also indexed by j for the (treatment and control) group. The dummy-variable d_t is a "time-dummy" with $d_t = 1$ if $t = 1$ and $= 0$ otherwise, and d^j is a "treatment-dummy" with $d^j = 1$ if $j = 1$ and $= 0$ otherwise, and d_t^j is the interaction of the two, with $d_t^j = 1$ if $t = 1$ and $j = 1$ and $= 0$ otherwise. d_t^j is a dummy-variable indicating that a unit is in the treatment group after it has received the treatment, and β is the true causal effect of the treatment on the outcome for this group. Moreover, α_1 captures effects of other unobserved events other than the experimental treatment affecting both groups that causes changes in the outcome between $t = 0$ and $t = 1$. And potential time-invariant differences in overall means between the groups are summarized in α^1 (Meyer 1995). As above, the key assumption is that β would be zero in the absence of the treatment, or $E(\varepsilon_{it}^j | d_t^j) = 0$. Then the unbiased difference-in-difference estimator $\hat{\beta}_{DD}$ can be obtained by the difference in the differences in the means of the groups as

$$\hat{\beta}_{DD} = \Delta \bar{y}^1 - \Delta \bar{y}^0$$
$$= \bar{y}_1^1 - \bar{y}_0^1 - (\bar{y}_1^0 - \bar{y}_0^0),$$

Equation 5.4: Obtaining the difference-in-differences estimator

where again a bar indicates an average over i, the subscript denotes the time period and the superscript denotes the group.

To test whether $\hat{\beta}_{DD}$ is statistically different from 0, one can either conduct a t-test testing the null hypothesis that $\Delta \bar{y}^1 = \Delta \bar{y}^0$, or directly estimate the parameters of *Equation 5.3* using regression analysis and pooled data from the two time periods.

The mentioned threats to validity – omitted variables bias and general trends in outcomes – are to some extent reduced by this approach (Meyer 1995). Extensions of the basic difference-in-differences design provide further robustness-checks for the results.

5.2.2.1 Inclusion of Control Variables for Individual Characteristics

An advantage of the regression formulation is that it allows including a vector z_{it}^j of background characteristics. As presented in paragraph 3.4.1.2, I gathered extensive information regarding individual background characteristics. By estimating the parameters of the following equation, I can control for differences along these characteristics between the units of observation within the two groups:

$$y_{it}^j = \alpha + \alpha_1 d_t + \alpha^1 d^j + \beta d_t^j + \delta z_{it}^j + \varepsilon_{it}^j.$$

Equation 5.5: Difference-in-differences estimation equation with controls

However, this method will not control for differences in these background variables between the two groups. In subsection 3.5.1, I tested the equivalency of treatment and control group and found differences along some background factors across groups. A matching procedure of observations in the treatment group to observations in the control group helps to reduce potential biases stemming from these differences.

5.2.2.2 Coarsened Exact Matching

Coarsened Exact Matching (CEM), presented in Iacus et al. (2008) is a matching method that reduces imbalance in chosen covariates between treatment and control group. The goal is to prune some observations from the data and thus reduce the imbalance between the remaining treatment and control group data.

The empirical distributions of the chosen covariates in the groups should then be more similar. When data is exactly balanced in a vector of covariates $X = (X_1, X_2, \ldots, X_k)$, then further controlling for X is unnecessary and the difference in means on the matched data estimates the true causal effect. Matching methods thus reduce model dependence and potential biases due to ex-ante differences between treatment and control group.

The CEM algorithm encompasses three steps (Iacus et al. 2009). First, it temporarily coarsens each chosen covariate. Then it sorts all units into strata, each of which has the same values of the coarsened X. Last, it prunes those units in any stratum that do not include at least one treated and one control unit. The analysis is then run on the uncoarsened, matched data.

So the algorithm creates a set of strata, $s \in S$, each with the same values of X. Only units in those strata will be retained for the further analysis that contain at least one treatment and one control group observation. Let $\mathcal{T}^s$ denote the treatment group units in stratum s and $m_{j=1}^s := \#\mathcal{T}^s$ the number of treatment group units in this stratum, and for the control group units similarly $\mathcal{C}^s$ with $m_{j=0}^s := \#\mathcal{C}^s$, and further $m_{j=1} := \bigcup_{s \in S} m_{j=1}^s$ as well as $m_{j=0} := \bigcup_{s \in S} m_{j=0}^s$. Then the algorithm assigns to each unit i in stratum s the following weights:

$$w_i = \begin{cases} 1, & i \in \mathcal{T}^s \\ \dfrac{m_{j=0}}{m_{j=1}} \dfrac{m_{j=1}^s}{m_{j=0}^s}, & i \in \mathcal{C}^s \end{cases}$$

and $w_i = 0$ for unmatched units. The CEM algorithm therefore eliminates imbalance beyond some chosen level. The remaining differences are within the strata. This allows getting a better estimate of the true causal effect of the treatment on the outcome variable and reduces the dependence on the empirical model.

Imbalance is measured by a statistic that is presented in more detail in Iacus et al. (2011). It reports the difference between the multivariate empirical distribution of the ex-ante covariates for the treatment $p(X|j = 1)$ and matched control group $p(\tilde{X}|j = 0)$. The authors' idea is to choose a number of "bins" for each continuous variable with a fine grid and with categorical variables left as is. Then they denote by $H(X_l)$, $l = 1, ..., k$, the set of distinct values generated by coarsening on variable X_l. Then, a multidimensional histogram is generated by the Cartesian product $H(X_1) \times ... \times H(X_k) =: H(X)$. Let f and g denote the relative empirical frequency distributions for the treatment and control group respectively, and $f_{l_1...l_k}$ the relative frequency for observations belonging to the cell with coordinates $l_1, ..., l_k$ of the multivariate cross-tabulation of the treatment group units, and $g_{l_1...l_k}$ for the control group units. Then Iacus et al. (2011) define the multivariate imbalance as

$$\mathcal{L}_1(f,g) := \frac{1}{2} \sum_{l_1,...,l_k \in H(X)} |f_{l_1...l_k} - g_{l_1...l_k}|.$$

Perfect global balance (up to coarsening) would be indicated by $\mathcal{L}_1 = 0$, which means that the two distributions overlap exactly. Larger values indicate larger imbalance between treatment and control group with a maximum of $\mathcal{L}_1 = 1$, which means that the two distributions are completely separated. If for example $\mathcal{L}_1 = 0.6$, then 40% of the density of the two histograms overlap. The $\mathcal{L}_1$ value is thus not meaningful on its own, but rather serves as an anchor for comparing matching solutions. Let f^m and g^m denote the empirical frequencies for matched treatment and control group units corresponding to the unmatched f and g frequencies. Then a "good" matching solution would give $\mathcal{L}_1(f^m, g^m) < \mathcal{L}_1(f,g)$.

All in all, this modification of the difference-in-differences estimation reduces biases due to ex-ante differences between the treatment and control group in the results of estimating the true causal effect of the treatment (i.e. the entrepreneurship course in this case) on the outcome variables of interest.

Another approach to exploit the gathered data on background characteristics is to explore whether the course had different effects on subsamples of the treatment group that are constructed along these characteristics. To compare these changes of the outcome variables in subsamples of the treatment group to the respective subsamples in the control group, a difference-in-difference-in-differences approach can be used.

5.2.3 Analyzing the Treatment Effect on Different Subsamples using a Difference-in-Difference-in-Differences Approach

In subsection 2.3.2 I argued that individuals interpret new information in a behavioral treatment differently according, e.g., to their personality or prior experiences. This could lead to different effects of the course on different subsamples. A further refinement of the definition of treatment and control group promises further insights in the effectiveness of the course with respect to subsamples of students. For example, one could be interested in the effects specifically on female students.

One possibility is to use data only on students in the treatment group and to define the subsample of female students as a "treatment group in the treatment group", with the male students as the control group. The potential problem with this difference-in-differences design is that there may be other and unobserved factors unrelated to the course, which might affect, for example, entrepreneurial intentions of females (for example government programs bringing forward female entrepreneurship). For later use I will call this type a "DD type 1".

Another way to set up a difference-in-differences design to further investigate effects on female students is to only take the female students from the treatment and control group and compare the difference of the differences in means regarding the outcome variable in question. Here the problem is that the changes in intentions could be systematically different across the treatment and control group, for example due to differences in other background variables. Parallel to above, I will call this a "DD type 2".

A more robust way to analyze the effects of the course on female students is to consider females as a "treated" group within the treatment group and compare the differences in the outcome variable to the "treated" group of females in the control group. This is called the difference-in-difference-in-differences approach in economics.

The underlying model of the difference-in-difference-in-differences approach is again a modification of *Equation 5.3*. This modification will include an additional dummy-variable resulting from the division of the sample in two subsamples according to the respective background factor in question. Thus the new version of *Equation 5.3* will have a higher-level interaction as the key explanatory variable with the coefficient β. This modification has also the advantage of removing any trends along the dimension of the background factor. The regression equation for this model is

$$y_{it}^{jk} \alpha + \alpha_1 d_t + \alpha^1 d^j + \gamma^1 e^k + \alpha_1^1 d_t^j + \gamma_1^1 e_t^k + \alpha^{11} d^{jk} + \beta d_t^{jk} + \delta z_{it}^j + \varepsilon_{it}^j.$$

Equation 5.6: Difference-in-difference-in-differences estimation equation

The outcome variable is now also indexed by k, $k = 0, 1$. e^k is a dummy-variable indicating if unit i exhibits the considered background factor, thus $e^k = 1$ if $k = 1$ (i.e. the unit exhibits the background factor in question) and $= 0$ otherwise ("subsample-dummy"). d_t^j, e_t^k, d^{jk} are the three possible interactions of two factors (the first-order interactions). Finally d_t^{jk} is a dummy-variable indicating that the unit is in the considered subsample in the treatment group after the treatment has taken place, hence $d_t^{jk} = 1$ if $k = 1, j = 1,$ and $t = 1$, and $= 0$ otherwise (Meyer 1995). And β is the effect of the treatment on the outcome (for the subsample that exhibits the background factor in question compared to changes in the outcome variable of the respective subsample in the control group). As above, z_{it}^j is a vector of control variables.

Again assuming that β is 0 in the absence of the treatment, the unbiased difference-in-difference-in-differences estimator $\hat{\beta}_{DDD}$ can be obtained by measuring the change in means for the subsample in the treatment group, where one nets out the change in means for the subsample in the control group and the change in means for the subsample not exhibiting the background factor in question in the treatment group:

$$\hat{\beta}_{DDD} = \Delta \bar{y}^{11} - \Delta \bar{y}^{01} - \Delta \bar{y}^{10}$$
$$= (\bar{y}_1^{11} - \bar{y}_0^{11}) - (\bar{y}_1^{01} - \bar{y}_0^{01}) - (\bar{y}_1^{10} - \bar{y}_0^{10}),$$

Equation 5.7: Obtaining the difference-in-difference-in-differences estimator

where again a bar indicates an average over the units i, the subscript denotes the time period and the superscript denotes the group and the subsample.[45]

As above, to test whether $\hat{\beta}_{DDD}$ is statistically different from 0 one can either conduct a t-test testing the null hypothesis that $\hat{\beta}_{DDD} = 0$, or directly estimate the parameters of *Equation 5.6* using regression analysis and pooled data from the two time periods. I will abstain from reporting results from a t-test in this case and only report the regression results with respect to several background factors.

This approach should control for two potentially confounding general trends: changes in the outcome variable of the subsample that exhibits the background factor in question across the treatment and control group and changes in the outcome variable of all units in the treatment group.

---

[45] Note that if one drops either the middle or last term, one obtains the DD type 1 and the DD type 2 difference-in-difference estimators respectively described in this paragraph.

5.3 Results

In this section I present the results of the difference-in-differences and difference-in-difference-in-differences estimations with the explained modifications to assess the impact of the entrepreneurship course. I proceed as follows: in the first part I look at average effects in the whole sample of all treatment and control units. As outcome variables I use the constructs of the Theory of Planned Behavior separately: entrepreneurial intentions, perceived desirability, perceived social norm, and perceived behavioral control. I report the differences and difference-in-differences estimators obtained by t-tests for the overall sample. Next I present the difference-in-differences estimations obtained by OLS regressions based on *Equation 5.3*. There I include additional variables to control for individual background (*Equation 5.5*) and perform the coarsened exact matching on the dataset. In the second part I look at various subsamples spanned by the background factors according to Table 3.13. There, I obtain difference-in-difference-in-differences estimates related to each subsample.

As already shown by equivalency-tests in subsection 3.5.1, the treatment and control group may be seen as statistically equivalent with respect to entrepreneurial intentions, perceived desirability, perceived social norm and perceived behavioral control when answering the ex-ante questionnaire. This provides an excellent basis for the interpretation of the results in this section, as these may not be biased due to differences in these central variables.

5.3.1 Differences

Table 5.1 sets out the results of the simple differences estimations using t-tests. Following this approach it seems that the course has significantly affected all of the considered outcome variables with the exception of *perceived desirability*. After adjusting the scale and spoken in absolute values, the mean *entrepreneurial intentions* have experienced the largest shift. Moreover, two issues are noteworthy. First, the shift in *entrepreneurial intentions* is negative. The average *entrepreneurial intentions* score (interpreting the scale as metric) has decreased from 4.179 to 3.859 ($|t| = 4.500, p = 0.001$), and so shows the same pattern as the results in the studies by Oosterbeek et al. (2010). Second, the means in *perceived social norm* and *perceived behavioral control* are higher after the course than before. At first sight this seems to contradict the Theory of Planned Behavior. At second sight this indicates that the students learned something about entrepreneurship and their own aptitude for it (see also section 3.6 for a self-reported assessment of entrepreneurial learning that corroborates this interpretation). But perhaps their entrepreneurial potential will not open out into the creation of a new business, but in entrepreneurial behavior in organizations where they are employed.

Table 5.1: Differences-approach – t-tests for ex-post/ex-ante differences

Variable	N	Ex-ante		Ex-post		Difference and test statistic			
		Mean	S.D.	Mean	S.D.	Mean	S.E.	|t|	p
entrepreneurial intentions	403	4.179	1.780	3.859	1.845	-0.320	0.071	4.500	0.000*
perceived desirability	403	4.280	1.418	4.333	1.519	0.053	0.059	0.890	0.374
perceived social norm	403	-4.856	29.121	-1.782	30.494	3.074	1.164	2.642	0.009*
perceived behavioral control	403	4.195	0.992	4.346	1.069	0.151	0.046	3.292	0.001*

Notes: * significant at 10%; ** significant at 5%; *** significant at 1% (for two-tailed t-tests)

However, as discussed, these results may be biased due to the reasons explained above. The results of the difference-in-difference estimation will be more reliable.

5.3.2 Difference-in-Differences

Difference-in-differences estimators obtained using t-tests are displayed in Table 5.2. The results reveal several interesting issues. First, the decrease of the mean in *entrepreneurial intentions* in the treatment group does not seem as drastic as in the simple differences design (shifts in means are -0.320 in the differences and -0.188 in the difference-in-differences approach). Moreover, the difference-in-differences in *entrepreneurial intentions* is not significant any more. Still significant is the increase in *perceived behavioral control*. And again, the size of the effect has changed compared to the differences design, now being higher (0.182 in the differences and 0.214 in the difference-in-differences design). This is a strong indicator that the students changed their control beliefs and thus feel that they acquired skills necessary to execute entrepreneurial roles. The sign of the coefficient on *perceived desirability* has changed, however the effect is near zero and not significant. Respecting the scale, the effect size in perceived social norm is almost equal to the one in the differences approach, but is not significant any more. The significant change in *perceived behavioral control* indicates that the students discover that they have increased knowledge about entrepreneurship and necessary skills to perform entrepreneurial roles after the course. However, it still seems that this increase in perceived behavioral control is not leading to more nascent entrepreneurs.

Table 5.2: Difference-in-differences approach – t-tests for ex-post/ex-ante differences

Variable (ex-post/ex-ante differences)	Treatment group			Control group			Difference-in-differences and test statistic			
	N	Mean	S.E.	N	Mean	S.E.	Mean	S.E.	|t|	p
entrepreneurial intentions	403	-0.320	0.071	106	-0.132	0.142	-0.188	0.157	1.200	0.231
perceived desirability	403	0.053	0.059	106	0.066	0.111	-0.014	0.128	0.109	0.913
perceived social norm	403	3.074	1.164	106	-0.368	2.453	3.442	2.595	1.327	0.185
perceived behavioral control	403	0.151	0.046	106	-0.064	0.075	0.214	0.097	2.205	0.028**

Notes: * significant at 10%; ** significant at 5%; *** significant at 1% (for two-tailed t-tests)

Figure 5.1 charts the calculation of the difference-in-differences estimators ß_DD for the variables of the Theory of Planned Behavior.

A positive difference-in-differences estimator implies that the entrepreneurship course had a positive impact on the value of the variable in question, and vice versa.

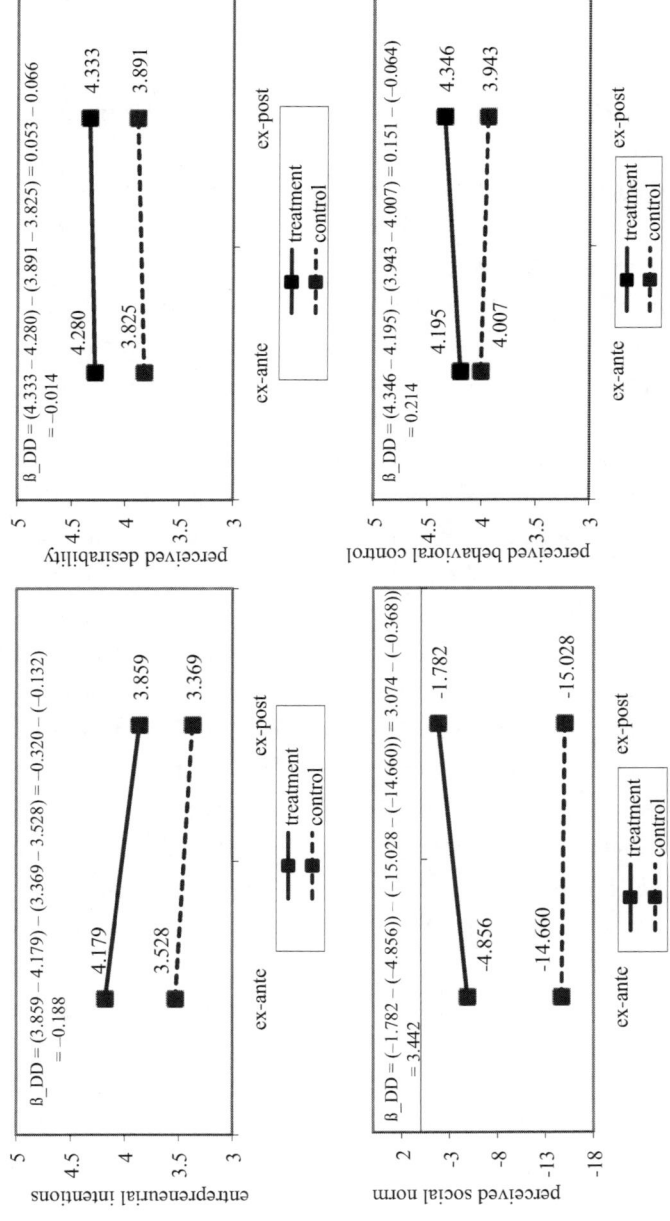

Figure 5.1: Difference-in-differences estimator calculated for Theory of Planned Behavior variables (calculations contain rounding errors)

Next I analyze the results of the OLS regressions to further investigate the average treatment effect on the four outcome variables. Table 5.3 sets out the results of the difference-in-differences estimations for each variable of the Theory of Planned Behavior in blocks of four models. Difference-in-differences estimators are set in bold.

Model 1 uses the specification of *Equation 5.3* without any control variables. Models 2 and 3 include two sets of control variables respectively using the specification of *Equation 5.5* to control for within-group initial differences in background: since I do not have data on the personality dimensions of the whole control group sample, I estimate one model without these variables and only with demographic and prior experiences variables in model 2. Model 3 contains these variables, resulting in a decrease of observations by 66. In model 4 I apply Coarsened Exact Matching to control for initial differences in background across treatment and control group. The equivalency-tests reported in Table 3.26 tell that I cannot rule out differences between the treatment and control group regarding the following variables: *female (0/1), foreign (0/1), parents self-employed (0/1), acquaintances self-employed (0/1), worked for start-up (0/1), entrepreneur (0/1), and attended entrepreneurship courses*. Therefore I chose to match the units in treatment and control group by applying the CEM algorithm along these variables. Checking for imbalance in these variables gives a multivariate imbalance of $\mathcal{L}_1 = .359$. After applying the matching algorithm the imbalance decreased to $\mathcal{L}'_1 = .100$. Seven units of the control group and 41 of the treatment group were pruned from the dataset leading to a decrease in observations by 96. Together with the 66 observations dropped due to missing values in the personality dimensions, the model 4 estimations are based on 856 observations.

Table 5.3: Difference-in-Differences estimations using OLS (part 1)

Dependent variable	entrepreneurial intention				perceived desirability			
	model 1 model only	model 2 with some controls	model 3 with all controls	model 4 with controls and CEM	model 1 model only	model 2 with some controls	model 3 with all controls	model 4 with controls and CEM
Model variables								
time dummy (ex-post = 1)	-0.132 (0.224)	-0.132 (0.213)	-0.155 (0.276)	-0.510* (0.274)	0.066 (0.179)	0.066 (0.171)	0.115 (0.226)	-0.205 (0.225)
treatment dummy (treatment = 1)	0.650*** (0.181)	0.612*** (0.175)	0.458** (0.221)	0.352 (0.217)	0.456*** (0.142)	0.423*** (0.135)	0.352* (0.180)	0.260 (0.179)
β_DD	**-0.188** (**0.258**)	**-0.188** (**0.244**)	**-0.165** (**0.299**)	**0.178** (**0.300**)	**-0.014** (**0.207**)	**-0.014** (**0.197**)	**-0.063** (**0.245**)	**0.237** (**0.246**)
Demographic variables								
age		-0.031 (0.028)	-0.030 (0.028)	-0.059** (0.027)		-0.036 (0.024)	-0.035 (0.025)	-0.068*** (0.022)
female (0/1)		-0.841*** (0.106)	-0.889*** (0.115)	-0.945*** (0.125)		-0.693*** (0.087)	-0.729*** (0.095)	-0.807*** (0.103)
foreign (0/1)		0.781*** (0.145)	0.829*** (0.149)	0.976*** (0.181)		0.421*** (0.118)	0.449*** (0.121)	0.696*** (0.149)
Prior experiences								
breadth of prior exposure		0.425*** (0.054)	0.329*** (0.057)	0.366*** (0.062)		0.314*** (0.045)	0.274*** (0.050)	0.284*** (0.051)
attended entrepreneurship courses		0.014 (0.043)	0.164 (0.128)	0.069 (0.247)		-0.057** (0.028)	-0.039 (0.120)	-0.051 (0.203)

Table 5.3 (continued): Difference-in-Differences estimations using OLS (part 1 continuted)

Dependent variable	entrepreneurial intention				perceived desirability			
	model 1 model only	model 2 with some controls	model 3 with all controls	model 4 with controls and CEM	model 1 model only	model 2 with some controls	model 3 with all controls	model 4 with controls and CEM
Personality dimensions								
extraversion			-0.006 (0.053)	0.029 (0.057)			-0.051 (0.046)	-0.013 (0.047)
agreeableness			-0.034 (0.071)	-0.043 (0.076)			-0.059 (0.066)	-0.098 (0.062)
conscientiousness			-0.081 (0.052)	-0.033 (0.053)			-0.073* (0.042)	-0.049 (0.043)
emotional stability			0.108** (0.050)	0.086 (0.053)			0.054 (0.043)	0.045 (0.043)
openness to experience			0.337*** (0.068)	0.333*** (0.069)			0.304*** (0.059)	0.286*** (0.056)
constant	3.528*** (0.158)	3.935*** (0.595)	2.490*** (0.766)	2.981*** (0.775)	3.825*** (0.123)	4.470*** (0.510)	3.593*** (0.673)	4.473*** (0.636)
Test statistics								
Observations	1,018	1,018	952	856	1,018	1,018	952	856
R-squared	0.022	0.156	0.196	0.197	0.016	0.128	0.171	0.182
F-test (df)	8.540(3)	24.75(8)	20.90(13)	16.11(13)	6.406(3)	18.94(8)	15.90(13)	14.60(13)
F-test sig	0.000	0.000	0.000	0.000	0.000	0.000	0.000	0.000

Notes: robust standard errors in parentheses; * significant at 10%; ** significant at 5%; *** significant at 1%

Table 5.3 (continued): Difference-in-Differences estimations using OLS (part 2)

Dependent variable	perceived social norms				perceived behavioral control			
	model 1 model only	model 2 with some controls	model 3 with all controls	model 4 with controls and CEM	model 1 model only	model 2 with some controls	model 3 with all controls	model 4 with controls and CEM
Model variables								
time dummy (ex-post = 1)	-0.368 (3.617)	-0.368 (3.462)	-1.535 (4.302)	-5.878 (4.465)	-0.064 (0.144)	-0.064 (0.134)	-0.035 (0.159)	-0.117 (0.156)
treatment dummy (treatment = 1)	9.804*** (2.874)	9.118*** (2.723)	3.459 (3.280)	3.116 (3.540)	0.188* (0.112)	0.178* (0.105)	0.101 (0.125)	0.033 (0.124)
β_DD	**3.442** **(4.183)**	**3.442** **(3.981)**	**4.610** **(4.702)**	**8.867*** **(4.883)**	**0.214** **(0.161)**	**0.214** **(0.151)**	**0.186** **(0.172)**	**0.270*** **(0.131)**
Demographic variables								
age		-0.074 (0.452)	0.028 (0.467)	-0.345 (0.444)		-0.015 (0.017)	-0.010 (0.017)	-0.020 (0.016)
female (0/1)		-11.232*** (1.748)	-11.31*** (1.934)	-11.192*** (2.033)		-0.470*** (0.062)	-0.504*** (0.062)	-0.531*** (0.071)
foreign (0/1)		7.064*** (2.445)	7.373*** (2.437)	8.768*** (2.946)		0.326*** (0.083)	0.347*** (0.084)	0.452*** (0.103)
Prior experiences								
breadth of prior exposure		8.045*** (0.864)	6.792*** (0.939)	7.078*** (1.001)		0.244*** (0.032)	0.190*** (0.035)	0.203*** (0.035)
attended entrepreneurship courses		0.024 (0.751)	2.383 (1.652)	-1.756 (4.028)		0.042 (0.036)	0.223*** (0.074)	0.137 (0.141)

Table 5.3 (continued): Difference-in-Differences estimations using OLS (part 2 continued)

Dependent variable	perceived social norms				perceived behavioral control			
	model 1 model only	model 2 with some controls	model 3 with all controls	model 4 with controls and CEM	model 1 model only	model 2 with some controls	model 3 with all controls	model 4 with controls and CEM
Personality dimensions								
extraversion			1.047 (0.873)	1.933** (0.921)			0.049 (0.033)	0.071** (0.032)
agreeableness			-0.230 (1.185)	-0.382 (1.234)			0.008 (0.053)	0.008 (0.043)
conscientiousness			-2.811*** (0.874)	-2.522*** (0.860)			0.039 (0.030)	0.046 (0.030)
emotional stability			2.244*** (0.843)	1.835** (0.856)			0.104*** (0.029)	0.098*** (0.030)
openness to experience			5.126*** (1.099)	4.741*** (1.117)			0.176*** (0.043)	0.176*** (0.039)
constant	-14.66*** (2.481)	-19.331** (9.779)	-41.603*** (12.792)	-34.274*** (12.61)	4.007*** (0.101)	4.181*** (0.366)	2.287*** (0.482)	2.458*** (0.442)
Test statistics								
Observations	1,018	1,018	952	856	1,018	1,018	952	856
R-squared	0.027	0.147	0.200	0.197	0.018	0.138	0.215	0.211
F-test (df)	10.73(3)	22.67(8)	19.92(13)	16.07(13)	5.799(3)	21.10(8)	22.33(13)	17.54(13)
F-test sig	0.000	0.000	0.000	0.000	0.001	0.000	0.000	0.000

Notes: robust standard errors in parentheses; * significant at 10%; ** significant at 5%; *** significant at 1%

Considering first models 1 only, the table tells that the difference-in-differences coefficients are reproduced compared to Table 5.2, however due to the additional controls the standard errors changed. In general, the significant treatment dummy in all model 1 regressions indicates that there are time-invariant differences in overall means between the groups. I now consider models 2 and 3 that contain control variables. Comparing the two models, the effects of the control variables remain largely robust under the inclusion of the personality dimensions. However, the coefficients on the difference-in-differences estimator remain insignificant. Models 4 control both for initial differences in background within and across groups, using the full set of available control variables and CEM. Comparing models 4 and 3, it seems that the size and nature of the effects are robust, with two exceptions: the coefficients of the difference-in-difference-estimators associated with the outcome-variables *perceived social norm* and *perceived behavioral control* are significant. They suggest an increase of 8.9 points (0.306 standard deviations with respect to the ex-ante distribution among the treated students) in *perceived social norm* and of 0.3 points (0.272 standard deviations) in *perceived behavioral control* as a consequence of attending the course.

Summing up the results of this subsection, I conclude that there is evidence for a positive average treatment effect of the course regarding perceived behavioral control and perceived social norm. I argue that students experience that they have increased knowledge about entrepreneurship and necessary skills to perform entrepreneurial roles after the course. This seems to be accompanied with an increase in perceived pressure to behave in an entrepreneurial way after the course, possibly due to feedback by important reference groups about the own performance during the course. On the other side, however, there is no indication that the course leads to an overall increase in the number of students who intend to start an own business. In the next subsection, I further explore the effects of the course by looking at the defined subsamples.

5.3.3 Difference-in-Difference-in-Differences

The goal here is to find out if the course had different effects on different subsamples. I will also interpret the results with respect to the findings in section 4.3. There I tested the hypotheses about relationships between background variables and entrepreneurial intentions. The findings there serve as "anchor", i.e. I am able to relate the effects on specific subsamples on the initial values of the entrepreneurial intentions of this subsample.

I will first elaborate more on the effects on entrepreneurial intentions. The reported results in Table 5.4 give an overview regarding the causal effects of the course on entrepreneurial intentions in each subsample. It tells the simple differences, DD type 1 and type 2 differences and also the difference-in-difference-in-differences estimates. The simple ex-post – ex-ante differences among the subsamples are in the first two lines of each "subsample-block", in column 4 for the treatment and column 8 for the control group. The value in the first line is the difference in entrepreneurial intentions among the group of students not exhibiting the respective background factor, in the second line the difference among the group of students who exhibit the background factor in question (e.g. -0.479 for female students in the treatment group).

The DD type 1 effects (i.e. the difference of the ex-post / ex-ante difference in means of the group who exhibit the factor and the group who do not) are in the same columns for treatment and control group in the third line of each "subsample-block" (e.g. the ex-post / ex-ante change of the mean entrepreneurial intentions on female vs. male students is -0.341).

DD type 2 effects (i.e. the difference of the ex-post / ex-ante difference in means among the subsample in the treatment compared to the same subsample in the control group) can be found in column 9 in the first two lines per "subsample" block (e.g. ex-post / ex-ante change of the mean entrepreneurial intentions on treated female students compared to the change in entrepreneurial intentions of untreated female students is -0.285).

Finally, the difference-in-difference-in-difference (DDD) estimates can be found in the third line in column 9 in every "subsample block". For example, the effect of the course on treated female students compared to treated male students and untreated female students is -0.192.

Considering column 4 (i.e. the DD type 1 effects), Table 5.4 informs that female students and students who have self-employed acquaintances alter their entrepreneurial intentions significantly in the negative direction (all else being equal). Oosterbeek et al. (2010) found the same effect for female students in their study. In section 4.3 I found that female students enter the course with lower entrepreneurial intentions than their male fellow students. Taking this finding into account, it seems that the career intentions of female students get more pronounced, in the sense that they probably got additional information through the course reinforcing them not to pursue an entrepreneurial career. On the other hand, students who already had attended another course before state that their entrepreneurial intentions changed positively during the course.

The difference-in-difference-in-differences approach promises more reliable results when analyzing variation in course-induced effects among subsamples. Table 5.5 presents the difference-in-difference-in-differences estimates (by estimating *Equation 5.6* with OLS) by subsamples and outcome variables. I only report the coefficients and robust standard errors of the regressions. The specifications of the models and the sets of control variables are the same as in Table 5.3. Complete regresseions are available from the author upon request.

First I consider demographic variables. The effect that female students experience a significant negative shift in entrepreneurial intentions as found using t-tests turns insignificant. Overall, the course does not seem to have a dedicated effect on demographically defined groups.

Table 5.4: t-tests for differences in entrepreneurial intentions by subsample

			Treatment group				Control group				Difference
			1	2	3	4	5	6	7	8	9
			sample size	ex-ante	ex-post	difference (3 - 4)	sample size	ex-ante	ex-post	difference (7 - 6)	difference (8 - 4)
demographics	female	no	188	4.537	4.399	-0.138	44	3.818	3.773	-0.045	-0.093
		yes	215	3.865	3.386	-0.479 ***	62	3.323	3.129	-0.194	-0.285
		difference (yes - no)	403	-0.672	-1.013	-0.341 **	106	-0.495	-0.644	-0.149	-0.192
	foreign	no	339	4.041	3.758	-0.283 ***	93	3.430	3.312	-0.118	-0.165
		yes	64	4.906	4.391	-0.515 ***	13	4.231	4.000	-0.231	-0.284
		difference (yes - no)	403	0.865	0.633	-0.232	106	0.801	0.688	-0.113	-0.119
prior experience	parents self-employed	no	210	3.824	3.433	-0.391 ***	53	3.151	3.000	-0.151	-0.240
		yes	193	4.565	4.321	-0.244 ***	53	3.906	3.792	-0.114	-0.130
		difference (yes - no)	403	0.741	0.888	0.147	106	0.755	0.792	0.037	0.110
	acquaintances self-employed	no	132	3.742	3.629	-0.113	45	3.444	3.444	0.000	-0.113
		yes	271	4.391	3.970	-0.421 ***	61	3.590	3.361	-0.229	-0.192
		difference (yes - no)	403	0.649	0.341	-0.308 **	106	0.146	-0.083	-0.229	-0.079

Notes: * significant at 10%; ** significant at 5%; *** significant at 1% (for two-tailed t-test); subsamples as defined by Table 3.13

Table 5.4 (continued): t-tests for differences in entrepreneurial intentions by subsample

			Treatment group				Control group				Difference
			1	2	3	4	5	6	7	8	9
			sample size	ex-ante	ex-post	difference (3 - 4)	sample size	ex-ante	ex-post	difference (7 - 6)	difference (8 - 4)
prior experience	worked for start-up	no	298	4.037	3.738	-0.299 ***	70	3.414	3.129	-0.285 *	-0.014
		yes	105	4.581	4.200	-0.381 **	36	3.829	3.971	0.142	-0.523 *
		difference (yes - no)	403	0.544	0.462	-0.082	106	0.415	0.842	0.427	-0.509
	entrepreneur	no	379	4.127	3.823	-0.304 ***	98	3.469	3.224	-0.245 *	-0.059
		yes	24	5.000	4.417	-0.583 *	8	4.250	5.500	1.250	-1.833 **
		difference (yes - no)	403	0.873	0.594	-0.279	106	0.781	2.276	1.495 **	-1.774
	attended course	no	385	4.187	3.834	-0.353 ***	95	3.400	3.295	-0.105	-0.248
		yes	18	4.000	4.389	0.389	11	4.636	4.273	-0.363	0.752 **
		difference (yes - no)	403	-0.187	0.555	0.742 **	106	1.236	0.978	-0.258	1.000
	high ECTS	no	181	4.348	4.133	-0.215 **		no data available			
		yes	222	4.041	3.635	-0.406 ***					
		difference (yes - no)	403	-0.307	-0.498	-0.191					

Notes: * significant at 10%; ** significant at 5%; *** significant at 1% (for two-tailed t-test); subsamples as defined by Table 3.13

Table 5.4 (continued): t-tests for differences in entrepreneurial intentions by subsample

			Treatment group				Control group				Difference
		1	2	3	4	5	6	7	8	9
		sample size	ex-ante	ex-post	difference (3 - 4)	sample size	ex-ante	ex-post	difference (7 - 6)	difference (8 - 4)
personality dimensions	extravert	no	165	3.915	3.661	-0.254 **	43	3.643	3.476	-0.167	-0.087
		yes	238	4.361	3.996	-0.365 ***	30	3.241	3.103	-0.138	-0.227
		difference (yes - no)	403	0.446	0.335	-0.111	73	-0.402	-0.373	0.029	-0.140
	agreeable	no	269	4.193	3.799	-0.394 ***	50	3.429	3.224	-0.205	-0.189
		yes	134	4.149	3.978	-0.171	23	3.591	3.545	-0.046	-0.125
		difference (yes - no)	403	-0.044	0.179	0.223	73	0.162	0.321	0.159	0.064
	conscientious	no	107	4.355	3.907	-0.448 ***	15	3.5	3.714	0.214	-0.662
		yes	296	4.115	3.841	-0.274 ***	58	3.474	3.228	-0.246	-0.028
		difference (yes - no)	403	-0.24	-0.066	0.174	73	-0.026	-0.486	-0.460	0.634
	emotionally stable	no	190	3.984	3.574	-0.41 ***	34	3.455	3.273	-0.182	-0.228
		yes	213	4.352	4.113	-0.239 **	39	3.500	3.368	-0.132	-0.107
		difference (yes - no)	403	0.368	0.539	0.171	73	0.045	0.095	0.050	0.121
	open to experience	no	102	3.755	3.373	-0.382 ***	28	3.296	3.259	-0.037	-0.345
		yes	301	4.322	4.023	-0.299 ***	45	3.591	3.364	-0.227	-0.072
		difference (yes - no)	403	0.567	0.65	0.083	73	0.295	0.105	-0.190	0.273

Notes: * significant at 10%; ** significant at 5%; *** significant at 1% (for two-tailed t-test); subsamples as defined by Table 3.13

Regarding the subsamples defined by the prior experiences-variables, students with self-employed parents seem to be affected by the course in two of the four outcome variables when looking at the CEM models. On average, perceptions of desirability and social norm of treated students with self-employed parents experience a stronger positive shift compared to their fellow students without a self-employed parent and to control group students with self-employed parents. Although the change in mean entrepreneurial intentions is insignificant for this subsample, it again seems that this group of students is receiving reinforcing information with respect to their career intentions: in section 4.3 I found that students with self-employed parents exhibit higher entrepreneurial intentions when entering the course compared to students without a self-employed parent. So I conclude that students with self-employed parents have more pronounced career intentions after the course than before, in the sense that they now even more pursue an entrepreneurial career. Students who have already attended an entrepreneurship course prior to "Business Planning" have experienced a stronger positive shift in perceived desirability compared to their fellow students who had not done so and the control group students who did so. At the time when the students entered the course, this background variable was not related to entrepreneurial intentions (see section 4.3). However, the relatively large shift in perceived desirability compared to other subsamples could indicate a certain openness of those students with respect to topics of entrepreneurship. The fact that they attended an entrepreneurship course prior to "Business Planning" could indicate a general interest in this topic and therefore they were probably more willing to exert effort and learn during the course. The effect on students who have already started an own business is rather surprising. They seem to lose their intent to found another start-up during the course. Even more surprising is the strong negative shift in perceived behavioral control. This argues for a decrease of perceptions of entrepreneurship-related skills among this subsample. It would be interesting to investigate if these students consider their started businesses as success or not. Lastly I look at subsamples defined by personality dimensions. The estimations do not suggest any dedicated effects of the course on any of these subsamples.

Table 5.5: Difference-in-difference-in-differences estimates using OLS and CEM (part 1)

dependent variable	entrepreneurial intentions			perceived desirability		
subsample-defining variable	some controls	all controls	with CEM	some controls	all controls	with CEM
demographic variables						
female (0/1)	-0.173 (0.515)	0.145 (0.623)	0.399 (0.610)	0.070 (0.422)	0.160 (0.511)	0.614 (0.502)
foreign (0/1)	-0.132 (0.759)	-0.125 (0.923)	-0.627 (0.886)	-0.323 (0.621)	0.029 (0.757)	-0.190 (0.728)
prior experiences						
parents self-employed (0/1)	0.087 (0.510)	0.075 (0.595)	0.597 (0.600)	0.486 (0.417)	0.527 (0.488)	**1.347*** (0.491)**
acquaintances self-employed (0/1)	-0.057 (0.521)	-0.187 (0.602)	0.153 (0.627)	0.204 (0.425)	0.395 (0.493)	0.693 (0.514)
worked for start-up (0/1)	-0.511 (0.549)	-0.768 (0.648)	-1.165 (0.738)	-0.216 (0.450)	-0.447 (0.532)	-0.396 (0.607)
entrepreneur (0/1)	**-1.788* (0.984)**	**-2.563** (1.282)**	**-2.939* (1.680)**	-0.170 (0.806)	0.216 (1.049)	-1.011 (1.374)
already attended course (0/1)	0.989 (0.929)	1.272 (1.028)	1.204 (1.079)	**1.258* (0.760)**	**1.618* (0.844)**	**1.830** (0.885)**
personality dimensions						
extravert (0/1)	-	-0.140 (0.604)	0.391 (0.616)	-	0.109 (0.495)	0.483 (0.505)
agreeable (0/1)	-	0.064 (0.641)	-0.027 (0.614)	-	-0.126 (0.527)	-0.351 (0.505)
conscientious (0/1)	-	0.635 (0.738)	0.915 (0.724)	-	-0.052 (0.604)	0.327 (0.594)
emotionally stable (0/1)	-	0.121 (0.597)	0.439 (0.603)	-	-0.344 (0.489)	0.349 (0.494)
open to experience (0/1)	-	0.274 (0.628)	0.522 (0.629)	-	0.307 (0.515)	0.470 (0.515)
Observations	1,018	952	865	1,018	952	865

Notes: subsamples as defined by Table 13.3; coefficients obtained by different OLS regressions; full models are available from the author upon request; the "some controls" models include *age, female (0/1), foreign (0/1), breadth of prior exposure*, and *attended entrepreneurship courses*; the "all controls" models additionally include the Big5 personality dimensions;
robust standard errors in parentheses; * significant at 10%; ** significant at 5%; *** significant at 1%

Table 5.5: Difference-in-difference-in-differences estimates using OLS and CEM (part 2)

dependent variable	perceived social norm			perceived behavioral control		
subsample-defining variable	some controls	all controls	with CEM	some controls	all controls	with CEM
demographic variables						
female (0/1)	4.029 (8.510)	3.686 (10.145)	9.281 (9.967)	0.132 (0.304)	0.165 (0.356)	0.181 (0.349)
foreign (0/1)	5.977 (12.534)	4.247 (14.999)	-3.112 (14.445)	0.387 (0.446)	0.561 (0.523)	0.498 (0.504)
prior experiences						
parents self-employed (0/1)	8.366 (8.415)	9.623 (9.665)	**20.970** (9.750)**	0.371 (0.300)	0.328 (0.338)	0.442 (0.343)
acquaintances self-employed (0/1)	1.309 (8.580)	1.014 (9.763)	6.870 (10.202)	-0.037 (0.307)	-0.128 (0.343)	-0.060 (0.359)
worked for start-up (0/1)	-2.613 (9.074)	-0.354 (10.540)	-0.175 (12.032)	-0.147 (0.323)	-0.297 (0.369)	-0.128 (0.423)
entrepreneur (0/1)	10.691 (16.283)	7.618 (20.854)	9.969 (27.366)	-0.410 (0.581)	-1.004 (0.731)	**-1.622* (0.960)**
already attended course (0/1)	13.098 (15.352)	13.732 (16.760)	24.593 (17.563)	0.542 (0.547)	0.399 (0.588)	0.777 (0.617)
personality dimensions						
extravert (0/1)	-	6.279 (9.842)	12.074 (10.040)	-	-0.009 (0.345)	0.082 (0.350)
agreeable (0/1)	-	-1.703 (10.425)	-3.525 (10.003)	-	-0.168 (0.365)	-0.331 (0.351)
conscientious (0/1)	-	-3.780 (11.982)	6.194 (11.808)	-	0.208 (0.419)	0.024 (0.414)
emotionally stable (0/1)	-	5.315 (9.718)	13.494 (9.826)	-	0.027 (0.341)	0.138 (0.346)
open to experience (0/1)	-	1.146 (10.210)	2.159 (10.244)	-	-0.128 (0.358)	-0.097 (0.360)
Observations	1,018	952	865	1,018	952	865

Notes: subsamples as defined by Table 13.3; coefficients obtained by different OLS regressions; full models are available from the author upon request; the "some controls" models include *age, female (0/1), foreign (0/1), breadth of prior exposure*, and *attended entrepreneurship courses*; the "all controls" models additionally include the Big5 personality dimensions;
robust standard errors in parentheses; * significant at 10%; ** significant at 5%; *** significant at 1%

5.4 Conclusion

I posed two research questions in this chapter: What is the size and nature of the course-induced effects on mean entrepreneurial attitudes and intentions? And do these effects appeal to some subsamples of students, defined by demographic variables, prior experiences, or personality dimensions, more than to others? To address these questions, I employed a quasi-experimental design, applying difference-in-differences to elicit the course-induced effects on mean entrepreneurial intentions and attitudes. Moreover, I used a difference-in-difference-in-differences framework to explore whether some subsamples of students do respond more to course-induced stimuli than others.

With respect to the first question, the results show that the post-course mean values of perceived social norm and perceived behavioral control are increased compared to the pre-course ones. However, mean entrepreneurial intentions at the end of the course are not significantly different from those at the beginning of the course. The significant increase in perceived social norm could reflect the creation of a new group of entrepreneurially minded acquaintances from the course (especially, as students did not self-select into the business planning teams, but were exogenously scheduled by faculty, and thus did not work together with already existing friends). As argued in subsection 2.5.1, perceived behavioral control is affected by course components focusing on the skills needed by an entrepreneur. The significant increase in this attitude may reflect the emphasis on the "learning-by-doing" component of the course "Business Planning". According to social learning theory (Bandura 1977, 1982), mastery experience as conveyed by this course component is the most powerful factor in shaping one's skills. Thus, "Business Planning" successfully conveys the skills needed to act entrepreneurially. On the other hand, the mean perceived desirability and mean entrepreneurial intentions are not significantly different after the course when compared to before. Especially the insignificant effect on intentions is somewhat disappointing at first sight, as the ultimate hope of many fund providers for entrepreneurship education is to increase the number of nascent entrepreneurs. But this does not have to be detrimental. On the one hand, small differences in the mean do not imply that there is no change in intentions at all. Overall, diametrical changes might cancel each other out, and another approach is needed to break these changes down to a more individual level to register them. On the other hand, together with the increase in perceived behavioral control, this suggests that the course does probably not produce more, but "better" entrepreneurs. Other students not striving for an entrepreneurial career might be more open for entrepreneurial thinking in organizations. Chapter 6 will provide more insight on this thought.

Regarding the second research question posed in this chapter, the findings suggest that entrepreneurship education has indeed not the same effects on all students as hypothesized by Franke and Lüthje (2004). According to the results, three subsamples of students are affected by the course: students who have self-employed parents, students who have started a business before, and students who have already attended an entrepreneurship course. The first subsample experiences positive changes in perceived desirability and perceived social norm, and the last one in perceived desirability. A possible explanation is that these students are open to learning about entrepreneurship due to previous impressions. Students who have already started a business, on the other hand, are affected differently and counter intuitively. Their intentions and their behavioral control decrease during the course. Maybe they do not intend to start another business, and somewhat lose their confidence in their skills because they are managing their business differently than proposed in the course or by the cooperating entrepreneur.

The findings have several implications for the design of entrepreneurship education. Taking the course "Business Planning" as a blueprint, a course planner can achieve an increase in mean perceptions of social norm and behavioral control. This argues for implementing teamwork and tutoring. Feedback by both team members and tutors probably affects social norm. Allowing more room for more extensive feedback promises positive effects. The positive effect on behavioral control proposes that students profit from being exposed to a "real-world" entrepreneurial project in the cooperation with a founder. According to previous arguments, entrepreneurship education should fulfill a function of skill-building for entrepreneurial tasks, regardless if in an own business or as an employee in an organization. Therefore, based on these results, entrepreneurship courses should contain learning-by-doing elements such as writing a business plan, pitching in front of investors, running start-up simulations or even setting up a small company.

The results, regarding the different effects on various subsamples of students, have implications for student admission to an entrepreneurship course. Due to restricted budgets course planners may face the challenge to select students for limited seminar places. According to the results – and taking "Business Planning" as a blueprint for entrepreneurship courses – three subsamples are significantly affected by the course: students with self-employed parents, students who already have started a business and students who have attended entrepreneurship courses before. As these subsamples seem to most likely respond to course-induced stimuli, these should be preferred with respect to selection. However, if the goal of the course is to increase overall entrepreneurial intentions and thus the number of nascent entrepreneurs, course planners should abstain from admitting students who already have started a business. The chapter has also implications for further research on the effects of entrepreneurship education. It provides methodological extensions of the basic difference-in-differences framework, delivering more robust estimations of the effects on mean entrepreneurial intentions and attitudes, and additional insight in the effects on entrepreneurship education on differently framed students. Future studies may follow this methodological approach and apply it to other student samples and course concepts to further validate and generalize the results.

6. A Bayesian Updating Approach to Evaluate Entrepreneurship Education

6.1 Introduction

In their recent study, employing a new approach to evaluate entrepreneurship education based on Bayesian Updating, Graevenitz et al. (2010) show that attending an entrepreneurship course helps students to find out about their entrepreneurial aptitude and supports them to better self-select into entrepreneurs and non-entrepreneurs. Although the overall intention to start a business decline during the course, students have stronger opinions about which career path, entrepreneur or not, suits them better. Depending on what they learn, students may adjust their opinions about their entrepreneurial aptitude upwards or downwards. This view of entrepreneurship education significantly differs from the notion in the literature. All of the studies presented in subsection 1.2.3 hypothesize a positive effect of entrepreneurship education on entrepreneurial attitudes and intentions. This misses the sorting – i.e. learning – benefits highlighted in von Graevenitz et al. (2010) and in this chapter.

This chapter tries to contribute to this new approach in the literature of the evaluation of entrepreneurship education. First, I build on the aforementioned Bayesian Updating-model introduced by von Graevenitz et al. (2010). It emphasizes the sorting effects, i.e. the discovery of one's own aptitude for entrepreneurship, as a goal of this type of course. Accordingly, an entrepreneurship course helps students to update their opinions about their entrepreneurial aptitude and can thus better self-select into an entrepreneurial or non-entrepreneurial career. Accordingly, mean entrepreneurial intentions will not change by much. Instead, career intentions become more "extreme", either in favor of an entrepreneurial or an employee-career. These separation effects may be responsible for the insignificant effect on mean entrepreneurial intentions found in chapter 5, as these changes would cancel each other out. I will test this model with the dataset described in section 3.5.[46] This test will be based on data on both the treated and the untreated students and thus extends the approach proposed by von Graevenitz et al. (2010), where we did not employ control group data. Moreover, this chapter extends the framework and integrates it with the Theory of Planned Behavior in order to better understand the updating processes. The combination of both, Bayesian Updating and the Theory of Planned Behavior, allows determining via which paths (perceived desirability, perceived social norm and perceived behavioral control) entrepreneurship education drives the updating of one's opinion. This in turn promises to deliver insights into how an entrepreneurship course should be designed which is meant to inform students about the career path they are most suited for. In addition, motivated by the results found in chapter 5, I also investigate whether certain subsamples of students are more receptive to informative signals provided during the course. Some students may be more likely to process the information and update their opinion about their entrepreneurial aptitude.

Although the sorting-effects of entrepreneurship education have been ignored in the previous literature, one does indeed find arguments backing this view of the goals of entrepreneurship education. A closer look at the classification and goals of entrepreneurship education (see subsection 1.2.2) reveals that it is not about "producing" entrepreneurs, but about providing them information about the option of pursuing an entrepreneurial career. That can also mean that overall entrepreneurial intentions can decline. For example, students learn that the average lifetime income of an entrepreneur is significantly below that one of an employee (Hamilton 2000) or that entrepreneurs work longer (Shelton 2006). As argued in section 2.5, the information received during the entrepreneurship course leads to an adjustment of behavioral, normative and control beliefs. One also has to take the audience into consideration. Undergraduate students, who mostly attend entrepreneurship courses, are typically younger and less experienced than graduate students. These students are largely naïve regarding entre-

---

[46] Note that in von Graevenitz et al. (2010) we used the 2008 cohort of the treatment group to test the proposed model. Now I will test the model with both cohorts.

preneurial processes (Cox et al. 2002). In the aforementioned studies, students are assumed to face no uncertainty regarding their own skills and interests when beginning an entrepreneurship course, while the process of learning itself is hardly modeled. I argue that researchers should not evaluate courses in terms of positive changes of attitudes or intentions or even in terms of created start-ups. The perspective taken in this chapter proposes to measure its effects differently. Researcher should investigate whether students, who were undecided about their future career before the course, had more decisive career intentions after the course, regardless of the direction they might choose, i.e. to become an entrepreneur or an employee. Entrepreneurship education is about educating better entrepreneurs, and not about convincing students to become entrepreneurs. It is about discovering one's own aptitude for entrepreneurship and thus about getting the skills to consciously decide for or against an entrepreneurial career.

The model presented in this chapter offers a new approach on how one should interpret the contradictory effects of previous studies on the effects of entrepreneurship education (see subsection 1.2.3). A decline in the overall entrepreneurial intentions after an entrepreneurship education course is not a detrimental effect. For example, a student who has learned that he would probably not be a good entrepreneur may now decide to enter a managerial career instead of performing a possibly costly "experiment" of starting a firm and failing the task (von Graevenitz et al. 2010). This should be considered a positive outcome, while most of the current literature (and many policy-makers) would proclaim it a case of failure.Shane (2009) argued that the typical start-up is not innovative, creates few jobs and generates little wealth. According to Shane, getting economic growth and job creation from entrepreneurs is not a numbers game, but it is about encouraging the formation of high quality companies. So maybe – to reach these mentioned ultimate goals – entrepreneurship education should not be about just getting more entrepreneurs, but about educating students to be more conscious and better entrepreneurs (or managers).

This chapter contains four sections. In the next section I present a theoretical model to measure the impact of entrepreneurship education based on Bayes' Rule and the Theory of Planned Behavior. Section three provides descriptive analysis backing the model and the empirical test of the predictions of the outlined model. Section four concludes and discusses further research.

6.2 Integrating the Theory of Planned Behavior with a Model of Learning

In this chapter the Theory of Planned Behavior is used as one half of a theoretical framework to analyze the effects of a university entrepreneurship course on students' entrepreneurial intentions. Such an intervention requires an evaluative response. People draw on relevant information, or beliefs, stored in memories, and then again form behavioral (perceived desirability), normative (perceived social norm) and control beliefs (perceived behavioral control) regarding entrepreneurship. The re-formation of attitudes in turn provides signals leading students to update their opinion about their own entrepreneurial aptitude (see also section 2.5).

In the case of entrepreneurship education, it is often hypothesized that this learning manifests itself in a uniform positive shift in attitudes and intentions.[47] In this chapter, I argue that learning in an entrepreneurship course is about discovering one's aptitude for entrepreneurship, which results either in updating one's opinion about entrepreneurial aptitude upwards, or downwards. Thus a closer look at the distribution of entrepreneurial intentions before and after the course promises valuable insights. If, for example, the average entrepreneurial intentions after the course are unchanged, but one can observe a greater polarization of intentions, one may declare the course a success. It separated more clearly the students who really want to pursue an entrepreneurial career from those who processed the new information and do not want to become entrepreneurs. With other words: discovering no significant differences in the average entrepreneurial intentions does not mean that – on an individual basis – students did not change their intention. It could be the case that these

---

[47] This hypothesis can be best tested by adopting a difference-in-differences approach used in chapter 5 of this book.

changes just cancel each other out. This aspect was completely ignored in the previous literature.

In the literature one does find some evidence backing this point of view. Liñán (2004) argues that the degree of realism in the perceptions has to be taken into account, and that specific knowledge – conveyed through an entrepreneurship course – would help to increase the realism of perceptions (and not just increase the perceived desirability or feasibility of starting a business). Ajzen (2002) stated that some people may have a wrong impression of their own capacity to carry out a behavior, which could be remedied through educational experiences. In this section, I present a model of Bayesian Updating, modeling the above-defined learning effects emanating from entrepreneurship education.

6.2.1 Updating Opinions of Entrepreneurial Aptitude through Entrepreneurship Education

Entrepreneurship education conveys knowledge and skills meant to reduce the cost of becoming an entrepreneur. However, there are generic components in the pedagogical approaches (e.g. knowing how to write a business plan is also helpful in established corporations). From this point of view, entrepreneurship education will not influence entrepreneurial intentions by much. However, according to the Theory of Planned Behavior, where such an intervention also affects behavioral, normative and control beliefs, it may affect intentions, and so downstream action.[48] Moreover, entrepreneurship education allows students to engage in entrepreneurial activity in an experimental setting, e.g. in start-up simulations or in real-life projects, which might help reduce their uncertainty about choosing an entrepreneurial career. The most important effect of entrepreneurship education may so lie in discovering – learning – about one's own aptitude for entrepreneurship.

---

[48] See subsection 2.5.1 for a more detailed discussion of how entrepreneurship education may affect behavioral, normative, and control beliefs.

Minniti and Bygrave (2001) stated, "(...) entrepreneurship is a process of learning, and a theory of entrepreneurship requires a theory of learning" (p. 7). And further, "entrepreneurs learn by updating a subjective stock of knowledge accumulated on the basis of past experiences" (p. 5). Together with Ajzen's (2002) and Liñán's (2004) assertions that learning increases the realism of perceptions of entrepreneurial attitudes, that means that an entrepreneurship course helps students to find out – or learn – about their true career intentions.

The theoretical learning framework I employ in this chapter has already been modeled in von Graevenitz et al. (2010). Learning about one's entrepreneurial aptitude – and thus about one's true career intentions – is seen as a process of Bayesian Updating based on signals generated before and during an entrepreneurship education course. These signals affect students' discovery of their aptitude for entrepreneurship. In this chapter I build on this model and extend it along the Theory of Planned Behavior: I argue that an entrepreneurship course provides informative signals along all three paths of the Theory of Planned Behavior. Students process information acquired during the course and change their behavioral, normative, and control beliefs. Based on these newly formed beliefs the students update their opinion about their career intentions towards their "true" career intentions.

Combining the Bayesian Updating approach with the Theory of Planned Behavior promises valuable insights whether it is the change of behavioral, normative, or control (or a combination of these) beliefs that leads students to update their opinion about their entrepreneurial aptitude either upwards or downwards. This would give hints how entrepreneurship courses have to be designed that are meant to increase the polarization in entrepreneurial intentions. Those courses would help students to better find out about their entrepreneurial aptitude and reduce the number of students who are unsure about their career intentions after the course.

So, in contrast to the previous literature on the evaluation of entrepreneurship education (and also to chapter 5), where only uniform shifts in entrepreneurial attitudes and intentions were of interest, I here focus on characterizing the distribution of entrepreneurial intentions before and after the course.

6.2.2 Assumptions

Here I review the most important aspects of the model presented in the paper I wrote with Georg von Graevenitz and Dietmar Harhoff (2010) and refer to this paper for more detailed specifications and the formal model itself. The model shows how informative signals generated before and during an entrepreneurship course affect the opinion about career intentions. Students can then better judge – or learn about – their own entrepreneurial aptitude, which manifests itself in stronger or weaker entrepreneurial intentions. This learning about one's own aptitude is modeled as a process of Bayesian Updating.

In the course of their lives the students may receive conflicting signals about their own entrepreneurial aptitude, and different students possibly receive signals of different quality (the results regarding different subsamples in subsection 5.2.3 give an indication for that). Assuming that a behavioral intervention like an entrepreneurship course can also generate informative signals (see section 2.5 for a theoretical discussion on this topic), there are three groups of students at the end of the course:

- those who learned nothing and know as much as before about their own entrepreneurial aptitude and therefore do not change their career intentions,
- students who received informative signals affecting their behavioral, normative and control beliefs and discover they like to be entrepreneurs,
- and students who receive signals affecting their beliefs and find out that they do not want to be entrepreneurs.

Through the data given in the questionnaires I can characterize the signals the students received before and during the course. This allows me to tell how sure a student is about his career intentions. A weak signal is equivalent to a signal that leaves the student unsure about his aptitude. The test for learning is executed by exploiting variation in the strength of signals students receive. The model focuses on consequences of such variation in signal strength.

The model assumes that there are two types of students: entrepreneurs (n) and employees (m). Being an entrepreneur means that one's own utility function from being in an entrepreneurial position is greater than the utility from being in an employee position. The starting point is the assumption that the students know that these two types exist, but are not certain about their own type, i.e. their "true" career intentions. However, they know the proportion of entrepreneurs in the population ϕ. Hence their prior of the probability that they are an entrepreneur is ϕ.

The students receive two independent signals about their aptitude for entrepreneurship: one in their pre-university life (period 1), and one during the entrepreneurship course (period 2). Students receive two signals, σ_1 in period 1 and σ_2 in period 2. Furthermore we distinguish between signals that entrepreneurs receive σ^n and signals employees receive σ^m.

The students' opinions about their career intentions are distributed on the interval [0,1]. An intention of 0 means that a student believes that he is an employee (i.e. he will pursue a career as employee), an intention of 1 means that he believes that he is an entrepreneur (i.e. he will pursue an entrepreneurial career).

Each type of student receives a positive signal of high entrepreneurial aptitude in each period with probability ψ^k where $\psi \in [0,1]$ and $k \in \{n, m\}$. Let $\varsigma_i, i \in \{1,2\}$ denote the precision of those positive signals. We made some simplifying assumptions about the signals the students receive.

a) Students are either entrepreneurs or employees.
b) The signaling process is informative. This assumption has two components:
   - the probability that entrepreneur-type students receive a positive signal that they are entrepreneurs is greater than the probability that employee-type students receive such a signal, and
   - signals always contain some information.

Now define the strength of signals that a student receives as

$$\sigma_i^n := \psi^n \cdot \varsigma_i, \qquad \sigma_i^m := \psi^m \cdot (1 - \varsigma_i)$$

Then signals will be informative ($\sigma_i^n > \sigma_i^m$), if $\varsigma_i > \frac{\psi^m}{\psi^m + \psi^n}$.

c) Finally, we assume that the students update their career intentions according to Bayes' Rule.

The assumption that signals are informative implies that the entrepreneurial intentions of an entrepreneur-type student will not decline if he receives a positive signal of entrepreneurial aptitude σ_i^n. An increase in the precision of signals simultaneously improves the strength of a positive signal received by entrepreneur-type students and reduces the strength of this signal as received by employee-type students. This implies that students who receive a "correct" signal about their type will revise their opinion about their career intentions more as the precision of the signal increases.

6.2.3 Definitions

In the course of their life, before entering the entrepreneurship course, the students receive a first signal about their entrepreneurial aptitude. This signal will differ according to the respective type of the student.

Career intentions after period 1

By Bayes' Rule the strength of the opinion of entrepreneur-type students that they are entrepreneurs after period one is

$$I_n^n = \frac{\sigma_1^n \phi}{\sigma_1^n \phi + \sigma_1^m (1 - \phi)} \quad \text{and} \quad I_m^n = \frac{(1 - \sigma_1^n)\phi}{(1 - \sigma_1^n)\phi + (1 - \sigma_1^m)(1 - \phi)}$$

where I_n^n is the strength of the pre-course opinion of entrepreneurs that they are entrepreneurs if they receive a positive signal, and I_m^n the strength of the pre-course opinion of entrepreneurs that they entrepreneurs if they receive a negative signal. Thus the period 1 signal divides the group of entrepreneur-type students in two sets. The first set is the group of entrepreneur-type students who believe more firmly that they are entrepreneurs (I_n^n), and the second set is the group of those entrepreneur-type students who no longer strongly believe that they are entrepreneurs (I_m^n). Given these definitions, the strength of the opinion employee-type students that they are employees after period one can be written as

$$I_n^m = 1 - I_n^n \quad and \quad I_m^m = 1 - I_m^n$$

As above the group of employee-type students is divided in two sets after reception of the period 1 signal: the group of employee-type students who believe more firmly that they are employees (I_m^m) and the group of employee-type students who no longer strongly believe that they are employees (I_n^m).

Career intentions after period 2

Applying Bayes' Rule once more, the strength of the opinion of entrepreneur-type students that they are entrepreneurs after period 2 (i.e. after the course) is given by

$$I_{n|n}^n = \frac{\sigma_2^n I_n^n}{\sigma_2^n I_n^n + \sigma_2^m I_n^m} \quad and \quad I_{n|m}^n = \frac{\sigma_2^n I_m^n}{\sigma_2^n I_m^n + \sigma_2^m I_m^m}$$

$$I_{m|n}^n = \frac{(1-\sigma_2^n) I_n^n}{(1-\sigma_2^n) I_n^n + (1-\sigma_2^m) I_n^m} \quad and \quad I_{m|m}^n = \frac{(1-\sigma_2^n) I_m^n}{(1-\sigma_2^n) I_m^n + (1-\sigma_2^m) I_m^m}$$

where $I_{n|n}^n$ is the strength of the opinion of entrepreneur-type students that they are entrepreneurs after receiving a period 2-signal that they are *entrepreneurs* and a period 1-signal that they are entrepreneurs. $I_{m|n}^n$ is the strength of entrepreneur-type students' opinion that they are entrepreneurs after receiving a period 2-signal that they are *employees* and a period 1-signal that they are entrepreneurs. The definitions for $I_{n|m}^n$ and $I_{m|m}^n$ are straightforward, analogous to the ones above. Thus after the course there are four groups of entrepreneur-type students having different strengths of their opinions about their entrepreneurial aptitude. This level of strength of the opinion is a function of the history of signals that students have received. There are two groups of entrepreneur-type students who have received signals going in the same direction (i.e. consistent signals) and now have the strongest ($I_{n|n}^n$) and the weakest ($I_{m|m}^n$) opinions that they are entrepreneurs. These two groups have reinforced their career intentions based on the received signals. The other two groups, in contrast, have received countervailing signals. Students in these groups update their opinion about their entrepreneurial aptitude upwards ($I_{n|m}^n$) and downwards ($I_{m|n}^n$) in period 2 (compared to period 1). Analogously there are four groups of employee-type students with different levels of information about their true career intention after the course:

$$I_{n|n}^m = 1 - I_{n|n}^n, \quad I_{n|m}^m = 1 - I_{n|m}^n, \quad I_{m|n}^m = 1 - I_{m|n}^n, \quad and \quad I_{m|m}^m = 1 - I_{m|m}^n$$

First, there are the employee-type students having received two consistent signals. They now have the strongest ($I_{m|m}^m$) and weakest ($I_{n|n}^m$) opinion that they are employees. Also, those employee-type students having received countervailing signals updated their opinion that they are entrepreneurs upwards ($I_{n|m}^m$) and downwards ($I_{m|n}^m$) in period 2 (compared to period 1).

Von Graevenitz et al. (2010) show that students' opinions about their entrepreneurial aptitude display a higher variance after the course, if uncertainty about true career intentions is sufficiently high before the course and if the course provided informative signals.

Next we show that a course that provides informative signals has two main effects: first it will leave students who receive consistent signals in period 1 and 2 with stronger opinions about their entrepreneurial aptitude than students who receive countervailing signals. Second, it will leave students who received stronger period 1-signals with stronger opinions about their entrepreneurial aptitude.

And finally we show that an entrepreneurship course that provides informative signals will change the participants' opinions about entrepreneurial aptitude less the stronger the period 1-signal is that they received, if the signals are consistent and sufficiently precise.

I use the theoretical model provided in von Graevenitz et al. (2010) and provide only the derived hypothesis in the next paragraph. For proofs of the propositions I refer to this article.

6.2.3.1 Opinions of Entrepreneurial Aptitude after Entrepreneurship Education

I begin with the most obvious implication of updating: if there are entrepreneurs and employees in the population of students, if these all receive informative signals, if entrepreneurs' period 1-signals that they are entrepreneurs are not too strong and if students update their opinion about their entrepreneurial intentions according to Bayes' Rule, then one can show that

Proposition 6.1
The distribution of opinions about entrepreneurial aptitude after the course will have greater variance than the distribution of opinions about entrepreneurial aptitude before, if signals before are not too strong and if signals are informative.

A course that provides informative signals will raise the number of students who have learned something about their aptitude for entrepreneurship, and will therefore increase sorting of students into two groups who are increasingly (not absolutely!) sure that they are entrepreneurs or not. The following hypothesis is tested in section three of this chapter:

Hypothesis 6.1
The variance of entrepreneurial intentions after the course is greater than the variance of entrepreneurial intentions before the course.

Further consider the period 1-signals effects on the period 2-opinions of entrepreneurs and employees. If signals are consistent, and the stronger the period 1-

signal is, the stronger are the opinions about entrepreneurial aptitude after the course.

Proposition 6.2
If the two signals received by students are consistent, then the opinion about entrepreneurial aptitude after the course will be stronger than if signals are inconsistent.
Stronger pre-course signals lead to stronger opinions after the course.

Note that opinions after the course will also be stronger for those students who receive conflicting signals. In section 6.3 the following hypotheses is tested:

Hypothesis 6.2
    i)   *If signals are consistent, then career intentions after the course are stronger.*
    ii)   *Stronger pre-course signals lead to stronger career intentions after the course.*

Hypothesis 6.2 i) a/b/c
If signals in the perceived desirability / perceived social norm / perceived behavioral control − path are consistent, then career intentions after the course are stronger.
Hypothesis 6.2 ii) a/b/c
Stronger pre-course signals in the perceived desirability / perceived social norm / perceived behavioral control − path lead to stronger career intentions after the course.

To test this hypothesis, a measure of strength of (the students' opinion about) career intentions is regressed on a measure of **S**trong **F**irst **P**eriod **S**ignals in each dimension of the Theory of Planned Behavior ($SFPS_{PD,PSN,PBC}$) and of **C**onsistent **S**ignals ($CS_{PD,PSN,PBC}$). The dependent variable is defined such that stronger career intentions increase the level of the dependent variable. The empirical model is

$$\bar{I} = \beta_0$$
$$+ \beta_1 SFPS_{PD} + \beta_2 CS_{PD} + \beta_3 CSX_{PD}$$
$$+ \beta_4 SFPS_{PSN} + \beta_5 CS_{PSN} + \beta_6 CSX_{PSN}$$
$$+ \beta_7 SFPS_{PBC} + \beta_8 CS_{PBC} + \beta_9 CSX_{PBC}$$
$$+ \beta'_{10} X + \varepsilon$$

Equation 6.1: Estimation equation of ex-post strength career intentions

where $\bar{I}$ captures the strength of students' career intentions after the course, $SFPS_*$ is a measure of strength of the period 1 signals, CS_* is a measure of consistent signals, and CSX_* is the interaction of the latter two variables. X is a vector of control variables. Hypothesis 6.2 predicts that $\beta_i > 0, i = 1,2,4,5,7,8$.

As a robustness-check, I will also estimate *Equation 6.1* after introducing interaction terms with a treatment dummy to control for signals that the students in the control group have received in periods 1 and 2. Hence, the extended empirical model is

$$\bar{I} = \beta_0$$
$$+ \beta_1 SFPS_{PD} + \beta_2 CS_{PD} + \beta_3 CSX_{PD}$$
$$+ \beta_4 SFPS_{PSN} + \beta_5 CS_{PSN} + \beta_6 CSX_{PSN}$$
$$+ \beta_7 SFPS_{PBC} + \beta_8 CS_{PBC} + \beta_9 CSX_{PBC}$$
$$+ \beta_{10} SFPS^T{}_{PD} + \beta_{11} CS^T{}_{PD} + \beta_{12} CSX^T{}_{PD}$$
$$+ \beta_{13} SFPS^T{}_{PSN} + \beta_{14} CS^T{}_{PSN} + \beta_{15} CSX^T{}_{PSN}$$
$$+ \beta_{16} SFPS^T{}_{PBC} + \beta_{17} CS^T{}_{PBC} + \beta_{18} CSX^T{}_{PBC}$$
$$+ \beta_{19} T + \beta'_{20} X + \varepsilon$$

Equation 6.2: Ext. estimation equation of ex-post strength career intentions

where the superscript T stands for the interaction of the respective variable with the treatment-dummy *treatment (0/1)*. Here, hypothesis 6.2 predicts that $\beta_i > 0, i = 10,11,13,14,16,17$.

6.2.3.2 The Change in Opinions about Entrepreneurial Aptitude after Entrepreneurship Education

In addition to the assumption above, that signals are informative, it is assumed here that the signaling process is reliable, i.e. students have a probability greater than ½ of receiving the correct signal for their type. Under these assumptions another proposition was proved in Graevenitz et al. (2010).

Proposition 6.3
If students receive sufficiently precise and reliable period 1-signals then those who receive consistent signals will update their opinion about their entrepreneurial aptitude less as period 1-signals become stronger.

Due to the additional assumption, Proposition 6.3 is weaker than Proposition 6.2. The corresponding hypothesis is:

Hypothesis 6.3
If students receive consistent signals, then those among them who have received stronger signals before the course will change their career intentions less.

To test this hypothesis, the absolute change[49] in career intentions due to the course is regressed on a measure of the strength of the period 1-signals and of consistent signals. The empirical model is

$$\overline{\Delta} = \gamma_0$$
$$+ \gamma_1 SFPS_{PD} + \gamma_2 CS_{PD} + \gamma_3 CSX_{PD}$$
$$+ \gamma_4 SFPS_{PSN} + \gamma_5 CS_{PSN} + \gamma_6 CSX_{PSN}$$
$$+ \gamma_7 SFPS_{PBC} + \gamma_8 CS_{PBC} + \gamma_9 CSX_{PBC}$$
$$+ \gamma'_{10} X + \varepsilon$$

Equation 6.3: Estimation equation of change of career intentions

---

[49] I will square the differences in intentions to capture that.

where $\overline{\Delta} = \Delta^2$ captures the absolute change in students' career intentions, the remaining variables defined as above. Hypothesis 6.3 predicts that $\gamma_i < 0, i = 3,6,9$.

As before, I also estimate the extended model introducing interaction terms with the treatment dummy. The extended empirical models is therefore

$$\overline{\Delta} = \gamma_0$$
$$+ \gamma_1 SFPS_{PD} + \gamma_2 CS_{PD} + \gamma_3 CSX_{PD}$$
$$+ \gamma_4 SFPS_{PSN} + \gamma_5 CS_{PSN} + \gamma_6 CSX_{PSN}$$
$$+ \gamma_7 SFPS_{PBC} + \gamma_8 CS_{PBC} + \gamma_9 CSX_{PBC}$$
$$+ \gamma_{10} SFPS^T{}_{PD} + \gamma_{11} CS^T{}_{PD} + \gamma_{12} CSX^T{}_{PD}$$
$$+ \gamma_{13} SFPS^T{}_{PSN} + \gamma_{14} CS^T{}_{PSN} + \gamma_{15} CSX^T{}_{PSN}$$
$$+ \gamma_{16} SFPS^T{}_{PBC} + \gamma_{17} CS^T{}_{PBC} + \gamma_{18} CSX^T{}_{PBC}$$
$$+ \gamma_{19} T + \gamma'_{20} X + \varepsilon$$

Equation 6.4: Extended estimation equation of change of career intentions

where again the superscript T stands for the interaction of the respective variable with the treatment-dummy T, which is 1 if the students attended the course and 0 if the students are in the control group. Hypothesis 6.3 predicts that $\gamma_i < 0, i = 12,15,18$.

6.3 Empirical Analysis

This section presents the description of dependent and explanatory variables, descriptive statistics, and hypotheses-tests. As a further extension of the analysis in von Graevenitz et al. (2010), I also employ the control group data for the tests.

6.3.1 Description of Variables

In the following I describe the construction of the variables needed for the hypothesis tests. The construction of the other variables I employ in the empirical analyses has already been discussed in chapter 3.

6.3.1.1 The Dependent Variables

Hypothesis 1 is tested using the variance of pre- and post-course *entrepreneurial intentions* (variable as defined in subsection 3.4.1) as a measure of career intentions. Hypothesis 2 focuses on the strength of students' opinions that they are (or are not) entrepreneurs after the course. Ex-ante, I take the squared deviation from the theoretical neutral value on the scale regarding the *entrepreneurial intentions* variable (which is 4 on the 7-point-scale), thus obtaining the variable *strength of ex-ante career intentions*. Based on the ex-post data I thus get a measure of the strength of students' opinions after the course (*strength of ex-post career intentions*, $\bar{I}$). Hypothesis 3 is based on the change in students' intentions due to the entrepreneurship course. The dependent measure here is the squared difference of the value of the *entrepreneurial intentions* variable before and after the course (*change in students' career intentions*, $\bar{\Delta}$).

6.3.1.2 Signals and their Strength

Naturally, the signals that students receive before and during the entrepreneurship course are not observable. However, these signals can be operationalized through the strength of behavioral, normative and control belief before and after the course and thus through the strength of the three attitudinal factors.

6.3.1.2.1 Period 1-Signals

The period 1-signals are measured using the scales for perceived desirability, perceived social norm, and perceived behavioral control. For each path in the Theory of Planned Behavior a signal is constructed.

The strength of the signal for each path is measured by comparing the individual's scale value to the point on the scale that indicates uncertainty about the beliefs belonging to the path. According to von Graevenitz et al. (2010) I set this point as the median of the ex-ante *perceived desirability, perceived social norm* and *perceived behavioral control* values. The strength of the period 1-signal is defined as the squared deviation from the respective point of uncertainty. The constructed variables *strength of period 1 perceived desirability / perceived social norm / perceived behavioral control signal* capture the strength. These variables do not capture the direction or level of the signal.

The direction of the respective signal (i.e. positive or negative regarding entrepreneurship) is also derived from the value on the ex-ante scale. If the value of an individual is larger (smaller) than the median, then he received a positive (negative) signal with respect to entrepreneurship.

6.3.1.2.2 Period 2-Signals

Period 2-signals are measured using the differences-scales of the perceptions of desirability, social norm, and behavioral control between the ex-post and ex-ante values.

The strength of the signals is measured by the squared deviation from the points of indecision on the differences-scales, this point being again the median on the scales (which is 0 for all of these scales). This gives the variables *strength of period 2 perceived desirability / perceived social norm / perceived behavioral control signal.* As above, these variables do not capture the direction of the signal.

The direction of the signals is obtained by using the differences of the perceptions of desirability, social norm and behavioral control respectively. If the simple difference between ex-post and ex-ante values was positive (negative), the student received a positive (negative) signal (regarding entrepreneurship) in the respective path.

6.3.1.2.3 Consistency of Signals

A sequence of signals is defined as consistent, if the direction of the signals received in period 1 and period 2 are both positive or both negative.

Signals are defined as consistently positive if both the period 1-signal and the period 2-signal are positive. Consistently negative signals regarding entrepreneurship are defined analogously. Thus I obtain a measure for *consistent perceived desirability / perceived social norm / perceived behavioral control signals*. On this definition about one third of students received consistent signals in each path of the Theory of Planned Behavior.

Finally, I construct interactions of strength of period 1-variables with the consistent signals variables and obtain measures for *strong and consistent perceived desirability / perceived social norm / perceived behavioral control signals*.

Table 6.1 and Table 6.2 set out descriptive statistics for all variables I employ, separately for the treatment and control group. At the top of the tables I present the dependent variables, below the explanatory variables. The descriptive statistics for the control variables are reported in section 3.5. The statistics are presented for the sample of 403 students of the treatment group and 106 students of the control group whose responses to the pre-course and post-course questionnaires I was able to match. I present additional descriptive results regarding the distribution of entrepreneurial intentions before and after the course in the next subsection.

Table 6.1: Descriptive statistics (treatment group)

variable	N	Mean	Median	S.D.	Min	Max
career intentions						
ex-ante entrepreneurial intentions	403	4.179	4	1.780	1	7
ex-post entrepreneurial intentions	403	3.859	4	1.845	1	7
strength of ex-ante career intention	403	3.191	1	3.177	0	9
strength of ex-post career intention (I)	403	3.417	4	3.267	0	9
change in students' career intentions (Δ)	403	2.136	1	4.230	0	36
perceived desirability						
ex-ante perceived desirability	403	4.280	4.2	1.418	1	7
ex-post perceived desirability	403	4.333	4.4	1.519	1	7
difference in perceived desirability (ex-post - ex-ante)	403	0.052	0	1.175	-6	4.6
strength of period 1 perceived desirability signal	403	2.013	1	2.462	0	10.24
strength of period 2 perceived desirability signal	403	1.380	0.4	3.614	0	36
consistent perceived desirability signals	403	0.323	-	-	0	1
strong and consistent perceived desirability signals	403	0.464	0	1.193	0	9

Table 6.1 (continued): Descriptive statistics (treatment group)

variable	N	Mean	Median	S.D.	Min	Max
perceived social norm						
ex-ante perceived social norm	403	-4.856	0	29.121	-78	84
ex-post perceived social norm	403	-1.782	0	30.494	-84	84
difference in perceived social norm (ex-post - ex-ante)	403	3.074	0	23.365	-77	90
strength of period 1 perceived social norm signal	403	869.491	361	1160.492	0	7056
strength of period 2 perceived social norm signal	403	554.027	196	974.978	0	8100
consistent perceived social norm signal	403	0.295	-	-	0	1
strong and consistent perceived social norm signal	403	206.933	0	632.674	0	6084
perceived behavioral control						
ex-ante perceived behavioral control	403	4.195	4	0.992	1	7
ex-post perceived behavioral control	403	4.346	4.3	1.069	1	7
difference in perceived behavioral control (ex-post - ex-ante)	403	0.151	0.3	0.919	-6	3
strength of period 1 perceived behavioral control signal	403	1.019	0.6	1.561	0	9
strength of period 2 perceived behavioral control signal	403	0.853	0.3	2.661	0	36
consistent perceived behavioral control signal	403	0.365	-	-	0	1
strong and consistent perceived behavioral control signals	403	0.295	0	0.784	0	5.062

Table 6.2: Descriptive statistics (control group)

variable	N	Mean	Median	S.D.	Min	Max
career intentions						
ex-ante entrepreneurial intentions	106	3.528	3	1.634	1	7
ex-post entrepreneurial intentions	106	3.396	3	1.637	1	7
strength of ex-ante career intention	106	2.868	1	2.781	0	9
strength of ex-post career intention (I)	106	3.019	1	3.210	0	9
change in students' career intentions (Δ)	106	2.132	1	4.705	0	36
perceived desirability						
ex-ante perceived desirability	106	3.825	3.6	1.275	1	7
ex-post perceived desirability	106	3.891	4	1.345	1	6.6
difference in perceived desirability (ex-post - ex-ante)	106	0.066	0.2	1.143	-4.4	2.6
strength of period 1 perceived desirability signal	106	1.661	1	2.060	0	11.56
strength of period 2 perceived desirability signal	106	1.313	0.36	2.703	0	21.16
consistent perceived desirability signals	106	0.340	-		0	1
strong and consistent perceived desirability signals	106	0.440	0	1.016	0	4.84

Table 6.2 (continued): Descriptive statistics (control group)

variable	N	Mean	Median	S.D.	Min	Max
perceived social norm						
ex-ante perceived social norm	106	-14.66	-12	25.612	-72	45
ex-post perceived social norm	106	-15.028	-16	27.173	-72	62
difference in perceived social norm (ex-post - ex-ante)	106	-0.368	0	25.258	-81	72
strength of period 1 perceived social norm signal	106	656.868	361	754.714	1	3600
strength of period 2 perceived social norm signal	106	632.104	182.5	1138.220	0	6561
consistent perceived social norm signal	106	0.245	-		0	1
strong and consistent perceived social norm signal	106	142.519	0	495.349	0	3249
perceived behavioral control						
ex-ante perceived behavioral control	106	4.007	4	1.040	1.25	6.75
ex-post perceived behavioral control	106	3.943	4	1.056	1	7
difference in perceived behavioral control (ex-post - ex-ante)	106	-0.064	0	0.773	-2	2.25
strength of period 1 perceived behavioral control signal	106	1.071	0.562	1.543	0	7.562
strength of period 2 perceived behavioral control signal	106	0.596	0.25	0.982	0	5.062
consistent perceived behavioral control signal	106	0.358	-		0	1
strong and consistent perceived behavioral control signals	106	0.254	0	0.642	0	4

6.3.2 Descriptive Results

In section 5.3 I already showed that the average *entrepreneurial intentions* score has decreased significantly from 4.179 to 3.859 ($|t| = 4.500$, $p = 0.000$)[50]. So I confirm the findings of previous work on the evaluation of entrepreneurship education (e.g. Cox et al. (2002), Oosterbeek et al. (2010), and von Graevenitz et al. (2010)). However, as argued above and already described in von Graevenitz et al. (2010), not only the shift in means, but also the ex-ante and ex-post distribution of entrepreneurial intentions is informative. This subsection provides descriptive results informing about possible separation-effects.

6.3.2.1 Strength and Change of Career Intentions

First, I have a look at mean strengths of career intentions before and after the course. Table 6.1 and Table 6.2 show that students of the treatment and the control group enter with a *strength of ex-ante career intention* of 3.191 and 2.868, respectively. This difference is not significant according to a two-tailed t-test ($|t| = 0.955$, $p = 0.340$). In fact, an equivalence test suggests that the two samples can be regarded as statistically equivalent ($|z| = 2.650$, $p = 0.004$)[51]. Again, this is an excellent basis for the following empirical analyses, as I do not expect major bias due to initial differences in strengths of career intentions across treatment and control group.

Regarding the ex-post values of this variable, the two tables suggest that treated students apparently have stronger ex-post career intentions than the control group students (3.417 vs. 3.019). A t-test reveals that this difference is significant at the 5% level ($|t| = 2.316$, $p = 0.021$; two-tailed). Regarding the differences in the *strength of career intentions,* Table 6.1 informs that the value of the variable increases from 3.191 to 3.417 among the treated students during

---

[50] However, this decrease is not significant when compared to the changes in the control group (see chapter 5).
[51] Westlake version; equivalence-criterion is 20% of the control group mean; only the highest p-value of the two one-sided tests are reported; further information on the equivalence-test in subsection 3.5.1.

the course. A two-tailed t-test on this difference reveals that this difference is – although only on the 10% level – statistically significant ($|t| = 1.486$, $p = 0.095$). A test on this difference among the control group students (increase from 2.868 to 3.019) yields no statistically significant result ($|t| = 0.526$, $p = 0.600$). Apparently, the mean increase in this variable was stronger among the treated students than among the control group students. Using a t-test to compare these two differences (+0.226 compared to +0.151) I can obtain a difference-in-differences estimator. However, this test reveals that this estimator is not statistically significant ($|t| = 0.205$, $p = 0.838$).

However, this latter measure does not give information about the absolute change in entrepreneurial intentions, as it may be the case that changes in opposite directions on the intentions-scale cancel each other out in the mean. The variable *change in students' career intentions* reflects the absolute change in intentions during the course. Apparently, the absolute change in intentions is very similar in both groups (2.132 in the treatment vs. 2.136 in the control group). A two-tailed t-test does not yield a statistical significance for this change ($|t| = 0.009$, $p = 0.993$).

These descriptive results support my assertion that the treated students are more separated into "entrepreneurs" and "employees" than the control group students. Having initially similar strengths of career intentions, the treated students exhibit stronger career intentions ex-post than their fellow students of the control group. Given this observation, the statistically not-distinguishable absolute changes in entrepreneurial intentions indicate that the treated students report "more extreme" career intentions ex-post (i.e. they choose a response category near the extremes of the scale), whereas the control group students seem to choose a response category near the middle of the scale ex-post (indicating that they are even more uncertain about their future career path than before). Figure 6.1 and Figure 6.2 below, showing the ex-ante and ex-post distribution of entrepreneurial intentions in the treatment and control group respectively, corroborate this interpretation. The treated students are more diverse regarding their entrepreneurial intentions after the course. Almost one third of the control group students, on the other hand, reported that they "rather disagree" with the statement to measure entrepreneurial intentions. An accumulation of this size was found with the response category "disagree" ex-ante. So the increase in uncertainty (statistically spoken, the increase of the share of students choosing a response category near the middle of the scale) about future career plans in the control group seems to be largely driven by students who changed from "disagree" ex-ante to "rather disagree" ex-post.

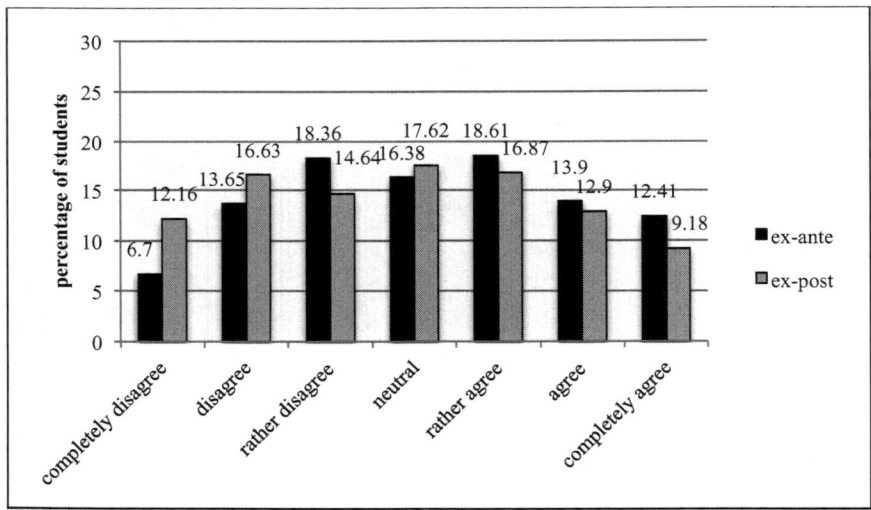

Figure 6.1: Ex-ante and ex-post entrepreneurial intentions of treatment group students

Notes: students were asked to indicate in how far they agree to the statement "I intend to start my own business in the next five to ten years"; N = 403.

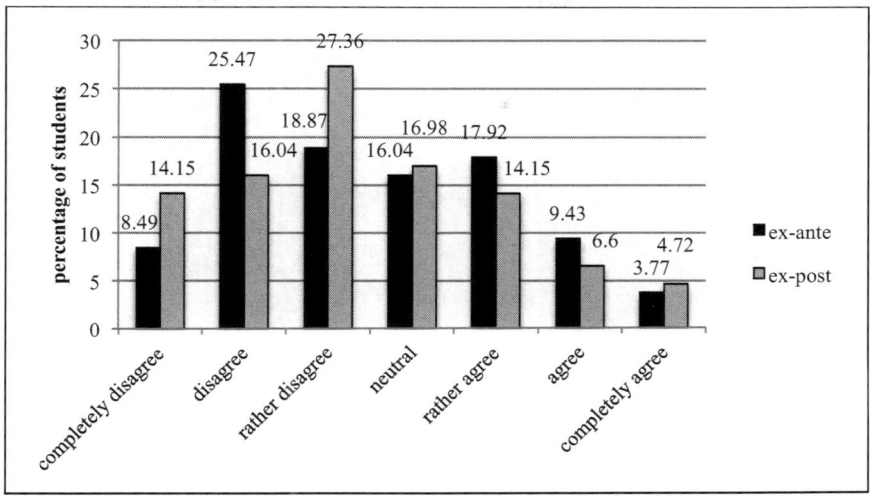

Figure 6.2: Ex-ante and ex-post entrepreneurial intentions of control group students

Notes: students were asked to indicate in how far they agree to the statement "I intend to start my own business in the next five to ten years"; N = 106.

6.3.2.2 Consistency and Strength of Signals

Next, I examine period 1 and period 2 signals that students of the two groups received. First of all, it is interesting to know if students of the treatment and control groups enter the course with differently strong period 1 signals. This is especially relevant for the multivariate analyses later. As already done in subsection 3.5.1, I perform an equivalence test on the three period 1 signal variables. The results are presented in Table 6.3.

Table 6.3: Equivalence test on strength of period 1 signals variables (treatment vs. control group)

variable	Treatment group (pooled) N=403		Control group (pooled) N=106		Difference (treatment-control)		Difference test two-tailed t-test		Equivalence test Westlake version		
	Mean	S.D.	Mean	S.D.	Mean	S.E.	|t|	p	criterion	|z|	p
strength of period 1 perceived desirability signal	2.013	2.462	1.661	2.060	0.352	0.260	1.354	0.176	0.332	0.078	0.469
strength of period 1 perceived social norm signal	869.491	1160.492	656.868	754.714	212.623	118.866	1.789	0.074	131.374	0.684	0.247
strength of period 1 perceived behavioral control signal	1.019	1.561	1.071	1.543	-0.052	0.170	0.308	0.758	0.214	0.952	0.171

Notes: equivalence criterion is +/- 20% of the control group's mean; the highest p-value of the two one-sided tests are reported; * significant at 5% for two-tailed t-test; + significant at 5% for equivalence test

Table 6.4: Comparison of the strengths of period 2 signals across groups

variable	treatment group (N = 403)		control group (N = 106)		Difference and test statistic (two-tailed t-test)			
	Mean	S.D.	Mean	S.D.	Mean	S.E.	|t|	p
strength of period 2 perceived desirability signal	1.380	3.614	1.313	2.703	0.067	0.376	0.178	0.859
strength of period 2 perceived social norm signal	554.027	974.978	632.104	1138.220	-78.077	110.353	0.708	0.480
strength of period 2 perceived behavioral control signal	0.853	2.661	0.596	0.982	0.257	0.263	0.976	0.330

Notes: * significant at 10%; ** significant at 5%; *** significant at 1% (for two-tailed t-tests)

Table 6.3 shows that the equivalence-tests on the strength of period 1 signal variables are inconclusive. This means that I cannot exclude biases in my results due to initial differences in these variables. To control for that in the following multivariate regressions, I will employ Coarsened Exact Matching on my data, as I already did in chapter 5.

Particularly interesting regarding the effect of the course are the consistency measures and the strengths of period 2 signals (i.e. the signals received during the time-period of the course). Table 6.4 shows results of t-tests comparing the values on the consistency-variables and the strengths of the period 2 signals across treatment and control group. The results show that the treatment group students received stronger period 2 desirability and behavioral control signals, and weaker social norm signals. However, the difference is not statistically significant in any case.

6.3.2.3 Separation Effects

Having discussed the means of the relevant variables, I now proceed to consider possible separation effects due to the course. This means I investigate further if students of the treatment group have more extreme career intentions after the course compared to their fellow students of the control group.

Table 6.5: Ex-post responses to the entrepreneurial intentions item, by ex-ante responses (treatment group)

			ex-post response							Total	
			1	2	3	4	5	6	7	N	%
ex-ante response	1	completely disagree	13	6	5	1	1	1	0	27	6.7
	2	disagree	18	23	7	7	0	0	0	55	13.6
	3	rather disagree	6	21	24	10	10	3	0	74	18.4
	4	neutral	3	12	14	21	11	5	0	66	16.4
	5	rather agree	7	2	4	20	29	9	4	75	18.6
	6	agree	0	3	3	8	13	20	9	56	13.9
	7	completely agree	2	0	2	4	4	14	24	50	12.4
		Total N	49	67	59	71	68	52	37	403	
		%	12.2	16.6	14.6	17.6	16.9	12.9	9.2		100.0

Table 6.5 shows that the share of responses indicating indecision about future career plans ("rather disagree", "neutral", "rather agree") declines from 53.3% to 49.1% among the treated students. Although this change is small, it provides an indication of the course's function to reduce uncertainty about future career plans.

The fact that students learn something about their true career intentions is more apparent in Table 6.6. There I cross-tabulate a discrete measure of changes in entrepreneurial intentions with ex-ante intentions. The table shows that respondents with stronger ex-ante intentions change their intentions less often than undecided students. Changes in intentions occur mostly among the respondents who took an ex-ante answer indicating uncertainty ("rather disagree", "neutral", "rather agree"), as one would expect in a world with Bayesian Updating during the course.

Table 6.6: Changes in the response to the entrepreneurial intentions item, by ex-ante responses (treatment group)

		ex-post response				Total
		Change		No change		
ex-ante response	completely disagree	14	51.9%	13	48.1%	27
	disagree	32	58.2%	23	41.8%	55
	rather disagree	50	67.6%	24	32.4%	74
	neutral	45	68.2%	21	31.8%	66
	rather agree	46	61.3%	29	38.7%	75
	agree	36	64.3%	20	35.7%	56
	completely agree	26	52.0%	24	48.0%	50
	Total	249	60.5%	154	39.5%	403

Further evidence is given in Table 6.7 and Table 6.8 where I display the changes in career intentions in the treatment and in the control group. The two panels show the pattern of changes between the low range ("completely disagree", "disagree"), the neutral range ("rather disagree", "neutral", "rather agree") and the high range ("agree", "completely agree") of responses to the entrepreneurial intentions question. The upper panel displays the changes in the treatment, the lower panel in the control group. The table suggests that students in the treatment group, who ex-ante gave responses in either the low or high range, tend to stay more in this range than students in the control group. On the other hand, treated students initially being undecided are more likely to change in one of the extreme ranges than untreated students. It seems that students in the control group predominantly either do not learn about their true career intentions (the high share of "neutral" students who stayed in the "neutral" range ex-post) or lose their initial certainty about their future career (the relatively high share of changers in the extreme ranges). In the treatment group, however, it seems that the students with initially strong career intentions tend more to stay with these and probably are even more certain about them ex-post. Moreover, the initially uncertain students seem to receive information leading them to form firmer career intentions.

As argued above, both groups have received signals affecting career intentions. However, signals emitted through general business administration courses seem to be weaker with respect to their ability to form firmer career plans than signals students receive who attend an entrepreneurship course during the same time. Therefore two developments can be identified. On the one hand, the course has apparently reduced entrepreneurial intentions of the participating students. On the other hand, students indicated that they learned something about entrepreneurship. The course has led to a reshaping of entrepreneurial intentions and seemingly to firmer career plans, even more when comparing the developments to those in the control group. In the next subsection I test the predictions of the theoretical model to monitor if Bayesian Updating along the Theory of Planned Behavior provides an explanation of what is observed.

Table 6.7: Pattern of changes in responses to the entrepreneurial intentions item (treatment group)

		Changed to		If changed: change to			Total
		Same range	Other range	to low	to neutral	to high	
ex-ante response	low	60 / 73.2%	22 / 26.8%		21 / 25.6%	1 / 1.2%	82
	neutral	143 / 66.5%	72 / 33.5%	51 / 23.7%		21 / 9.8%	215
	high	67 / 63.2%	39 / 36.8%	5 / 4.7%	34 / 32.1%		106

Table 6.8: Pattern of changes in responses to the entrepreneurial intentions item (control group)

		Changed to		If changed: change to			Total
		Same range	Other range	to low	to neutral	to high	
ex-ante response	low	24 66.7%	12 33.3%		11 30.6%	1 2.8%	36
	neutral	44 78.6%	12 21.4%	7 12.5%		5 8.9%	56
	high	6 42.9%	8 57.1%	1 7.1%	7 50.0%		14

6.3.3 Test of Hypotheses

To test the hypotheses, I employed the following tests: i) difference-of-variance tests to investigate the effect of the course on entrepreneurial intentions, ii) OLS regressions to test the strength of beliefs after the course, and iii) OLS regressions for the extent of changes in intentions during the course.

6.3.3.1 Hypothesis 6.1

The presented model of Bayesian Updating predicts that students' post-course career intentions will have greater variance if students receive informative signals regarding their true career intentions from the course and if the period 1-signal is not too strong.

Before comparing the ex-ante and ex-post variances within the treatment group and also the differences in variances between the two groups, I look at the ex-ante variance of entrepreneurial intentions in the treatment and control group as some sort of equivalency-test in Table 6.9. I displayed the ex-ante distribution of entrepreneurial intentions by treatment and control group in Figure 3.6, paragraph 3.5.2.1. This figure suggests that the distributions are shaped differently, therefore I have to address the question of a possible difference in ex-ante entrepreneurial intentions among the treatment and control group. This table sets out the standard-deviations of ex-ante entrepreneurial intentions in the treatment and control group. I present test statistics (p-values) for four difference-of-variance tests: the traditional F-test, Levene's robust test (Levene 1960) that is robust under non-normality, and Brown and Forsythe's median and trimmed mean test (Brown and Forsythe 1974) that are more robust with respect to skewed populations. This table shows that I cannot reject the null-hypothesis of equal variances of ex-ante entrepreneurial intentions among the treatment and control group. Moreover, according to a two-sample Kolmogorov-Smirnov-Test for equality of distributions I cannot reject the null-hypothesis of equal ex-ante distributions of entrepreneurial intentions among the treatment and control group ($p = 0.630$). Thus I may compare the differences in variances between the treatment and control group due to the course.

Table 6.9: Comparison of ex-ante standard deviation of entrepreneurial intentions by group

		estimation sample
	Observations	1018
		S.D.
group	treatment	1.780
	control	1.634
	difference (treatment-control)	0.146
test statistic (p-value)	F-test	0.294
	Levene's robust test	0.294
	Brown and Forsythe's median test	0.281
	Brown and Forsythe's trimmed mean test	0.215

Now I look at the ex-ante and ex-post variances. Table 6.10 sets out the standard deviations of students' entrepreneurial intentions ex-ante and ex-post, the left panel for the treatment group, the right panel for the control group. These results are first provided for the full set of students whose responses I was able to match. Second I show the results when students who had very strong pre-course intentions or (i.e. indicated an "extreme" value on the *entrepreneurial intentions* scale: "completely disagree" or "completely agree") are excluded (restriction 1). In a second step I also excluded those students who did not change their intentions at all (restriction 2). My preferred estimation sample is the "restriction 1" sample where I excluded the students with extreme ex-ante intentions. Per definition of the entrepreneurial intentions scale, their intentions cannot get any more polarized due to the course.[52] If not written otherwise, I will concentrate on the results derived from this sample.

The table shows that the variance of entrepreneurial intentions among the treated students increases: entrepreneurial intentions have greater variance than before. Although I cannot reject the hypothesis that the variances are statistically identical for the full sample, I find statistically significant increases in the variance among the preferred sample. Looking at the ex-ante and ex-post variances of entrepreneurial intentions among the control group, I do not find a statistically significant change in the variances. Although the variance increased slightly also here, the increase was larger among the treated students. This "difference-in-differences" is even larger when considering the restriction-2-sample. These results confirm Hypothesis 6.1 and thus confirm the results of the study by von Graevenitz et al. (2010).

---

[52] I discussed these floor/ceiling – disadvantages when employing questionnaires in paragraph 2.3.3.2.

Table 6.10: Test of Hypothesis 6.1 (variance in entrepreneurial intentions, ex-ante and ex-post by group)

		treatment group			control group		
		estimation sample	estimation sample, restriction 1	estimation sample, restriction 2	estimation sample	estimation sample, restriction 1	estimation sample, restriction 2
	Observations	806	652	418	212	186	122
			S.D.			S.D.	
response time	ex-ante	1.780	1.351	1.330	1.634	1.375	1.389
	ex-post	1.845	1.663	1.779	1.637	1.446	1.481
	difference (ex-post - ex-ante)	0.065	0.312	0.449	0.003	0.071	0.092
test statistic (p-values)	F-test	0.467	0.000	0.000	0.986	0.629	0.620
	Levene's robust test	0.435	0.000	0.000	0.592	0.858	0.754
	Brown and Forsythe's median test	0.459	0.000	0.000	0.515	0.634	0.610
	Brown and Forsythe's trimmed mean test	0.285	0.000	0.000	0.436	0.632	0.682

I also investigate sorting effects in subsamples of the treatment group to find out whether certain background characteristics facilitate or impede the sorting effects[53]. Table 6.11 informs in which subsamples (defined by the dummy-variables given in Table 3.13) hypothesis 1 holds. Results are presented by group (treatment and control). I only report results of Levene's robust test for the "restriction 1" treatment sample. The upper panel displays the ex-ante and ex-post standard deviations as well as the ex-post − ex-ante difference of standard deviations of entrepreneurial intentions in the group of students not exhibiting the respective background factor. The lower panel shows the results for the group of students who do exhibit the background factor. The "Difference-in-Differences" line gives the difference-in-differences in standard deviations within one group (treatment and control respectively). The last line displays a "Difference-in-Difference-in-Differences" estimation, where I compare changes in standard deviations in intentions in subsamples within the treatment group with the changes in standard deviations in intentions in subsamples within the control group.[54]

When considering only the treatment group, hypothesis 1 seems to hold in all subsamples except for students who have self-employed parents, who already have been self-employed themselves, and who already attended an entrepreneurship course. For students in these subsamples, the variance of entrepreneurial intentions does not change significantly. However, for the students who do not have a self-employed parent, who have not been self-employed yet and who have not attended an entrepreneurship course yet, the variance increased significantly. The increase in variance also holds when looking at difference-in-differences in standard deviations. The difference-in-difference-in-differences line gives additional information about the changes in standard deviations. When comparing the subsample in question to the respective subsample in the control group, one learns that the variances in entrepreneurial intentions

---

[53] See subsection 2.5.3 for the importance of background characteristics when interpreting the information received during entrepreneurship education.

[54] I did not employ a statistical test to determine if the difference-in-differences or the difference-in-difference-in-differences in standard-deviations are statistically different from zero. These values are best considered to deliver qualitative arguments about the changes in the standard-deviations of intentions.

increase for female students, for students who already worked for a start-up, and for students who are open to experience. This is an indication that for members of these subsamples the course fulfills a sorting function with respect to entrepreneurship i.e. they had a relatively low predisposition towards or against entrepreneurship. Variances decrease for students who have self-employed parents, who have started a business themselves, for extravert and for emotionally stable students. The difference-in-difference-in-differences are rather small for female and foreign students, for students who have self-employed acquaintances, for agreeable and conscientious students.[55]

---

[55] The difference-in-difference-in-differences interpretation should be noticed with caution, because they assume all else being equal.

Table 6.11: Variance in entrepreneurial intentions by subsample (part 1)

group (T = treatment, C = control)	subsample-defining variable		demographic variables						prior experiences						
			female (0/1)		foreign (0/1)		parents self-employed (0/1)		acquaintances self-employed (0/1)		worked for start-up (0/1)		entrepreneur (0/1)		already attended course (0/1)
			T	C	T	C	T	C	T	C	T	C	T	C	T	C
no		N	288	76	558	162	350	96	226	82	514	128	628	176	626	166
	response time	ex-ante S.D.	1.350	1.324	1.351	1.387	1.290	1.362	1.374	1.267	1.355	1.332	1.353	1.385	1.344	1.365
		ex-post S.D.	1.659	1.445	1.650	1.447	1.648	1.383	1.736	1.378	1.657	1.528	1.682	1.440	1.659	1.419
		difference (ex-post - ex-ante)	0.309	0.121	0.299	0.060	0.358	0.021	0.362	0.111	0.302	0.196	0.329	0.055	0.315	0.054
		Levene's robust test (p-value)	0.019	0.713	0.000	0.759	0.000	0.514	0.003	0.789	0.000	0.515	0.000	0.669	0.000	0.700
yes		N	364	110	94	24	302	90	426	104	138	58	24	10	26	20
	response time	ex-ante S.D.	1.326	1.421	1.330	1.279	1.385	1.352	1.325	1.462	1.345	1.473	1.348	1.304	1.536	1.265
		ex-post S.D.	1.590	1.456	1.705	1.422	1.631	1.466	1.624	1.507	1.697	1.203	1.087	0.894	1.772	1.563
		difference (ex-post - ex-ante)	0.264	0.035	0.375	0.143	0.246	0.114	0.299	0.045	0.352	-0.270	-0.261	-0.410	0.236	0.298
		Levene's robust test (p-value)	0.013	0.583	0.180	0.802	0.249	0.627	0.003	0.601	0.041	0.049	0.275	0.341	0.490	0.591
	Diff-in-Diff (yes - no)		-0.045	-0.086	0.076	0.083	-0.112	0.093	-0.063	-0.066	0.050	-0.466	-0.590	-0.465	-0.079	0.244
	Diff-in-Diff-in-Diff (DD treatment - DD control)		0.041		-0.007		-0.205		0.003		0.516		-0.125		-0.323	

Notes: subsamples as defined by Table 3.13; sample sizes get smaller when considering the personality dimensions in the control group, as I do not have data on these variables for the 2008 cohort;

Table 6.11: Variance in entrepreneurial intentions by subsample (part 2)

group (T = treatment, C = control)	subsample-defining variable		extravert (0/1)		agreeable (0/1)		personality dimensions conscientious (0/1)		emotionally stable (0/1)		open to experience (0/1)	
			T	C	T	C	T	C	T	C	T	C
no	response time	N	268	76	426	84	168	22	314	58	170	46
		ex-ante S.D.	1.312	1.516	1.323	1.517	1.400	1.362	1.328	1.524	1.384	1.403
		ex-post S.D.	1.673	1.441	1.672	1.590	1.819	1.502	1.697	1.575	1.712	1.642
		difference (ex-post - ex-ante)	0.361	-0.075	0.349	0.073	0.419	0.140	0.369	0.051	0.328	0.239
	Levene's robust test (p-value)		0.002	0.180	0.000	0.927	0.005	1.000	0.000	0.952	0.008	0.385
yes	response time	N	384	50	226	42	484	104	338	68	482	80
		ex-ante S.D.	1.366	1.528	1.400	1.521	1.336	1.550	1.371	1.518	1.335	1.528
		ex-post S.D.	1.657	1.796	1.654	1.532	1.610	1.607	1.618	1.596	1.636	1.502
		difference (ex-post - ex-ante)	0.291	0.268	0.254	0.011	0.274	0.057	0.247	0.078	0.301	-0.026
	Levene's robust test (p-value)		0.007	0.341	0.087	0.761	0.001	0.748	0.055	0.776	0.003	0.490
	Diff-in-Diff (yes - no)		-0.070	0.343	-0.095	-0.062	-0.145	-0.083	-0.122	0.027	-0.027	-0.265
	Diff-in-Diff-in-Diff (DD treatment - DD control)		-0.413		-0.033		-0.062		-0.149		0.238	

Notes: subsamples as defined by Table 3.13; sample sizes get smaller when considering the personality dimensions in the control group, since I do not have data on these variables for the 2008 cohort;

Going back to subsection 5.3.3, I found that students who already have started a business themselves experience a strong negative shift in entrepreneurial intentions and perceived behavioral control (diff-in-diff-in-diff-in means estimations). In addition, students with self-employed parents positively alter their perceptions of desirability and social norm, and students who already attended an entrepreneurship course experienced a shift in perceived desirability. Together with the findings in this chapter, this may mean that for these groups of students the course does not fulfill a function of sorting. Students who have self-employed parents entered the course with relatively high entrepreneurial intentions (section 4.3), and experience a rather uniform positive shift in means of entrepreneurial attitudes. Students who have already attended an entrepreneurship course seem to uniformly change their intentions positively with respect to an entrepreneurial career. Students who already started an own business, on the other hand, lose their intent to start a business again during the course.

6.3.3.2 Hypothesis 6.2

Table 6.12 below sets out results from regressions performed to test Hypothesis 2, estimating *Equation 6.1* based on the treatment data only. I set out six regressions. The first contains only control variables and shows that none of these is able to explain the strength of students' opinions about their entrepreneurial aptitude, i.e. whether to become entrepreneurs or not. Models 2 - 4 consider each attitudinal factor in the Theory of Planned Behavior separately, perceived desirability (2), perceived social norm in (3), and perceived behavioral control in (4) respectively. In each regression, measures of the strength of period 1-signals, of consistent signals, and the interaction of these two measures are included. Considering each attitudinal factor alone, hypothesis 2 can be fully confirmed for the social norm and behavioral control signals, but only partly for attitude towards self-employment. Especially model 4 is interesting, as here the study by von Graevenitz et al. (2010) is replicated and confirmed. The full model is presented in model 5, using the specification of *Equation 6.1*. The first column reports the coefficients of the OLS regression. The coefficient for the strength of the period 1-signal has a positive sign and is significant for perceived desirability and perceived social norm. The consistent signal coefficient has a positive sign and is significant for social norm and behavioral control. All other relevant explanatory variables are not significant. Considering the full model, hypothesis 2 is further fully confirmed for perceived social norm, and only partly for perceived desirability and perceived behavioral control. Probably the students cannot separate the signals they receive according to the path of the Theory of Planned Behavior. In model 6 I drop all those controls that are insignificant above the 20% level. I arrive at the specification by iteratively removing the least significant control variables one by one. The R-squared for the reported specification is the highest and the estimated coefficients seem not much affected by this procedure. The effects I identify are robust. I also report the standardized coefficients of the OLS estimations of this model to discuss the influence of consistent signals on the ex-post strength of career intentions. This variable is the most relevant in the model when discussing implications for the design of entrepreneurship courses meant to help students better self-select into their true career intentions. Consistent behavioral control signals seem to exert a stronger significant influence than the consistent social norm signals. Paired with the high strength of the period 2 behavioral control signal, it seems that it was the information provided along this path of the Theory of Planned Behavior that led to the discovery of "true" career intentions.

Table 6.12: Test of Hypothesis 6.2 (OLS regressions, treatment group data only, part 1)

dependent variable strength of ex-post career intentions	model 1 controls	model 2 perceived desirability only	model 3 perceived social norm only	model 4 perceived behavioral control only
perceived desirability				
strength of period 1 signal		0.476*** (0.069)		
consistent signals		0.311 (0.417)		
strong and consistent signals		0.457*** (0.166)		
strength of period 2 signal		0.100** (0.043)		
perceived social norm				
strength of period 1 signal			0.737*** (0.160)	
consistent signals			1.067*** (0.403)	
strong and consistent signals			0.791** (0.322)	
strength of period 2 signal			0.358** (0.162)	
perceived behavioral control				
strength of period 1 signal				0.249** (0.123)
consistent signals				1.316*** (0.395)
strong and consistent signals				0.705*** (0.267)
strength of period 2 signal				0.178*** (0.068)

Table 6.12 (continued): Test of Hypothesis 6.2 (OLS regressions, treatment group data only, part 1 continued)

dependent variable strength of ex-post career intentions	model 1 controls	model 2 perceived desirability only	model 3 perceived social norm only	model 4 perceived behavioral control only
demographic variables				
age	0.008	-0.014	-0.007	-0.013
	(0.080)	(0.071)	(0.073)	(0.075)
female (0/1)	-0.331	-0.143	-0.436	-0.115
	(0.356)	(0.321)	(0.328)	(0.334)
foreign (0/1)	-0.328	-0.196	-0.383	-0.175
	(0.469)	(0.423)	(0.432)	(0.439)
prior experiences				
breadth of prior exposure	0.105	-0.084	-0.090	-0.161
	(0.176)	(0.161)	(0.165)	(0.169)
attended entrepreneurship courses	0.206	-0.013	0.059	-0.107
	(0.481)	(0.433)	(0.443)	(0.451)
ECTS	0.001	0.002	-0.001	0.001
	(0.013)	(0.012)	(0.012)	(0.012)
personality dimensions				
extraversion	0.077	0.134	-0.024	0.084
	(0.163)	(0.147)	(0.151)	(0.152)
agreeableness	-0.145	-0.229	-0.098	-0.127
	(0.225)	(0.203)	(0.207)	(0.215)
conscientiousness	-0.188	-0.254*	-0.261*	-0.177
	(0.157)	(0.142)	(0.145)	(0.149)
emotional stability	-0.032	0.073	0.047	-0.049
	(0.156)	(0.141)	(0.145)	(0.147)
openness to experience	-0.057	-0.122	-0.050	-0.026
	(0.199)	(0.179)	(0.184)	(0.189)
constant	5.035**	4.536**	4.743**	4.411*
	(2.437)	(2.190)	(2.265)	(2.285)
test statistics				
Observations	403	403	403	403
R-squared	-0.013	0.188	0.143	0.120
F-test (df)	0.526(11)	7.210(15)	5.463(15)	4.646(15)
F-test sig	0.886	0.000	0.000	0.000

Notes: robust standard errors in parentheses; * significant at 10%; ** significant at 5%; *** significant at 1%

Table 6.12 (continued): Test of Hypothesis 6.2 (OLS regressions, treatment group data only, part 2)

dependent variable strength of ex-post career intentions	model 5 full model	model 6 restricted model	
		coefficient	beta
perceived desirability			
strength of period 1 signal	0.321*** (0.073)	0.313*** (0.072)	0.236
consistent signals	0.133 (0.396)	0.097 (0.386)	0.014
strong and consistent signals	0.287* (0.165)	0.299* (0.162)	0.109
strength of period 2 signal	0.036 (0.054)	0.033 (0.053)	0.036
perceived social norm			
strength of period 1 signal	0.489*** (0.168)	0.488*** (0.165)	0.172
consistent signals	0.804** (0.374)	0.847** (0.367)	0.121
strong and consistent signals	0.335 (0.305)	0.311 (0.300)	0.059
strength of period 2 signal	0.164 (0.154)	0.152 (0.151)	0.045
perceived behavioral control			
strength of period 1 signal	-0.037 (0.126)	-0.034 (0.124)	-0.016
consistent signals	0.944** (0.365)	0.905** (0.356)	0.133
strong and consistent signals	0.463* (0.253)	0.520** (0.243)	0.125
strength of period 2 signal	0.128 (0.079)	0.129* (0.077)	0.105

Table 6.12 (continued): Test of Hypothesis 6.2 (OLS regressions, treatment group data only, part 2 continued)

dependent variable strength of ex-post career intentions	model 5 full model	model 6 restricted model	
		coefficient	beta
demographic variables			
age	-0.015		
	(0.068)		
female (0/1)	-0.176		
	(0.306)		
foreign (0/1)	-0.193		
	(0.401)		
prior experiences			
breadth of	-0.274*	-0.280*	-0.085
prior exposure	(0.156)	(0.146)	
attended entrepreneurship	-0.197		
courses	(0.411)		
ECTS	-0.001		
	(0.011)		
personality dimensions			
extraversion	0.046		
	(0.140)		
agreeableness	-0.153		
	(0.197)		
conscientiousness	-0.283**	-0.316**	-0.107
	(0.136)	(0.128)	
emotional stability	0.066		
	(0.135)		
openness to experience	-0.077		
	(0.174)		
constant	4.142**	3.307***	
	(2.092)	(0.765)	
Test statistics			
Observations	403	403	
R-squared	0.275	0.288	
F-test (df)	7.628(23)	12.6(14)	
F-test sig	0.000	0.000	

Notes: robust standard errors in parentheses; * significant at 10%; ** significant at 5%, *** significant at 1%

Table 6.13: Test of Hypothesis 6.2 (OLS regressions, treatment and control group data, part 1)

Dependent variable strength of ex-post career intentions sample	model 1	model 2	model 3	model 4	model 5	model 6
	Controls only		Perceived desirability only		Perceived social norm only	
	treated only	with control group	treated only	with control group	treated only	with control group
treatment (yes = 1)		0.345 (0.364)		-0.240 (0.531)		-0.517 (0.542)
Perceived desirability						
strength of period 1 signal			0.463*** (0.068)	0.139 (0.170)		
consistent signals			0.289 (0.412)	0.036 (0.835)		
strong and consistent signals			0.454*** (0.165)	0.748* (0.407)		
strength of period 2 signal			0.100** (0.042)	0.157 (0.119)		
strength of period 1 signal x treatment				0.324* (0.182)		
consistent signals x treatment				0.262 (0.932)		
strong and consistent signals x treatment				-0.295 (0.440)		
strength of period 2 signal x treatment				-0.057 (0.126)		
Perceived social norm						
strength of period 1 signal * 1000					0.653*** (0.154)	0.202 (0.496)
consistent signals					0.855** (0.417)	-0.004 (0.864)
strong and consistent signals * 1000					0.862*** (0.320)	1.937** (0.862)
strength of period 2 signal * 1000					0.380** (0.160)	-0.091 (0.273)
strength of period 1 signal x treatment * 1000						0.448 (0.518)
consistent signals x treatment						0.870 (0.957)
strong and consistent signals x treatment * 1000						-1.077 (0.919)
strength of period 2 signal x treatment * 1000						0.469 (0.316)

Table 6.13 (continued): Test of Hypothesis 6.2 (OLS regressions, treatment and control group data, part 1 continued)

Dependent variable strength of ex-post career intentions sample	model 1	model 2	model 3	model 4	model 5	model 6
	Controls only		Perceived desirability only		Perceived social norm only	
	treated only	with control group	treated only	with control group	treated only	with control group
Perceived behavioral control						
strength of period 1 signal						
consistent signals						
strong and consistent signals						
strength of period 2 signal						
strength of period 1 signal x treatment						
consistent signals x treatment						
strong and consistent signals x treatment						
strength of period 2 signal x treatment						
Demographics						
age	0.007	0.027	-0.017	0.006	-0.008	0.007
	(0.077)	(0.070)	(0.070)	(0.065)	(0.072)	(0.066)
female (0/1)	-0.442	-0.439	-0.363	-0.354	-0.635**	-0.581**
	(0.331)	(0.294)	(0.299)	(0.272)	(0.309)	(0.277)
foreign (0/1)	-0.303	-0.380	-0.182	-0.261	-0.326	-0.353
	(0.455)	(0.410)	(0.411)	(0.377)	(0.421)	(0.384)
Prior experiences						
breadth of prior exposure	0.123	0.111	-0.050	-0.055	-0.013	-0.002
	(0.168)	(0.150)	(0.153)	(0.140)	(0.158)	(0.142)
attended entrepreneurship courses	0.163	-0.087	-0.028	-0.104	-0.031	-0.131
	(0.473)	(0.164)	(0.428)	(0.151)	(0.441)	(0.153)
constant	3.350**	2.615*	2.711*	2.478*	2.784*	2.943**
	(1.683)	(1.497)	(1.518)	(1.408)	(1.564)	(1.448)
Test statistics						
Observations	403	509	403	509	403	509
R-squared	-0.004	-0.001	0.188	0.163	0.140	0.129
F-test (df)	0.657(5)	0.933(6)	11.32(9)	8.089(14)	8.281(9)	6.373(14)
F-test sig	0.656	0.471	0.000	0.000	0.000	0.000

Notes: robust standard errors in parentheses; * significant at 10%; ** significant at 5%, *** significant at 1%

Table 6.13 (continued): Test of Hypothesis 6.2 (OLS regressions, treatment and control group data, part 2)

Dependent variable strength of ex-post career intentions sample	model 7 Perceived behavioral control only treated only	model 8 Perceived behavioral control only with control group	model 9 Full model treated only	model 10 Full model with control group	model 11 Full model with CEM
treatment (yes = 1)		0.127 (0.528)		-0.586 (0.670)	-1.332* (0.758)
Perceived desirability					
strength of period 1 signal			0.309*** (0.073)	0.084 (0.177)	0.972** (0.378)
consistent signals			0.128 (0.393)	0.052 (0.826)	1.156* (0.643)
strong and consistent signals			0.281* (0.163)	0.485 (0.432)	-0.918 (0.693)
strength of period 2 signal			0.025 (0.053)	0.202* (0.116)	-0.268* (0.145)
strength of period 1 signal x treatment				0.223 (0.191)	0.829 (0.576)
consistent signals x treatment				0.066 (0.917)	-1.007 (0.868)
strong and consistent signals x treatment				-0.200 (0.463)	1.272 (0.953)
strength of period 2 signal x treatment				-0.176 (0.128)	0.517** (0.201)
Perceived social norms					
strength of period 1 signal * 1000			0.427*** (0.162)	-0.103 (0.489)	0.067 (0.915)
consistent signals			0.614* (0.356)	-0.085 (0.835)	0.165 (0.817)
strong and consistent signals * 1000			0.448 (0.302)	1.730** (0.839)	4.290 (3.114)
strength of period 2 signal * 1000			0.172 (0.153)	-0.342 (0.278)	0.381 (0.284)
strength of period 1 signal x treatment * 1000				0.528 (0.516)	0.435 (1.284)
consistent signals x treatment				0.682 (0.921)	0.782 (1.078)
strong and consistent signals x treatment * 1000				-1.274 (0.894)	-2.147 (3.610)
strength of period 2 signal x treatment * 1000				0.515 (0.318)	0.205 (0.482)

Table 6.13 (continued): Test of Hypothesis 6.2 (OLS regressions, treatment and control group data, part 2 continued)

	model 7	model 8	model 9	model 10	model 11
Dependent variable strength of ex-post career intentions	Perceived behavioral control only		Full model		
sample	treated only	with control group	treated only	with control group	with CEM
Perceived behavioral control					
strength of period 1 signal	**0.251****	0.361	**-0.032**	0.192	0.143
	(0.122)	(0.231)	**(0.126)**	(0.245)	(0.755)
consistent signals	1.316***	0.471	0.932**	0.508	1.415**
	(0.387)	(0.789)	(0.360)	(0.738)	(0.587)
strong and consistent signals	0.692***	0.497	0.490**	0.159	2.696*
	(0.259)	(0.594)	(0.248)	(0.605)	(1.608)
strength of period 2 signal	0.187***	0.308	0.158**	0.339	1.452***
	(0.064)	(0.338)	(0.077)	(0.323)	(0.473)
strength of period 1 signal x treatment		-0.119		-0.229	0.415
		(0.262)		(0.277)	(1.020)
consistent signals x treatment		0.841		0.417	1.102
		(0.880)		(0.825)	(0.868)
strong and consistent signals x treatment		0.192		0.329	-0.860
		(0.646)		(0.652)	(2.269)
strength of period 2 signal x treatment		-0.123		-0.183	-1.009*
		(0.344)		(0.332)	(0.533)
Demographics					
age	-0.014	0.021	-0.017	0.004	-0.003
	(0.073)	(0.067)	(0.066)	(0.062)	(0.098)
female (0/1)	-0.199	-0.266	-0.383	-0.381	-0.646*
	(0.311)	(0.279)	(0.289)	(0.265)	(0.352)
foreign (0/1)	-0.150	-0.249	-0.156	-0.175	-0.525
	(0.424)	(0.389)	(0.389)	(0.363)	(0.546)
Prior experiences					
breadth of prior exposure	-0.139	-0.134	-0.214	-0.198	-0.580***
	(0.160)	(0.145)	(0.149)	(0.137)	(0.195)
attended entrepreneurship courses	-0.144	-0.102	-0.266	-0.148	-0.148
	(0.444)	(0.155)	(0.409)	(0.145)	(0.104)
constant	2.963*	2.133	2.201	2.312	3.288
	(1.577)	(1.469)	(1.449)	(1.408)	(2.087)
Test statistics					
Observations	403	509	403	509	331
R-squared	0.128	0.112	0.273	0.242	0.256
F-test (df)	7.531(9)	5.570(14)	9.880(17)	6.407(30)	4.754(30)
F-test sig	0.000	0.000	0.000	0.000	0.000

Notes: robust standard errors in parentheses; * significant at 10%; ** significant at 5%, *** significant at 1%

As a robustness check, I also test Hypothesis 6.2 after including the control group data. In Table 6.13 I report the results of OLS regressions estimating *Equation 6.2*. I set out eleven models in total in four blocks of two and one block of three models. The first model of each block is a copy of the models estimated in Table 6.12, however with a restricted set of control variables as I do not have data on the personality dimensions for a part of the control group sample. The second models each consider one attitudinal factor of the Theory of Planned Behavior separately. The fourth block (models 9, 10, and 11) presents the estimation of the full model, where model 10 represents the estimation of *Equation 6.2*. To control for differences across the treatment and control group, I additionally apply Coarsened exact matching on the data in model 11. Like in subsection 5.3.2 I chose the following variables to match treated and control units: *female (0/1), foreign (0/1), parents self-employed (0/1), acquaintances self-employed (0/1), worked for start-up (0/1), entrepreneur (0/1), and attended entrepreneurship courses*. As already denoted in subsection 6.3.2, I add the strengths of the period 1 signals to these variables. Checking for imbalance in these variables gives a multivariate imbalance of $\mathcal{L}_1 = .766$. After applying the matching algorithm the imbalance decreased to $\mathcal{L}'_1 = .552$. As a consequence the overall sample size decreases to 331 (278 units of the treatment and 53 units of the control group). With respect to the hypothesis test, model 11 would be the preferred model to look at.

In the table I set the relevant explanatory variables of Hypothesis 6.2 in bold. The results show that the models based on the treatment group data only are robust to the changed specification of the models by using the restricted set of control variables. The estimations based on the data from treated and control students, however, show that the coefficients of the main explanatory variables turn insignificant both in the models for each attitudinal factor of the Theory of Planned Behavior separately, as well as in the full model. One exception is the coefficient on the interaction of the strength of the perceived desirability period 1 signal with the treatment dummy in model 4, which is significant at the 10% level. Therefore, based on the complete data on treated and control students, Hypothesis 6.2 is rejected.

6.3.3.3 Hypothesis 6.3

Finally I consider how students who received consistent signals and strong period 1-signals adjust their opinions about their entrepreneurial aptitude during the course. Table 6.14 shows coefficients of six OLS regressions for the extent of changes in entrepreneurial intentions based on *Equation 6.3* and the treatment group data only. The variables are also the same as above. Model 5 is the full model. Hypothesis 6.3 predicts that the consistent and strong signal coefficients have a negative sign. Model 1 contains only control variables as above. It seems that extravert students are less likely to change their career intentions at all. Models 2 to 4 only consider one single path of the Theory of Planned Behavior, model 5 contains the full model. There is no significant influence of consistent and strong signals in either dimension of the Theory of Planned Behavior in any of the eight models. Therefore Hypothesis 6.3 is rejected. Still, one interesting observation is that the coefficients on the strength of the period 2 signals (i.e. the signals the students receive during the course) are significant and positive. So the stronger the signals are, the more they change their career intentions, as one would expect. In the full model the coefficients on the desirability and social norm signals are significant at the 1% level.

Like above, I also present the results of estimating *Equation 6.4* based on data from both the treatment and control group in Table 6.15. The structure of the table corresponds to the structure of Table 6.13 above. Model 10 contains the full model, model 11 the full model after the application of CEM. Considering the models based on the treatment group data only, the results are robust under the different specification of the models due to the restricted dataset. As before, none of the relevant explanatory variables is significant, neither in the models with a single factor of the Theory of Planned Behavior, nor in the full model. So Hypothesis 3 is still rejected. Regarding the strength of the second period signal, model 11 reveals a different pattern than the full model of Table 6.15. After comparing the signal strengths across treatment and control group, it seems that the behavioral control-signal is the most relevant with respect to the absolute change in entrepreneurial intentions.

Table 6.14: Test of Hypothesis 6.3 (OLS regressions, treatment group data only)

Dependent variable change in career intentions	model 1 controls only	model 2 perceived desirability only	model 3 perceived social norm only	model 4 perceived behavioral control only	model 5 full model
perceived desirability					
strength of period 1 signal		-0.167* (0.085)			-0.229** (0.092)
consistent signals		-0.205 (0.519)			-0.298 (0.502)
strong and consistent signals		**-0.004 (0.207)**			**-0.071 (0.208)**
strength of period 2 signal		0.615*** (0.053)			0.568*** (0.068)
perceived social norm					
strength of period 1 signal * 1000			0.030 (0.212)		0.325 (0.213)
consistent signals			0.434 (0.535)		0.618 (0.474)
strong and consistent signals * 1000			**-0.400 (0.427)**		**-0.352 (0.386)**
strength of period 2 signal * 1000			1.450*** (0.215)		0.988*** (0.195)
perceived behavioral control					
strength of period 1 signal				-0.387** (0.163)	-0.226 (0.160)
consistent signals				-0.152 (0.520)	0.135 (0.462)
strong and consistent signals				**0.095 (0.468)**	**-0.311 (0.474)**
strength of period 2 signal				0.549*** (0.089)	-0.029 (0.100)

Table 6.14 (continued): Test of Hypothesis 6.3 (OLS regressions, treatment group data only)

Dependent variable change in career intentions	model 1 controls only	model 2 perceived desirability only	model 3 perceived social norm only	model 4 perceived behavioral control only	model 5 full model
demographic variables					
age	-0.035	-0.063	-0.030	-0.043	-0.033
	(0.103)	(0.089)	(0.097)	(0.099)	(0.086)
female (0/1)	0.359	0.388	0.318	0.555	0.331
	(0.460)	(0.399)	(0.435)	(0.440)	(0.387)
foreign (0/1)	-0.251	-0.013	-0.195	-0.122	0.050
	(0.605)	(0.526)	(0.572)	(0.578)	(0.508)
prior experiences					
breadth of prior exposure	0.038	-0.183	-0.028	-0.230	-0.242
	(0.227)	(0.200)	(0.219)	(0.222)	(0.198)
attended entrepreneurship courses	-0.799	-0.656	-0.695	-0.880	-0.637
	(0.621)	(0.539)	(0.588)	(0.594)	(0.521)
ECTS	-0.001	0.002	0.008	0.005	0.008
	(0.017)	(0.015)	(0.016)	(0.016)	(0.014)
personality dimensions					
extraversion	-0.473**	-0.196	-0.417**	-0.407**	-0.209
	(0.210)	(0.183)	(0.200)	(0.200)	(0.177)
agreeableness	-0.153	-0.380	-0.265	-0.302	-0.325
	(0.290)	(0.252)	(0.275)	(0.283)	(0.249)
conscientiousness	0.032	0.171	0.002	0.123	0.076
	(0.203)	(0.176)	(0.192)	(0.196)	(0.172)
emotional stability	0.164	0.254	0.261	0.210	0.290*
	(0.202)	(0.175)	(0.193)	(0.193)	(0.171)
openness to experience	0.315	0.497**	0.399	0.545**	0.496**
	(0.257)	(0.223)	(0.244)	(0.249)	(0.220)
constant	3.170	0.880	1.318	1.401	-0.408
	(3.144)	(2.727)	(3.002)	(3.012)	(2.648)
test statistics					
Observations	403	403	403	403	403
R-squared	-0.006	0.249	0.101	0.088	0.307
F-test (df)	0.774(11)	9.898(15)	4.016(15)	3.581(15)	8.731(23)
F-test sig	0.666	0.000	0.000	0.000	0.000

Notes: robust standard errors in parentheses; * significant at 10%; ** significant at 5%; *** significant at 1%

Table 6.15: Test of Hypothesis 6.3 (OLS regressions, treatment and control group data, part 1)

Dependent variable change in career intentions / sample	model 1 treated only	model 2 with control group	model 3 treated only	model 4 with control group	model 5 treated only	model 6 with control group
	Controls only		Perceived desirability only		Perceived social norm only	
treatment (yes = 1)		-0.061 (0.485)		1.372** (0.671)		-0.444 (0.740)
Perceived desirability						
strength of period 1 signal			-0.161* (0.086)	0.872*** (0.215)		
consistent signals			-0.145 (0.517)	0.036 (1.056)		
strong and consistent signals			**0.008** **(0.207)**	-0.624 (0.515)		
strength of period 2 signal			0.590*** (0.052)	0.497*** (0.150)		
strength of period 1 signal x treatment				-1.035*** (0.230)		
consistent signals x treatment				-0.211 (1.178)		
strong and consistent signals x treatment				**0.634** **(0.556)**		
strength of period 2 signal x treatment				0.094 (0.159)		
Perceived social norm						
strength of period 1 signal * 1000					-0.115 (0.205)	0.413 (0.677)
consistent signals					-0.152 (0.554)	-1.718 (1.178)
strong and consistent signals * 1000					**-0.051** **(0.425)**	-0.511 (1.176)
strength of period 2 signal * 1000					1.441*** (0.212)	0.736** (0.373)
strength of period 1 signal x treatment * 1000						-0.552 (0.707)
consistent signals x treatment						1.509 (1.306)
strong and consistent signals x treatment * 1000						**0.496** **(1.254)**
strength of period 2 signal x treatment * 1000						0.715* (0.432)

Table 6.15 (continued): Test of Hypothesis 6.3 (OLS regressions, treatment and control group data, part 1 continued)

Dependent variable change in career intentions sample	model 1	model 2	model 3	model 4	model 5	model 6
	Controls only		Perceived desirability only		Perceived social norm only	
	treated only	with control group	treated only	with control group	treated only	with control group
Perceived behavioral control						
strength of period 1 signal						
consistent signals						
strong and consistent signals						
strength of period 2 signal						
strength of period 1 signal x treatment						
consistent signals x treatment						
strong and consistent signals x treatment						
strength of period 2 signal x treatment						
Demographics						
age	-0.044	0.052	-0.063	0.029	-0.045	0.068
	(0.100)	(0.094)	(0.087)	(0.082)	(0.095)	(0.090)
female (0/1)	0.319	0.302	0.382	0.313	0.209	0.170
	(0.429)	(0.392)	(0.375)	(0.343)	(0.411)	(0.378)
foreign (0/1)	-0.168	-0.413	0.032	-0.130	-0.194	-0.482
	(0.589)	(0.547)	(0.516)	(0.477)	(0.559)	(0.523)
Prior experiences						
breadth of prior exposure	0.007	0.032	-0.082	-0.191	0.016	0.016
	(0.217)	(0.199)	(0.192)	(0.177)	(0.209)	(0.194)
attended entrepreneurship courses	-0.750	-0.204	-0.475	-0.120	-0.589	-0.163
	(0.613)	(0.219)	(0.537)	(0.191)	(0.586)	(0.209)
constant	2.974	0.940	2.995	-0.163	2.406	0.473
	(2.181)	(1.997)	(1.906)	(1.780)	(2.077)	(1.975)
Test statistics						
Observations	403	509	403	509	403	509
R-squared	-0.007	-0.008	0.236	0.243	0.095	0.082
F-test (df)	0.468(5)	0.366(6)	14.83(9)	12.65(14)	5.691(9)	4.252(14)
F-test sig	0.800	0.900	0.000	0.000	0.000	0.000

Notes: robust standard errors in parentheses; * significant at 10%; ** significant at 5%, *** significant at 1%

Table 6.15 (continued): Test of Hypothesis 6.3 (OLS regressions, treatment and control group data, part 2)

Dependent variable change in career intentions sample	model 7 Perceived behavioral control only treated only	model 8 Perceived behavioral control only with control group	model 9 Full model treated only	model 10 Full model with control group	model 11 Full model with CEM
treatment (yes = 1)		-0.509 (0.726)		0.128 (0.862)	-0.702 (0.734)
Perceived desirability					
strength of period 1 signal			-0.223** (0.093)	0.939*** (0.228)	-0.161 (0.366)
consistent signals			-0.165 (0.501)	0.245 (1.064)	0.446 (0.623)
strong and consistent signals			**-0.068** **(0.208)**	-0.447 (0.557)	-0.486 (0.671)
strength of period 2 signal			0.576*** (0.068)	0.503*** (0.149)	0.276* (0.141)
strength of period 1 signal x treatment				-1.165*** (0.247)	-0.421 (0.558)
consistent signals x treatment				-0.439 (1.181)	-0.850 (0.841)
strong and consistent signals x treatment				**0.381** **(0.596)**	**0.867** **(0.923)**
strength of period 2 signal x treatment				0.073 (0.164)	0.142 (0.194)
Perceived social norm					
strength of period 1 signal * 1000			0.194 (0.207)	-0.394 (0.629)	0.598 (0.886)
consistent signals			-0.034 (0.492)	-1.537 (1.076)	-1.863** (0.791)
strong and consistent signals * 1000			**-0.029** **(0.386)**	0.090 (1.081)	0.395 (3.016)
strength of period 2 signal * 1000			0.962*** (0.195)	0.417 (0.358)	0.865*** (0.275)
strength of period 1 signal x treatment * 1000				0.593 (0.664)	-1.396 (1.243)
consistent signals x treatment				1.488 (1.186)	1.481 (1.044)
strong and consistent signals x treatment * 1000				**-0.107** **(1.151)**	**-2.701** **(3.497)**
strength of period 2 signal x treatment * 1000				0.552 (0.410)	-0.540 (0.467)

Table 6.15 (continued): Test of Hypothesis 6.3 (OLS regressions, treatment and control group data, part 2 continued)

Dependent variable change in career intentions sample	model 7	model 8	model 9	model 10	model 11
	Perceived behavioral control only		Full model		
	treated only	with control group	treated only	with control group	with CEM
Perceived behavioral control					
strength of period 1 signal	-0.380** (0.163)	0.236 (0.318)	-0.193 (0.161)	-0.262 (0.315)	-0.875 (0.731)
consistent signals	-0.207 (0.515)	-0.471 (1.085)	0.109 (0.460)	-0.134 (0.951)	-0.496 (0.569)
strong and consistent signals	**0.137 (0.344)**	-0.358 (0.817)	**0.143 (0.316)**	-0.414 (0.779)	0.330 (1.558)
strength of period 2 signal	0.496*** (0.085)	-0.368 (0.464)	-0.098 (0.098)	-0.445 (0.416)	-0.796* (0.458)
strength of period 1 signal x treatment		-0.648* (0.360)		0.050 (0.356)	0.843 (0.988)
consistent signals x treatment		0.224 (1.210)		0.226 (1.062)	1.910** (0.841)
strong and consistent signals x treatment		**0.470 (0.988)**		**1.064 (0.840)**	**-1.099 (2.198)**
strength of period 2 signal x treatment		0.861* (0.472)		0.348 (0.427)	1.478*** (0.516)
Demographics					
age	-0.047 (0.097)	0.051 (0.092)	-0.038 (0.085)	0.054 (0.080)	-0.028 (0.095)
female (0/1)	0.557 (0.414)	0.501 (0.384)	0.257 (0.369)	0.215 (0.341)	0.098 (0.341)
foreign (0/1)	-0.055 (0.565)	-0.370 (0.535)	0.050 (0.497)	-0.137 (0.467)	-0.771 (0.529)
Prior experiences					
breadth of prior exposure	-0.186 (0.213)	-0.105 (0.199)	-0.098 (0.190)	-0.173 (0.177)	-0.355* (0.189)
attended entrepreneurship courses	-0.782 (0.591)	-0.175 (0.214)	-0.502 (0.523)	-0.107 (0.187)	-0.036 (0.101)
constant	2.902 (2.098)	1.270 (2.020)	2.099 (1.851)	0.148 (1.813)	2.869 (2.021)
Test statistics					
Observations	403	509	403	509	331
R-squared	0.079	0.050	0.292	0.288	0.188
F-test (df)	4.805(9)	2.905(14)	10.77(17)	7.862(30)	3.524(30)
F-test sig	0.000	0.000	0.000	0.000	0.000

Notes: robust standard errors in parentheses; * significant at 10%; ** significant at 5%, *** significant at 1%

6.4 Discussion and Conclusion

Entrepreneurship is not a numbers game. Just having more entrepreneurs will not meet the hopes of politicians for a prospering economy or more jobs. It is the high-quality start-ups that have this desired outcome (Shane 2009). Transferring this to entrepreneurship education at tertiary educational institutions – a measure politicians take in order to "produce" more entrepreneurs – its goals may need reconsideration. Is it the right goal to convince students to become entrepreneurs, even if they are not willing to engage in an entrepreneurial career?

In this chapter I argue that entrepreneurship education should rather support students' self-selection into entrepreneurial activities or not. Based on this postulated goal of entrepreneurship education, I present a theoretical model that grounds on learning processes and updating of the opinion about one's own entrepreneurial aptitude according to Bayes' Rule. I extend the model by von Graevenitz et al. (2010), both theoretically along the Theory of Planned Behavior and empirically by employing data from a control group. It is assumed that students enter an entrepreneurship course with a prior opinion about their career intentions, and update their opinion during the entrepreneurship course towards their "true" career intentions. In the course they get signals along the three paths of the Theory of Planned Behavior, perceived desirability, perceived social norm, and perceived behavioral control regarding entrepreneurship. Based on this model I derived three hypotheses that on the one hand are grounded in the Theory of Planned Behavior, and on the other hand link post-course intentions and changes in intentions due to the course to the strength and the consistency of signals received by students prior to and during the entrepreneurship course. To test these hypotheses, I used the dataset described in section 3.5.

I confirm the hypothesis that the variance of entrepreneurial intentions significantly increases. This is a first indication that entrepreneurship education fulfills a separation function. The students' entrepreneurial intentions become more pronounced. A further investigation of these separation effects across several subsamples reveal that an entrepreneurship course fulfills this sorting function especially for female students, for students who already worked for a start-up, and for students who are open to experience. In addition, together with the findings in chapter 5, students with self-employed parents and students who already have attended an entrepreneurship course experience a more uniform positive shift in their opinion about their entrepreneurial aptitude. Next, the results show that strong pre-course signals along the perceived desirability and perceived social norm paths lead to stronger post-course opinions about one's entrepreneurial aptitude, as do consistent signals in the perceived social norm and perceived behavioral control paths. The herein presented extension of the model by von Graevenitz et al. (2010) provides valuable information about the paths of the Theory of Planned Behavior in which students process new information and subsequently update their opinion about their entrepreneurial aptitude. However, these findings do not hold when employing the data from a control group. Probably, with only 106 observations the control group data lacks statistical power (see section 3.7). In addition, changes of entrepreneurial intentions during the course were not related to strong and consistent pre-course signals.

The reconsideration of the goals of entrepreneurship education is one practical implication of this study. The evaluation of entrepreneurship education – often also as a report to an external fund provider to offer this kind of education – is based either on estimating possible increases in the actual or anticipated start-up rate and then trading these benefits off against program costs, or on mere positive shifts of entrepreneurial intentions and attitudes. These approaches miss the sorting effects highlighted in this chapter. Informing a student about an entrepreneurial career and help him discover that he is not willing to engage in such a career should be considered as much a success as to help a student strengthen his entrepreneurial intentions, since the student could be prevented from entering a very costly real-world experiment of starting and failing a company. Also other possible welfare effects have to be taken into account: in the context of funding of entrepreneurial ventures it has been argued that subsidies for new entrepreneurs could be socially wasteful (De Meza and Southey 1996; De Meza 2002). By analogy, one might expect that entrepreneurship education could have negative effects if it succeeded in convincing those not suited to entrepreneurship that they should become entrepreneurs. Alternatively, and more positively, it could be that such education actually informs students and allows them to discover their specific abilities. In this case, even a decline in entrepreneurial intentions could be socially valuable, since it may indicate that subsequent matches in the labor market will be improved (von Graevenitz et al. 2010).

The results also give insights into how an entrepreneurship course could be designed which is meant to inform students about the career path they are most suited for. The Theory of Planned Behavior delivers a suitable framework for deriving implications. Consistent social norm-signals and consistent behavioral control signals strengthen students' beliefs that they are (or are not) entrepreneurs. There should be enough room for more extensive feedback by educators than just giving grades, or letting students discuss their performance in a team project with a feedback round. Also, feedback on the students' course performance (for example in writing a business plan or playing in a start-up simulation) could generate social norm signals. On the other hand the behavioral control signal seems to be the most important. In entrepreneurship courses students should be put in situations where they can discover if they have control over the tasks associated with starting a company. This was also the most important implication of the findings in chapter 5. The results regarding the different strength of the sorting effect across several subsamples deliver first implications for student admission to an entrepreneurship course. If a course planner aims at informing students about their entrepreneurial aptitude, he should preferably admit female students, students who already worked for a start-up, and students who are open to experience to the course. From a methodological point of view this chapter adds to the approach taken by von Graevenitz et al. (2010) by exploiting data from a control group. This promises to deliver more robust estimations. However, as mentioned above, the control group data lacks statistical power in this chapter.

The framework outlined here opens up several avenues for future work. It is intended to further test this theoretical framework and to reapply it to other entrepreneurship courses, or even to other types of education using both treatment and control group data with appropriate sample sizes. Second, possible interactions along the Theory of Planned Behavior framework should be considered. Third, the effects of particular course characteristics on entrepreneurial attitudes (and indirectly on entrepreneurial intentions) – as discussed above – should be integrated in the model. One could gain more insights how entrepreneurship education, which is intended to inform students rather than convincing them to be entrepreneurs, should be designed. Moreover, the further investigation of the different effects across subsamples defined by background characteristics promises additional insights into optimal student selection.

7. Peer Effects in Entrepreneurship Education

7.1 Introduction

Although important both for educational production (e.g. Sacerdote 2001) and the formation of entrepreneurial activity (e.g. Nanda and Sørensen 2010), the effects of social interactions on the development of entrepreneurial skills in entrepreneurship education have been completely ignored so far. At the same time there is a large potential for leveraging social interaction effects to increase the formation of entrepreneurial skills among the students: team-based business planning is a prevalent component of entrepreneurship education (Krueger et al. 2000). And due to restricted education budgets, an efficient measure, for example the reshuffling of teams to maximize beneficial social interaction effects for skill formation, is welcome to instructors and course planners. A quantification of externalities deriving from social interactions would be valuable to several stakeholder groups involved in entrepreneurship education, that are concerned about efficient educational production given heterogeneous student quality (Foster 2006).

Presently, none of the studies on the effects of entrepreneurship education at tertiary institutions, although aiming at deriving implications about optimal course design, has taken into account social multiplier effects on the formation of entrepreneurial skills due to social interaction in the business planning teams. Since a central function of entrepreneurship education is increasing entrepreneurial skills among students (see previous chapters), an investigation of these externalities may provide an important contribution to the literature. In this chapter I investigate whether social interaction effects in an entrepreneurship course foster the formation of entrepreneurial skills. The course "Business Planning" (described in chapter 3) provides an attractive setting for such an analysis. In this course the students work together in teams of four to six to create business plans. The ongoing social interactions in this teamwork may enhance students' entrepreneurial abilities. I survey students on their skill-perceptions before and after the course and link the changes to the influence of their team members.

I investigate three main questions: first, do social interaction effects exist in the context of entrepreneurship education at all? Second, I determine the size and nature of these effects. More specifically, are "receiving students" (those with initially low skills) more subject to input by their team members than highly skilled students (or vice versa)? Also regarding "sending students", is the size and nature of the effect dependent on the skill level of a focal student's team members? And third, how can course planners achieve a maximum "social gain" in entrepreneurial skills across the whole population of students by composing teams according to the students' initial skill level?

To answer these questions I build on previous research on education and entrepreneurship dealing with social interactions. Researchers already pursue these questions with respect to general education at all levels of schooling. They identify the quality of students as an important input factor regarding educational production apart from teachers and infrastructure. Social scientists emphasize the importance of social interactions among students. The existence of such interactions may affect learning and skill building in classrooms, which in turn has implications for the optimal organization of those. Economists, in particular, are interested in effects emerging from social interactions among students because some of these effects – which are, by definition, externalities – are not internalized (Hoxby 2001). Hence the existence of these effects opens avenues for increasing overall skill building in a classroom by leveraging "social multipliers". Several empirical papers deal with the evaluation of size and nature of these effects and derive implications for a better organization of schooling at tertiary institutions (e.g. Sacerdote 2001; Zimmerman 2003; Hanushek et al. 2003, Arcidiacono and Nicholson 2005).

Social interactions are also of interest for entrepreneurship researchers. The formation of regions with high levels of entrepreneurial activity such as Silicon Valley raises the question whether powerful social interactions within a defined (geographical, social) environment impact the decision to become an entrepreneur (Lerner and Malmendier 2011). Central to the studies on social interactions and entrepreneurial activity is the role that coworkers play in the formation of entrepreneurial attitudes and activity (e.g. Nanda and Sørensen (2010), or Stuart and Ding (2006) for university scientists). Lerner and Malmendier (2011) provide first insight into social interaction effects among university students, exploiting data on a section-level at Harvard Business School.

To my knowledge, for the first time this chapter explores social interaction effects regarding the formation of entrepreneurial skills in entrepreneurship education. This brings together the two research streams. It thus gives first information about the question if these effects do play a role in entrepreneurship education at all, and how course planners can leverage these effects in order to maximize the overall formation of entrepreneurial skills among students.

The results suggest that social interaction effects exist. A focal student's mean entrepreneurial skills increase the higher are the skills of his team members. This even holds when introducing fixed effects, taking into account commonly shared resources used by several teams of students (in this case the tutorial teaching assistant). The further investigation of the nature of social interaction effects reveals, however, that this effect is driven by a significant negative effect on a student's skills when working together with low-skilled team members. Additional analyses suggest that male students are more susceptible to social interaction effects than female ones, and students with few prior entrepreneurship-related experiences more than students with a broad prior exposure to entrepreneurship. Regarding non-linearities in the social interaction effects the findings suggest that students in the middle of the entrepreneurial skill distribution should be grouped together with high skilled team members. Other combinations do not yield significant positive effects on entrepreneurial skills of a focal student. By exploiting these findings course planners may extract a net social gain in entrepreneurial skills among the population of students. High skilled students may be moved away from low skilled or other high skilled students, since these two groups do not seem to profit from their team members anyway.

I argue that these findings are reliable, since my research design overcomes several challenges that other studies face that have dealt with social interaction effects. First, the boundaries of the social interaction (the business planning team) in question are precise and unambiguous. Although other reference persons may play a role in the formation of skills emanating from social interactions, most likely the surveyed students spend most of the time they spend on entrepreneurship topics in their respective team. Second, estimation of social interaction effects is often seriously biased by selection. In settings where students can self-select into the teams, they may group themselves with other students who are very similar. In the case of entrepreneurial skills, the researcher cannot distinguish whether a potential increase in skills is an *effect* of belonging to the group or a *reason* for belonging to it (Hoxby 2001). In this chapter I argue that I can build on a "quasi-random" assignment to teams. Although students are grouped according to the amount of previously completed university education, my tests suggest that the assignment is random regarding previous exposure to entrepreneurship and additional individual background characteristics. Thus I do not expect the results to be biased by self-selection. And finally, due to the ex-ante ex-post design, I am able to take the same variable measuring entrepreneurial skills both as an exogenous determinant of a student's own and his team's skill level as well as endogenous outcome variable. This minimizes measurement errors in comparison to other studies in a schooling setting, which take the high school SAT (Scholastic Aptitude Test) score as exogenous determinant of skill level and GPA (Grade Point Average) at college as endogenous variable (e.g. Sacerdote (2001) or Zimmerman (2003)).

The remainder of this chapter is organized as follows. Section 2 provides a literature review on social interaction effects in schooling and entrepreneurship. Moreover I discuss how entrepreneurial skills may be mutually enhanced in a student team in an entrepreneurship course. Section 3 lays out the econometric framework based upon which I estimate the size and nature of these effects. The ensuing section introduces the relevant measures and provides descriptive statistics. Results are provided in section 5. Section 6 concludes and discusses the implications of the findings.

7.2 Social Interactions in Education and Entrepreneurship

The analysis of social interactions is central to sociology and social psychology, and has also become an important area of research regarding economic outcomes (Manski 1993, 2010). These analyses aim at explaining group behaviors emerging from interdependencies across individuals belonging to the same group. Models of social interactions have been applied to a wide range of context within these domains: neighborhood influences on socioeconomic outcomes, determining location decisions (leading for example to agglomerations of economic activity such as Silicon Valley), the adoption of technology standards, the evolution of political parties according to voter preferences, types of "undesirable behavior" sustained by peer effects, information cascades (learning by observing one's peers), or the evolution of science (conformity effects in scientific communities, just to name a few (this list is taken from Brock and Durlauf (2001).

Manski (1993) stated three hypotheses regarding the observation that individuals belonging to the same group tend to behave similarly. He suggests that there are three types of effects at work:

a) endogenous social (or peer-) effects[56]: the propensity of an individual to behave in some way varies with the behavior of the group

b) exogenous (or contextual) social effects: the propensity of an individual to behave in some way varies with the exogenous characteristics of the group, and

c) correlated effects: individuals belonging to the same group tend to behave similarly due to similar individual characteristics or similar institutional environments.

---

[56] There are many terms that all refer to endogenous social effects. These effects mean an individual's formation of attitudes or behavior according to the variation of attitudes or behavior in some reference group containing this individual. With other words, individuals belonging to the same group tend to share similar attitudes or behave similarly (Manski 1993). These effects may be called "social norms" (see subsection 2.3.1), "peer influences" or "peer effects", "neighbourhood effects", "conformity", "imitation", "contagion", "epidemics", "bandwagons", "herd behavior", "interdependent preferences", or "social interactions" (Manski 1993).

In the next subsection (7.2.1) I will discuss these three effect types and their differing policy implications by means of the setting I am dealing with – an educational intervention – and the goal an educational interventions has – increasing overall learning or achievement. This is followed by a closer look at social interaction effects in the formation of entrepreneurial attitudes and intentions as well as behavior. In a synthesis in subsection 7.2.3 I will argue that social interactions may be used to leverage the formation of entrepreneurial skills in an entrepreneurship course.

7.2.1 Social Interaction Effects in Schooling

Research on social interactions in schooling has become an important aspect of the analysis of achievement outcomes. Understanding the nature and size of social interactions effects are critical to social scientists. They are interested in their contribution to the overall learning of students compared to other inputs such as teachers and infrastructure and whether or not those interactions lead to large social multipliers (Sacerdote 2001, Epple and Romano 1998). The fundamental assumption is that students learn from their teachers and also from their classmates through observation and imitation. The members of the reference group (classmates) and their behavior are seen as a source of information. The presence of such social interaction effects might affect the optimal organization of schooling, when the aim is to increase the overall learning.

Within the issue of the organization of schooling, the composition of classes is one of the most important issues discussed in the literature (Schneeweis and Winter-Ebmer 2007). For example, should high-achieving, highly-skilled students or students from a certain socio-economic background be grouped together ("tracking") or not? There are arguments for both sides when one aims at increasing of overall learning. Tracking students allows teachers to respond to the specific needs of certain groups or to purposefully advance high-achieving and low-achieving students. On the other hand, bringing together skilled students with less skilled students (or students belonging to one socio-economic group and students from another) may promise stimulating learning-effects for the latter group. If these effects are asymmetric, reshuffling students into classes to increase overall learning will be an issue of economic efficiency. For example, if "good" students are more subject to influences of the reference group than "bad" students, then tracking would be the optimal strategy. If, by contrast, "bad" students are more sensitive towards these effects, then one should try to bring both groups together in one class. These organizational changes can have sizeable effects on student achievement (Woessmann 2003).

According to the three hypotheses stated by Manski (1993, 2010) social interaction effects on a student in schools can have the following impact on students:

- an endogenous effect on their achievement occurs, if their individual achievements vary with the average achievement of his reference group (which one can think of as their class, for example). Here, the interaction is not completed – the rise in achievement of one student further advances the achievement of his classmates.
- exogenous effects will occur if their achievements vary with, for example, the socio-economic composition of their reference group/class. This means that the achievement of student i rises, when a classmate j with an achievement-advancing background arrives.
- correlated effects mean that that their achievements are similar to those of his reference group because they have similar backgrounds or face the same institutional environment, e.g. when the same teacher teaches them.

As in other fields dealing with social interactions, research in the field of schooling can be divided into the investigation of exogenous effects (mostly reflecting sociologists' interest in background variables), and endogenous effects (mostly reflecting the interest of economists in externalities) (Gaviria and Raphael 2001).[57]

---

[57] Of course, there are also studies concerned to the investigation of correlated effects, e.g. with class size effects (e.g. Woessmann and West 2006), or with the congestion problem that arises because a classroom of students share a common resource (e.g. Hanushek (1998)).

It is increasingly important to be able to distinguish between exogenous and endogenous effects, because their predictions regarding the impact of policies are different.

Implications derived from exogenous effects became a major field of research in sociology in the 1960s. Scholars exerted high effort in order to analyze effects of school and neighborhood environment on students. Making classes for example more diverse (socially, racially, intellectually) may affect students' attitudes and achievements. This research primarily focused on primary and secondary education. The most noticed study in this field – studying exogenous effects – is the "Coleman Report" from 1966 (Coleman et al. 1966). They observed over half a million students from more than 3.000 primary and secondary schools. A key finding is that a student's achievement varies with the educational background and aspirations of the other students in the school. These effects were found to be even more important than characteristics of the teachers or than the school's environmental characteristics. Exploiting the database generated by the STAR (Student Teacher Achievement Ratio) project in Tennessee, Whitmore (2005) found that girls have a positive spillover effect onto both male and female peers in kindergarten through second grade. Her findings corroborate those of Hoxby (2001), who also found that a higher share of girls in one's cohort raises achievement.

From an economist's point of view, the most important question in this field of research is one of efficiency: is it possible, by enhancing the achievement of one student in class, to promote the achievement of other students in the class as well? Exogenous or correlated effects may not generate these "social multiplier" effects (Manski 2000). Probably due to the availability of large datasets, the research here is strongly concerned with primary and secondary schools.

For example, using data of over one million third-graders at over 3.000 Texas public elementary schools Hanushek et al. (2003) find that peer average achievement strongly influences learning across test score distributions. A 0.1 standard deviation increase in average peer (classmates) achievement (from one grade to the next) leads to a 0.02 increase in a student's achievement.

Kang (2007) uses the international data set from the Third International Mathematics and Science Study (TIMSS). He examines effects on achievements among classroom peers for each country and uses within-student differences to minimize the biases inherent in analyses of endogenous effects. The results provide evidence of a positive relationship between own and classmates' achievements for most of the TIMSS countries.

Another large international dataset has been used to assess peer effects. Schneeweis and Winter-Ebmer (2007) exploit the Austrian part of the Programme for International Student Assessment (PISA) dataset. Their results suggest that peer effects in reading seem to be asymmetric in favor of students with a lower ability, meaning that the returns to peers are higher for these students.

Fewer studies deal with peer effects in higher education. Sacerdote (2001) makes an important contribution in the investigation of social multiplier effects in higher education. He exploits random housing assignment to assess peer effects among students of Dartmouth College and provides strong evidence for the existence of these effects. Accordingly, roommate peer effects are important influences on first-year Grade Point Average (GPA). Additionally, his findings suggest that students from the bottom 25% of the GPA distribution may do better when sharing a room with a student who is in the top 25% of the distribution.

Zimmerman (2003) uses data from Williams College students on students' and their roommates' math and verbal SAT (Scholastic Aptitude Test) scores to measure peer effects in academic outcomes (GPA). He finds that peer effects are linked more strongly with the verbal than with the math scores, although the effects are not very large. Moreover, he investigates asymmetric effects: students in the middle SAT distribution may have worse grades when sharing a room with a student who is in the bottom 15% of the verbal SAT distribution.

Using data of over one million third-graders at over 3.000 Texas public elementary schools Hanushek et al. (2003) find that peer average achievement strongly influences learning across test score distributions. An increase in average peer (classmates) achievement (from one grade to the next) leads to an increase in a student's achievement.

Looking at a very selected group of students, Arcidiacono and Nicholson (2005) assess peer effects among the population of students (N = 47.755) attending a medical school in the US. They find that the ability of a person's peer group affects this person's own ability. However, this effect disappears when introducing school fixed-effects. They also analyze peer effects in specialty preferences. Their findings suggest that when attending a medical school with students who plan choosing a high-income specialty, own ability as well as the probability of choosing a high income-specialty increase.

Foster (2006), on the other hand, cannot confirm robust residential peer effects on undergraduate performance, using data on over 50.000 students of the University of Maryland. Moreover, she compares the influence of random and chosen peers on college performance, and found that "friends" do not impact performance more than randomized peers.

This review of literature on peer effects in schooling is far from being complete, but gives a good overview about the findings when looking at class composition and social multiplier effects. Few peer effects studies have been conducted at tertiary level although this setting would provide a more convenient one for the measurement of peer effects. These effects are difficult to isolate for young children, as the parental influence at this stage of their lives is probably too strong and may cancel out any positive or negative effects from student interaction. The peer effects discovered there are mostly modest and not robust to sample modifications or alternative specifications (Foster 2006). Also, there are several difficulties in measuring peer effects, and especially in empirically distinguishing between endogenous and exogenous effects I did not mention so far. I will discuss these issues in section 7.3 together with my empirical strategy. However, the vast majority of conducted research suggests that peer effects contribute to overall learning and achievement within the defined peer group. I will argue that those peer and social multiplier effects are also existent in educational interventions such as entrepreneurship education in tertiary institutions.

But first, I review the literature on peer effects and their role in the formation of entrepreneurial attitudes and activity.

7.2.2 Social Interaction Effects and Entrepreneurial Intentions and Activity

The review of literature in the previous subsection already referred to one article, which suggests that peers may have an impact on occupational choice (Arcidiacono and Nicholson 2005). In this subsection I review the literature on the role of peers in the formation of entrepreneurial attitudes and activity. In the previous chapters I have emphasized the role of perceived social norm in the formation of entrepreneurial intentions. As argued in this chapter, social norm are a form of peer effect. Only recently, however, has the role of social interaction with peers in the formation of entrepreneurial attitudes, intentions and activity explicitly been highlighted. Here, too, researchers ask whether interactions among high-skilled individuals lead to large social multipliers. The formation of regions with high levels of entrepreneurial activity such as Silicon Valley raises the question whether powerful social interactions within a defined (geographical, social) environment impact the decision to become an entrepreneur (Lerner and Malmendier 2011). And Bernardo and Welch (2001) discuss "entrepreneurial cascades", a concept derived from Bikhchandani's et al. (1998) "informational cascades": the decision of an individual to become an entrepreneur will encourage others to do likewise, even if the imitating individual has prior information that returns to this activity are poor.

Taking a sociological perspective and using data on local labor markets in Sweden, Giannetti and Simonov (2009) show that the probability of entry into entrepreneurship is higher for individuals in neighbourhoods with a high level of entrepreneurial activity.

Some studies look at the role workplace peers play in the formation of entrepreneurial activity. Stuart and Ding (2006) examine the conditions leading university-employed scientists to become entrepreneurs. They find that scientists are more likely to become entrepreneurs when they work in departments where other scientists have previously become entrepreneurs.

Based on data from the Integrated Database for Labor Market Research in Denmark (IDA), Nanda and Sørensen (2010) examine whether the likelihood of entrepreneurial activity is related to prior career experiences of an individual's coworkers. They find that an individual is more likely to become an entrepreneur when her coworkers have previously been entrepreneurs.

Exploiting the assignments of MBA students at Harvard Business School into sections (i.e. groups of typically 80 to 90 students), Lerner and Malmendier (2011) provide counter-intuitive effects. They find that a higher share of students with an entrepreneurial background in a given section leads to lower subsequent rates of entrepreneurship among their peers (i.e. section members).

The environment closest to the one I am studying is considered by Falck et al. (2010). They exploit PISA 2006 data to examine peer effects on entrepreneurship among students at the age of 15 to 16. Their results suggest that having entrepreneurial peers (i.e. classmates whose parents are entrepreneurs) at school contributes to the formation of entrepreneurial intentions.

Although the empirical work backing this assertion is rather scarce, this stream of literature lends support to the notion that one's peer group does influence one's own entrepreneurial attitudes, intentions and activity. However, the subjects observed in these articles did not explicitly work on projects of entrepreneurial nature. This means that the impact of peers on the formation of individual entrepreneurial attitudes may be underestimated. This impact is rather a result of observing peers and not of cooperating with them on entrepreneurial tasks. The social multiplier effects may be even stronger when researchers look at cooperative teams who work on entrepreneurial projects together compared to cooperative teams who share the same workplace but do not work on projects that are entrepreneurial in nature or even non-cooperative teams, who share the same workplace but do not really interact.

Here I exploit the structure of the entrepreneurship course "Business Planning", where students are "quasi-randomly"[58] assigned to teams working

---

[58] Faculty staff assigns students to their project-teams based on the number of previously completed university courses.

cooperatively on entrepreneurial projects. Thus I integrate the two streams of literature on peer effects regarding schooling outcomes and the formation of entrepreneurial attitudes and examine the impact of peers on the formation of entrepreneurial skills. To my knowledge, no study has so far assessed the role of peer effects in the formation of entrepreneurial skills in entrepreneurship education. Therefore my research contributes to both literature streams:

- First, the goal of a university is to increase (overall) the entrepreneurial skills of their students, regardless of whether they become entrepreneurs or organizationally employed (and act as entrepreneurially skilled employees). I investigate the nature and size of the peer effects towards this goal and derive implications about how to group students in teams to increase the overall learning of entrepreneurial skills, when an entrepreneurship course involves teamwork, and
- Second, I contribute to the literature on the impact of workplace peers on the formation of entrepreneurial skills, when the team works cooperatively on a project that is entrepreneurial in nature.

In the next subsection I present the theoretical foundations regarding the role of peer effects in the formation of entrepreneurial skills in teams who work on entrepreneurial projects.

7.2.3 Peer Effects and the Formation of Entrepreneurial Skills during Entrepreneurship Education

Entrepreneurship education aims at increasing entrepreneurial skills among students. A vast amount of literature has dealt with optimal course design to increase learning (and also ex-post entrepreneurial intentions) in such settings. Substantial efforts have been made to support tertiary institutions in this task. However, the "quality" of students itself may be an important factor in the production of entrepreneurial skills at universities. In many entrepreneurship courses, students work in cooperative teams on entrepreneurial projects, for example creating a business plan or running a start-up simulation. They may learn more and acquire more entrepreneurial skills, when they work on projects together with strong students during an entrepreneurship course. Close ties between students may lead to accelerated learning processes regarding entrepreneurship and favor social learning and knowledge spillovers (Saxenian 1996). To identify peer effects in the formation of entrepreneurial skills, I rely on Bandura's (1977, 1982) concept of self-efficacy and the notion of entrepreneurial self-efficacy.

7.2.3.1 Entrepreneurial Self-Efficacy

"Perceived self-efficacy" is derived from Bandura's "Social Learning Theory" (Bandura 1977, 1982). Bandura (1997, p. 257) defines perceived self-efficacy as "(...) people's belief about their capabilities to exercise control over their own level of functioning and over events that affect their lives." It thus describes the self-assessment of the ability to execute necessary courses of action and accomplish future tasks. It is also related to an individual's effectiveness in transforming these skills into desired outcomes. It is based upon past experience and anticipation of future obstacles and determines perceptions whether or not certain goals are attainable. An important aspect is that perceived self-efficacy is considered to be task- and domain-specific. Hence, an individual can exhibit a very strong self-efficacy in one domain and be convinced to be able to successfully perform the behavior, whereas in another domain the opposite is true (Bandura 1977; 1982, 1997).

Self-efficacy is affected by experience and social influence in four ways (Bandura 1982): mastery experience (or "learning by doing"), observational (or "vicarious") learning (through the presence of role models that may be one's peers), social persuasion (feedback by others helps evaluating one's own capability to perform a task (Gist and Mitchell 1992)), and finally also the judgment of the own physiological state.

The concept of self-efficacy has been increasingly emphasized in the study of entrepreneurial activity and entrepreneurship education (Chen et al. 1998; Zhao et al. 2005; Wilson et al. 2007; Kickul et al. 2009). Chen et al. (1998, p. 301) define "entrepreneurial self-efficacy" as "the strength of an individual's belief that he or she is capable of successfully performing the roles and tasks of an entrepreneur". Krueger and Carsrud (1993) state that entrepreneurial self-efficacy is influenced by the acquisition of management tools and the exposure to entrepreneurial situations, and that entrepreneurship education seems to be an ideal setting for the development of self-efficacy. Also peer evaluations should play a role therein.

My basic but rational assumption is grounded on Bandura's research into the phenomenon of self-efficacy, i.e., that people with high perceived self-efficacy will actually carry out the roles and tasks in question (Bandura 1997). Accordingly, when working in a cooperative team on an entrepreneurial project, team members will act according to their entrepreneurial self-efficacy and will learn from each other.

7.2.3.2 Mutual Development of Entrepreneurial Self-Efficacy in Cooperative Teams

According to social learning theory, direct observation of other people can provide vicarious experience that affects attitudes by a process of social comparison with the potential role models (Wood and Bandura 1989). When an individual perceives similarities between herself and the role model (in terms of personality or skills) and when the observed behavior produces obvious consequences or measurable success (Bandura 1986; Gist and Mitchell 1992), individuals tend to infer that the same outcomes would occur when performing the behavior themselves. The peer group, i.e. members of the own cooperative project-team in an entrepreneurship course, can act as role models. Previous research suggests that similarity in perceived competence (i.e. in perceived entrepreneurial self-efficacy) increases the likelihood of observational learning (Bandura 1986). The team members should therefore experience higher self-efficacy for performing a task when they observe their team members performing it well: "The people, with whom one regularly associates – either through preference or imposition –, delimit the behavioral patterns that will be repeatedly observed, and hence, learned most thoroughly" (Bandura 1986, p. 55).

Mutual benefits through peer effects are also discussed in the literature on learning in small groups. Each individual contributes to the team's knowledge, and individuals integrate team knowledge into personal meaning schemes. The conducted research has presented a favorable picture of cooperative learning (Webb 1982). Scholars emphasize the importance of interaction in small teams for learning: "It is through the medium of this interaction and communication process within small groups cooperating on academic tasks that these team-learning methods strive to influence pupils' cognitive learning" (Sharan 1980, p. 242). When every team member's performance influences the rewards of the team, team members will support each other's academic efforts, which in turn will lead to increased individual effort.

In sum, work on social psychology and cooperative learning states that the mentioned social comparison processes in groups lead to a strong tendency to conform or to uniformity. People who exhibit a very high (or very low) entrepreneurial self-efficacy may act as "trendsetters", establishing a "social identity" within the group (Bicchieri and Fukui 1999). The team members may want to conform to what they think is the group norm. This "peer pressure" is even stronger when profits (i.e. grades in this case) are shared (Kandel and Lazear 1992)[59]. On the other hand the theory suggests that self-efficacy gets higher during the teamwork, the more a team member contributes to the successful completion of the project. However, it is of course important to mention that these peer effects may not always be beneficial. In a team with many members who exhibit a very low entrepreneurial self-efficacy and act accordingly, other team members may be influenced negatively. This means that the latter may also do poorly in the entrepreneurial project and therefore experience a decrease in their perception of entrepreneurial self-efficacy.

In the following I investigate the size and nature of peer-effects when working in small teams on an entrepreneurial project during entrepreneurship education using the data collected from students in the "Business Planning" course. The first goal is to elicit whether peer effects in these small teams do

---

[59] In "Business Planning", the profit is also shared among team members, as grading is based on the business plan that is largely a team-achievement.

exist at all. The models will also allow for nonlinearity in peer quality to test whether peers in a special area of the entrepreneurial self-efficacy distribution affect the own self-efficacy differently. Besides the asymmetric influence of the "information-sending" peers, I will also allow for a varying own entrepreneurial self-efficacy to assess whether peers differently influence certain subgroups of students. As argued, the existence of asymmetric peer effects is interesting from an economic efficiency point of view, as regrouping students in teams may evoke beneficial effects on the development of individual entrepreneurial self-efficacy. Finally I will try to derive policy guidelines for entrepreneurship course planners who employ cooperative learning how to optimally distribute students based on their own and team members' entrepreneurial self-efficacy to maximize the "social gain" in entrepreneurial self-efficacy, i.e. to maximize the average increase among the whole population of course attendees.

7.3 Econometric Framework

In this section I present the econometric models I use to estimate mean and asymmetric peer effects. Estimating these models in the next section I provide answers to the questions raised at the end of the previous section.

7.3.1 Mean Peer-Effects

There is a common framework for estimating peer effects regarding academic achievement in high schools in the studies presented in subsection 7.2.1. It involves the student's GPA, which is dependent on the own level of academic ability (before being exposed to the peer effects in question, often the student's SAT as a proxy for this ability), and the peers' GPA. Hence, the basic econometric model (following Sacerdote (2001)) is often specified as follows, whereby I assume that student i has only one peer, student j (an extension of this model to more peers is straightforward by using the average of the peers' characteristics):

$$GPA_i = \alpha'_0 + \alpha'_1 SAT_i + \alpha'_2 SAT_j + \alpha'_3 GPA_j + \alpha'_4 X_i + \epsilon_i$$
$$GPA_j = \beta'_0 + \beta'_1 SAT_j + \beta'_2 SAT_i + \beta'_3 GPA_i + \beta'_4 X_i + \epsilon_j$$

where GPA_* and SAT_* stand for the GPA and the SAT of student i or j respectively, μ_* represents the measurement error from taking the SAT as a proxy for academic ability, and X_* is a vector of background characteristics of the students.

In my case, the ex-ante ex-post survey design allows me to measure the outcome of interest – entrepreneurial self-efficacy – before and after the exposure to peer effects. Therefore I employ the following model:

$$ESE_i^{ex-post} = \alpha_0 + \alpha_1 ESE_i^{ex-ante} + \alpha_2 ESE_j^{ex-ante} + \alpha_3 ESE_j^{ex-post} + \alpha_4 X_i + \epsilon_i$$

$$ESE_j^{ex-post} = \alpha_0 + \alpha_1 ESE_j^{ex-ante} + \alpha_2 ESE_i^{ex-ante} + \alpha_3 ESE_i^{ex-post} + \beta_4 X_i + \epsilon_j$$

where ESE_*^{time} represents the entrepreneurial self-efficacy of student *i* or *j* ex-ante or ex-post respectively.

The identification of peer effects is complicated due to the "reflection problem" (Manski 1993), as the student's (*i*) and the peer's (*j*) entrepreneurial self-efficacy are determined simultaneously. To overcome this complexity, researchers suggest using a reduced form equation when the dataset delivers a "lagged" value of the outcome under consideration (Sacerdote 2001), which is given here with $ESE_j^{ex-ante}$. Therefore I substitute one equation into the other and obtain the following reduced form:

$$ESE_i^{ex-post} = \gamma_0 + \gamma_1 ESE_i^{ex-ante} + \gamma_2 ESE_j^{ex-ante} + \gamma_3 X_i + \gamma_4 X_j + \eta_i$$

Next I translate this equation to my setting where normally the peer group is larger than one. Following past convention I use the average value among a student's peers of the respective construct. I denote the ("endogenous") peer-variables as $\overline{ESE_{(-i)}^{ex-ante}}$ (average peer entrepreneurial self-efficacy ex-ante) and $\overline{X_{(-i)}}$ (average background characteristics of peers), where the subscript (-i) means that these variables represent the average values computed over all students in the peer group other than the vocal student i.

$$ESE_i^{ex-post} = \gamma_0 + \gamma_1 ESE_i^{ex-ante} + \gamma_2 \overline{ESE_{(-i)}^{ex-ante}} + \gamma_3 X_i + \gamma_4 \overline{X_{(-i)}} + \eta_i$$

Equation 7.1: Reduced form for estimating peer effects

The peer-effect is given by the coefficient γ_2. Manski's (1993) hypothesis about peer-effects predicts that $\gamma_2 \neq 0$.

Estimating this last model still faces some conceptual and empirical hurdles. The first issue is the definition of the "right" peer group. I argue that the business planning teams of four to six students is a meaningful context of locating peer-effects. Another (observable) possibility for the peer group is of course the tutorial that four to five teams attend together every week. However, due to the higher interaction between students in the team than compared to the tutorial, I define the team as the relevant peer group. The big advantage in my research design is that students are forced to interact with a fixed, well-defined team. Unlike statistical proxies for neighbourhoods (see e.g. Giannetti and Simonov (2009)), the boundaries of interaction here are precise and unambiguous. However, this choice does not rule out the possibility that other factors, including peers who are not team members (friends, siblings, etc.), also influence the ex-post entrepreneurial self-efficacy. But most likely the students – in this stage of their life – spend most of their time on topics of entrepreneurship (during the semester under consideration) in their respective teams to write the business plan that is demanded at the end of the course. My estimates of peer effects based on team members alone will be a lower bound on the total peer effects that influence the ex-post entrepreneurial self-efficacy. Henceforth I will also refer to the term "team" for a student's peer group. Another severe problem arises if students are not randomly assigned their peers. Then the estimated peer effect γ_2 will be biased, as $cov(ESE_j^{ex-ante}; \eta_i) \neq 0$. This is most likely the case when students self-select into their peer group or neighborhood, a context most of the presented studies above are confronted with. In "Business Planning", students cannot self-select into teams because the faculty staff exogenously assigns the team members. However, this assignment is not completely random: the teams are formed homogeneously regarding previous academic achievement measured in previously gained ECTS credits. This means that every team has students from the low, the middle, and the top area of the ECTS credits distribution. However, in the next section I run a test whether the team assignment can be considered as random regarding entrepreneurship-related background characteristics. This "quasi-random" assignment minimizes this bias. Finally I have to take "common shocks" into account that affect the teams together. Common shocks arise when several teams share a common resource that other teams do not use. Most likely in my setting the quality of the tutor will cause such shocks. An often-proposed measure to address this concern is to add tutorial-level fixed-effects (e.g. Sacerdote (2001)).

Summing up, separating out exogenous from endogenous effects in this framework is equivalent to recovering the original structural parameters α_3 and β_3 from the equations above. To identify those structural parameters, I further make the restrictive assumption that the student's and the peers' ex-ante entrepreneurial self-efficacy are measured without error and that no unobserved background characteristics matter. My final econometric model (without adding tutorial-fixed-effects) for an individual i, being a member of team k attending tutorial m is

Econometric Framework

$$ESE_{ikm}^{ex-post} = \gamma_0 + \gamma_1 ESE_{ikm}^{ex-ante} + \gamma_2 \overline{ESE_{(-i)km}^{ex-ante}}$$
$$+ \gamma_3 X_{ikm} + \gamma_4 \overline{X_{(-i)km}} + \gamma_5 Y_{km} + \gamma_6 Z_m + \xi_{ikm}$$

Equation 7.2: Econometric model to estimate peer effects

where Y_{km} and Z_m are vectors of team- and tutorial-variables and ξ_{ikm} is an error term.

In addition, I estimate models allowing for non-linearities in the peer effect and also in own ex-ante entrepreneurial self-efficacy. In particular, I allow those to vary based on whether the student and her peers are in the lowest 25 percent, the middle 50 percent, or the top 25 percent ("ranges") of the ex-ante self-efficacy distribution. Formally I estimate

$$ESE_{ikm}^{ex-post} = \gamma'_0 + \sum_{g=1}^{3} \gamma'_{1,g} ESE_{ikm,g}^{D,ex-ante} + \sum_{h=1}^{3} \gamma'_{2,h} \overline{ESE_{(-i)km,h}^{D,ex-ante}}$$
$$+ \gamma'_3 X_{ikm} + \gamma'_4 \overline{X_{(-i)km}} + \gamma'_5 Y_{km} + \gamma'_6 Z_m + \xi'_{ikm}$$

Equation 7.3: Econometric model allowing for non-linearities in peer effects

where $ESE_{ikm,g}^{D,ex-ante}$ and $\overline{ESE_{(-i)km,h}^{D,ex-ante}}$ are dummy variables for the ex-ante self-efficacy range (indexed by g and h respectively) and $\gamma_{*,+}$ the effect associated with this range.

I estimate all these models using ordinary least squares and interpret the coefficients on peers' ex-ante ESE to be estimates of the peer-effect on the increase of own entrepreneurial self-efficacy. This is the econometric strategy to investigate whether peer effects do exist at all and whether and how these mean peer effects depend on the peers' level of ex-ante ESE. In the following I present two models with which I can assess nonlinear peer-effects to investigate whether students are differently influenced by peers, depending on their own level of ESE.

7.3.2 Non-Linear Peer-Effects

I conclude the empirical investigations with another model that allows assessing the size and nature of peer effects in dependence of a focal student's own level of ex-ante self-efficacy. The results I obtain from this estimation allows me to derive implications for the grouping of students based on their initial ESE to achieve the optimal "social gain" in ex-post ESE among the population of students. Following Sacerdote (2001) I run a regression of own ex-post self-efficacy on binary indicator variables for the level of own and peers' ex-ante self-efficacy:

$$\begin{aligned}
ESE_{ikm}^{ex-post} = \pi_0 \\
+\pi_1 \cdot ESE_{km}^{ex-ante}(own = bottom, peers = bottom) \\
+\pi_2 \cdot ESE_{km}^{ex-ante}(own = bottom, peers = middle) \\
+\pi_3 \cdot ESE_{km}^{ex-ante}(own = bottom, peers = top) \\
+\pi_4 \cdot ESE_{km}^{ex-ante}(own = middle, peers = bottom) \\
+\pi_5 \cdot ESE_{km}^{ex-ante}(own = middle, peers = middle) \\
+\pi_6 \cdot ESE_{km}^{ex-ante}(own = middle, peers = top) \\
+\pi_7 \cdot ESE_{km}^{ex-ante}(own = top, peers = bottom) \\
+\pi_8 \cdot ESE_{km}^{ex-ante}(own = top, peers = middle) \\
+\pi_9 \cdot ESE_{km}^{ex-ante}(own = top, peers = top) \\
+\zeta_{ikm}
\end{aligned}$$

Equation 7.4: Econometric model allowing for non-linearities in peer effects and own quality

To investigate whether certain student/peers combinations outperform others, I compare the coefficients $\pi_k, k = 1, \ldots, 9$. Based on these comparisons I can also derive implications about how to optimally group students based on their initial ESE to achieve a maximum "net social gain" in ESE among the population of students.

7.3.3 Further Methodological Issues

Finally I address two additional methodological issues. First, given that I do not always observe a student's whole peer group, I consider the estimate for the peer effect as a lower bound for the true causal effect of peers on own self-efficacy (Ammermueller and Pischke 2009). To minimize this bias I will also estimate this model taking only those students into consideration for whom I observe more than 60% of their peers. And second, I have to respect the "grouped" nature of my explanatory variables. This nature may bias the estimates of standard errors. When the true specification of the residual variance-covariance matrix follows a grouped structure, the estimates of standard errors from simple OLS will be biased downwards (Gaviria and Raphael 2001). As a consequence, I estimate all models using Huber-White robust estimators in which the residual covariance matrix is clustered by team.

7.4 Dataset and Additional Measures

This section mainly serves to introduce my measure for entrepreneurial self-efficacy and to describe how I constructed the peer-variables. The empirical analyses are again based on the dataset introduced in section 3.5.

7.4.1 Entrepreneurial Self-Efficacy

To measure entrepreneurial self-efficacy, I included in total 19 items in both the ex-ante and ex-post questionnaire (see Table 7.1). I used items developed by De Noble et al. (1999), Chen et al. (1998) and Anna et al. (2000) that have subsequently been used in Kolvereid and Isaaksen's (2006) study. Again I employed the seven-point Likert scale presented in Table 3.4 and asked students, in how far they feel capable of performing the following roles and tasks of an entrepreneur. I averaged the scores to obtain an overall measure of ex-ante and ex-post *entrepreneurial self-efficacy* (abbreviated by *ESE*). The high values of

Cronbach's alpha (0.925 for the ex-ante and 0.939 for the ex-post measure) suggest high reliability of the scales. The three dummy variables *own ESE bottom 25%, own ESE middle 50%,* and *own ESE top 25%* indicate the position of a student's ESE in the distribution of the ex-ante ESE.

Table 7.1: Items for measuring Entrepreneurial Self-Efficacy

Item	German item in the questionnaire	English translation (based on Kolvereid and Isaaksen (2006)
-	Ich fühle mich fähig, ...	I feel capable ...
1	neue Marktchancen für neue Produkte bzw. Dienstleistungen zu erkennen.	of seeing new market opportunities for new products/services.
2	neue Wege zu finden, bestehende Produkte und Dienstleistungen zu verbessern.	of discovering new ways to improve existing products/services.
3	neue Bereiche mit Wachstumspotential zu identifizieren.	of identifying new areas for potential growth.
4	Produkte und Dienstleistungen zu entwerfen, die aktuelle Probleme lösen.	of designing products/services that solve current problems.
5	Produkte und Dienstleistungen zu erschaffen, die unbefriedigte Kundenbedürfnisse erfüllen.	of creating products/services that fulfill unmet customer needs.
6	eine Produktidee rechtzeitig umzusetzen und auf den Markt zu bringen.	of bringing a product concept to market in a timely manner.
7	eine Marktrecherche durchzuführen.	of conducting a market research.
8	ausreichende Finanzmittel für zukünftiges Unternehmenswachstum zu sammeln.	of obtaining sufficient funds for future growth.
9	vorteilhafte Beziehungen mit potentiellen Investoren aufzubauen und zu pflegen.	of developing and maintaining favorable relationships with potential investors.
10	Beziehungen zu Schlüsselpersonen aufzubauen, die Zugang zu Finanzierungsquellen haben.	of developing relationships with key people who are connected to capital sources.
11	potentielle Quellen zur Finanzierung von Investitionen zu identifizieren.	of identifying potential sources of funding for investments.
12	unter anhaltendem Stress, Druck und Konflikten produktiv zu arbeiten.	of working productively under continuous stress, pressure and conflict.
13	unerwartete Veränderungen in den wirtschaftlichen Rahmenbedingungen auszuhalten.	of tolerating unexpected changes in business conditions.
14	trotz Widrigkeiten hartnäckig zu bleiben.	of persisting in the face of adversity.
15	kalkulierte Risiken einzugehen.	of taking calculated risks.
16	Entscheidungen unter Unsicherheit und Risiko zu treffen.	of making decisions under uncertainty and risk.
17	Risiken und Unsicherheit zu reduzieren.	of reducing risk and uncertainty.
18	einen Überblick über die Geschäftskosten zu behalten.	of managing expenses.
19	Ausgaben zu kontrollieren.	of controlling business costs.
20	Zahlungseingänge zu verwalten.	of managing cash flows.

7.4.2 Additional Explanatory and Control Variables

The main explanatory variables in this chapter are peers' ex-ante ESE and the three dummy-variables indicating the peers' position in the distribution of the ex-ante ESE, *peers' ESE bottom 25%, peers' ESE middle 50%,* and *peers' ESE top 25%*. These peer variables and the ones mentioned below are constructed by taking the peers' (i.e. team members') mean value for the respective variable without the contribution of the respective focal student.

Peer background variables that enter the empirical analyses are *share of female peers, share of foreign peers, peers' age, share of peers with self-employed parents, share of peers with self-employed acquaintances, share of peers who worked for a start-up, share of peers who are entrepreneurs, peers' breadth of prior exposure* and *entrepreneurship courses attended by peers*[60].

As additional controls I include team- and tutorial-level variables, basically the *team size, team size squared*, the *tutorial size*, and the *tutorial size squared*. All other control variables are the same as before. Table 7.2 in the next subsection provides descriptive statistics to these variables.

7.4.3 Descriptive Statistics

Basically the pooled dataset (i.e. data on the 2008 and 2009 cohort of "Business Planning") contains data on 160 teams and 36 tutorials.[61] When I observed no or just one member of a team (which means that I did not observe any one of her

---

[60] Note: I included all ex-ante observations in the calculation of the peer variables, i.e. these values are based on 710 observations (see Table 3.3) and are not affected by a potential non-response bias.

[61] As before I ran the Westlake version of equivalence test to investigate whether the two cohorts can be regarded as statistically equivalent regarding ex-ante entrepreneurial self-efficacy. This test reveals that this is indeed the case ($|z| = 11.641$, $p = 0.000$ for the Westlake test, the highest p-value reported; $|t| = 1.125$, $p = 0.261$ for a two-tailed t-test). Therefore pooling the two cohorts is justified. For more information on the Westlake version of equivalence test, I refer to subsection 3.5.1.
I also tested for attrition bias in this variable. According to a two-tailed t-test, the variable entrepreneurial self-efficacy is not affected by this kind of bias ($|t| = 0.157$, $p = 0.876$)
The general setup for these tests is the same as presented in subsection 3.5.1.

or his peers in the latter case), I excluded this observation from the analysis. For two teams I did not observe any team member at all, and for 17 teams I only observed one member each. This leaves me with 388 observations, which is the sample for the following empirical analyses.

The team- and tutorial level variables at the bottom of the table indicate that the average team size was five students and that I was able to observe three peers per student on average. The maximum value of observed peers is four, so apparently I do not have complete data on any of the six-students-teams. The average tutorial size was about 22 students. Per student, I was able to observe 15 attendees of the same tutorial on average.[62]

Looking at the group of individual variables first, one can see that students in the bottom 25% of the ex-ante ESE distribution have an ESE lower than 4.450 (applies to 105 of 403 students), those in the top 25% have an ESE higher than 5.450 (111 of 403). Moreover, the mean ESE did not change by much in terms of simple mean differences (a two-tailed t-test gives a test statistic of $|t| = 0.398, p = 0.691$). However, this does not mean that the individual ESE did not change by much, as negative and positive shifts may have canceled each other out in means.

---

[62] I am able to report these values for all 403 students, as this data was provided by the "Business Planning" faculty staff.

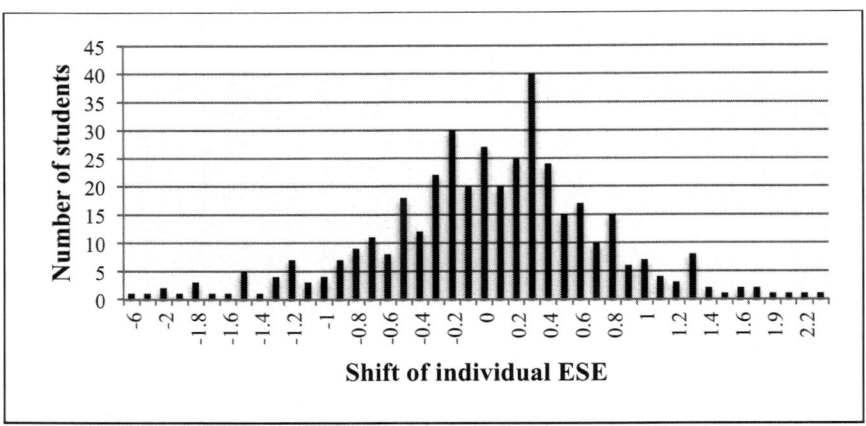

Figure 7.1: Shift in individual entrepreneurial self-efficacy during the course

Figure 7.1 presents more detailed information about the change in students' ESE.[63] About 8.4% of the students experience a rather large negative (below or equal to −1.0), and about 6.5% a rather large positive shift (above or equal to +1.0) in ESE. About one third of the students leave the course with slightly more negative ESE than before, another third with slightly more positive ESE. For 27 students their ESE did not change at all.

---

[63] Values are rounded to one decimal place.

Table 7.2: Descriptive statistics

variable	N	Mean	S.D.	P25	Median	P75	Min	Max
individual variables								
Entrepreneurial Self-Efficacy								
own ex-ante ESE	403	4.957	0.741	4.450	4.950	5.450	2.300	7.000
own ESE bottom 25%	105	4.049	0.393	-	-	-	2.300	4.450
own ESE middle 50%	187	4.932	0.262	-	-	-	4.500	5.400
own ESE top 25%	111	5.859	0.370	-	-	-	5.450	7.000
own ex-post ESE	403	4.972	0.814	4.450	5.000	5.500	1.000	7.000
difference in ESE (ex-post - ex-ante)	403	0.016	0.782	-0.350	0.050	0.450	-6.000	3.200
control variables								
ex-ante entrepreneurial intentions	403	4.179	1.780	3.000	4.000	6.000	1.000	7.000
female (0/1)	403	0.533	-	-	-	-	0.000	1.000
foreign (0/1)	403	0.159	-	-	-	-	0.000	1.000
age	403	21.660	2.135	20.000	21.000	22.000	19.000	34.000
self-employed parents (0/1)	403	0.479	-	-	-	-	0.000	1.000
self-employed acquaintances (0/1)	403	0.672	-	-	-	-	0.000	1.000
worked for start-up (0/1)	403	0.261	-	-	-	-	0.000	1.000
entrepreneur (0/1)	403	0.060	-	-	-	-	0.000	1.000
breadth of prior exposure	403	1.471	0.991	1.000	1.000	2.000	0.000	4.000
attended entrepreneurship courses	403	0.065	0.347	0.000	0.000	0.000	0.000	4.000

Table 7.2 (continued): Descriptive statistics

variable	N	Mean	S.D.	P25	Median	P75	Min	Max
peer variables								
Entrepreneurial Self-Efficacy								
peers' ex-ante ESE	388	4.925	0.506	4.600	4.908	5.235	3.400	7.000
peers' ESE bottom 25%	70	4.192	0.218	-	-	-	3.400	4.450
peers' ESE middle 50%	266	4.951	0.252	-	-	-	4.463	5.438
peers' ESE top 25%	52	5.780	0.257	-	-	-	5.467	7.000
peers' ex-post ESE	372	4.967	0.628	4.600	5.000	5.381	2.175	6.750
peers' difference in ESE (ex-post - ex-ante)	372	0.022	0.564	-0.267	0.050	0.350	-2.133	2.000
control variables								
peers' ex-ante entrepreneurial intentions	388	4.130	1.079	3.333	4.000	4.750	1.000	7.000
share of female peers	388	0.548	0.264	0.333	0.500	0.750	0.000	1.000
share of foreign peers	388	0.202	0.242	0.000	0.000	0.333	0.000	1.000
peers' age	388	21.743	1.289	21.000	21.667	22.333	19.000	28.500
share of peers with self-employed parents	388	0.506	0.331	0.250	0.500	0.750	0.000	1.000
share of peers with self-employed acquaintances	388	0.675	0.298	0.500	0.667	1.000	0.000	1.000
share of peers who worked for a start-up	388	0.261	0.264	0.000	0.250	0.500	0.000	1.000
share of peers who are entrepreneurs	388	0.066	0.149	0.000	0.000	0.000	0.000	1.000
peers' breadth of prior exposure	388	1.071	0.574	0.750	1.000	1.500	0.000	2.500
entrepreneurship courses attended by peers	388	0.088	0.242	0.000	0.000	0.000	0.000	2.000

Table 7.2 (continued): Descriptive statistics

variable	N	Mean	S.D.	P25	Median	P75	Min	Max
team variables								
team size	403	5.069	0.405	5.000	5.000	5.000	4.000	6.000
number of own peers observed	403	2.873	1.052	2.000	3.000	4.000	0.000	4.000
share of observed own team members	403	0.768	0.215	0.600	0.800	1.000	0.167	1.000
tutorial variables								
tutorial size	403	22.129	2.648	20.000	21.000	25.000	19.000	26.000
number of tutorial members observed	403	15.489	2.568	14.000	16.000	17.000	9.000	19.000

Next I discuss the peer variables. Based on the distribution of the individual ESE, for 70 students their peer group is among the top 25%, for 266 students in the middle 50%, and for the other 52 students in the top 25% area.[64] The peer control variables give information about the composition of a student's peer group. Accordingly one half of one's peer group is female and 20% of the team members are foreign (which means that, according to the number of observed peers, every observed student has on average one non-German team member). The value of peers' breadth of prior exposure suggests that every student has – on average – at least one team member who already gathered entrepreneurial experiences before entering the course. Table 7.3 provides additional information. There I present the data aggregated on team- and tutorial-level.

---

[64] I will also call students among the top 25% "top", "good", or "high-quality" students, students among the bottom 25% "bad" or "low-quality" students

Table 7.3: Descriptive statistics (data aggregated on team- and tutorial level)

variable	N	Mean	SD	P25	Median	P75	Min	Max
team level								
Entrepreneurial Self-Efficacy								
team's ex-ante ESE	158	4.948	0.438	4.650	4.969	5.250	3.983	6.300
team's ex-post ESE	154	4.957	0.512	4.625	4.937	5.350	2.633	6.100
control variables								
team members' ex-ante entrepreneurial intentions	158	4.197	1.016	3.500	4.200	5.000	1.667	7.000
share of female team members	158	0.533	0.224	0.400	0.600	0.600	0.000	1.000
share of foreign team members	158	0.188	0.240	0.000	0.000	0.333	0.000	1.000
team members' age	158	21.661	1.175	21.000	21.667	22.250	19.667	26.000
share of team members with self-employed parents	158	0.491	0.316	0.250	0.500	0.750	0.000	1.000
share of team members with self-employed acquaintances	158	0.689	0.278	0.500	0.750	1.000	0.000	1.000
share of team members who worked for a start-up	158	0.259	0.258	0.000	0.250	0.400	0.000	1.000
share of team members who are entrepreneurs	158	0.061	0.130	0.000	0.000	0.000	0.000	0.500
team members' breadth of prior exposure	158	1.001	0.527	0.600	1.000	1.400	0.000	2.200
attended entrepreneurship courses by team members	158	0.078	0.208	0.000	0.000	0.000	0.000	1.600
team variables								
team size	160	5.081	0.434	5.000	5.000	5.000	4.000	6.000
observed team members	160	3.873	1.052	3.000	4.000	5.000	0.000	5.000
share of observed team members	160	0.667	0.264	0.500	0.708	0.800	0.000	1.000

Table 7.3 (continued): Descriptive statistics (data aggregated on team- and tutorial level)

variable	N	Mean	SD	P25	Median	P75	Min	Max
tutorial level								
Entrepreneurial Self-Efficacy								
tutorial members' ex-ante ESE	36	4.942	0.177	4.799	4.947	5.049	4.592	5.330
tutorial members' ex-post ESE	36	4.954	0.224	4.830	4.930	5.117	4.414	5.338
control variables								
tutorial members' ex-ante entrepreneurial intentions	36	4.192	0.458	3.941	4.215	4.500	2.818	4.933
share of female tutorial members	36	0.536	0.106	0.462	0.532	0.577	0.333	0.857
share of foreign tutorial members	36	0.191	0.103	0.092	0.188	0.264	0.000	0.400
tutorial members' age	36	21.726	0.492	21.432	21.743	21.971	20.765	22.875
share of tutorial members with self-employed parents	36	0.492	0.142	0.408	0.471	0.573	0.182	0.765
share of tutorial members with self-employed acquaintances	36	0.684	0.148	0.588	0.690	0.812	0.375	1.000
share of tutorial members who worked for a start-up	36	0.266	0.108	0.185	0.294	0.333	0.056	0.538
share of tutorial members who are entrepreneurs	36	0.066	0.073	0.000	0.059	0.108	0.000	0.250
tutorial members' breadth of prior exposure	36	1.027	0.309	0.765	1.050	1.244	0.500	1.650
attended entrepreneurship courses by tutorial members	36	0.084	0.121	0.000	0.057	0.118	0.000	0.562
tutorial variables								
tutorial size (in students)	36	22.583	2.781	20.000	21.000	26.000	19.000	26.000
share of observed tutorial members	36	0.684	0.191	0.500	0.762	0.850	0.375	0.950
teams per tutorial	36	4.444	-	-	-	-	4.000	5.000

Table 7.4: Test for random team assignment

estimation method		OLS	OLS	Probit	Probit	OLS	Probit
dependent variable		ex-ante ESE	entrepreneurial intentions	female (0/1)	foreign (0/1)	age	self-employed parents (0/1)
peers level	individual level						
ex-ante ESE		0.074 (0.111)					
ex-ante entrepreneurial intention			-0.109 (0.100)				
female (share)				0.310 (0.288)			
foreign (share)					0.099 (0.360)		
age						-0.157* (0.091)	
self-employed parents (share of peers)							0.356 (0.240)
self-employed acquaintances (share of peers)							
worked for start-up (share of peers)							
entrepreneurs (share)							
breadth of prior exposure							
attended entrepreneurship courses							
constant		4.587*** (0.545)	4.627*** (0.433)	-0.085 (0.163)	-1.026*** (0.105)	25.090** (2.011)	-0.219 (0.138)
test statistics							
Observations		388	388	388	388	388	388
adj. R-squared		0.000	0.002			0.006	
F-test		0.446(1)	1.178(1)			3.011(1)	
F-test sig		0.505	0.280			0.085	
Pseudo R-squared				0.003	0.000		0.006
Log-Likelihood				-277.6	-168.7		-267.1

Notes: robust standard errors in parentheses are clustered at team level; * significant at 10%; ** significant at 5%; *** significant at 1%

Table 7.4 (continued): Test for random team assignment

estimation method		Probit	Probit	Probit	OLS	OLS	OLS
dependent variable		self-employed acquaintances (0/1)	worked for start-up (0/1)	entrepreneur (0/1)	breadth of prior exposure	attended entrepreneurship courses	ex-ante ESE
peers level	individual level						
ex-ante ESE							0.025
							(0.115)
ex-ante entrepreneurial intention							-0.038
							(0.038)
female (share)							-0.187
							(0.159)
foreign (share)							0.173
							(0.175)
age							-
							(0.026)
self-employed parents (share of peers)							0.165
							(0.124)
self-employed acquaintances (share of peers)		0.236					0.074
		(0.260)					(0.135)
worked for start-up (share of peers)			-0.141				0.138
			(0.384)				(0.154)
entrepreneurs (share)				0.081			0.036
				(0.779)			(0.275)
breadth of prior exposure					0.037		
					(0.085)		
attended entrepreneurship courses						-0.072	-0.070
						(0.069)	(0.139)
constant		0.275	-0.598***	-1.545***	1.432***	0.073***	6.276**
		(0.176)	(0.119)	(0.114)	(0.108)	(0.021)	(0.911)
test statistics							
Observations		388	388	388	388	388	388
adj. R-squared					-0.002	0.000	0.002
F-test					0.185(1)	3.414(1)	1.343(1)
F-test sig					0.668	0.067	0.213
Pseudo R-squared		0.002	0.001	0.000			
Log-Likelihood		-246.2	-223.4	-90.03			

Notes: robust standard errors in parentheses are clustered at team level; * significant at 10%; ** significant at 5%; *** significant at 1%

7.5 Results

This section contains the estimations of the models specified in section 7.3. Before I present those, I address the issue of "quasi-random" assignment of teams and present descriptive results regarding the size and nature of peer effects.

7.5.1 Test for Random Team Assignment

Table 7.4 shows that – except for *age* – conditional on a student's responses to the questionnaire items there is no relationship between her own ex-ante ESE or background characteristics and the respective average values of the ESE or the background characteristics of her peers. The columns show OLS or probit regressions of own values on peers' values of the respective variables. In the last column I regress *own ex-ante ESE* on all considered peer-variables. The reported F-test statistics indicate that the model is uninformative. Although there is a significant correlation between the own and the peers' age, I conclude that the team-assignment process resembles a randomized experience regarding individual entrepreneurial background. Hence this issue is not likely to introduce any bias in the results.

7.5.2 Descriptive Results regarding Peer Effects

Figure 7.2 provides first descriptive results regarding the influence of the team members on own entrepreneurial self-efficacy. I present the mean effect for the whole sample in the first set of columns, and the effects for four subsamples: female and male students as well as for students with low and with high prior exposure to entrepreneurship (low means, that the variable *breadth of prior exposure* has a value of 0 or 1). Each sample is analyzed with respect to different effects dependent on the peers' position in the ex-ante ESE distribution: each first column indicates the effect on own ESE when the peer group is among the bottom 25%, each second column when the peers are among the middle 50%, and each third column when the peer group is among the top 25%. Table 7.5 informs about the sample sizes.

Table 7.5: Sample size by level of ex-ante entrepreneurial self-efficacy and background variables

Subsample peers' ex-ante ESE	gender		breadth of prior exposure	
	female	male	low	high
bottom 25%	37	33	40	30
middle 50%	144	122	147	119
top 50%	25	27	27	25

According to the figure, the peer effects are moderate at best, and the nature of the effect is quite unusual. Considering the mean peer effects, it seems that a student benefits most with regard to own ESE when her peers are among the middle 50% of the ex-ante ESE distribution. Having "bad" or "good" peers is both detrimental for the own ESE, but more when one has a peer group from the bottom 25%.

Female students seem to benefit from having bottom or middle peers, while experiencing a relatively large negative shift in own ESE when grouped together with top peers. The look at male students reveals a different picture. A bad peer group has a rather large negative impact on own ESE, while they experience a positive shift when working together with top peers. Probably female students lack confidence to contribute enough to the teamwork when grouped together with strong students. Male students, on the other hand, seem to get encouraged to contribute to the teamwork when working together with strong students, and get discouraged when working with bad students.

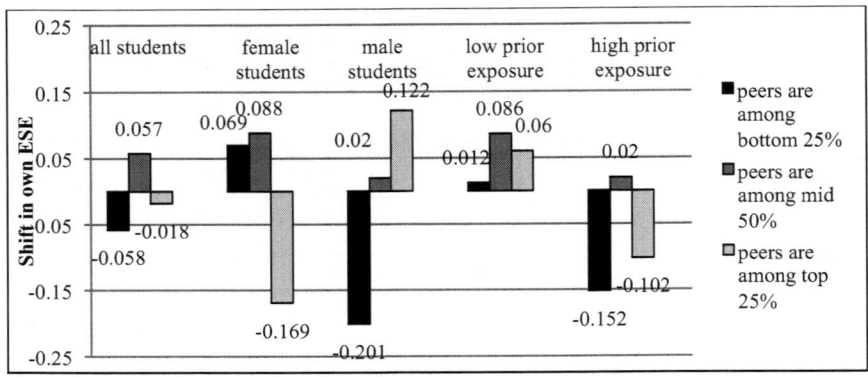

Figure 7.2: Shift in entrepreneurial self-efficacy by background characteristics

Considering prior exposure to entrepreneurship, students with low prior exposure to entrepreneurship apparently always profit from the teamwork, but most when they are grouped together with peers from the middle area of the ex-ante ESE distribution. Those students who already collected substantial entrepreneurial experiences, however, almost always experience a negative shift in own ESE, except when they work together with peers from the middle area. This indicates that students who did not collect much entrepreneurial experience profit from their peers, as those may become role models for entrepreneurial acting, even if the entrepreneurial project they work on is more or less an academic exercise. Students with many entrepreneurial experiences seem on the one hand to get "negative" role models when grouped together with peers from the bottom 25%, and on the other hand get probably "blocked" in their aspirations when working together with strong peers who may take on a leadership role in the team themselves. Figure 7.3 below shows the shift in entrepreneurial self-efficacy due to peers' ex-ante level of ESE by own ex-ante level of ESE (also differentiated by bottom, middle, and top). The first set of columns again displays the mean peer effects, the second set shows the peer effects for the subsample of students who are in the low area of the ex-ante ESE distribution, followed by subsample of students in the middle and finally in the top areas of this distribution. Table 7.6 reports the sample sizes.

Table 7.6: Sample size by own and peers' level of ex-ante entrepreneurial self-efficacy

Own ex-ante ESE Peers' ex-ante ESE	bottom 25%	middle 50%	top 25%
bottom 25%	23	34	13
middle 50%	71	121	74
top 25%	10	23	19

Apparently students who are in the low area of the ex-ante ESE distribution benefit from peers throughout the distribution, most when working together with peers from the middle area. Probably when working together with "weak" peers the increase in own ESE is driven by mastery experience (i.e. they have to contribute more to the project when the team lacks a "leader" and thus increase their efficacy through "learning-by-doing"), and when grouped with strong students then they learn from these role models. When having mediocre peers these two influences may come together, resulting in the largest benefit with respect to own ESE.

Peer effects are generally smaller for students who are in the middle area of the ex-ante ESE distribution, and their nature follows an intuitive pattern. These students profit from working together with high-ESE students and lose self-efficacy when grouped together with a weak peer group. Both effects are probably generated by role modeling, however in different directions. Having peers from the middle area of the distribution does not seem to have an impact on own ESE at all.

Students with a high ex-ante ESE experience detrimental effects independent from the quality of their team members. Negative role modeling effects may occur when these students are grouped together with weak and mediocre students, who drag them to a lower level. Working together with other strong students may evoke a mutual blocking of their activity within the entrepreneurial project. However, the negative effect for strong students is smallest when having peers from the middle area of the ex-ante ESE distribution.

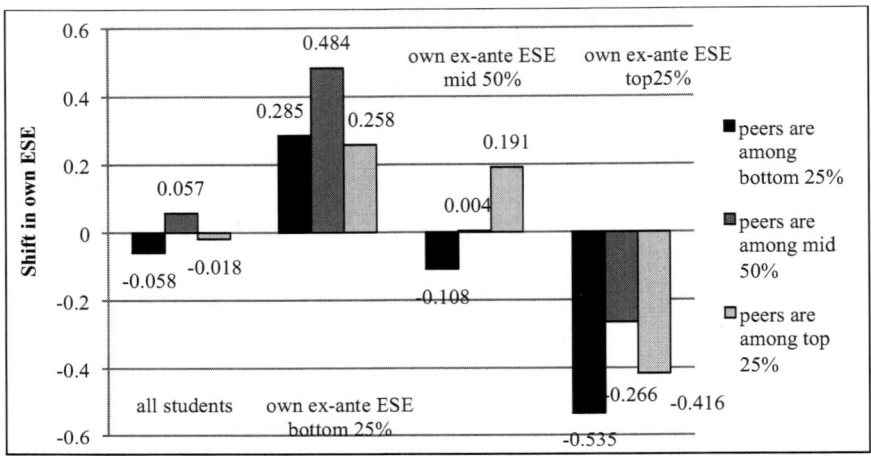

Figure 7.3: Shift in own entrepreneurial self-efficacy during the course by own and peers' level of ex-ante entrepreneurial self-efficacy

All in all, it seems that in the case of entrepreneurship education students from the middle area of the ex-ante ESE distribution seem to be a valuable resource when course planners intend to increase overall entrepreneurial self-efficacy among the population of students through peer-effects. Mediocre students grouped with similar peers do not experience any change in their self-efficacy, whereas these students maximize the positive effect for initially low-ESE students and minimize the detrimental effect for initially high-ESE students. In contrast, mediocre students themselves do not experience very large shifts in own ESE. Therefore grouping students from the middle area of the ex-ante ESE distribution with weak and strong students should increase the "social gain" in entrepreneurial self-efficacy during the entrepreneurship course.

7.5.3 Mean Peer-Effects

Table 7.7 presents the results of the estimation of *Equation 7.2*, i.e. the mean effects of peers' entrepreneurial self-efficacy on own ex-post ESE. Twice it sets out three estimations. In each triad I first run the regression based on the whole sample of 388 students for whom I observed peers. This is followed by an estimation where I only consider students for whom I observed more than 60% of their team members (i.e. when the team size was six students, then I only considered students for whom I observed three of their peers, the same for students whose team consisted of five students, and when students worked together in teams of four I only take students into account for whom I observed two other team members). The last regression in each triad uses the second specification and adds tutorial fixed-effects.

In models 1 to 3 I regress own ex-post ESE on own and peers' background variables. Effects associated with the latter variables may be interpreted as exogenous effects according to Manski's (1993) differentiation (see section 7.2). According to model 2 female students score 0.279 points lower than male students, and a broader prior exposure to entrepreneurship is associated with a higher ex-post ESE. These effects remain significant after adding tutorial fixed-effects in model 3. In addition, older peers seem to have a small negative impact on own ex-post ESE. Models 4 to 6 present the estimates of *Equation 7.2*. Given the empirical framework, these coefficients can be interpreted as causal and not subject to the reflection problem. I include the main explanatory variable – *peers' ex-ante ESE* – and control for *own ex-ante ESE*. The effect of own ex-ante ESE is rather large and significant in all three models. Looking at model 5, own ex-ante ESE significantly raises own ex-post ESE by 0.496 points, the peers' ESE significantly by 0.161 points. These numbers imply that a one standard-deviation increase in peers' ESE is associated with a 0.08 increase in own ex-post ESE.[65] This coefficient is moderate in size, as already suggested by the descriptive results in the previous subsection. The peer effect is robust to adding tutorial fixed-effects in model 6.

---

[65] Using the same specification with the subsamples considered in subsection 7.5.1 (regressions not reported), a one standard deviation in peers' ESE is associated with a 0.14 increase in ex-post ESE for male students and an increase of 0.12 for students with a low breadth of prior exposure to entrepreneurship. The coefficients for mean peer effects for female students and students with a high breadth of prior exposure are insignificant.

Table 7.7: Estimation of mean peer effects (OLS regressions)

dependent variable own ex-post ESE	Model 1 full sample	Model 2 min 60% of peers observed	Model 3 min 60% of peers observed tutorial fixed-effects	Model 4 full sample	Model 5 min 60% of peers observed	Model 6 min 60% of peers observed tutorial fixed-effects
own ESE						
own ex-ante ESE				0.500***	0.496***	0.481***
				(0.077)	(0.084)	(0.074)
peers' ESE						
peers' ex-ante ESE				0.060	0.161**	0.147*
				(0.074)	(0.070)	(0.087)
own background variables						
female (0/1)	-0.285***	-0.279***	-0.237**	-0.116*	-0.133*	-0.075
	(0.084)	(0.089)	(0.095)	(0.070)	(0.075)	(0.084)
foreign (0/1)	0.048	-0.010	-0.055	0.096	0.044	-0.018
	(0.114)	(0.109)	(0.121)	(0.106)	(0.104)	(0.105)
age	-0.029	-0.024	-0.037	-0.023	-0.018	-0.022
	(0.023)	(0.025)	(0.026)	(0.023)	(0.025)	(0.026)
breadth of prior exposure	0.164***	0.161***	0.139***	0.072**	0.074*	0.052
	(0.045)	(0.047)	(0.051)	(0.036)	(0.038)	(0.044)
attended entrepr-neur ship courses	0.113	0.096	0.107	0.052	0.030	0.045
	(0.118)	(0.118)	(0.104)	(0.088)	(0.088)	(0.082)
peers' background variables						
share of female peers	-0.212	-0.243	0.003	-0.069	-0.050	0.135
	(0.188)	(0.199)	(0.177)	(0.157)	(0.158)	(0.155)
share of foreign peers	0.218	0.311	0.137	0.143	0.213	0.030
	(0.173)	(0.196)	(0.228)	(0.144)	(0.165)	(0.170)
peers' age	-0.031	-0.038	-0.068**	-0.002	0.005	-0.001
	(0.030)	(0.037)	(0.033)	(0.026)	(0.030)	(0.029)
peers' breadth of prior exposure	0.018	0.067	-0.006	-0.065	-0.050	-0.144
	(0.090)	(0.101)	(0.101)	(0.078)	(0.086)	(0.102)
attended entrepre-neurship courses by peers	-0.051	-0.028	-0.033	-0.022	0.002	0.006
	(0.129)	(0.137)	(0.123)	(0.101)	(0.101)	(0.087)

Table 7.7 (continued): Estimation of mean peer effects (OLS regressions)

dependent variable own ex-post ESE	Model 1 full sample	Model 2 min 60% of peers observed	Model 3 min 60% of peers observed tutorial fixed-effects	Model 4 full sample	Model 5 min 60% of peers observed	Model 6 min 60% of peers observed tutorial fixed-effects
team control variables						
team size	0.733	0.955	-0.111	-0.061	-0.648	-1.699
	(1.080)	(1.300)	(1.189)	(1.064)	(1.181)	(1.087)
team size squared	-0.047	-0.066	0.037	0.016	0.072	0.178*
	(0.105)	(0.126)	(0.115)	(0.101)	(0.113)	(0.106)
tutorial control variables						
tutorial size	-0.126	-0.003		0.174	0.377	
	(0.543)	(0.584)		(0.507)	(0.549)	
tutorial size squared	0.002	-0.001		-0.004	-0.009	
	(0.012)	(0.013)		(0.011)	(0.012)	
Constant	5.501	3.517	6.776**	1.003	-0.460	6.439**
	(6.447)	(6.963)	(3.195)	(6.234)	(6.721)	(2.909)
test statistics						
Observations	388	349	349	388	349	349
R-squared	0.070	0.072	0.110	0.246	0.251	0.261
F-test (df)	3.096(14)	2.606(14)	3.609(12)	7.776(16)	7.511(16)	11.78(14)
F-test sig.	0.000	0.003	0.000	0.000	0.000	0.000

Notes: robust standard errors in parentheses are clustered at team level; * significant at 10%;
** significant at 5%; *** significant at 1%

Therefore I accept the hypothesis that a student's ex-post ESE is significantly affected by her peers' entrepreneurial self-efficacy. In the next subsection, I replace the mean values of own and peers' ESE by dummy-variables indicating the level of ex-ante ESE.

Table 7.8: Estimation of peer effects (OLS regressions, allowing for non-linearities in peer quality)

dependent variable own ex-post ESE	Model 1 full sample	Model 2 min 60% of peers observed	Model 3 min 60% of peers observed tutorial fixed-effects	Model 4 full sample	Model 5 min 60% of peers observed	Model 6 min 60% of peers observed tutorial fixed-effects
own ESE						
own ex-ante ESE	0.500***	0.496***	0.477***			
	(0.077)	(0.084)	(0.075)			
own ex-ante ESE bottom 25%				-0.413***	-0.413***	-0.426***
				(0.087)	(0.092)	(0.089)
own ex-ante ESE top 25%				0.554***	0.586***	0.603***
				(0.093)	(0.098)	(0.111)
peers' ESE						
peers' ex-ante ESE bottom 25%	-0.132	-0.212**	-0.161	-0.079	-0.170*	-0.095
	(0.091)	(0.093)	(0.108)	(0.096)	(0.098)	(0.121)
peers' ex-ante ESE top 25%	0.009	0.044	0.052	0.021	0.058	0.077
	(0.088)	(0.089)	(0.125)	(0.093)	(0.093)	(0.127)
own background variables						
female (0/1)	-0.117*	-0.138*	-0.084	-0.165**	-0.180**	-0.098
	(0.070)	(0.075)	(0.083)	(0.075)	(0.080)	(0.084)
foreign (0/1)	0.092	0.038	-0.026	0.059	0.006	-0.050
	(0.106)	(0.103)	(0.105)	(0.106)	(0.104)	(0.106)
age	-0.022	-0.018	-0.023	-0.025	-0.021	-0.026
	(0.023)	(0.024)	(0.026)	(0.021)	(0.023)	(0.023)
breadth of prior exposure	0.072**	0.077**	0.055	0.087**	0.088**	0.059
	(0.036)	(0.038)	(0.044)	(0.039)	(0.041)	(0.046)
attended entrepreneurship courses	0.055	0.032	0.043	0.075	0.052	0.074
	(0.090)	(0.091)	(0.085)	(0.098)	(0.098)	(0.083)

Table 7.8 (continued): Estimation of peer effects (OLS regressions, allowing for non-linearities in peer quality)

dependent variable own ex-post ESE	Model 1 full sample	Model 2 min 60% of peers observed	Model 3 min 60% of peers observed tutorial fixed-effects	Model 4 full sample	Model 5 min 60% of peers observed	Model 6 min 60% of peers observed tutorial fixed-effects
peers' background variables						
share of female peers	-0.077 (0.158)	-0.085 (0.162)	0.098 (0.156)	-0.030 (0.173)	-0.042 (0.175)	0.211 (0.153)
share of foreign peers	0.150 (0.143)	0.230 (0.164)	0.028 (0.170)	0.157 (0.143)	0.252 (0.164)	0.059 (0.170)
peers' age	0.002 (0.026)	0.006 (0.031)	-0.004 (0.028)	0.004 (0.028)	0.012 (0.033)	0.006 (0.032)
peers' breadth of prior exposure	-0.072 (0.078)	-0.050 (0.088)	-0.135 (0.101)	-0.053 (0.080)	-0.030 (0.091)	-0.130 (0.095)
attended entrepreneurship courses by peers	-0.029 (0.101)	0.000 (0.100)	-0.001 (0.090)	0.003 (0.106)	0.033 (0.108)	0.082 (0.094)
team control variables						
team size	-0.195 (1.049)	-0.623 (1.158)	-1.587 (1.039)	-0.218 (1.039)	-0.664 (1.183)	-1.891* (1.031)
team size squared	0.028 (0.100)	0.069 (0.111)	0.167 (0.102)	0.031 (0.100)	0.075 (0.115)	0.198* (0.101)
tutorial control variables						
tutorial size	0.175 (0.506)	0.388 (0.549)		0.168 (0.507)	0.359 (0.546)	
tutorial size squared	-0.004 (0.011)	-0.009 (0.012)		-0.004 (0.011)	-0.009 (0.012)	
constant	1.586 (6.116)	0.174 (6.618)	6.993** (2.854)	4.148 (5.977)	2.885 (6.452)	9.822*** (2.655)
test statistics						
Observations	388	349	349	388	349	349
R-squared	0.246	0.250	0.259	0.236	0.251	0.288
F-test (df)	7.586(17)	7.203(17)	9.552(15)	10.13(18)	11.05(18)	12.65(16)
F-test sig	0.000	0.000	0.000	0.000	0.000	0.000

Notes: robust standard errors in parentheses are clustered at team level; * significant at 10%; ** significant at 5%; *** significant at 1%

7.5.4 Effects of Peers of Different Self-Efficacy Levels

Models 1 to 3 in Table 7.8 show the results of regressions of own ex-post ESE on dummy variables that indicate the level of the peers' ex-ante ESE controlling for own ex-ante ESE and all background variables. The *peers' ESE middle 50%* (and *own ESE middle 50%* in the second triad) is the omitted category. The results are again presented in triads, following the same pattern as in Table 7.7 above. For example, Model 2 shows the regression of own ex-post ESE on dummies for peers' ex-ante ESE bottom 25% and peers' ex-ante ESE top 25% based on all students for whom I observed at least 60% of her peers. The results there suggest that the significant positive mean peer-effect in Table 7.7 above is largely driven by a significant negative effect of low ex-ante ESE-peers. The coefficient on *peers ex-ante ESE top 25%* is not significant. The significance of the peer effect vanishes when adding tutorial fixed effects. Regressions 4 to 6 show that the nature of peer effects remain the same when I add dummy variables for *own ex-ante ESE bottom 25%* and *own ex-ante ESE top 25%*. The omitted category is again the middle 50% area of the distribution. The coefficients on the dummy variables for the level of own ex-ante ESE are highly significant and have the intuitively expected sign. The significance level on *peers ex-ante ESE bottom 25%* drops from 5 percent to 10 percent. Being a student in the bottom 25% area of the ex-ante ESE distribution lowers own ex-post ESE by 0.413 relative to the omitted category. Having peers among the bottom 25% lowers own ex-post ESE by 0.170. These numbers imply that the peer effect is 41 percent as large as the own effect, which is quite large. Unfortunately, this finding is not robust to the addition of tutorial fixed-effects in model 6.

Table 7.9 and Table 7.10 below provide results of the regressions of own ex-post ESE on the four dummy-variables that indicate own and peers' levels of ex-ante ESE for the four subsamples female and male students as well as students with low and high breadth of prior exposure to entrepreneurship. The findings there corroborate the descriptive results in subsection 7.5.2. The effects of peers on own ex-post ESE are not significant for female students, however the male students experience a negative shift in own ex-post ESE when

Results 311

working together with peers from the bottom 25% area of the ex-ante ESE distribution (according to the second specification with the reduced sample). Compared to the negative and significant coefficient on *own ex-ante ESE bottom 25%* the number implies that this peer effect for male students is 71% as large as the own effect, which is very large. However, again this effect turns insignificant when introducing tutorial fixed effects.

Table 7.9: Estimation of peer effects by gender

dependent var own ex-post ESE	female students			male students		
	full sample	min 60% of peers observed	min 60% of peers observed tutorial fixed-effects	full sample	min 60% of peers observed	min 60% of peers observed tutorial fixed-effects
peers' ESE						
peers' ex-ante ESE bottom 25%	0.112	-0.038	0.145	-0.219	-0.271*	-0.262
	(0.129)	(0.123)	(0.174)	(0.147)	(0.149)	(0.185)
peers' ex-ante ESE top 25%	-0.104	-0.016	-0.072	0.140	0.163	0.032
	(0.129)	(0.115)	(0.160)	(0.135)	(0.156)	(0.216)
controls included	yes	yes	yes	yes	yes	yes
constant	-0.681	-1.683	8.766**	14.600	13.370	9.184**
	(8.020)	(8.452)	(4.380)	(10.410)	(11.400)	(3.722)
test statistic						
Observations	206	188	188	182	161	161
R-squared	0.225	0.273	0.376	0.226	0.234	0.188
F-test (df)	4.913(17)	5.598(17)	6.628(15)	7.719(17)	7.568(17)	6.195(15)
F-test sig	0.000	0.000	0.000	0.000	0.000	0.000

Notes: robust standard errors in parentheses are clustered at team level; * significant at 10%; ** significant at 5%; *** significant at 1%; the usual set of control variables is included

Table 7.10: Estimation of peer effects by prior exposure to entrepreneurship

dependent var own ex-post ESE	students with low prior exposure			students with high prior exposure		
	full sample	min 60% of peers observed	min 60% of peers observed tutorial fixed-effects	full sample	min 60% of peers observed	min 60% of peers observed tutorial fixed-effects
peers' ESE						
peers' ex-ante ESE bottom 25%	0.004 (0.112)	-0.139 (0.113)	0.076 (0.166)	-0.138 (0.160)	-0.214 (0.177)	-0.206 (0.186)
peers' ex-ante ESE top 25%	0.127 (0.154)	0.254* (0.151)	0.228 (0.180)	-0.011 (0.173)	-0.016 (0.190)	0.113 (0.307)
controls included	yes	yes	yes	yes	yes	yes
constant	1.082 (7.279)	-2.932 (7.580)	11.04*** (3.619)	4.674 (8.862)	6.079 (9.278)	5.852 (5.833)
test statistics						
Observations	214	192	192	174	157	157
R-squared	0.313	0.331	0.471	0.102	0.141	0.086
F-test (df)	7.941(17)	8.031(17)	9.319(15)	4.648(17)	5.864(17)	7.008(15)
F-test sig	0.000	0.000	0.000	0.000	0.000	0.000

Notes: robust standard errors in parentheses are clustered at team level; * significant at 10%; ** significant at 5%; *** significant at 1%; the usual set of control variables is included

Looking at the two subsamples defined by the differentiation along breadth of prior exposure, I find a positive and significant effect for students with a low breadth of prior exposure who work together with a peer group from the top 25% of the ex-ante ESE distribution (according to the second specification). Comparing this coefficient to the coefficient of *own ex-ante ESE top 25%* I find that this peer-effect is 31% as large as the own effect.

Summing up the results, the average effect on own ex-post ESE from (randomly) assigned team members in teamwork-based entrepreneurship education are modest in size and statistical significance. This pattern is comparable to the findings of Sacerdote (2001) or Zimmerman (2003), who also examine peer effects at tertiary institutions though for general academic achievement. The significant relation between peers' ESE and own ESE seems to be largely driven by a negative influence from weak peers. I interpret my findings as supporting the existence of peer effects regarding perceptions of entrepreneurial self-efficacy. Probably working in teams on an entrepreneurial project injects some sort of realism into the students that helps them to better adjust their initially overestimated entrepreneurial self-efficacy. Another explanation would be that the students let themselves be dragged to a lower level of entrepreneurial self-efficacy due to a negative role-model effect.

The results suggest that planners of a teamwork-based entrepreneurship course should bear these effects, although small, in mind during the team-composition, when their goal is the overall increase in entrepreneurial self-efficacy (the "net social gain"). In opposition to the findings by e.g. Sacerdote (2001), a reshuffling of teams is not a measure to increase the overall level of ex-post ESE, but apparently a measure to minimize the overall negative influences from peers. In the next subsection I report the estimates of *Equation 7.4* allowing the peer effect to depend on the student's own position in the ex-ante ESE distribution to derive implications for team-composition in order to increase the net social gain.

7.5.5 Non-Linearities in Peer-Effects

As argued, nonlinear peer-effects are a question of economic interest. Table 7.8 above informs that own ex-post ESE seems to suffer from having bad ex-ante ESE peers, and having top peers does not appear to have any effect. To assess whether certain student/peers combinations outperform others and to derive implications for reshuffling students to achieve an optimal "social gain" in ex-post ESE, I estimate *Equation 7.4* following Sacerdote (2001). Comparable to this article and to Zimmerman (2003) I find evidence that interactions between own and peers' level of ex-ante ESE influence own ex-post ESE. To examine non-linearities, I use the three dummy-variables each that indicate the levels of own and peers' position in the ex-ante distribution (bottom 25%, middle 50%, top 25%) and interact those. Table 7.11 below shows the coefficients from a regression of own ex-post ESE on the interaction terms. The combination *(own=middle,peers=middle)* is the omitted category.

Table 7.11: Estimation of peer effects by own and peers' ex-ante entrepreneurial self-efficacy

		peers' ex-ante ESE		
		bottom 25%	middle 50%	top 25%
own ex-ante ESE	bottom 25%	-0.484*** (0.164)	-0.442*** (0.111)	-0.648*** (0.243)
	middle 50%	-0.118 (0.128)	0	0.220* (0.116)
	top 25%	0.487** (0.200)	0.645*** (0.127)	0.535*** (0.187)

Notes: coefficients obtained by a single regression; (own=middle,peers=middle) is omitted category; robust standard errors in parentheses are clustered at team level; * significant at 10%; ** significant at 5%; *** significant at 1%;

Not surprising, own ex-post ESE is higher when own ex-ante ESE is high and vice versa. But also the peers' ex-ante ESE level affects own ex-post ESE dependent on the own ex-ante ESE. Looking at the line of *own ex-ante ESE bottom 25%*, the effect of the combination *(own=bottom,peers=top)* is worse than *(own=bottom,peers=bottom)*, a result already suggested by Figure 7.3. Accordingly the effect of *(own=top,peers=bottom)* is worse than *(own=top,peers=top)*, what is also a consequent result according to Figure 7.3. More generally, rows 1 and 3 propose that peers in the middle 50% of the ex-ante distribution help both bottom and top students most, compared to having peers from other levels. The second row tells that middle students profit most from top students. To assess whether the differences between these coefficients are significant and thus to find out if certain student/peers combinations outperform others, I conduct F-tests on the coefficients. Table 7.12 reports the results of these tests.

Table 7.12: Peer effects by different team combinations

combination 1		combination 2		test statistic	
own	peers	own	peers	F-test	F-test sig
bottom	bottom	bottom	middle	0.07 (1 , 138)	0.791
bottom	bottom	bottom	top	0.35 (1 , 138)	0.557
bottom	middle	bottom	top	0.68 (1 , 138)	0.411
middle	bottom	middle	middle	0.84 (1 , 138)	0.360
middle	**bottom**	**middle**	**top**	**5.48 (1 , 138)**	**0.021**
middle	**middle**	**middle**	**top**	**3.61 (1 , 138)**	**0.060**
top	bottom	top	middle	0.53 (1 , 138)	0.467
top	bottom	top	top	0.03 (1 , 138)	0.853
top	middle	top	top	0.28 (1 , 138)	0.599

Note: post-estimation comparisons based on the regression results presented in Table 7.11; N = 388

These results show that, first, middle students grouped with top students significantly outperform middle students matched with bottom students. The same is true for middle students matched with top peers when compared to pairings of middle students with middle peers. If these results held more generally, then planners of an entrepreneurship course may retrieve a net social gain in entrepreneurial self-efficacy. Top peers may be moved away from bottom or top students since these two groups do not seem to profit from top peers anyway. But apparently top peers may be helpful to students from the middle of the ex-ante ESE distribution regarding an increase in the latter's ex-post ESE. To visualize this, I give an example as an experiment of thought[66]:

Consider two teams. Team 1 is *(own=middle,peers=bottom)*, and team 2 is *(own=top,peers=top)*. Now rearrange these two teams into team 1a that is *(own=middle,peers=top)* and team 2a that is *(own=top,peers bottom)*. Due to

---

[66] The construction of these experiments of thought follows Sacerdote (2001). He admits that the results from these experiments are more suggestive than conclusive, and so do I. In addition, the calculations done here are only valid if I assume that a student's peer group consists of only one student.

this rearranging, the focal student (own = middle) of team 1 is estimated to gain 0.220 − (− 0.118) = 0.338, and her peers are estimated to lose a benefit to ex-post ESE of − 0.648 − (− 0.442) = − 0.206. Therefore the focal student and his peers are responsible for a social gain of 0.132 in ESE related to the whole population of students. The same calculation on team 2 delivers a social gain of 0.062. Therefore, rearranging the two teams 1 and 2 into 1a and 2a gives a social gain of 0.194. However, an F-test on this gain yields a p-value of 0.708. Hence this redistribution experiment does not yield statistically significant gains. Table 7.13 below reports social gains and test-statistics of F-tests on these gains for every possible team combinations where middle students can be assigned to bottom or top peers. Although the values of yielded social gains by redistribution are relatively high, the effect is not statistically significant.

Although course planners may probably not create a net social gain in ex-post ESE among the population of students by reshuffling the teams, they should bear nonlinear effects in mind. Apparently students from the middle area of the ex-ante ESE distribution significantly profit from working together with middle, and even more when grouped with top peers. Similar nonlinear effects are not significant for bottom or top students, though.

Table 7.13: Social gain in entrepreneurial self-efficacy by reshuffling teams

initial situation				after reshuffling				social gain		
team 1		team 2		team 1		team 2		value	F-test	F-test sig
own	peers	own	peers	own	peers	own	peers			
middle	bottom	top	top	middle	top	top	bottom	0.192	0.14 (1 , 138)	0.708
middle	middle	top	top	middle	top	top	middle	0.660	0.25 (1 , 138)	0.619
middle	bottom	bottom	top	middle	top	bottom	bottom	0.618	2.03 (1 , 138)	0.156
middle	middle	bottom	top	middle	top	bottom	middle	0.466	1.53 (1 , 138)	0.218

Note: post-estimation comparisons based on the regression results presented in Table 7.11; N = 388

7.6 Conclusion

Building entrepreneurial skills is a central function of entrepreneurship education. The contribution of social interaction (or more specific, peer-) effects to the formation of entrepreneurial skills among students in an entrepreneurship course has been completely ignored up to now. Studies on the effects of entrepreneurship education focused largely on deriving implications about optimal course content and thus on how to optimally allocate faculty resources. A resource that has not been considered in these studies is the quality of the students themselves who attend the course. Team-based business planning components are prevalent in entrepreneurship education anyway (Krueger et al. 2000). By bestowing greater care on team composition course planners may leverage this quality to increase entrepreneurial skills among the course audience based on social multiplication effects.

To investigate whether peer effects deliver this lever, I posed three research questions in this chapter: Do social interaction effects exist in the context of entrepreneurship education at all? Are students with initially low skills more subject to input by their team members than highly skilled students (or vice versa)? And how can course planners achieve a maximum "social gain" in entrepreneurial skills across the whole population of students by composing teams according to the students' initial skill level? I investigate these questions using data on 158 student teams of four to six working on a business planning project during an entrepreneurship course. The empirical analysis is based on 388 observations at the individual level.

The results suggest that student quality in terms of initial entrepreneurial self-efficacy is indeed a resource that course planners should bear in mind when setting up an entrepreneurship course. The quality of a focal student's team has a significant impact on the development of own entrepreneurial skills (i.e. entrepreneurial self-efficacy) during a course. Allowing for asymmetry in peer effects reveals that this mutual average impact of the focal student's skills and his team members' skills is largely driven by a significant negative effect emanating from the teamwork of low skilled students with low-skilled team members. This implies that course planners can more *prevent a decrease* of entrepreneurial skills among the population of students by careful planning on team composition, rather than to *achieve an increase* in skills by grouping students thoroughly. Further the results show that students in the middle area of the pre-course entrepreneurial self-efficacy distribution should be grouped together with students high on ex-ante entrepreneurial self-efficacy. This significantly increases the self-efficacy for the former students during the course. The estimations do not deliver similar results for either low or top quality students. Going further into this finding, there is weak (however not significant) evidence that course planners may achieve a "net social gain" in entrepreneurial self-efficacy during the course by moving away top students from low quality students and reassign them to initially middle-skilled students who are grouped together with low-skilled students. A possible explanation why the initially middle-skilled students are valuable in the process of reassigning students to achieve a "net social gain" in entrepreneurial skills can be found in the social learning theory (Bandura 1977; 1982). Middle students can profit both from low- and high-quality students. Working together with the former, they have to take the initiative in the business planning project and learn about entrepreneurial actions by executing them. Working together with high-skilled students, on the other hand, enables these students to learn by observing their team members.

However, several caveats apply in addition to those mentioned in section 3.7 (e.g. sample selection issues, pooling of two survey datasets), emanating from the assumptions made. First, due to the assignment of students to teams based on the amount of their previously completed university courses might introduce some kind of "self-selection" bias, since as a consequence the teams are equally staffed to this effect. Although the students in each team do not exhibit any similarities regarding most demographic variables and all variables concerning prior entrepreneurial experiences, a true randomized assignment will deliver even more reliable results. Second, it is questionable if the concept of entrepreneurial self-efficacy measures entrepreneurial skills without error (beyond measurement errors introduced by asking for skills with questionnaires). And third, the estimated peer effects represent a lower bound of all social interaction effects affecting the formation of entrepreneurial skills. The assumption that the team members are all relevant peers and that no unobserved background characteristics matter to this effect is very restrictive.

This chapter takes first steps into the investigation of social interaction effects in entrepreneurship education. It delivers valuable insight into how course planners can leverage the existing quality among the attending students to increase overall entrepreneurial skills. At the same time it opens up several avenues for future research. First and foremost, it would seem important to study social interaction effects in successive courses to be sure that my conclusions from this first study hold true. Second, my results on the different importance of social interaction effects on males versus females and on students with few versus many prior entrepreneurship-related experiences indicate that it is worthwhile to explicitly consider background characteristics when measuring peer effects. I found that male students are more subject to peer effects than females, and students with few prior experiences more than students with broad prior experiences. Further research into background variables may deliver important implications for the organization of teamwork in entrepreneurship courses. And finally, other outcome variables aiming at different questions may be of interest. For example: do some teams, after being grouped together randomly, in fact start own businesses after having completed the mere academic task in the entrepreneurship course?

8. Conclusion and Avenues for Further Research

Entrepreneurship is an important driver of the economy and plays an important role for social welfare in general (e.g. Fritsch and Müller 2008). By contrast, failure as an entrepreneur can be costly both for society and for the individual. On the one hand, for example in the context of funding of entrepreneurial ventures, it has been argued that subsidizing finance for new entrepreneurs may be socially wasteful (De Meza and Soutey 1996; De Meza 2002; Shane 2009). Having the "wrong" person driving an entrepreneurial venture could lead to missed opportunities and therefore to missed benefits in terms of job and value creation. On the other hand, a failed entrepreneurial "experiment" might be devastating to the entrepreneur in terms of psychological and financial (losses and opportunity costs) impacts (Zhao et al. 2010).

For all these reasons, different stakeholders are increasingly interested in informing about and preparing for entrepreneurship as a career option. Especially students at tertiary institutions of education are assigned a substantial role in this regard. According to empirical evidence this group creates more jobs than entrepreneurs without a university degree (Dietrich 1999), and they invest more in their own start-up (Reynolds et al. 1994). Entrepreneurship education is considered to play an essential role in shaping attitudes, skills and culture (World Economic Forum 2009). Several stakeholder groups conceive of entrepreneurship courses as reducing the cost of becoming an entrepreneur. However, although considered an important input factor, the effects emanating from entrepreneurship education are still poorly understood. Research on entrepreneurship education has not provided resilient empirical determination of the size and nature of its effects (Cox et al. 2002; Souitaris et al. 2007). This research project seeks to make several contributions to bring forward the understanding of the importance of entrepreneurship education at tertiary institutions.

Following widely recognized definitions of entrepreneurship education and previous work on its effects, I argue that courses in this field have two purposes: to improve students' entrepreneurial skills and to help students to learn if they are suited to entrepreneurship or not. The second aspect helps students to better self-select into the "right" career path.

Based on these fundamental assumptions, I posed three major research questions: Has entrepreneurship education any impact on students' career plans at all, and how large is this impact? How can this impact be characterized on an individual level in terms of skill-building and pronouncing career intentions? And third, how can the population of course attendees as input factor in an educational production function be used to leverage this impact, especially with respect to conveying skills?

To answer these questions, I study the effects of a large-scale compulsory entrepreneurship course at a major German university, using a pre-test–post-test control group design. Data was collected before and after an entrepreneurship course from 509 business administration students (403 in the treatment group who took the course and 106 in the control group). The analyses are grounded theoretically on the Theory of Planned Behavior. This theory identifies three sufficient antecedents of behavioral intentions, which in turn are the single best predictors of actual behavior: perceived desirability (the perceived attractiveness of the behavior, in this case pursuing an entrepreneurial career), perceived social norm (the perceived pressure to execute the behavior), and perceived behavioral control (the perceived capability to perform tasks related to the behavior).

By and large, the findings reported in the empirical analyses (chapters 5 through 7) can be summarized as follows[67]:

a) Following approaches taken by previously conducted studies, I analyze the effects of entrepreneurship education on mean entrepreneurial attitudes and intentions in chapter 5 employing a difference-in-differences approach. The results suggest that mean entrepreneurial intentions

---

[67] I only review the most important findings here. For a more detailed report on the results, I refer to concluding remarks at the end of each chapter.

among the treatment group do not change significantly. Regarding the antecedents of intentions, I found that the mean perceptions of social norm and behavioral control significantly increased during the course.

An investigation of the effects on subsamples among the students using a difference-in-difference-in-differences approach revealed that students are not equally subject to course-induced influences. Based on their demographic and personality characteristics as well as on their prior experiences they respond differently to the new information received during the course. This becomes visible in different adjustments of both intentions and their antecedents.

b) The insignificant effect on mean entrepreneurial intentions raises the question if the course has any effect on this most important outcome variable at all. The results reported in chapter 6 indicate that individual adjustments of entrepreneurial intentions might cancel each other out. Therefore a significant change in mean entrepreneurial intentions is not observed. By contrast, the variance of entrepreneurial intentions increases during the course. This finding suggests that students discover if they are suited to an entrepreneurial career or not and self-select into the "right" career path accordingly.

c) Leaving the framework of the Theory of Planned Behavior I investigate whether social interactions among students can foster the development of entrepreneurial skills during entrepreneurship education in chapter 7. Since team-based business planning is a prevalent component in entrepreneurship education, I investigate the possibility of leveraging mutual learning in teams. The results suggest that course planners may exploit teamwork on an entrepreneurial project to foster individual skill development by bestowing greater care on team composition according to pre-course entrepreneurial skills.

The concepts and results introduced and reported in this book have important implications both for all stakeholder groups introduced in section 1.1 that are involved in entrepreneurship education. The findings reported under a) and b) support the proposition that entrepreneurship education has to major functions:

develop the necessary skills to fulfill entrepreneurial tasks among students, and help them to better assess their own aptitude for an entrepreneurial career. The result reported in c) suggests an efficient way to increase skill-development.

Overall, the results support educational policies considering entrepreneurship training as a way of informing students about career options. This information should help students to adjust and strengthen their career plans. Discouraging students who are not suited to an entrepreneurial career should be considered as much a success as encouraging the right students to start a new business after graduation. Shane (2009) argues that entrepreneurship is not a numbers game. Just having more entrepreneurs will not meet hopes of politicians towards the creation of jobs and social welfare. Only high quality start-ups will have this desired outcome, and high-quality entrepreneurs manage these. If entrepreneurship education sorts students and thus helps identifying these entrepreneurs, politicians can subsidize promising new ventures more targeted. This reduces the risk of wasting public resources by broadly supporting graduating students who are mentally unprepared and lack necessary skills for an entrepreneurial career. As noted in von Graevenitz et al. (2010), I also have no means to assess how costly a mistake like this is for society, and quantifying the economic impact of entrepreneurship education is difficult. However, a "production" of just more entrepreneurs might not be a good objective and should not be the reason for including entrepreneurship education into university curricula.

Building on this, my results may also add to the exchange between providers and receivers of funds for the establishment and extension of entrepreneurship education. The view of entrepreneurship education as a measure to help students strengthen their career intention – together with the results reported under b) – may provide both parties with a new criterion to evaluate the success of entrepreneurship education. Moreover, the findings reported under a) suggest that students do acquire skills necessary to fulfill entrepreneurial tasks. Both public and private fund providers may profit from this. High-skilled students with strong entrepreneurial intentions might become entrepreneurs and create jobs and economic impact. Students who discovered that they are not suited for an entrepreneurial career but acquired the necessary skills to do so may fulfill important functions in established corporations as entrepreneurially minded managers.

This study delivers valuable insights to course planners into ways of improving the design of entrepreneurship courses by taking the course considered in this book as a "blueprint". They might use the results to alter their own courses by comparing and adjusting the used concepts. I argue that course planners should distinguish between two stages of entrepreneurship education.

First, they should offer a mandatory entrepreneurship course at the beginning of the curriculum, allowing students to conduct the self-assessment regarding entrepreneurial aptitude. Suggestions for the design of such courses may be drawn from the results reported in chapter 6. For example, the importance of perceived social norm calls for more room for feedback by fellow students and instructors to support this self-assessment.

In a second step, they should offer elective courses aiming at further developing the necessary skills for an entrepreneurial career. Students who consciously decide to take these courses should be determined to become entrepreneurs by then. Here, the results reported under a) and c), or in chapter 5 and 7, respectively, have important implications. Since chapter 5 shows that students' entrepreneurial skills increase during the course (identified by the increase in perceived behavioral control), course planners may copy the "blueprint"-course to achieve this goal. Moreover, the analysis of the course-impact on different subsamples of students help them in the selection of students for course admission when seminar places are limited, as the information conveyed in the course do not appeal to all students. In addition, chapter 7 proposes a concrete implication regarding the importance of teamwork and team composition. The results there suggest that students do not only learn from instructors, but also from their fellow students. Course planners can make use of these social interactions and leverage them to increase the formation of entrepreneurial skills among the student population.

Of course, the results are also of interest for the students attending entrepreneurship courses. In contrast to other courses taught at university aiming at transferring practical knowledge, entrepreneurship education deals with students' career attitudes and intentions. My results inform students that entrepreneurship courses have a prominent function at universities. They help them to develop stronger career intentions and thus minimize the risk of taking the "wrong" career decision, which can be costly in either way. Failing as entrepreneur due to a lack of preparation may be devastating to the individual in terms of financial and psychological impact. Being unhappy in a managerial role, when an entrepreneurial career would have been the better decision, has at least negative psychological consequences.

Finally, this research project bears several implications for the last identified stakeholder group. Other researchers in this field might use the introduced concepts and methods to repeat the empirical studies. The detailed description of the theoretical model as well as the data generation procedure may support them in doing so.

Three major avenues for future research can be identified[68]. First, with the exception of the study by von Graevenitz et al. (2010), the view of entrepreneurship as a measure to support students in their self-assessment of entrepreneurial aptitude is radically different from the one that has dominated the literature. More evaluations taking this perspective are necessary to validate the findings in this work. Second, a further investigation of social interaction effects in entrepreneurship education promises insights into an efficient way to achieve intended course-goals. Third, an application of the proposed methods on secondary school level entrepreneurship education might be worthwhile. It would be interesting if students could conduct the self-assessment regarding their entrepreneurial aptitude already there. Tertiary institutions could then concentrate on conveying skills. This division of labor may result in significant cost advantages for both school-levels.

Following are several smaller suggestions for further research. The internal validity won by exploiting data from a treatment and control group comes at the cost of the lack of external validity. My implications are all based on just one course. As proposed by Oosterbeek et al. (2010), more studies assessing the

---

[68] I already proposed several smaller extensions and modifications of the conducted empirical studies in the concluding sections of the respective chapters.

effectiveness of several variants of entrepreneurship courses would be instructive. Variants could include, among others, the duration of the course, mandatory versus voluntary participation, number of credit points earned, or addressed target group (e.g. different fields of study, interdisciplinary student population, students' progress in their course of study, etc.). Of course, there are several more obvious limitations of this research project, such as the sample composition (I exclusively surveyed business administration students) as well as the sample size (especially of the control group). Moreover, allocation of the students to the treatment and control group was not random – a true experiment would provide even more reliable results.

As already argued, the intention behind the detailed description of the theoretical framework and data generation process was to reduce other researchers' costs to conduct similar studies whose results are comparable mine. They might use the concepts and instruments presented in this book to overcome the limitations of this study and extend the scope of this literature stream. Thus they should be able to deepen our understanding of the effects emanating from entrepreneurship education and derive further implications for the design of courses.

Bibliography

Abelson, R. P. (1982): "Three modes of attitude behavior consistency" in: Zanna, M. P. (Ed.): *Consistency in social behavior*, Ontario 1982, pp. 131-146

Ajzen, I. (1985): "From intentions to actions: A theory of planned behavior" in: Kuhl, J. and Beckman, J. (Eds.): *Action-control: From cognition to behavior*, pp. 11-39, Heidelberg

Ajzen, I. (1987): "Attitudes, traits, and actions: Dispositional prediction of behavior in personality and social psychology" in: Berkowitz, L. (Ed.): *Advances in experimental social psychology*, New York 1987, pp. 1-63

Ajzen, I. (1991): "The theory of planned behavior" in: *Organizational Behavior and Human Decision Processes,* Vol. 50, No. 2, pp. 179-211

Ajzen, I. (2002): "Perceived Behavioral Control, Self-Efficacy, Locus of Control, and the Theory of Planned Behavior" in: *Journal of Applied Social Psychology,* Vol. 32, No. 4, pp. 665-683

Ajzen, I. and Fishbein, M. (1980): *Understanding attitudes and predicting social behavior*, New York

Ajzen, I. and Madden, T. J. (1986): "Prediction of goal-directed behavior: Attitudes, intentions, and perceived behavioral control" in: *Journal of experimental social psychology,* Vol. 22, No. 5, pp. 453-474

Akerlof, G. A. and Kranton, R. E. (2000): "Economics and Identity" in: *Quarterly Journal of Economics,* Vol. 115, No. 3, pp. 715-753

Alberti, F. (1999): "Entrepreneurship education: scope and theory" in: Salvato, C., Davidsson, P. and Persson, A. (Eds.): *Entrepreneurial knowledge and learning: conceptual advances and directions for future research*, Research Report No 1999-6, Jonkoping, Jonkoping International Business School

Ammermueller, A. and Pischke J. S. (2009): "Peer effects in european primary schools: Evidence from the progress in international reading literacy study" in: *Journal of Labor Economics,* Vol. 27, No. 3, pp. 315-348

Anna, A. L., Chandler, G. N., Jansen, E. and Mero, N. P. (2000): "Women business owners in traditional and non-traditional industries" in: *Journal of Business Venturing,* Vol. 15, No. 3, pp. 279-303

Arcidiacono, P. and Nicholson, S. (2005): "Peer effects in medical school" in: *Journal of Public Economics,* Vol. 89, No. 2-3, pp. 327-350

Armitage, C. J. and Conner, M. (1999): "The theory of planned behaviour: Assessment of predictive validity and'perceived control" in: *British Journal of Social Psychology,* Vol. 38, No. 1, pp. 35-54

Armitage, C. J. and Conner, M. (2001): "Efficacy of the Theory of Planned Behaviour: A meta-analytic review" in: *British Journal of Social Psychology,* Vol. 40, No. 4, pp. 471-499

Armitage, C. J., Norman, P. and Conner, M. (2002): "Can the Theory of Planned Behaviour mediate the effects of age, gender and multidimensional health locus of control?" in: *British Journal of Health Psychology,* Vol. 7, No. 3, pp. 299-316

Autio, E., Keeley, R. H., Klofsten, M. and Ulfstedt, T. (1997): "Entrepreneurial intent among students: testing an intent model in Asia, Scandinavia and USA", Frontiers of Entrepreneurship Research, Babson

Autio, E., Keeley, R. H., Klofsten, M., Parker, G. G. C. and Hay, M. (2001): "Entrepreneurial Intent among Students in Scandinavia and in the USA" in: *Enterprise & Innovation Mgmt Std,* Vol. 2, No. 2, pp. 145 - 160

Bagozzi, R. P. and Yi, Y. (1989): "The degree of intention formation as a moderator of the attitude-behavior relationship" in: *Social Psychology Quarterly,* Vol. 52, No. 4, pp. 266-279

Bandura, A. (1977): "Self-efficacy: Toward a unifying theory of behavioral change" in: *Psychological review,* Vol. 84, No. 2, pp. 191-215

Bandura, A. (1982): "Self-efficacy mechanism in human agency" in: *American psychologist,* Vol. 37, No. 2, pp. 122-147

Bandura, A. (1986): *Social foundations of thought and action: A social cognitive theory,* Englewood Cliffs

Bandura, A. (1992): "Exercise of personal agency through the self-efficacy mechanism" in: Schwartzer, R. (Ed.): *Self-efficacy: Thought control of action*, Washington, D.C. 1992, pp. 3-38

Bandura, A. (1997): *Self-efficacy: The exercise of control*, New York

Bandura, A., Barbaranelli, C., Caprara, G. V. and Pastorelli, C. (2001): "Self Efficacy Beliefs as Shapers of Children's Aspirations and Career Trajectories" in: *Child development,* Vol. 72, No. 1, pp. 187-206

Baron, R. A. (2004): "The cognitive perspective: a valuable tool for answering entrepreneurship's basic "why" questions" in: *Journal of Business Venturing,* Vol. 19, No. 2, pp. 221-239

Barrick, M. R. and Mount, M. K. (1991): "The Big Five Personality Dimensions and Job Performance: A Meta-Analysis" in: *Personnel Psychology,* Vol. 44, No. 1, pp. 1-26

Béchard, J. P. and Grégoire, D. (2005): "Entrepreneurship education research revisited: the case of higher education" in: *Academy of Management Learning & Education,* Vol. 4, No. 1, pp. 22-43

Béchard, J. P. and Toulouse, J. M. (1998): "Validation of a didactic model for the analysis of training objectives in entrepreneurship" in: *Journal of Business Venturing,* Vol. 13, No. 4, pp. 317-332

Bernardo, A. E. and Welch, I. (2001): "On the Evolution of Overconfidence and Entrepreneurs" in: *Journal of Economics & Management Strategy,* Vol. 10, No. 3, pp. 301-330

Bicchieri, C. and Fukui, Y. (1999): "The Great Illusion: Ignorance, Informational Cascades, and the Persistence of Unpopular Norms" in: *Business Ethics Quarterly,* Vol. 9, No. 1, pp. 127-155

Bikhchandani, S., Hirshleifer, D. and Welch, I. (1998): "Learning from the Behavior of Others: Conformity, Fads, and Informational Cascades" in: *The Journal of Economic Perspectives,* Vol. 12, No. 3, pp. 151-170

Bird, B. (1988): "Implementing entrepreneurial ideas: The case for intention" in: *Academy of Management Review,* Vol. 13, No. 3, pp. 442-453

Block, Z. and Stumpf, S. A. (1992): "Entrepreneurship education research: experience and challenge" in: Sexton, D. L. and Kasarda, J. M. (Eds.): *The state of the art of entrepreneurship*, pp. 17-45, Boston

Boyd, N. G. and Vozikis, G. S. (1994): "The influence of self-efficacy on the development of entrepreneurial intentions and actions" in: *Entrepreneurship: Theory and Practice*, Vol. 18, No. 4, pp. 63-77

Brock, W. A. and Durlauf, S. N. (2001): "Interactions-based models" in: *Handbook of econometrics*, Vol. 5, No. pp. 3297-3380

Brockhaus, R. H. (1980): "Risk taking propensity of entrepreneurs" in: *Academy of Management Journal*, Vol. 23, No. 3, pp. 509-520

Brockhaus, R. H. (1987): "Entrepreneurial Folklore" in: *Journal of Small Business Management*, Vol. 25, No. pp. 1-6

Brockhaus, R. H. (1994): "Entrepreneurship and Family Business Research: Comparisons, Critique, and Lessons" in: *Entrepreneurship: Theory and Practice*, Vol. 19, No. 1, pp. 25-38

Brockhaus, R. H. and Horwitz, P. S. (1982): "The psychology of the entrepreneur" in: Kent, C., Sexton, D. and Vesper, K. (Eds.): *The Encyclopaedia of Entrepreneurship*, pp. 25-48, Englewood Cliffs

Brown, R. (1990): "Encouraging enterprise: Britain's graduate enterprise program" in: *Journal of Small Business Management*, Vol. 28, No. 4, pp. 71-77

Brown, M. B. and Forsythe, A. B. (1974): "Robust tests for the equality of variances" in: *Journal of the American Statistical Association*, Vol. 69, No. 346, pp. 364-367

Budd, R. J. (1987): "Response bias and the theory of reasoned action" in: *Social Cognition*, Vol. 5, No. 2, pp. 95-107

Burris, R. W. (1976): "Human Learning" in Dunnette, M. D. (Ed.): *Handbook of industrial and organizational psychology*, Chicagoi IL

Carland, J. W., Hoy, F., Boulton, W. R. and Carland, J. A. C. (1984): "Differentiating entrepreneurs from small business owners: A conceptualization" in: *Academy of Management Review*, Vol. 9, No. 2, pp. 354-359

Carrier, C. (2005): "Pedagogical challenges in entrepreneurship education" in: Kyrö, P. and Carrier, C. (Eds.): *The dynamics of learning entrepreneurship in a cross-cultural university context*, pp. 136-158, Hämmeenlinna

Carsrud, A. L., Gaglio, C. M. and Olm, K. W. (1987): "Entrepreneurs-mentors, networks, and successful new venture development: an exploratory study" in: *American Journal of Small Business*, Vol. 12, No. 2, pp. 13-18

Cattell, R. B. (1943): "The description of personality: Basic traits resolved into clusters" in: *Journal of Abnormal and Social Psychology*, Vol. 38, No. 4, pp. 476-506

Chamard, J. (1989): "Public education: Its effect on entrepreneurial characteristics" in: *Journal of Small Business and Entrepreneurship*, Vol. 6, No. 2, pp. 23-30

Chamorro-Premuzic, T. and Furnham, A. (2005): *Personality and intellectual competence*, Mahwah NY

Chandler, G. N. and Lyon, D. W. (2001): "Issues of Research Design and Construct Measurement in Entrepreneurship Research: The Past Decade" in: *Entrepreneurship: Theory and Practice*, Vol. 25, No. 4, pp. 101-114

Chen, C. C., Greene, P. G. and Crick, A. (1998): "Does entrepreneurial self-efficacy distinguish entrepreneurs from managers?" in: *Journal of Business Venturing*, Vol. 13, No. 4, pp. 295-316

Chrisman, J. J. (1997): "Program Evaluation and the Venture Development Program at the University of Calgary: A Research Note" in: *Entrepreneurship Theory and Practice*, Vol. 22, No. 1, pp. 59-74

Clark, B. W., Davis, C. H. and Harnish, V. C. (1984): "Do courses in entrepreneurship aid in new venture creation?" in: *Journal of Small Business Management*, Vol. 22, No. 2, pp. 26-31

Coleman, J. S., Campbell, E., Hobson, C., McPartland, J., Mood, A., Weinfield, F. and York, R. (1966): "Equality of educational opportunity Washington", U.S. Department of Health, Education, and Welfare, Office of Education

Colquit, J. A., LePine, J. A. and Noe, R. A. (2000): "Toward an integrative theory of training motivation: A meta-analytic path analysis of 20 years of research" in: *Journal of Applied Psychology*, Vol. 85, No. 5, pp. 678-707

Conner, M. and Armitage, C. J. (1998): "Extending the Theory of Planned Behavior: A Review and Avenues for Further Research" in: *Journal of Applied Social Psychology*, Vol. 28, No. 15, pp. 1429-1464

Cooper, A. C. (1985): "The role of incubator organizations in the founding of growth-oriented firms" in: *Journal of Business Venturing*, Vol. 1, No. 1, pp. 75-86

Cooper, A. C. (1993): "Challenges in predicting new firm performance" in: *Journal of Business Venturing*, Vol. 8, No. 3, pp. 241-253

Costa, P. T., McCrae, R. R. and Holland, J. L. (1984): "Personality and vocational interests in an adult sample" in: *Journal of Applied Psychology*, Vol. 69, No. 3, pp. 390-400

Cox, L. W. (1996): "The Goals and Impact of Educational Interventions in the Early Stages of Entrepreneur Career Development", Internationalising Entrepreneurship Education and Training Conference, Arnhem

Cox, L. W., Mueller, S. L. and Moss, S. E. (2002): "The impact of entrepreneurship education on entrepreneurial self-efficacy" in: *International Journal of Entrepreneurship Education*, Vol. 1, No. 2, pp. 229-245

Curran, J. and Stanworth, J. (1989): "Education and training for enterprise: Problems of classification, evaluation, policy and research" in: *International Small Business Journal*, Vol. 7, No. 2, pp. 11-22

Davidsson, P. (1995): "Determinants Of Entrepreneurial Intentions", RENT IX Workshop, Piacenza

Dean, M. A., Conte, J. M. and Blankenhorn, T. R. (2006): "Examination of the predictive validity of Big Five personality dimensions across training performance criteria" in: *Personality and Individual Differences*, Vol. 41, No. 7, pp. 1229-1239

Delmar, F. and Davidsson, P. (2000): "Where do they come from? Prevalence and characteristics of nascent entrepreneurs" in: *Entrepreneurship and Regional Development*, Vol. 12, No. 1, pp. 1-23

De Meza, D. (2002): "Overlending?" in: *Economic Journal*, Vol. 112, No. 477, pp. 17-31

De Meza, D. and Southey, C. (1996): "The borrower's curse: Optimism, finance and entrepreneurship" in: *The Economic Journal*, Vol. 106, No. 435, pp. 375-386

De Noble, A. F., Jung, D. and Ehrlich, S. B. (1999): "Entrepreneurial self-efficacy: The development of a measure and its relationship to entrepreneurial action", Frontiers of Entrepreneurship Research, Babson

De Raad, B. and Schouwenburg, H. C. (1996): "Personality in learning and education: a review" in: *European Journal of Personality*, Vol. 10, No. 5, pp. 303-336

Dietrich, H. (1999): "Empirische Befunde zur selbständigen Erwerbstätigkeit unter besonderer Berücksichtigung scheinselbständiger Erwerbsverhältnisse" in: *Mitteilungen aus der Arbeitsmarkt-und Berufsforschung*, Vol. 32, No. 1, pp. 85-101

Donckels, R. (1991): "Education and entrepreneurship experiences from secondary and university education in Belgium" in: *Journal of Small Business*, Vol. 9, No. 1, pp. 35-42

Drucker, P. F. (1985): *Innovation and Entrepreneurship*, New York

Epple, D. and Romano, R. E. (1998): "Competition between private and public schools, vouchers, and peer-group effects" in: *The American Economic Review*, Vol. 88, No. 1, pp. 33-62

Epstein, S. (1984): "Entwurf einer integrativen Persönlichkeitstheorie" in: *Selbstkonzeptforschung. Probleme, Befunde, Perspektiven*, Vol. 2, No. pp. 15-45

Epstein, S. and O'Brien, E. J. (1985): "The personñsituation debate in historical and current perspective" in: *Psychological Bulletin*, Vol. 98, No. 3, pp. 513-537

European Commission (2006): "Entrepreneurship Education in Europe: Fostering Entrepreneurial Mindsets through Education and Learning"

Eysenck, H. J. (1992): "Personality and education: The influence of extraversion, neuroticism and psychoticism" in: *Zeitschrift für Pädagogische Psychologie/German Journal of Educational Psychology*, Vol. 2, No. pp. 133-144

Facteau, J. D., Dobbins, G. H., Russell, J. E. A., Ladd, R. T. and Kudisch, J. D. (1995): "The influence of general perceptions of the training environment on pretraining motivation and perceived training transfer" in: *Journal of Management,* Vol. 21, No. 1, pp. 1-25

Falck, O., Heblich, S. and Luedemann, E. (2010): "Identity and entrepreneurship: do school peers shape entrepreneurial intentions?" in: *Small Business Economics,* Vol. 35, No. pp. 1-21

Fayolle, A., Gailly, B. and Lassas-Clerc, N. (2006a): "Effect and Counter-effect of Entrepreneurship Education and Social Context on Student'sIntentions" in: *Estudios de Economía Aplicada,* Vol. 24, No. 2, pp. 509-523

Fayolle, A., Gailly, B. and Lassas-Clerc, N. (2006b): "Assessing the impact of entrepreneurship education programmes: a new methodology" in: *Journal of European Industrial Training,* Vol. 30, No. 9, pp. 701-720

Fiet, J. O. (2001): "The theoretical side of teaching entrepreneurship" in: *Journal of Business Venturing,* Vol. 16, No. 1, pp. 1-24

Fishbein, M. and Ajzen, I. (1975): *Belief, attitude, intention and behavior: An introduction to theory and research,* Reading

Fishbein, M. and Ajzen, I. (2010): *Predicting and changing behavior: The reasoned action approach,* New York

Foster, G. (2006): "It's not your peers, and it's not your friends: Some progress toward understanding the educational peer effect mechanism" in: *Journal of Public Economics,* Vol. 90, No. 8-9, pp. 1455-1475

Frank, H., Lueger, M. and Korunka, C. (2007): "The significance of personality in business start-up intentions, start-up realization and business success" in: *Entrepreneurship & Regional Development,* Vol. 19, No. 3, pp. 227-251

Franke, N. and Lüthje, C. (2004): "Entrepreneurial Intentions of Business Students: A Benchmarking Study" in: *International Journal of Innovation and Technology Management,* Vol. 1, No. 3, pp. 269-288

Fritsch, M. and Müller, P. (2008): "The effect of new business formation on regional development over time: the case of Germany" in: *Small Business Economics,* Vol. 30, No. 1, pp. 15-29

Garavan, T. N. and O'Cinneide, B. (1994a): "Entrepreneurship Education and Training Programmes: A Review and Evaluation - Part 1" in: *Journal of European Industrial Training,* Vol. 18, No. 11, pp. 13-21

Garavan, T. N. and O'Cinneide, B. (1994b): "Entrepreneurship Education and Training Programmes:: A Review and Evaluation - Part 2" in: *Journal of European Industrial Training,* Vol. 18, No. 11, pp. 13-21

Gartner, W. B. (1988): "Who is an entrepreneur? Is the wrong question" in: *American Journal of Small Business,* Vol. 12, No. 4, pp. 11-32

Gasse, Y. (1985): "A strategy for the promotion and identification of potential entrepreneurs at the secondary school level", Frontiers of Entrepreneurship Research, Babson

Gatewood, E. J., Shaver, K. G., Powers, J. B. and Gartner, W. B. (2002): "Entrepreneurial Expectancy, Task Effort, and Performance" in: *Entrepreneurship: Theory and Practice,* Vol. 27, No. 2, pp. 187-207

Gaviria, A. and Raphael, S. (2001): "School-Based Peer Effects and Juvenile Behavior" in: *Review of Economics and Statistics,* Vol. 83, No. 2, pp. 257-268

Giannetti, M. and Simonov, A. (2009): "Social interactions and entrepreneurial activity" in: *Journal of Economics & Management Strategy,* Vol. 18, No. 3, pp. 665-709

Gibb, A. A. (1987): "Education for enterprise: training for small business initiation – some contrasts" in: *Journal of Small Business and Entrepreneurship,* Vol. 4, No. 3, pp. 42-70

Gibb Dyer, W. (1994): "Toward a Theory of Entrepreneurial Careers" in: *Entrepreneurship Theory and Practice,* Vol. 19, No. 2, pp. 7-21

Giner-Sorolla, R. (1999): "Affect in attitude" in: Chaiken, S. and Trope, Y. (Eds.): *Dual process theories in social psychology,* pp. 441-461, New York

Gist, M. E. and Mitchell, T. R. (1992): "Self-efficacy: A theoretical analysis of its determinants and malleability" in: *Academy of Management Review,* Vol. 17, No. 2, pp. 183-211

Goldberg, L. R. (1992): "The development of markers for the Big-Five factor structure" in: *Psychological assessment,* Vol. 4, No. 1, pp. 26-42

Goldstein, I. and Ford, J. (2002): *Training in organizations: Needs assessment, development, and evaluation*, Belmont CA

Gompers, P., Lerner, J. and Scharfstein, D. (2005): "Entrepreneurial Spawning: Public Corporations and the Genesis of New Ventures, 1986 to 1999" in: *The Journal of Finance*, Vol. 60, No. 2, pp. 577-614

Gorman, G., Hanlon, D. and King, W. (1997): "Some Research Perspectives on Entrepreneurship Education, Enterprise Education and Education for Small Business Management: A Ten Year Literature Review" in: *International Small Business Journal*, Vol. 15, No. 3, pp. 56-77

Gosling, S. D., Rentfrow, P. J. and Swann, W. B. (2003): "A very brief measure of the Big-Five personality domains" in: *Journal of Research in Personality*, Vol. 37, No. 6, pp. 504-528

Gough, H. G. (1966): "Graduation from high school as predicted from the California psychological inventory" in: *Psychology in the Schools*, Vol. 3, No. 3, pp. 208-216

Gundry, L. K. and Welch, H. P. (2001): "The ambitious entrepreneur: High growth strategies of women-owned enterprises" in: *Journal of Business Venturing*, Vol. 16, No. 5, pp. 453-470

Gupta, A. (1992): "The informal education of the Indian entrepreneur" in: *Journal of Small Business and Entrepreneurship*, Vol. 9, No. 4, pp. 63-70

Hack, A., Rettberg, F. and Witt, P. (2008): "Grundungsausbildung und Grundungsabsicht: eine empirische Untersuchung an der TU Dortmund" in: *ZfKE-Zeitschrift fur KMU und Entrepreneurship*, Vol. 56, No. 3, pp. 148-171

Hagen, E. E. (1962): *On the Theory of Social Change. How Economic Growth Begins*, Homewood, IL

Hamilton, B. H. (2000): "Does entrepreneurship pay? An empirical analysis of the returns of self-employment" in: *Journal of Political Economy*, Vol. No. pp. 604-631

Hansemark, O. C. (1998): "The effects of an entrepreneurship programme on need for achievement and locus of control of reinforcement" in: *International Journal of Entrepreneurial Behaviour & Research*, Vol. 4, No. 1, pp. 28-50

Hansemark, O. C. (2003): "Need for achievement, locus of control and the prediction of business start-ups: A longitudinal study" in: *Journal of Economic Psychology,* Vol. 24, No. 3, pp. 301-319

Hanushek, E. A. (1998): "Conclusions and controversies about the effectiveness of school resources" in: *Economic Policy Review,* Vol. 4, No. 1, pp. 11-27

Hanushek, E. A., Kain, J. F., Markman, J. M. and Rivkin, S. G. (2003): "Does peer ability affect student achievement?" in: *Journal of Applied Econometrics,* Vol. 18, No. 5, pp. 527-544

Harhoff, D. (1999): "Firm formation and regional spillovers-evidence from Germany" in: *Economics of Innovation and New Technology,* Vol. 8, No. 1, pp. 27-55

Hayton, J. C., George, G. and Zahra, S. A. (2002): "National Culture and Entrepreneurship: A Review of Behavioral Research" in: *Entrepreneurship: Theory and Practice,* Vol. 26, No. 4, pp. 33-53

Heckman, J. J. (1979): "Sample selection bias as a specification error" in: *Econometrica: Journal of the econometric society,* Vol. 47, No. 1, pp. 153-161

Henry, C., Hill, F. M. and Leitch, C. M. (2004): "The Effectiveness of Training for New Business Creation: A Longitudinal Study" in: *International Small Business Journal,* Vol. 22, No. 3, pp. 249-269

Henry, C., Hill, F. and Leitch, C. (2005): "Entrepreneurship education and training: can entrepreneurship be taught? Part I" in: *Education+ Training,* Vol. 47, No. 2, pp. 98-111

Hills, G. E. (1988): "Variations in university entrepreneurship education: an empirical study of an evolving field" in: *Journal of Business Venturing,* Vol. 3, No. 2, pp. 109-22

Hills, G. E. and Morris, M. H. (1998): "Entrepreneurship education: A conceptual model and review" in: Scott, M. G., Rosa, P. and Klandt, H. (Eds.): *Educating entrepreneurs for wealth creation,* pp. 38-58, Hants

Honig, B. (2004): "Entrepreneurship education: Toward a model of contingency-based business planning" in: *Academy of Management Learning & Education,* Vol. 3, No. 3, pp. 258-273

Hornaday, J. A. (1982): "Research about living entrepreneurs" in: Kent, C. A., Sexton, D. and Vesper, K. H. (Eds.): *Encyclopedia of entrepreneurship*,, pp. 21-22, Englewood Cliffs,

Hostager, T. J. and Decker, R. L. (1999): "The effects of an entrepreneurship program on achievement motivation: A preliminary study", Small Business Institute Director's Association, San Francisco

Hoxby, C. M. (2001): "Peer effects in the classroom: Learning from gender and race variation", National Bureau of Economic Research Cambridge, MA

Iacus, S. M., King, G. and Porro, G. (2008): "Matching for causal inference without balance checking", Working Paper, Harvard University

Iacus, S. M., King, G. and Porro, G. (2009): "CEM: Software for Coarsened Exact Matching" in: *Journal of Statistical Software,* Vol. 30, No. 9, pp. 1-27

Iacus, S. M., King, G. and Porro, G. (2011): "Multivariate matching methods that are monotonic imbalance bounding" in: *Journal of the American Statistical Association,* Vol. 106, No. 493, pp. 345-361

Isfan, K., Moog, P. and Backes-Gellner, U. (2004): "Die Rolle der Hochschullehrer für Gründungen aus deutschen Hochschulen–erste empirische Erkenntnisse" in: Achleitner, A.-K. (Ed.): *Jahrbuch Entrepreneurship*, Berlin 2004, pp. 339-361

Jamieson, I. (1984): "Schools and enterprise" in: Watts, A. G. and Moran, P. (Eds.): *Education for Enterprise,* pp. 19-27, Cambridge

Johannisson, B. (1991): "University training for entrepreneurship: Swedish approaches" in: *Entrepreneurship & Regional Development,* Vol. 3, No. 1, pp. 67-82

Kaiser, H. F. (1970): "A second generation little jiffy" in: *Psychometrika,* Vol. 35, No. 4, pp. 401-415

Kandel, E. and Lazear, E. P. (1992): "Peer Pressure and Partnerships" in: *The Journal of Political Economy,* Vol. 100, No. 4, pp. 801-817

Kang, C. (2007): "Academic interactions among classroom peers: a cross-country comparison using TIMSS" in: *Applied Economics,* Vol. 39, No. 12, pp. 1531-1544

Kantor, J. (1988): "Can entrepreneurship be taught?–a Canadian experiment" in: *Journal of Small Business and Entrepreneurship*, Vol. 5, No. 4, pp. 12-19

Katz, J. (1992): "Modeling entrepreneurial career progressions: Concepts and considerations" in: *Entrepreneurship Theory and Practice*, Vol. 19, No. 2, pp. 23-39

Katz, J. and Gartner, W. B. (1988): "Properties of emerging organizations" in: *Academy of Management Review*, Vol. 13, No. 3, pp. 429-441

Kelley, D., Bosma, N. and Amorós, J. E. (2010): "Global Entrepreneurship Monitor: 2010 Global Report"

Kickul, J., Gundry, L. and Whitcanack, L. (2009): "Intuition versus Analysis?: Testing differential models of cognitive style on entrepreneurial self-efficacy and intentionality" in: *Entrepreneurship Theory and Practice*, Vol. March 2009, No. pp. 439-453

Kim, M. S. and Hunter, J. E. (1993): "Relationships among attitudes, behavioral intentions, and behavior: A meta-analysis of past research, part 2" in: *Communication Research*, Vol. 20, No. 3, pp. 331-364

Klandt, H. and Heil, A. H. (2001): "FGF-Report: Gründungslehrstühle 2001. Eine Studie zum Stand der Gründungsprofessuren an deutschsprachigen Hochschulen." Förderkreis Gründungs-Forschung eV, Oestrich-Winkel

Klandt, H., Koch, L. T., Schmude, J. and Knaup, U. (2008): "Entrepreneurship-Professuren and deutschsprachigen Hochschulen: Ausrichtung, Organisation und Vernetzung." Förderkreis Gründungs-Forschung eV, Oestrich-Winkel

Kolvereid, L. (1996a): "Prediction of Employment Status Choice Intentions" in: *Entrepreneurship: Theory and Practice*, Vol. 21, No. 1, pp. 47-57

Kolvereid, L. (1996b): "Organizational Employment versus Self-Employment: Reasons for Career Choice Intentions" in: *Entrepreneurship: Theory and Practice*, Vol. 20, No. 3, pp. 23-31

Kolvereid, L. and Isaksen, E. (2006): "New business start-up and subsequent entry into self-employment" in: *Journal of Business Venturing*, Vol. 21, No. 6, pp. 866-885

Kolvereid, L. and Moen, Ø. (1997): "Entrepreneurship among business graduates: does a major in entrepreneurship make a difference?" in: *Journal of European Industrial Training*, Vol. 21, No. 4, pp. 154-160

Kourilsky, M. L. (1995): "Entrepreneurship education: Opportunity in search of curriculum", Kauffman Center for Entrepreneurial Leadership, Kauffman Foundation

Kourilsky, M. L. and Walstad, W. B. (1998): "Entrepreneurship and female youth: knowledge, attitudes, gender differences, and educational practices" in: *Journal of Business Venturing*, Vol. 13, No. 1, pp. 77-88

Krueger, N. F. (1993): "The Impact of Prior Entrepreneurial Exposure on Perceptions of New Venture Feasibility and Desirability" in: *Entrepreneurship: Theory and Practice*, Vol. 18, No. 1, pp. 5-21

Krueger, N. F. and Brazeal, D. V. (1994): "Entrepreneurial Potential and Potential Entrepreneurs" in: *Entrepreneurship: Theory and Practice*, Vol. 18, No. 3, pp. 91-104

Krueger, N. F. and Carsrud, A. L. (1993): "Entrepreneurial intentions: Applying the theory of planned behaviour" in: *Entrepreneurship & Regional Development*, Vol. 5, No. 4, pp. 315-330

Krueger, N. F., Reilly, M. D. and Carsrud, A. L. (2000): "Competing models of entrepreneurial intentions" in: *Journal of Business Venturing*, Vol. 15, No. 5-6, pp. 411-432

Kulicke, M. (2006): *EXIST - Existenzgründungen aus Hochschulen - Bericht der wissenschaftlichen Begleitung zum Förderzeitraum 1998 bis 2005*, Stuttgart

Kuratko, D. F. (2005): "The emergence of entrepreneurship education: development, trends, and challenges" in: *Entrepreneurship Theory and Practice*, Vol. 29, No. 5, pp. 577-598

Lent, R. W. (1994): "Toward a unifying social cognitive theory of career and academic interest, choice, and performance" in: *Journal of Vocational Behavior*, Vol. 45, No. 1, pp. 79-122

Lerner, J. and Malmendier, U. (2011): "With a little help from my (random) friends: Success and failure in post-business school entrepreneurship", National Bureau of Economic Research

Levene, H. (1960): "Robust Tests for Equality of Variances" in: Olkin, I., Ghurye, S. G., Hoeffding, W., Madow, W. G. and Mann, H. B. (Eds.): *Contributions to probability and statistics: Essays in honor of Harold Hotelling*, pp. 278-292, Menlo Park

Liñán, F. (2004): "Intention-based models of entrepreneurship education" in: *Piccolla Impresa/Small Business,* Vol. 3, No. pp. 11–35

Liñán, F. and Chen, Y. W. (2009): "Development and cross-cultural application of a specific instrument to measure entrepreneurial intentions" in: *Entrepreneurship Theory and Practice,* Vol. 33, No. 3, pp. 593-617

Lindsay, P. H. and Norman, D. A. (1977): *An introduction to psychology*, New York

Lüthje, C. and Franke, N. (2002): "Fostering entrepreneurship through university education and training: Lessons from Massachusetts Institute of Technology", Innovative Research in Management, Stockholm

Manski, C. F. (1993): "Identification of endogenous social effects: The reflection problem" in: *The Review of Economic Studies,* Vol. 60, No. 3, pp. 531-542

Manski, C. F. (2000): "Economic analysis of social interactions" in: *The Journal of Economic Perspectives,* Vol. 14, No. 3, pp. 115-136

Manski, C. F. (2010). "Identification of treatment response with social interactions." Northwestern University Department of Economics working paper.

Markman, G. D., Balkin, D. B. and Baron, R. A. (2002): "Inventors and New Venture Formation: The Effects of General Self-Efficacy and Regretful Thinking" in: *Entrepreneurship: Theory and Practice,* Vol. 27, No. 2, pp. 149-166

Matthews, C. H. and Moser, S. B. (1996): "A longitudinal investigation of the impact of family background and gender on interest in small firm ownership" in: *Journal of Small Business Management,* Vol. 34, No. 2, pp. 29–43

McCall, M. W., Lombardo, M. M. and Morrison, A. M. (1988): *The lessons of experience: How successful executives develop on the job*, Lexington

McClelland, D. C. (1961): *The Achieving society*, New York

McMullan, W. E., Chrisman, J. J. and Vesper, K. (2001): "Some problems in using subjective measures of effectiveness to evaluate entrepreneurial assistance programs" in: *Entrepreneurship: Theory and Practice,* Vol. 26, No. 1, pp. 37-55

McMullan, W. E. and Gillin, L. M. (1998): "Developing technological start-up entrepreneurs: a case study of a graduate entrepreneurship programme at Swinburne University" in: *Technovation,* Vol. 18, No. 4, pp. 275-293

McMullan, W. E. and Long, W. (1987): "Entrepreneurship education in the nineties" in: *Journal of Business Venturing,* Vol. 2, No. 3, pp. 261-275

McMullan, E., Long, W. and Wilson, A. (1985): "MBA concentration on entrepreneurship" in: *Journal of Small Business,* Vol. 3, No. 1, pp. 18-22

Meyer, B. (1995): "Natural and Quasi-Experiments in Economics" in: *Journal of Business and Economic Statistics,* Vol. 13, No. 2, pp. 151-161

Middleton Jr, G. and Guthrie, G. M. (1959): "Personality syndromes and academic achievement" in: *Journal of Educational Psychology,* Vol. 50, No. 2, pp. 66-69

Miller, G. A. (1956): "The magical number seven, plus or minus two: some limits on our capacity for processing information" in: Psychological review, Vol. 63, No. 2, pp. 81-97

Minniti, M. and Bygrave, W. (2001): "A Dynamic Model of Entrepreneurial Learning" in: *Entrepreneurship: Theory and Practice,* Vol. 25, No. 3, pp. 5-16

Mischel, W. (1968): *Personality and assessment*, New York

Mitchell, R. K., Busenitz, L., Lant, T., McDougall, P. P., Morse, E. A. and Smith, J. B. (2002): "Toward a Theory of Entrepreneurial Cognition: Rethinking the People Side of Entrepreneurship Research" in: *Entrepreneurship Theory and Practice,* Vol. 27, No. 2, pp. 93-104

Mueller, S. L. and Thomas, A. S. (2001): "Culture and entrepreneurial potential: A nine country study of locus of control and innovativeness" in: *Journal of Business Venturing,* Vol. 16, No. 1, pp. 51-75

Nanda, R. and Sørensen, J. B. (2010): "Workplace Peers and Entrepreneurship" in: *Management Science,* Vol. 56, No. 7, pp. 1116-1126

Norman, W. T. (1963): "Toward an adequate taxonomy of personality attributes: Replicated factor structure in peer nomination personality ratings" in: *Journal of Abnormal and Social Psychology,* Vol. 66, No. 6, pp. 574-583

Notani, A. S. (1998): "Moderators of perceived behavioral control's predictiveness in the theory of planned behavior: A meta-analysis" in: *Journal of Consumer Psychology,* Vol. 7, No. 3, pp. 247-271

Nunnally, J. C. (1978): *Psychometric theory,* New York

Oakland, J. A. (1969): "Measurement of personality correlates of academic achievement in high school students" in: *Journal of Counseling Psychology,* Vol. 16, No. 5, Part 1, pp. 452-457

Ogden, J. (2003): "Some problems with social cognition models: A pragmatic and conceptual analysis" in: *Health Psychology -Hillsdale-,* Vol. 22, No. 4, pp. 424-428

Oosterbeek, H., van Praag, M. and Ijsselstein, A. (2010): "The impact of entrepreneurship education on entrepreneurship skills and motivation" in: *European Economic Review,* Vol. 54, No. 3, pp. 442-454

Ouellette, J. A. and Wood, W. (1998): "Habit and intention in everyday life: The multiple processes by which past behavior predicts future behavior" in: *Psychological Bulletin,* Vol. 124, pp. 54-74

Peter, J. P. (1979): "Reliability: A review of psychometric basics and recent marketing practices" in: *Journal of Marketing Research,* Vol. 16, No. 1, pp. 6-17

Peterman, N. E. and Kennedy, J. (2003): "Enterprise Education: Influencing Students' Perceptions of Entrepreneurship" in: *Entrepreneurship Theory and Practice,* Vol. 28, No. 2, pp. 129-144

Plaschka, G. R. and Welsch, H. P. (1990): "Emerging structures in entrepreneurship education: curricular designs and strategies" in: *Entrepreneurship Theory and Practice,* Vol. 14, No. 3, pp. 55-71

Randall, D. M. and Wolff, J. A. (1994): "The time interval in the intention-behaviour relationship: Meta-analysis" in: *British Journal of Social Psychology*, Vol. 33, No. pp. 405-418

Rauch, A. and Frese, M. (2007): "Born to be an entrepreneur? Revisiting the personality approach to entrepreneurship" in: Baum, J. R., Frese, M. and Baron, R. A. (Eds.): *The psychology of entrepreneurship*, pp. 41-65

Reuber, R., Dyke, L. and Fischer, E. M. (1990): "Experientially acquired knowledge and Entrepreneurial venture success", Academy of Management Best Paper Proceedings

Reynolds, P. D. (1997): "Who Starts New Firms?--Preliminary Explorations of Firms-in-Gestation" in: *Small Business Economics*, Vol. 9, No. 5, pp. 449-462

Reynolds, P., Storey, D. J. and Westhead, P. (1994): "Cross-national Comparisons of the Variation in New Firm Formation Rates" in: *Regional Studies*, Vol. 28, No. 4, pp. 443-456

Robinson, P. B., Stimpson, D. V., Huefner, J. C. and Hunt, H. K. (1991): "An attitude approach to the prediction of entrepreneurship" in: *Entrepreneurship Theory and Practice*, Vol. 15, No. 4, pp. 13-31

Rogers, J. L., Howard, K. I. and Vessey, J. T. (1993): "Using significance tests to evaluate equivalence between two experimental groups" in: *Psychological Bulletin*, Vol. 113, No. 3, pp. 553-565

Rondstadt, R. (1990): "The educated entrepreneur: A new era of entrepreneurial education is beginning" in: Kent, C. (Eds.): *Entrepreneurship education: Current developments, future directions*, pp. 69-88, Westport

Ross, L. and Ward, A. (1996): "Naive realism in everyday life: Implications for social conflict and misunderstanding" in: Brown, T., Reed, E. and Turiel, E. (Eds.): *Values and knowledge*, pp. 103-136, Mahwah

Rothstein, M. G., Paunonen, S. V., Rush, J. C. and King, G. A. (1994): "Personality and Cognitive Ability Predictors of Performance in Graduate Business School" in: *Journal of Educational Psychology*, Vol. 86, No. 4, pp. 516-530

Sacerdote, B. (2001): "Peer Effects with Random Assignment: Results for Dartmouth Roommates" in: *Quarterly Journal of Economics*, Vol. 116, No. 2, pp. 681-704

Salgado, J. F. (1997): "The Five Factor Model of Personality and Job Performance in the European Community" in: *Journal of Applied Psychology*, Vol. 82, No. 1, pp. 30-43

Sandberg, T. and Conner, M. (2008): "Anticipated regret as an additional predictor in the theory of planned behaviour: A meta-analysis" in: *British Journal of Social Psychology*, Vol. 47, No. 4, pp. 589-606

Sapsford, R. (2007): *Survey research*, London

Saxenian, A. L. (1996): *Regional advantage: Culture and competition in Silicon Valley and Route 128*, Cambridge MA

Scherer, R. F., Adams, J. S., Carley, S. S. and Wiebe, F. A. (1989): "Role model performance effects on development of entrepreneurial career preference" in: *Entrepreneurship Theory and Practice*, Vol. 13, No. 3, pp. 53-71

Schmit, M. J. and Ryan, A. M. (1993): "The Big Five in Personnel Selection: Factor Structure in Applicant and Nonapplicant Populations" in: *Journal of Applied Psychology*, Vol. 78, No. 6, pp. 966-974

Schneeweis, N. and Winter-Ebmer, R. (2007): "Peer effects in Austrian schools" in: *Empirical Economics*, Vol. 32, No. 2, pp. 387-409

Scott, M. G. and Twomey, D. F. (1988): "The Long-Term Supply of Entrepreneurs: Students' Career Aspirations in Relation to Entrepreneurship" in: *Journal of Small Business Management*, Vol. 26, No. 4, pp. 5-13

Shadish, W. R., Cook, T. D. and Campbell, D. T. (2002): *Experimental and quasi-experimental designs for generalized causal inference*, Boston, MA

Shane, S. (2000): "Prior Knowledge and the Discovery of Entrepreneurial Opportunities" in: *Organization Science*, Vol. 11, No. 4, pp. 448-469

Shane, S. (2004): *Academic entrepreneurship: University spinoffs and wealth creation*, Northampton

Shane, S. (2009): "Why encouraging more people to become entrepreneurs is bad public policy" in: *Small Business Economics,* Vol. 33, No. 2, pp. 141-149

Shane, S., Locke, E. A. and Collins, C. J. (2003): "Entrepreneurial motivation" in: *Human Resource Management Review,* Vol. 13, No. 2, pp. 257-279

Shane, S. and Venkataraman, S. (2000): "The promise of entrepreneurship as a field of research" in: *Academy of Management Review,* Vol. 25, No. 1, pp. 217-226

Shapero, A. (1975): "The displaced uncomfortable Entrepreneur" in: *Psychology Today,* Vol. 8, No. pp. 83–88

Shapero, A. and Sokol, L. (1982): "The social dimensions of entrepreneurship" in: Kent, C., Sexton, D. and Vesper, K. (Eds.): *Encyclopedia of entrepreneurship*, pp. 72-90, Englewood Cliffs

Sharan, S. (1980): "Cooperative Learning in Small Groups: Recent Methods and Effects on Achievement, Attitudes, and Ethnic Relations" in: *Review of Educational Research,* Vol. 50, No. 2, pp. 241-271

Shelton, L. M. (2006): "Female entrepreneurs, work-family conflict, and venture performance: New insights into the work-family interface" in: *Journal of Small Business Management,* Vol. 44, No. 2, pp. 285-297

Shepherd, D. A. and DeTienne, D. R. (2005): "Prior Knowledge, Potential Financial Reward, and Opportunity Identification" in: *Entrepreneurship: Theory and Practice,* Vol. 29, No. 1, pp. 91-113

Shook, C. L., Priem, R. L. and McGee, J. E. (2003): "Venture creation and the enterprising individual: A review and synthesis" in: *Journal of Management,* Vol. 29, No. 3, pp. 379-399

Souitaris, V., Zerbinati, S. and Al-Laham, A. (2007): "Do entrepreneurship programmes raise entrepreneurial intention of science and engineering students? The effect of learning, inspiration and resources" in: *Journal of Business Venturing,* Vol. 22, No. 4, pp. 566-591

Stevenson, H. H., Roberts, M. J. and Grousbeck, H. I. (1989): *New business ventures and the entrepreneur*, Homewook, IL

Stewart, W. H. (2001): "Risk Propensity Differences Between Entrepreneurs and Managers: A Meta-Analytic Review" in: Journal of Applied Psychology, Vol. 86, No. 1, pp. 145-153

Stewart, W. H. and Roth, P. L. (2007): "A Meta Analysis of Achievement Motivation Differences between Entrepreneurs and Managers" in: *Journal of Small Business Management*, Vol. 45, No. 4, pp. 401-421

Storey, D. J. (2000): *Six steps to heaven: evaluating the impact of public policies to support small businesses in developed economies*, Warwick

Stuart, T. E. and Ding, W. W. (2006): "When Do Scientists Become Entrepreneurs? The Social Structural Antecedents of Commercial Activity in the Academic Life Sciences" in: *American Journal of Sociology*, Vol. 112, No. 1, pp. 97-144

Timmons, J. A. (1994): *New Venture Creation: Entrepreneurship For The 21st Century, revised 4th Edition*, Chicago

Tkachev, A. and Kolvereid, L. (1999): "Self-employment intentions among Russian students" in: *Entrepreneurship & Regional Development*, Vol. 11, No. 3, pp. 269-280

Tubbs, M. E. and Ekeberg, S. E. (1991): "The role of intentions in work motivation: Implications for goal-setting theory and research" in: *Academy of Management Review*, Vol. 16, No. 1, pp. 180-199

van der Sluis, J., van Praag, M. and Vijverberg, W. (2005): "Entrepreneurship Selection and Performance: A Meta-Analysis of the Impact of Education in Developing Economies" in: *The World Bank Economic Review*, Vol. 19, No. 2, pp. 225-261

van Praag, C. and Versloot, P. (2007): "What is the value of entrepreneurship? A review of recent research" in: *Small Business Economics*, Vol. 29, No. 4, pp. 351-382

Veciana, J. M., Aponte, M. and Urbano, D. (2005): "University students' attitudes towards entrepreneurship: A two countries comparison" in: *International Entrepreneurship and Management Journal*, Vol. 1, No. 2, pp. 165-182

Venkataraman, S. (1997): "The distinctive domain of entrepreneurship research" in: *Advances in entrepreneurship, firm emergence and growth,* Vol. 3, No. 1, pp. 119-138

Vesper, K. H. and Gartner, W. B. (1997): "Measuring progress in entrepreneurship education" in: *Journal of Business Venturing,* Vol. 12, No. 5, pp. 403-421

Vesper, K. and McMullan, E. (1997): "New venture scholarship versus practice: When entrepreneurship academics try the real thing as applied research" in: *Technovation,* Vol. 17, No. 7, pp. 349-358

von Graevenitz, G., Harhoff, D. and Weber, R. (2010): "The effects of entrepreneurship education" in: *Journal of Economic Behavior & Organization,* Vol. 76, No. 1, pp. 90-112

Walter, S. G. and Walter, A. (2008): "Deutsche Universitäten als Gründungsinkubatoren: Der Beitrag der Gründungsausbildung zur Gründungsintention von Studierenden" in: *Schmalenbachs Zeitschrift für betriebswirtschaftliche Forschung,* Vol. 60, September 2008, pp. 542-569

Webb, N. M. (1982): "Student Interaction and Learning in Small Groups" in: *Review of Educational Research,* Vol. 52, No. 3, pp. 421-445

Webb, T. L. and Sheeran, P. (2006): "Does changing behavioral intentions engender behavior change? A meta-analysis of the experimental evidence" in: *Psychological Bulletin,* Vol. 132, No. 2, pp. 249-268

Webster, J. and Martocchio, J. J. (1995): "The differential effects of software training previews on training outcomes" in: *Journal of Management,* Vol. 21, No. 4, pp. 757-787

Weinrauch, J. D. (1984): "Educating the entrepreneur: understanding adult learning behaviour" in: *Journal of Small Business Management,* Vol. 22, No. 2, pp. 32-37

Westlake, W. J. (1976): "Symmetrical confidence intervals for bioequivalence trials" in: *Biometrics,* Vol. 32, No. 4, pp. 741-744

Westlake, W. J. (1988): "Bioavailability and bioequivalence of pharmaceutical formulations" in: Peace, K. E. (Eds.): *Biopharmaceutical statistics for drug development,* pp. 329-352, New York

Wilson, F., Kickul, J. and Marlino, D. (2007): "Gender, Entrepreneurial Self-Efficacy, and Entrepreneurial Career Intentions: Implications for Entrepreneurship Education 1" in: *Entrepreneurship Theory and Practice*, Vol. 31, No. 3, pp. 387-406

Whitlock, D. M. and Masters, R. J. (1996): "Influences on business students' decisions to pursue entrepreneurial opportunities or traditional career paths", Proceedings of the Small Business Institute Directors Association

Whitmore, D. (2005): "Resource and peer impacts on girls' academic achievement: Evidence from a randomized experiment" in: *American Economic Review*, Vol. 95, No. 2, pp. 199-203.

Woessmann, L. (2003): "Schooling resources, educational institutions and student performance: the international evidence" in: *Oxford Bulletin of Economics and Statistics*, Vol. 65, No. 2, pp. 117-170

Woessmann, L. and West, M. (2006): "Class-size effects in school systems around the world: Evidence from between-grade variation in TIMSS" in: *European Economic Review*, Vol. 50, No. 3, pp. 695-736

Wood, R. and Bandura, A. (1989): "Impact of conceptions of ability on self-regulatory mechanisms and complex decision making" in: *Journal of Personality and Social Psychology*, Vol. 56, No. 3, pp. 407-415

World Economic Forum (2009): "Educating the Next Wave of Entrepreneurs: Unlocking Entrepreneurial Capabilities to Meet the Global Challenges of the 21st Century: A Report of the Global Education Initiative", Switzerland

Wortman, M. S. (1986): "A unified framework, research typologies, and research prospectuses for the interface between entrepreneurship and small business" in: Sexton, D. and Smilor, R. (Eds.): *The Art and Science of Entrepreneurship*, pp. 273-332, Cambridge

Wyckham, R. G. (1989): "Ventures launched by participants of an entrepreneurial education program" in: *Journal of Small Business Management*, Vol. 27, No. 2, pp. 54-61

Zhao, H., Seibert, S. E. and Hills, G. E. (2005): "The Mediating Role of Self-Efficacy in the Development of Entrepreneurial Intentions" in: *Journal of Applied Psychology*, Vol. 90, No. 6, pp. 1265–1272

Zhao, H., Seibert, S. E. and Lumpkin, G. T. (2010): "The Relationship of Personality to Entrepreneurial Intentions and Performance: A Meta-Analytic Review" in: *Journal of Management,* Vol. 36, No. 2, pp. 381-404

Zimmerman, D. J. (2003): "Peer effects in academic outcomes: Evidence from a natural experiment" in: *Review of Economics and Statistics,* Vol. 85, No. 1, pp. 9-23

Springer Gabler RESEARCH

„Innovation und Entrepreneurship"
Herausgeber: Prof. Dr. Nikolaus Franke, Prof. Dietmar Harhoff, Ph. D.
und Prof. Dr. Joachim Henkel
zuletzt erschienen:

Rudolf Dömötör
**Erfolgsfaktoren der Innovativität
von kleinen und mittleren Unternehmen**
2011. XIV, 156 S., 14 Abb., 23 Tab., Br. € 49,95
ISBN 978-3-8349-2738-5

Timo Fischer
Managing Value Capture
Empirical Analyses of Managerial Challenges in Capturing Value
2011. XXVI, 222 S., 60 Abb., 23 Tab., Br. € 59,95
ISBN 978-3-8349-3251-8

Florian Jell
Patent Filing Strategies and Patent Management
An Empirical Study
2012. XXII, 214 S., 14 Abb., 31 Tab., Br. € 59,95
ISBN 978-3-8349-3247-1

Richard Weber
Evaluating Entrepreneurship Education
2012. XXII, 352 S., 22 Abb., 68 Tab., Br. € 69,95
ISBN 978-3-8349-3653-0

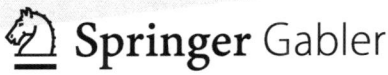

Änderungen vorbehalten. Stand: Februar 2012. Erhältlich im Buchhandel oder beim Verlag.
Abraham-Lincoln-Str. 46 . 65189 Wiesbaden . www.springer-gabler.de